Radio's Golden Years

Also by **Vincent Terrace:**
The Complete Encyclopedia
of Television Programs

Radio's Golden Years

The Encyclopedia of Radio Programs
1930 • 1960

Vincent Terrace

San Diego • New York
A. S. Barnes & Company, Inc.
In London:
The Tantivy Press

First Edition
Manufactured in the United States of America

For information write to:
A.S. Barnes & Company, Inc.
P.O. Box 3051
La Jolla, California 92038

The Tantivy Press
Magdalen House
136-148 Tooley Street
London, SE1 2TT, England

Library of Congress Cataloging in Publication Data

Terrace, Vincent, 1948-
    Radio's golden years.

    Includes index.
    1. Radio programs — United
States — Dictionaries.   I.   Title.
PN1991.3.U6T47   791.44'03   79-87791
ISBN 0-498-02393-1

1 2 3 4 5 6 7 8 9   84 83 82 81

CONTENTS

Preface

Radio's Golden Years, 1930-1960, is an alphabetical listing of 1,500 nationally broadcast network and syndicated entertainment programs. Covered within the thirty year period are the following types of series: adventure, anthology, children's, comedy, crime (police, detective), drama, game (quiz, audience participation), gossip, human interest, interview, musical variety, mystery, science fiction, serial, talk-interview, variety, western, and women's programs. The entries provide story line information, cast lists (character, performer, and relationship to other characters), announcer and music credits, sponsors, program openings, network and/or syndication information, and length and date of broadcasts. Also included are ninety photographs, an index, and the first-run programs broadcast during the 1970s.

While not an encyclopedia of every program that was ever broadcast, *Radio's Golden Years* is the most complete reference work yet published on the subject of old-time radio. What was the name of the Broadway play in which "Myrt and Marge" were performers? Who or what is "The Green Lama"? Who are the nine actors who portrayed "Sherlock Holmes"? What radio programs became the basis for television series? What radio programs were based on TV series? What radio series used edited TV soundtracks? You'll find the answers to these and many other questions within the nostalgia-packed pages of *Radio's Golden*

Years—a journey down memory lane for those who remember, and a new experience for those of us who are too young to recall a world without television: a world in which that little box that now sits on the kitchen windowsill blurting out loud music and endless D.J. talk, once provided hours of laughter, sorrow, chills, and daring adventures. It was a time from the Depression-ridden 1930s to the war-torn years of the 1940s, from a brief peace to a war in Korea, and from the birth of television to the demise of radio as it was. We never saw what the performers looked like, we only heard them; there were never any expensive sets or fancy colors to impress us; whether it came from outer space and attempted to destroy the world, or out of a mad scientist's lab, makeup was never used. We shared the laughter of "Blondie," the excitement of "Jack Armstrong," and the tears of Mary Noble, "Backstage Wife." We listened and we enjoyed. The picture tube was our imagination: we envisioned that creature from outer space, that mad scientist, or whatever radio could create. The impossible could be presented—and we could "see" it. It's gone now, our imagination no longer provides the picture; television has taken its place. The days of "Captain Midnight," "Ma Perkins," and "Frontier Gentleman" are no longer with us. Our minds can relive them; *Radio's Golden Years* can help you recall or acquaint you with them, and with a time that will never be again.

Acknowledgments

The author wishes to thank the following people for their help in making this book possible: Robert A. Evans, Alvin H. Marill, Charles K. Stumpf, Sylvia Lawler, Bert and Mary Stangler.

Most of the photographs used in this book are from the collections of Charles K. Stumpf, author of *Ma Perkins, Little Orphan Annie,* and *Heigh Ho Silver* (Carlton Press, 1971) and the *Call-Chronicle* Newspapers, Allentown, Pa.

Author's Notes

Networks:

ABC: The American Broadcasting Company. Formed in 1944; see NBC for further information.

CBS: The Columbia Broadcasting System. Formed in 1927 when two companies, United Independent Broadcasters and The Columbia Phonograph Broadcasting Company, merged.

Mutual: The Mutual Broadcasting System. Formed in 1934; also known as MBS.

NBC: The National Broadcasting Company. The first American network, formed in 1926 by General Electric, R.C.A., and Westinghouse under the leadership of David Sarnoff. From1926 to 1943, NBC owned two separate networks: NBC Red and NBC Blue. When the Federal Communications Commission began its investigation of chain broadcasting and monopolies, NBC sold the Blue Network to Life Savers Candy Company owner Edward J. Noble who, a year later, formed ABC. The Red Network became simply NBC. In the text, NBC Blue is listed as either NBC Blue or Blue, NBC Red as NBC.

Program Openings:

All of the program openings (and closes), except those for "The Adventures of Ellery Queen" and "Manhattan Mother," which came from reviews, are taken from the actual programs. Many radio programs used different themes or openings throughout their runs. In cases where several different openings were found, the one which best describes the program has been used.

Program Types:

All programs are listed alphabetically by title. Religious, sports, and audition programs, specials, and news series have been excluded. See the preface for a full list of the types used.

Radio Legends

The Abbott and Costello Show

Type: Variety
Format: Music, songs, and sketches that high-lighted the comedic talents of Bud Abbott and Lou Costello.
Starring: Bud Abbott and Lou Costello.
Regulars: Mel Blanc, Connie Haines, Lou Krogman, Frank Nelson, Martha Wentworth, Si Wills, Wally Brown, Verna Felton, Sharon Douglas, Pat McGeehan, Artie Auerbrook, Ken Niles, Sid Fields, Iris Adrian, Elvia Allman, Benay Venuta.
Vocalists: Marilyn Maxwell, Connie Haines, Susan Miller, The Les Baxter Singers, The Delta Rhythm Boys.
Announcers: Ken Niles, Jim Doyle, Frank Bingman, Michael Roy.
Orchestra: Leith Stevens, Freddie Rich, Skinnay Ennis, Jack Meakin, Will Osborne, Peter Van Steeden, Matty Matlock.
Program Opening:
Lou: Heyyyyy Abbott!!! What time is it?
Bud: Why it's time for The Abbott and Costello Show. We're on the air for ABC here in Hollywood.
Lou: Well, what are we waiting for? Let's go with The Abbott and Costello Show.
Length: 30 minutes.
Network: NBC (1942), ABC (1947).
First Broadcast: 1942.
Note: In addition to their prime-time series on ABC, Bud and Lou were the stars of "The Abbott and Costello Kid Show," a thirty minute, Saturday morning series featuring games and quizzes for children.

Abbott Mysteries

Type: Mystery.
Format: The series, based on the novel by Frances Crane, followed the investigations of Pat and Jean Abbott, a newly wed couple who solved various crimes.
Cast: Pat Abbott   Charles Webster
                              Les Tremayne
            Jean Abbott   Julie Stevens
                              Alice Reinheart
Stock Performers: Jean Ellyn, Sidney Slon.
Announcer: Frank Gallop, Cy Harrice.
Music: Hank Sylvern, Albert Buhrman.
Length: 30 minutes.
Network: Mutual.
First Broadcast: 1945.

The Abe Burrows Show

Type: Comedy
Format: Humorous nonsense geared for an adult audience.
Host: Abe Burrows.
Announcer: Michael Fitzmaurice.
Music: The Milton DeLugg Quartet.
Length: 15 minutes.
Network: CBS.
First Broadcast: 1947.

Abie's Irish Rose. Richard Coogan and Mercedes McCambridge.

Abie's Irish Rose

Type: Comedy-Drama

Format: Ethnic differences as seen through the marriage of a Jewish Boy (Abie) and an Irish Catholic girl (Rosemary) in New York City in 1942. A story "dedicated to the spirit of freedom and equality which gives to this nation the greatness that is America." Based on the Broadway play by Anne Nichols; also served as the basis for the television series "Bridget Loves Bernie."

Cast: Abie Levy   Richard Bond
                                Sydney Smith
                                Richard Coogan
                                Bud Collyer
        Rosemary Levy   Betty Winkler
                                Mercedes
                                  McCambridge
                                Julie Stevens
                                Marion Shockley
        Pat Murphy   Walter Kinsella
        Soloman Levy   Alfred White
                                Charlie Cantor
                                Alan Reed

Abie's Irish Rose. Anna Appel and Menasha Skulnick.

Mr. Cohen	Menasha Skulnik
Mrs. Cohen	Anna Appel
Father Whelan	Bill Adams
Casey	Ann Thomas
David Lerner	Carl Eastman
Dr. Mueller	Fred Sullivan
Mrs. Mueller	Charme Allen
The maid	Amanda Randolph
The twins	Dolores Gillen
Mrs. Brown	Florence Freeman

Announcer: Howard Petrie.
Orchestra: Joe Stopak.
Sponsor: Drene.
Length: 30 minutes.
Network: NBC.
First Broadcast: 1942 (ended in 1944).

Academy Award Theatre

Type: Anthology
Format: Adaptations of Academy Award-winning motion pictures.

Included:

The Maltese Falcon. Dashiell Hammett's tale of detective Sam Spade's efforts to recover the Maltese Falcon, a priceless statue stolen by Casper Gutman, "The Fat Man."
Starring: Humphrey Bogart, Sydney Greenstreet, Mary Astor.

The Front Page. The Hecht and MacArthur story of a newspaper reporter and his attempts to cover one last story—that of a convicted murderer who has escaped—before he retires.
Starring: Pat O'Brien, Adolph Menjou.

Suspicion. About a woman who belives that her husband is planning to murder her.
Starring: Cary Grant, Ann Todd.

Portrait of Jennie. The story of an impoverished New York artist who believes he has found the ideal model—beautiful and captivating—until she begins to mature with incredible speed.
Starring: Joan Fontaine, John Lund.
Length: 30 minutes.
Network: CBS.
First Broadcast: 1946 (March 30, to December 18, 1946).

Add a Line

Type: Quiz
Format: Called for players to add the final line to a rhyme given to them by the host.
Host: John Nelson.
Length: 30 minutes.
Network: ABC.
First Broadcast: 1949.

The Adele Clark Show

Type: Musical Variety.
Hostess: Adele Clark.
Announcer: Gene Kirby.
Orchestra: Jack Kelly.
Length: 30 minutes.
Network: CBS.
First Broadcast: 1946.

Adventure Parade

Type: Anthology
Format: Dramatizations of novels for children. Stories ran one week (Monday through Friday), with a new story beginning the following Monday.
Host-Story Teller: John Griggs (as "Roger Elliott" for the first six weeks only; from then on Griggs used his own name).
Announcer: George Hogan.
Program Opening:
Announcer: Adventurers atten-shun! Fall in for Adventure Parade. The Mutual Broadcasting Company cordially invites all adventurers from six to sixty to join in a parade of the world's most famous stories; stories of action! mystery! and adventure! on Adventure Parade...
Length: 15 minutes.
Network: Mutual.
First Broadcast: 1946.

Adventures By Morse

Type: Adventure
Format: The global exploits of Bart Friday, a ship's captain, and his mate, Skip Turner. Created by Carleton E. Morse.
Cast: Captain Bart
      Friday   Elliott Lewis
                    Russell Thorson
      Skip Turner   Barton
                    Yarborough
Length: 30 minutes.
Syndicated.
First Broadcast: 1940s.

The Adventures of Archie Andrews

Type: Comedy
Format: The series, adapted from the comic strip by Bob Montana, dealt with the misadventures of a group of high school students in the town of Riverdale: Archie, Jughead, Veronica, Betty, and Reggie.
Cast: Archie Andrews   Charles Mullen
                         Jack Grimes

	Burt Boyer
	Bob Hastings
Jughead Jones	Harlan Stone
	Cameron Andrews
Veronica Lodge	Gloria Mann
	Vivian Smolen
Betty Cooper	Doris Grundy
	Joy Geffen
	Rosemary Rice
Reggie Mantle	Paul Gordon
Fred Andrews, Archie's Father	Vinton Hayworth
	Arthur Kohl
	Reese Taylor
Mary Andrews, Archie's Mother	Alice Yourman
	Peggy Allenby
Mr. Weatherby, the school principal	Arthur Maitland
Mr. Lodge, Veronica's Father	Bill Griffis

Announcer: Ken Banghart, Dick Dudley.
Organist: George Wright.
Program Opening:
Announcer: Yes, here he is, the youngster millions of readers of *Archie Comics* magazine know so well; brought to you by Swift and Company... Archie Andrews and all his gang.
Length: 15 and 30 minute versions.
Network: Mutual (1943) Blue (1943) NBC (1945).
First Broadcast: 1943.

The Adventures of Bill Lance

Type: Crime Drama.
Format: The cases of Bill Lance, a private detective working out of Los Angeles, California.
Starring: Gerald Mohr as Bill Lance.
Announcer: Owen James.
Length: 30 minutes.
Network: ABC.
First Broadcast: 1947.

The Adventures of Bulldog Drummond

Type: Mystery
Format: A whodunit series dealing with the exploits of Captain Hugh Drummond, a dashing police sleuth nicknamed "Bulldog" for his tireless pursuit of lawbreakers. Based on a series of books by H.C. McNeile.
Cast: Hugh "Bulldog"
     Drummond   George Coulouris
                Santos Ortega
                Ned Weaver

     Denny, his assistant   Everett Sloane
                Luis Van Rooten
                Rod Hendrickson
Announcer: Ted Brown, Henry Morgan.
Organist: Lew White.
Programming Opening:
Announcer: Out of the fog, out of the night, and into his American adventures comes Bulldog Drummond.
Length: 30 minutes.
Network: Mutual (1941), Syndicated (1947).
First Broadcast: 1941.

The Adventures of Casanova

Type: Adventure
Format: Based on the legend of a world-famous lover, the series followed the romantic exploits of Christopher Casanova, a modern day roué whose name forced him into affairs with beautiful women the world over.
Starring: Errol Flynn as Christopher Casanova.
Length: 30 minutes.
Network: Mutual.
First Broadcast: 1952.

The Adventures of Champion

Type: Western
Format: The exploits of Gene Autry's wonder horse, Champion.
Starring: Gene Autry.

Length: 15 minutes.
Network: Mutual.
First Broadcast: 1949.

The Adventures of Charlie Chan

See title: "Charlie Chan"

The Adventures of Christopher Wells

Type: Crime Drama
Format: The exploits of Christopher Wells, a newspaper reporter seeking to corrupt the inner workings of organized crime.
Cast: Christopher
     Wells   Myron McCormick
              Les Damon

     Stacy McGill his assistant Charlotte Lawrence
              Vicki Vola
Orchestra: Peter Van Steeden.
Length: 30 minutes.
Network: CBS.
First Broadcast: 1947.

The Adventures of Dick Cole

Type: Adventure
Format: The exploits of Dick Cole, a cadet at the Farr Military Academy. Based on characters appearing in *Bluebolt and Foremost Comics*.
Starring: Leon Janney as Dick Cole.
Announcer: Paul Luther.
Music: Lew White.
Sponsor: Bluebolt and Foremost Comics.
Length: 30 minutes.
Syndicated.
First Broadcast: 1946.

The Adventures of Ellery Queen

Type: Mystery
Format: The cases of Ellery Queen, a sophisticated gentleman detective and writer working out of New York City.

Based on the stories by Frederic Dannay and Manfred B. Lee. Became the basis for a television series of the same title.

Cast: Ellery Queen — Hugh Marlowe, Carleton Young, Sidney Smith, ?*, Larry Dobkin

Richard Queen, his father — Santos Ortega, Bill Smith

Nikki Porter, Ellery's secretary — Marion Shockley, Barbara Terrell, Virginia Gregg, Charlotte Keane, Gertrude Warner

Sgt. Velie, Richard's assistant — Howard Smith, Ted deCorsia, Ed Latimer

The Medical Examiner — Arthur Allen

Announcer: Paul Masterson, Roger Krupp.

Organist: Rex Koury, Chet Kingsbury.

Orchestra: Bernard Herrmann.

Program Opening:

Announcer: This program is being presented in the interest of a safer community and is dedicated against crime; against the crime of bad citizenship, which is a crime against America.

Note: Gimmick of the series was the presence of a guest celebrity who served as "The Armchair Detective." Just prior to the conclusion of the program, Ellery Queen would step out of his role and ask the guest to identify the culprit, Following his prediction, Queen would reveal the actual murderer.

Length: 60 and 30 minute versions.

Network: CBS (1939), NBC (1941), ABC (1947).

First Broadcast: 1939.

*In 1947, the name of the actor portraying Ellery Queen was withheld in an attempt to make the fictitious character seem real.

The Adventures of Father Brown

Type: Crime Drama

Format: The exploits of Father Brown, an eccentric Roman Catholic priest with a knack for solving crimes. Based on the fictional detective priest created by G.K. Chesterton. On April 23, 1979, NBC-TV presented "Sanctuary of Fear," a two hour pilot film with Barnard Hughes portraying Father Brown.

Starring: Karl Swenson as Father Brown.

Announcer: Jack Irish.

Length: 30 minutes.

Network: Mutual.

First Broadcast: 1945.

The Adventures of Frank Merriwell

Type: Adventure

Format: The series followed the life and times of Frank Merriwell, a late 19th century fictional character created by Burt L. Standish.

Cast: Frank Merriwell — Lawson Zerbe
Inza Burrage — Jean Gillespie, Elaine Rost
Bart Hodge — Harold Studer
Elsie Bellwood — Patricia Hosley

Also: Al Hodge.

Announcer: Harlow Wilcox.

Orchestra: Paul Taubman.

Program Opening:

Announcer (over hoof beats): There it is, an echo of the past; an exciting past, a romantic past; the era of the horse and carriage, gas-lit streets, and free-for-all football games. The era of one of the most beloved heroes in American fiction, Frank Merriwell, the character created by Burt L. Standish. Merriwell is loved as much today as he ever was. And so, the National Broadcasting Company brings him to radio in a brand new series of stories. Today, The Riddle of the Wrong Answer; or Gambling Is the Devil's Pastime.

Length: 30 minutes.

Network: NBC.

First Broadcast: 1946.

The Adventures of Helen and Mary

Type: Children's.
Format: The fairy tale adventures of Helen and Mary, two children, as they wander through a storybook world of make-believe.
Cast: Helen   Estelle Levy
      Mary   Patricia Ryan
Orchestra: Maurice Brown
Length: 30 minutes.
Network: CBS.
First Broadcast: 1930.
Note: In 1934 the series became "Let's Pretend," which see.

The Adventures of Leonidas Witherall

Type: Mystery
Format: The cases of Leonidas Witherall, a British criminology professor and amateur detective, as he attempted to solve crimes through scientific knowledge and common sense.
Cast: Leonidas
      Witherall   Walter Hampden
      Mrs. Mollet, his
      assistant   Agnes
                         Moorehead
Length: 30 minutes.
Network: Mutual.
First Broadcast: 1943.

The Adventures of Maisie

See title "Maisie."

The Adventures of Michael Shayne

Type: Crime Drama
Format: The cases of Michael Shayne, a private detective working out of New York City.

Cast: Michael Shayne   Jeff Chandler
                        Robert Sterling
      His Assistant   Judith Parrish
Length: 30 minutes.
Network: ABC.
First Broadcast: 1952.
Note: Also known as "Michael Shayne, Private Detective."

The Adventures of Mr. Meek

See title: "Meet Mr. Meek."

The Adventures of Nero Wolfe

Type: Mystery
Format: The cases of Nero Wolfe, a private detective working out of New York City. Based on the Rex Stout character.
Cast: Nero Wolfe   Santos Ortega
                        Sydney Green-
                        street

      Archie, his
      assistant   Joseph Julian
                        Louis Vittes
Announcer: Carl Eastman.
Organist: Lew White.
Length: 30 minutes.
Network: NBC Blue.
First Broadcast: 1943.

The Adventures of Ozzie and Harriet

Type: Comedy
Format: A domestic comedy series that followed the home life of the Nelson family: parents Ozzie and Harriet and their children David and Ricky. Became the basis for the television series of the same title.
Cast: Ozzie Nelson   Himself
      Harriet Hilliard
      Nelson   Herself
      David Nelson   Tommy Bernard
                        David Nelson
                        Henry Blair
      Ricky Nelson   Ricky Nelson

Thorny, their neighbor	John Brown
Harriet's mother	Lurene Tuttle
Gloria, the Nelson's maid	Bea Benaderet
Emmy Lou, a friend	Janet Waldo
Roger, a friend	Dink Trout

Vocalists: The King Sisters, Harriet Hilliard, Ozzie Nelson.

Announcer: Jack Bailey, Verne Smith

Orchestra: Ozzie Nelson, Billy May.

Program Opening:

Announcer: The solid silver with beauty that lives forever is International Sterling. From Hollywood, International Silver Company, creator of International Sterling, present The Adventures of Ozzie and Harriet, starring America's favorite young couple, Ozzie Nelson and Harriet Hilliard.

Length: 30 minutes.

Network: CBS.

First Broadcast: 1944. Originally titled "The Ozzie Nelson-Harriet Hilliard Show."

The Adventures of Philip Marlowe

Type: Crime Drama

Format: The investigations of private detective Philip Marlowe. Based on the character created by Raymond Chandler.

Cast: Philip Marlowe   Van Heflin
                                    Gerald Mohr

Announcer: Wendell Niles.

Music: Lyn Murray.

Program Opening:

Announcer: From the pen of Raymond Chandler, outstanding author of mystery, comes his most famous character and crime's most deadly enemy, as we present The Adventures of Philip Marlowe.

Length: 30 minutes.

Network: NBC (1947); CBS (1949).

First Broadcast: 1947.

The Adventures of Philip Marlowe. Van Heflin.

The Adventures of Sam Spade

See title: "Sam Spade."

The Adventures of Sherlock Holmes

See title: "Sherlock Holmes."

The Adventures of Superman

Type: Adventure Serial

Format: Faraway in the outer regions of space there existed the planet Krypton which, inhabited by super-intelligent beings, was being drawn closer to the sun and destruction. When Jor-El, a scientist discovered this, but failed to convince anyone of its reality, he began preparations to save his wife Lara and their infant son Kal-El. Having had time only to complete a miniature experimental rocket ship when the planet began to explode, Jor-El and Lara placed Kal-El in it and set its controls for the planet Earth. Shortly after the rocket's take-off Krypton exploded. During the long journey of the rocket ship to Earth the infant had become a man. The ship landed in a desert where a strange being, dressed in a red and blue costume, emerged. While exploring his new surroundings, the being, "a Superman in our world," rescued a boy and his father from a runaway trolley. With their help and their promise to keep his secret, he became Clark Kent and, wanting to use his great abilities to benefit mankind, he acquired a job as a reporter for the *Daily Planet*, a crusading newspaper in Metropolis. Stories depict Clark's battle against crime as the mysterious Superman. (Story line culled from the first two episodes).

Cast: Clark Kent/
      Superman   Bud Collyer
                       Michael Fitz-
                        maurice

      Lois Lane, his
      girlfriend, a
      reporter   Joan Alexander
      Jimmy Olsen, a
      reporter   Jackie Kelk
      Perry White, the
      editor   Julian Noa
      Beanie, the office
      boy   Jackson Beck
      Batman, the
      caped crusader
      who aided
      Superman   Stacy Harris
                       Gary Merrill
                       Matt Crowley
      Robin, Batman's
      aide   Ronald Liss

Narrator-Announcer: Jackson Beck, George Lowther, Frank Knight, Dan McCullough.

Organist: John Gart.

Sponsor: Kellogg's cereals.

Program Opening:

    Announcer: Boys and girls, your attentions please. Presenting a new, exciting radio program featuring the thrilling adventures of that amazing and incredi-

ble personality. Faster than a speeding bullet, more powerful than a locomotive, impervious to bullets.

Voices: Up in the sky, look! It's a giant bird! It's a plane! It's Superman!

Announcer: And now, Superman, a being no larger than an ordinary man but possessed of powers and abilities never before realized on Earth. Able to leap into the air an eighth of a mile at a single bound, hurtle a twenty story building with ease, race a high powered bullet to its target, lift tremendous weights, and bend solid steel in his bare hands as though it were paper. Superman, the strange visitor from a distant planet, champion of the oppressed, physical marvel extraordinary who has sworn to devote his existance on Earth to helping those in need.

Program Closing:

Announcer: Fellows and girls, follow The Adventures of Superman, brought to you everyday, Monday through Friday, same time, same station by the makers of that super delicious cereal, Kellogg's Pep. Superman is a copyrighted feature appearing in *Superman-D.C. Publications.* This is Mutual.

Length: 15 minutes.

Network: Mutual.

First Broadcast: 1940.

The Adventures of the Falcon

See title: "The Falcon."

The Adventures of the Scarlet Pimpernel

Type: Adventure

Format: Set against the background of England during the 1790's, the series followed the exploits of Sir Percy Blakeney, a man of wealth and social status who adopts the guise of the mysterious Scarlet Pimpernel (named after a small, red flower that is common to the English countryside). Appearing as the Scarlet Pimpernel whenever trouble is apparent, he battled injustice in his endeavor to aid the oppressed. Became the basis for the television series of the same title.

Starring: Marius Goring as Sir Percy Blakeney.
Music: Sidney Torch.
Length: 30 minutes.
Network: NBC.
First Broadcast: 1954.

The Adventures of Topper

Type: Comedy
Format: The story of Cosmo Topper, a henpecked bank vice president who is haunted by the spirits of George and Marion Kerby, a fun-loving young couple who were killed in an automobile accident and now appear and talk to only him. Topper's misadventures, as George and Marion attempt to bring a little fun into his dull life, were the focal point of the program. Based on the characters created by Thorne Smith.

Cast: Cosmo Topper   Roland Young
      Henrietta Top-
        per, his wife   Hope Emerson
      George Kerby   Paul Mann
      Marion Kerby   Frances Chaney
      Mr. Borris, Top-
        per's employer   Ed Latimer
Sponsor: Post Toasties cereal; Maxwell House Coffee.
Length: 30 minutes.
Network: NBC.
First Broadcast: 1945.

The Affairs of Ann Scotland

Type: Crime Drama
Format: The investigations of Ann Scotland, a witty female private detective.
Starring: Arlene Francis as Ann Scotland.
Announcer: Ken Niles.
Orchestra: Del Castillo.
Length: 30 minutes.
Network: ABC.
First Broadcast: 1946.

The Affairs of Peter Salem

Type: Crime Drama
Format: The cases of Peter Salem, a suave and sophisticated private detective who used his deductive abilities rather than the two fisted approach as he and his sidekick Marty attempted to solve baffling crimes.

Cast: Peter Salem   Santos Ortega
      Marty   Jack Grimes
Length: 30 minutes.
Network: Mutual.
First Broadcast: 1949.

The Affairs of Tom, Dick, and Harry

Type: Variety.
Format: Music, songs, and comedy vignettes.
Cast: Tom   Bud Vandover
      Dick   Marlin Hart
      Harry   Gordon Vandover
Vocalist: Edna O'Dell.
Announcer: Jack Brickhouse.
Orchestra: Robert Trendler.
Length: 30 minutes.
Network: Mutual.
First Broadcast: 1941.

African Trek

Type: Variety
Host: Josef Marais.
Regulars: Juano Hernandez, The Burford Hampden Chorus.
Orchestra: Burford Hampden.
Length: 25 minutes.
Network: NBC Blue.
First Broadcast: 1939.

Against the Storm

Type: Serial
Format: The story of Catherine Allen, a refugee from Central Europe, as she struggled to adjust to a new life in the United States. In later episodes, following

Catherine's marriage to Philip Cameron, stories related incidents in the lives of the Cameron family.

Cast: Catherine Allen   Gertrude Warner
                                  Claudia Morgan
       Philip Cameron   Arnold Moss
                                  Alexander
                                   Scourby
                                  Elliott Reid
       Jason Allen   Roger DeKoven
       Margaret Allen   May Seymour
                                  Florence Malone
                                  Katherine Raht
       Siri Allen   Dolores Gillian
                                  Joan Tompkins
                                  Ethel Owen
       Mark Scott   Chester Stratton
                                  Eddie Mayehoff
       Nichole Scott   Ruth Mattheson
       Kathy Reimer   Charlotte Holland
       Lucretia Hale   Jane Erskine
       Penny   Leslie Bingham
       Dr. Reimer   Philip Clarke
       Reid Wilson   James Meighan
                                  Walter Vaughn
       Mr. Fullerton   Rex Ingram
       Ebba   Lenore Kingston
       Lisa   Sarah Burton
       Guy Aldis   William Quinn
       Kip Taylor   Mary Hunter
       Pascal Taylor   Lawson Zerbe
       Manuel   Michael Ingram
       Nathan   Ian Martin

Announcer: Nelson Case, Ralph Edwards, Richard Stark.
Sponsor: Ivory Soap.
Length: 15 minutes.
Network: NBC (1939), Mutual (1944), ABC (1951).
First Broadcast: 1939.

The Air Adventures of Jimmy Allen

Type: Adventure
Format: The exploits of Jimmy Allen, a sixteen-year-old messenger boy for the Kansas City Airport during the 1930s.
Starring: Murray McLean as Jimmy Allen.
Program Opening:

Voice: The Air Adventures of Jimmy Allen.
Announcer: You have just heard the inspirational identification tag known in radio as the signature of The Air Adventrues of Jimmy Allen. And now to episode one thousand and one . . .
Length: 15 minutes.
Syndicated.
First Broadcast: 1946.

Al Goodman's Musical Album

Type: Musical Variety
Host: Al Goodman.
Regulars: Elaine Malbin, Felix Knight.
Orchestra: Al Goodman.
Length: 30 minutes.
Network: NBC.
First Broadcast: 1951.

The Al Jolson Show

Type: Variety
Format: Sketches, music, and songs.
Host: Al Jolson.
Regulars: Douglas Corrigan, Martha Raye, Harry Einstein, Tiny Ruffner.
Orchestra: Lud Gluskin.
Length: 30 minutes.
Network: CBS.
First Broadcast: 1938.

Al Pearce and His Gang

Type: Comedy
Format: Outlandish sketches featuring an array of buffoons, most notably Elmer Blurt, the shy door-to-door salesman.
Starring: Al Pearce as Elmer Blurt.
Cast: The Human
          Chatterbox   Arlene Harris
       The Laughing
          Lady   Kitty O'Neil
       Tizzie Lish   Bill Comstock
       Yahbut   Jennison Parker
       Lord Bilegwater   Monroe Upton
       Yogi Yorgeson   Harry Stewart

Regulars: Billy House, Don Reid, Earl Hodgins, Martha Mears, Mabel Todd, Hazel Werner, Gary Brechner, Cal Pearce, Harry Foster, Tony Romano, Morey Amsterdam, Orville and Andy Andrews, The Sportsmen, The Three Cheers, Marie Green and Her Merry Men.

Announcer: Ken Roberts.

Orchestra: Carl Hoff, Harry Sosnik, Ivan Ditmars, Larry Marsh.

Length: 30 minutes.

Network: NBC Blue (1933), CBS (1939), NBC (1947).

First Broadcast: 1933.

The Alan Young Show

Type: Comedy.

Format: The series dealt with the antics of Alan Young, a young man who found misadventures in everything he did.

Cast:

Alan Young	Himself
Betty, his girl-friend	Doris Singleton
Hubert Updike, the millionaire	Jim Backus
Zero	Charlie Cantor
Papa Dittenfeller	Ed Begley
Mrs. Johnson	Ruth Perrott

Also: Ken Christy, The Smart Set.

Announcer: Jimmy Wallington, Larry Elliott, Michael Roy.

Orchestra: George Wyle.

Length: 30 minutes.

Network: ABC (1944), NBC (1946).

First Broadcast: 1944.

Album of Manhattan

Type: Gossip

Format: Inside reports of the people and events in New York City.

Host: Louis Sobol.

Length: 15 minutes.

Network: Mutual.

First Broadcast: 1940.

The Aldrich Family

Type: Comedy

Format: The series dealt with the comic escapades of Henry Aldrich, a mischievous high school student, and his friends Homer and Dizzy. Became the basis for a TV series of the same title.

Cast:

Henry Aldrich	Ezra Stone
	Norman Tokar
	Raymond Ives
	Dick Jones
	Bobby Ellis
Sam Aldrich, his father	Clyde Fillmore
	House Jameson
	Tom Shirley
Alice Aldrich, his mother	Lea Penman
	Katharine Raht
	Regina Wallace
Mary Aldrich, Henry's sister	Betty Field
	Jone Allison
	Mary Mason
	Charita Bauer
	Mary Shipp
	Mary Rolfe
	Ann Lincoln
Homer Brown	Jackie Kelk
Dizzy Stevens	Eddie Bracken
Kathleen Anderson, Henry's girlfriend	Mary Shipp
	Ann Lincoln
	Ethel Blume
	Jean Gillespie
Will Brown, Homer's father	Ed Begley
	Howard Smith
	Arthur Vinton
Toby Smith, Henry's friend	Dick Van Patten
Mrs. Anderson, Kathleen's mother	Alice Yourman
Willie Marshall, the pesty little boy	Norman Tokar

Announcer: Dwight Weist, Dan Seymour,

Ralph Paul, George Bryan, Harry Von Zell.
Orchestra: Jack Miller.
Program Opening:
Mrs. Aldrich: Henry, Henry Aldrich!
Henry: Coming, Mother.
Announcer: Yes, it's "The Aldrich Family," based on characters created by Clifford Goldsmith, and starring Ezra Stone as Henry and Jackie Kelk as Homer . . .
Length: 30 minutes.
Network: NBC.
First Broadcast: 1939.

Alec Templeton Time

Type: Musical Variety
Host: Alec Templeton.
Regulars: Edna O'Dell, Billy Mills, Pat O'Malley, The William Miller Chorus.
Announcer: Fort Pearson.
Orchestra: Alec Templeton, Daniel Sardenberg, Ray Noble.
Length: 30 minutes.
Network: NBC.
First Broadcast: 1939.

The Alfredo Antonini Orchestra

Type: Classical Music
Host: Alfredo Antonini.
Regulars: Harry Kramer, Arthur Whiteside.
Orchestra: Alfredo Antonini.
Length: 30 minutes.
Network: Mutual.
First Broadcast: 1939.

Alias Jane Doe

Type: Drama
Format: The story of a beautiful and adventurous girl magazine editor who, in an attempt to acquire material, dons various disguises and writes of her experiences under the alias Jane Doe.
Cast: Jane Doe   Kay Phillips

Allen Prescott Presents. Allen Prescott.

The editor   Tudor Owen
Also: Eric Sinclair, Lamont Johnson.
Announcer: Frank Martin.
Length: 30 minutes.
Network: CBS.
First Broadcast: 1951.

Alias Jimmy Valentine

Type: Drama
Format: The series, based on the character created by O. Henry, followed the exploits of Jimmy Valentine, a famous safe-cracker.
Cast: Jimmy Valentine   Bert Lytell
                            James Meighan
Length: 15 minutes.
Network: NBC Blue.
First Broadcast: 1937.

Alka-Seltzer Time

Type: Musical Variety
Host: Herb Shriner.

Announcer: Durward Kirby.
Music: The Raymond Scott Quintet.
Sponsor: Alka-Seltzer.
Length: 15 minutes.
Network: CBS.
First Broadcast: 1948.

Allen Prescott Presents

Type: Variety
Format: Music, comedy, and songs.
Host: Allen Prescott.
Regulars: Diane Courtney, Jack and a Dame, The Hi-Lo's.
Orchestra: Jimmy Lytell.
Length: 30 minutes.
Network: NBC.
First Broadcast: 1941.

The Amazing American

Type: Quiz
Format: The object was for contestants to associate the travel services of the Greyhound Bus Lines with facts about America. A lecture, reconstructed to resemble a parlor game and containing facts about an unknown American locale, was read to the studio audience. Contestants chosen from the audience were asked questions concerning the lecture; they were permitted to receive two clues, but each clue diminished the point value of the question. Failure to respond within the allotted time disqualified a player from receiving points for the particular question. The winner. "The Amazing American," was the player with the highest point total at the end of the game.
Host: Bob Brown.
Vocalists: The Ranch Boys.
Orchestra: Roy Shield.
Length: 30 minutes.
Network: NBC.
First Broadcast: 1940.

The Amazing Mr. Malone

Type: Crime Drama
Format: The investigations and cases of John J. Malone, a light-hearted criminal attorney.
Cast: John J. Malone   Eugene Raymond
                                 Frank Lovejoy
                                 George Petrie
          The Police Lt.   Larry Haines
Length: 30 minutes.
Network: ABC (1948), NBC (1951).
First Broadcast: 1948.

The Amazing Mr. Smith

Type: Comedy-Mystery
Format: The cases of Gregory Smith, an amateur sleuth with an uncanny knack for attracting trouble.
Cast: Gregory Smith   Keenan Wynn
           His valet   Charlie Cantor
Announcer-Commentator: Harry Von Zell.
Orchestra: Harry Salter.
Length: 30 minutes.
Network: Mutual.
First Broadcast: 1941.

The Amazing Mr. Tutt

Type: Comedy-Drama
Format: The trials and tribulations of Ephriam Tutt, an uncanny and cantankerous New England attorney.
Starring: Willard Wright as Ephriam Tutt.
Announcer: Roy Rowan.
Orchestra: Lud Gluskin.
Length: 30 minutes.
Network: ABC.
First Broadcast: 1948.

The Amazing Mrs. Danbury

Type: Comedy
Format: The misadventures of Mrs. Jon-

athan Danbury, a sharp-tongued old woman, the owner of a department store, as she struggled to cope with life both at home and at work.

Cast: Mrs. Jonathan
      Danbury   Agnes
                      Moorehead
      Her daughter Cathy Lewis
      Her son   Dan Wolfe
Also: Bill Johnstone.
Announcer: Ken Niles.
Length: 30 minutes.
Network: CBS.
First Broadcast: 1946.

America Calling

Type: Variety
Format: A series devoted to playing the record requests of servicemen overseas. Highlight of the program was its efforts to help wives and girlfriends talk to servicemen via on-the-air telephone conversations.
Hostess: Rebel Randall.
Announcer: George Walsh.
Music: Recorded.
Length: 30 minutes.
Network: CBS.
First Broadcast: 1952.

American Melody Hour

Type: Musical Variety
Hostess: Vivian Della Chiesa.
Regulars: Conrad Thibault, Frank Munn, Frank Black.
Length: 30 minutes.
Network: NBC.
First Broadcast: 1941.

American Music Festival

Type: Classical Music
Host-Commentator: Nicolai Berzowski.
Orchestra: Howard Barlow.
Length: 30 minutes.

The Amos and Andy Show. Freeman Gosden (left) and Charles Correll in makeup for Amos and Andy respectively.

The Amos and Andy Show. Pictured are Freeman Gosden (left) and Charles Correll, out of makeup and in the midst of listener mail offering suggestions for naming the baby "born" to Amos and Ruby. The photograph is dated December 8, 1936.

Network: CBS.
First Broadcast: 1941.

The Amos and Andy Show

Type: Comedy
Format: The misadventures of Andrew Halt Brown, the naive and dim-witted president of the Fresh Air Taxi Cab Company of America, Inc., Amos Jones, his level-headed partner and the cab driver, and George "Kingfish" Stevens, a con artist and the head of the "Mystic Knights of the Sea" fraternity.

Cast: Amos Jones   Freeman Gosden
        Andrew H. Brown   Charles Correll
        George Stevens   Freeman Gosden
        Ruby Jones,
          Amos's wife   Elinor Harriot
        Arbadella Jones,
          Amos and
          Ruby's daugh-
          ter   Terry Howard
        Madame Queen,
          Andy's roman-
          tic interest   Harriette Widmer
                          Amanda Randolph
        Lightnin', the cab
          company jan-
          itor   Freeman Gosden
        Sapphire Stevens,
          George's wife   Ernestine Wade
        Mama, Sapphire's
          mother   Lillian Randolph
        Algonquin J. Cal-
          houne, the in-
          ept lawyer   Johnny Lee
        Shorty, the bar-
          ber   Lou Lubin
        Henry Van Port-
          er, a friend   Charles Correll
        Genevieve Blue,
          cab company
          secretary   Madaline Lee
Also, various roles: Millie Bruce.
Announcer: Bill Hay, Del Sharbutt, Olan Soule, Burrett Wheeler, Harlow Wilcox, Ned LeFevre, John Lake, Art Gilmore, Jim Ameche.
Vocalists: The Jubalaires, The Four Knights, The Jeff Alexander Chorus.
Orchestra: Jeff Alexander, Lud Gluskin.
Sponsor: Pepsodent tooth paste, Campbell's Soup Company, Rinso soap, Rexall drugs, Chrysler automobiles.
Program Opening:
Amos: Andy, listen, the man is just about to say it.
Andy: Yea, let's everybody listen.
Announcer: Rinso, the new Rinso with Solium, brings you "The Amos and Andy Show." Yes sir, Rinso, the soap that contains Solium, the sunlight ingredient, brings you a full half-hour of entertainment with the Jubalaires, Jeff Alexander's Orchestra and Chorus, and radio's all-time favorites, Amos and Andy.
Length: 15, 30, and 25 minute versions.
Network: NBC (1929), CBS (1950).
First Broadcast: 1926.
Note: In 1926, over station WGN in Chicago, Freeman Gosden and Charles Correll brought two blackface characters to radio in a series called "Sam and Henry." In 1928, over station WMAQ, the series title changed to "Amos and Andy" and one year later began its network run over NBC. In 1954, four years after switching to CBS, Gosden and Correll became the stars of "The Amos and Andy Music Hall," a twenty-five minute series of chatter between the two hosts, which originated from the mythical Grand Ballroom of the Mystic Knights of the Sea lodge. The series ended in 1960. Became the basis for a television series of the same title.

The Andrews Sisters Eight-to-the-Bar Ranch

Type: Musical Variety
Hosts: The Andrews Sisters (Patty, Maxene, and LaVerne).
Regulars: George "Gabby" Hayes, The Riders of the Purple Sage.
Announcer: Marvin Miller.
Orchestra: Vic Schoen.
Length: 30 minutes.
Network: NBC Blue (1944), ABC (1945).
First Broadcast: 1944.

The Andrews Sisters Show

Type: Musical Variety
Hostesses: The Andrews Sisters (Patty, Maxene, and LaVerne).
Regulars: Curt Massey, Jane Froman.
Announcer: Andre Baruch.
Orchestra: Vic Schoen.
Length: 30 minutes.
Network: CBS.
First Broadcast: 1945.

The Answer Man

Type: Information
Format: Over-the-air responses to listener's questions.
Starring: Albert Mitchell.
Sponsor: Trommer's beer, Post Grape-Nuts Flakes, Colgate toothpaste, Rayve shampoo.
Length: 15 minutes.
Network: Mutual.
First Broadcast: 1937.
Note: In 1954 the series was syndicated, with each market's own host serving as the Answer Man.

Appointment with Music

Type: Musical Variety
Host: Snooky Lanson.
Regulars: Dorothy Dillard, The Dixie Doms, The Varieteers.
Announcer: Ernie Kelly.
Orchestra: Beasley Smith.
Length: 30 minutes.
Network: NBC.
First Broadcast: 1948.

Arch Oboler Plays

Type: Anthology
Format: Dramatic presentations.
Host: Arch Oboler.
Included:
Mr. Pyle. The story of Ernie Pyle, a dissillusioned war correspondent as he searched the Pacific theater of war seeking to find the meaning of war and what this country stood for them.
Starring: Burgess Meredith.
Mr. Ten percent. The story of a theatrical agent and his efforts to make a superstar out of a woman of stunning beauty who has no interest in films.
Starring: Elliott Lewis, Bob Bailey.
Length: 30 minutes.
Network: NBC (1939), Mutual (1945).
First Broadcast: 1939 (NBC run: March 25, 1939 to March 23, 1940).

Archie Andrews

See title: "The Adventures of Archie Andrews."

Armchair Adventures

Type: Drama
Format: Both original plays and adaptations of stories, with one actor portraying all the parts.
Starring: Marvin Miller.
Length: 15 minutes.
Network: CBS.
First Broadcast: 1952.

Armstrong of the SBI

Type: Adventure
Format: The exploits of Jack Armstrong, chief investigator for the Scientific Bureau of Investigation. A spin-off from "Jack Armstrong, the All-American Boy."
Cast: Jack Armstrong   Charles Flynn
        Vic Hardy, head
          of the SBI   Ken Griffin
                              Carlton KaDell

        Betty Fairfield,
          Jack's assist-
          ant   Patricia Dunlap
        Billy Fairfield,
          Jack's assist-
          ant   Dick York
Announcer: Ken Nordine, Ed Prentiss.

Arthur Godfrey Time. Janette Davis and Arthur Godfrey.

Length: 30 minutes.
Network: ABC.
First Broadcast: 1950.

The Armstrong Theatre of Today

Type: Anthology
Format: Dramatic presentations.
Starring: Elizabeth Reller as the Armstrong Girl (later played by Julie Conway).
Announcer: George Bryan.
Sponsor: Armstrong.
Length: 30 minutes.
Network: CBS.
First Broadcast: 1941.

The Art Van Damme Quintet

Type: Musical Variety
Starring: Louise Carlyle, Benny Week, Lew Skalinder, Max Marlash, Chuck Calzoetta.
Announcer: George Stone.
Music: The Art Van Damme Quintet.

Length: 15 minutes.
Syndicated.
First Broadcast: 1945.

Arthur Godfrey Time

Type: Variety
Host: Arthur Godfrey.
Substitute Host: Robert Q. Lewis.
Regulars: Patti Clayton, Julius LaRosa, Marshall Young, Frank Parker, Bill Lawrence, Lu Ann Simms, Janette Davis, The McGuire Sisters, The Polka Dots, The Mariners, The Symphonettes, The Chordettes, The Jubalaires, The Four Clubmen.
Announcer: Tony Marvin.
Orchestra: Hank Sylvern, Archie Bleyer.
Length: 30 minutes.
Network: CBS.
First Broadcast: 1945.

Arthur Godfrey's Digest

Type: Variety
Host: Arthur Godfrey.
Regulars: Bill Lawrence, Janette Davis, The Cordettes, The Mariners.
Announcer: Tony Marvin.
Orchestra: Archie Bleyer.
Length: 30 minutes.
Network: CBS.
First Broadcast: 1950.

Arthur Godfrey's Talent Scouts

Type: Variety
Format: Performances by undiscovered professional talent. Became the basis for a TV series of the same title.
Host: Arthur Godfrey.
Vocalists: Peggy Marshall and the Holidays.
Announcer: George Bryan.
Orchestra: Archie Bleyer.
Sponsor: Lipton Tea.
Length: 30 minutes.
Network: CBS.
First Broadcast: 1946.

Arthur's Place

Type: Comedy Variety
Format: The misadventures of Arthur Moore, the owner-operator of a Midwest beanery.
Starring: Arthur Moore.
Also: Sara Berner.
Orchestra: Jeff Alexander.
Length: 30 minutes.
Network: CBS.
First Broadcast: 1947.

Arthur Tracy, Your Street Singer

Type: Variety
Starring: Arthur Tracy
Length: 15 minutes.
Network: NBC.
First Broadcast: 1942.

As the Twig is Bent

Type: Serial
Format: The struggles of Andrea Reynolds, a young school teacher, as she attempted to establish a new life in Beachmont, a small rural community.

Cast:

Andrea Reynolds	Barbara Terrell
	Joan Banks
	Betty Worth
Frank Harrison, the school board chairman	George Coulouris
	Horace Braham
Miss Blakely, the principal	Effie Palmer
The Music Teacher	Karl Swenson
The janitor	Henry M. Neely
Bill Peters	Frank Lovejoy
Taffy Grahame	Mitzi Gould
Kit Collins	Don MacLaughlin
Mrs. Van Cleave	Grace Keddy
Her butler	Bill Podmore
Dixie	Ann Thomas
Thelma	Sybil Trent
Mickey	Lesley Woods
Mrs. Wickes	Ethel Everett
Laura	Sarah Burton
Peter	Norman Rose
Madame Sophie	Barbara Weeks
	Lilli Darvas
Mrs. Carlton	Charme Allen
Abraham Watts	Juano Hernandez
Carlo	Carlo DeAngelo

Also: Ethel Owen, Larry Robinson, Jackie Grimes, Betty Jane Taylor.
Announcer: Tom Shirley, Dick Dunham, Adele Ronson, Fred Uttal.
Organist: Charles Paul, Hershel Leucke.
Length: 15 minutes.
Syndicated: (1941), CBS (1942).
First Broadcast: 1941. Later titled "We Love and Learn." Spin-off series: "The Story of Ruby Valentine," which see.

Ask Eleanor Nash

Type: Women's
Format: Beauty and fashion advice.
Hostess: Eleanor Nash.
Length: 15 minutes.
Network: NBC.
First Broadcast: 1941.

The Ask-It-Basket

Type: Quiz
Format: Called for contestants to answer general knowledge questions in return for cash prizes.
Host: Jim McWilliams, Ed East.
Sponsor: Colgate Dental Cream.
Length: 30 minutes.
First Broadcast: 1938.

At Home with Faye and Elliott

Type: Variety
Format: Celebrity interview, husband and wife chatter, household tips, and other items of interest to women.
Hostess: Faye Emerson.
Host: Elliott Roosevelt (Faye's husband at the time).
Announcer: Jim Ameche.

Length: 15 minutes.
Syndicated.
First Broadcast: 1946.

Attorney-at-Law

Type: Serial
Format: The dramatic story of Terry Regan, a young attorney.
Cast: Terry Regan   Jim Ameche
                            Henry Hunter

    Sally Dunlap,
      his secretary   Fran Carlon
                            Betty Winkler

    Mrs. Regan,
      Terry's mother   Grace Lockwood
    Mr. Regan,
      Terry's father   Fred Sullivan
    Terry's sister   Lucy Gilman
Length: 15 minutes.
Network: NBC Blue.
First Broadcast: 1937.

Attorney for the Defense

Type: Crime Drama
Format: The cases of Roger Allen, a crusading young San Francisco attorney who specialized in helping people with problems far beyond the norm.
Cast: Roger Allen (later
    changed to
    Jonathan Brix-
    ton)   Michael Raffetto
                            Al Hodge
    His assistant   Barton
                            Yarborough
Also: Forrest Lewis.
Length: 30 minutes.
Network: Mutual.
First Broadcast: 1946.

Auction Quiz

Type: Quiz
Format: The studio audience was divided into seven sections representing different subject categories. Questions (submitted by listeners) were offered at auction to the members of the appropriate section, with raises limited to one dollar. The high bid became the prize for that question, and the high bidder was given the opportunity to answer. If he answered correctly, he shared the prize money with the listener who submitted the question; if not, the listener received a consolation prize.
Host-Quizmaster: Chuck Acree.
Auctioneer: Bob Brown.
Announcer: Dan Donaldson.
Length: 30 minutes.
Network: NBC.
First Broadcast: 1941.

Aunt Jemima

Type: Variety
Format: Music and songs of the Old South.
Cast: Aunt Jemima   Tess Gardell
                            Harriette
                            Widmer
Host-Announcer: Marvin Miller.
Vocalists: Vera Lane, Mary Ann Mercer, Bill Miller, William Muelle, The Mixed Chorus, The Old Plantation Sextet.
Orchestra: Harry Walsh.
Sponsor: Aunt Jemima Pancake Mix.
Length: 5 and 15 minute versions.
Network: CBS.
First Broadcast: 1942.

Aunt Jenny's Real Life Stories

Type: Serial
Format: Dramatizations of real life stories. Various casts and presentations.
Hostess — Storyteller: Edith Spencer as Aunt Jenny.
Announcer: Dan Seymour as Danny, her assistant.
Sounds of Aunt Jenny's Canary: Henry Boyd.
Organist: Elsie Thompson.
Sponsor: Spry.
Length: 15 minutes.
Network: CBS.
First Broadcast: 1936.
Note: Also known as "Aunt Jenny's Thrilling Real Life Stories."

Author, Author

Type: Game
Format: The program challenged a well-known author to match wits with the fictional detective and author Ellery Queen. A short dramatic or humorous sequence was read to Ellery and his guest, each of whom had to design a complete plot around it. A later format found famous authors supplying endings to stories sent in by listeners.
Host: S.J. Pearlman, Ogden Nash.
Ellery Queen portrayed by: Manfred B. Lee and Frederic Dannay.
Announcer: Robert L. Shayon. Frank Knight.
Length: 30 minutes.
Network: Mutual.
First Broadcast: 1939.

Autumn in New York

Type: Musical Variety
Hosts: Jimmy Carroll, Frances Green.
Orchestra: Alfredo Antonini.
Length: 30 minutes.
Network: CBS.
First Broadcast: 1952.

Avalon Time

Type: Variety
Format: Music and comedy set against the background of a sophisticated hillbilly barn dance.
Host: Red Foley.
Regulars: Red Skelton, Janette Davis, Kitty O'Neil, Del King, The Neighbors Boys.
Orchestra: Phil Davis.
Sponsor: Avalon cigarettes.
Length: 30 minutes.
Network: NBC.
First Broadcast: 1938.

The Avenger

Type: Crime Drama
Format: The story of Jim Brandon, a biochemist who invented a secret diffusion capsule that cloaked him in a black light of invisibility. The series followed Brandon's attempts to uphold the law, equipped with the diffusion capsule and a telepathic indicator, which enabled him to pick up thought flashes.
Cast: Jim Brandon   James Monks
Fern Collier, his
assistant   Helen Adamson
Also: Allyn Edwards, Winston O'Keefe, Jean Vitez.
Orchestra: Doc Whipple.
Length: 30 minutes.
Syndicated.
First Broadcast: 1945.

The Baby Snooks Show

Type: Comedy
Format: The program focused on the life of Baby Snooks, an unpredictable and mischievous girl, and her harassed parents, Mr. and Mrs. Higgins.
Cast: Baby Snooks   Fanny Brice
Mr. Higgins
(Daddy)   Hanley Stafford
Mrs. Higgins
(Mummy)   Lalive Brownell
Lois Corbett
Arlene Harris
Robespierre,
Snook's brother   Leone Ledoux
Regulars: Elvia Allman, Martha Wentworth, Celeste Rush, Stan Farr, Georgia Ellis, Sara Berner.
Announcer: Don Wilson, Ken Roberts, Harlow wilcox.
Vocalist: Bob Graham.
Orchestra: Carmen Dragon.
Length: 30 minutes.
Network: NBC.
First Broadcast: 1939.

Backstage Wife

Type: Serial
Format: The dramatic story of Mary Noble, the wife of Broadway matinee idol

Larry Noble.

Cast:
Mary Noble	Vivian Fridell
	Claire Niesen
Larry Noble	Ken Griffin
	James Meighan
	Guy Sorel
Clara Noble,	
Larry's mother	Ethel Owen
Goldie	Eileen Palmer
Pop	Alan MacAteer
Arnold Carey	John M. James
Ada	Kay Renwick
Sandra Carey	Luise Barclay
Doris	Virginia Dwyer
Sylvia King	Dorothy Francis
Mercy	Charme Allen
Tom Bryson	Frank Dane
	Charles Webster
	Mandel Kramer
Katharine	
Monroe	Betty Smith
Regina	Anne Burr
Margot	Dorothy Sands
Larry Noble,	
Jr., Mary and	
Larry's son	Wilda Hinkel

Also, various roles: Marvin Miller, Eloise Kummer, Gail Henshaw.

Announcer: Harry Clark, Ford Bond, Roger Krupp, Sandy Becker.

Organist: Chet Kinsbury.

Sponsor: Dr. Lyon's Tooth Powder.

Program Opening:

Announcer: We present again today "Backstage Wife," the story of Mary Noble, an Iowa girl who marries Larry Noble, handsome matinee idol, dream sweetheart of a million other women, and her struggles to keep his love in the complicated atmosphere of backstage life.

Length: 15 minutes.

Network: Mutual (later NBC).

First Broadcast: 1935.

The Baron and the Bee

Type: Quiz

Format: Two two-member teams competed in a spelling bee in return for cash prizes. The "Baron" of the title was derived from Baron Munchausen, the teller of tall tales character created by Jack Pearl in 1933. See also "The Jack Pearl Show."

Host: Jack Pearl.

Co-Host: Cliff Hall (as Sharlie, his straight man).

Organist: Paul Taubman.

Length: 30 minutes.

Network: NBC.

First Broadcast: 1953.

Barry Cameron

Type: Serial

Format: Dramatic incidents in the lives of marrieds Barry and Anna Cameron.

Cast:
Barry Cameron	Spencer Bentley
Anna Cameron	Florence Williams
Vinnie	Doris Rich
Mary Ann Clark	Dorothy Sands
John Nelson	Scott McKay
Josephine	Elsie Hitz
Will Stevenson	King Calder
Frances	Colleen Ward
Martha Stevenson	Mary Hunter

Announcer: Larry Elliott.

Length: 15 minutes.

Network: NBC.

First Broadcast: 1945.

Barry Crane, Confidential Investigator

Type: Crime Drama

Format: The cases of Barry Crane, a confidential private investigator who undertook the causes of people unable to turn to the police for help.

Cast:
Barry Crane	William Gargan
the bartender	John Gibson

Length: 30 minutes.

Network: NBC.

First Broadcast: 1951.

The Barton Family

Type: Serial

Format: The dramatic story of the Barton family.

Cast: Bud Barton   Dick Holland
        Grandmother
        Barton   Kathryn Card

Also: Fern Parsons, Bill Bouchey, Ian Keith, Betty Jeffries, Jackie Harrison, Bob Jellison, Cliff Soubier, Ed Prentiss.

Length: 15 minutes.

Network: NBC.

First Broadcast: 1939. Also known as "Bud Barton," "The Story of Bud Barton," and "Those Bartons."

The Battle of the Sexes

Type: Quiz

Format One, 1938:

Two four-member teams, men vs. women, competed. A general knowledge question was read and the first player to respond through a buzzer signal received a chance to answer. If correct, he or she scored points. The members of the highest scoring team each received a wristwatch as a prize.

Format Two, 1942:

Shortly after America's involvement in World War II, the program altered its format to accommodate servicemen. Soldiers and girl canteen workers competed in a spelling bee; war bonds and cash prizes were awarded for correct answers.

Host, captain of the male team: Frank Crumit.

Hostess, captain of the female team: Julia Sanderson.

Later Hosts: Jay C. Flippen, Walter O'Keefe.

Announcer: Ben Grauer.

Length: 30 minutes.

Network: NBC.

First Broadcast: 1938.

The Baxters

Type: Drama

Format: The series focused on the difficulties of an average American family during wartime.

Cast: The father   Arthur Peterson
        The mother   Fern Parsons
        Their daughter   Jane Webb
        Their daughter   Eva Grant
        Their son   Arthur Young

Length: 15 minutes.

Network: NBC.

First Broadcast: 1943.

Beat the Band

Type: Quiz

Format: A music-oriented question, submitted by a home listener, was read to the studio orchestra. If an orchestra member failed to identify the song to which the question referred, the listener won $10 ($25 in a later format), and 50 cents was placed in the kitty (bass drum) by the orchestra. The orchestra member who identified the most songs won the money in the kitty.

Host: Garry Moore.

Hostess: Hildegarde Loretta Sell.

Vocalists: Marilyn (Marvel) Maxwell, Marilyn Thorne.

Announcer: Marvin Miller, Tom Shirley.

Orchestra: Ted Weems, Harry Sosnik.

Sponsor: Raleigh Cigarettes.

Length: 30 minutes.

Network: CBS.

First Broadcast: 1940.

The Beatrice Kay Show

Type: Musical Variety

Hostess: Beatrice Kay.

Regulars: Peter Lind Hayes, Lon Clark, The Elm City Four.

Announcer: Jay Jackson.

Orchestra: Hank Sylvern, Henry Levine.

Length: 30 minutes.

Network: Mutual.

First Broadcast: 1946.

Behind the Front Page

Type: Anthology
Format: Dramatizations of front page newspaper stories.
Host-Narrator: Gabriel Heatter.
Length: 30 minutes.
Network: Mutual.
First Broadcast: 1948.

Behind the Mike

Type: Anthology
Format: Dramatizations of behind-the-scenes stories in broadcasting.
Host: Graham McNamee.
Announcer: Harry Von Zell.
Length: 15 minutes.
Network: CBS.
First Broadcast: 1931.

Believe It Or Not. Robert Ripley.

Length: 30 minutes.
Network: NBC (1930) CBS (1939).
First Broadcast: 1930.

Behind the Story

Type: Anthology
Format: Dramatizations of little known incidents in the lives of famous people.
Host-Narrator and voices of all characters: Marvin Miller.
Length: 15 minutes.
Network: Mutual.
First Broadcast: 1949.

The Bell Telephone Hour

Type: Music
Host: James Melton.
Regulars: Francia White, The Ken Christy Chorus.
Orchestra: Donald Voorhees, The Bell Symphony Orchestra.
Length: 30 minutes.
Network: NBC.
First Broadcast: 1940.

Believe It Or Not

Type: Variety-Drama
Format: Dramatizations of the unusual happenings that appeared in the *Ripley's Believe It Or Not* newspaper column.
Host: Robert L. Ripley.
Substitute Host: George Abbott, Gregory Adams.
Regulars: Linda Lee, Harriet Hilliard, The Men About Town.
Announcer: Bill Griffis, Don Hancock.
Orchestra: B.A. Rolfe, Frank Novak, Ozzie Nelson.

The Ben Bernie Show

Type: Variety
Format: Music, songs, and comedy sketches.
Host: Ben Bernie.
Regulars: Lew Lehr, Mary Small, Manny Prager, Buddy Clark, Jackie Heller, Jane Pickens, Pat Kennedy, Bill Wilgus, Dick Stabile, Frank Prince.
Announcer: Harlow Wilcox, Bob Brown,

Harry Von Zell.
Orchestra: Bob Gibson.
Length: 30 minutes.
Network: CBS.
First Broadcast: 1936.

Ben Bernie's Musical Quiz

Type: Quiz
Format: A music-oriented quiz wherein two teams, men vs. women, competed in a series of question and answer rounds in return for merchandise prizes.
Host: Ben Bernie.
Regulars: Carol Bruce, The Bailey Sisters.
Announcer: Dan Seymour.
Orchestra: Bob Gibson.
Length: 30 minutes.
Network: NBC.
First Broadcast: 1940.

The Benny Goodman Show

Type: Musical Variety
Host: Bert Parks.
Starring: Benny Goodman.
Regulars: Art Lund, Martha Tilton, Peter Donald.
Announcer: Bud Collyer.
Music: The Benny Goodman Orchestra and Sextet.
Length: 30 minutes.
Network: NBC.
First Broadcast: 1939.

The Benny Rubin Show

Type: Variety
Format: Music coupled with talk and comedy routines.
Host: Benny Rubin.
Regulars: Edith Fellows, Jackie Coogan, Vinnie Monte, Lou and Lillian Bernard, The Andrews Twins.
Announcer: Don Ward.
Orchestra: Rex Maupin.
Length: 30 minutes.
Network: NBC (1949) ABC (1951).
First Broadcast: 1949.

Bert Lytell Dramas

Type: Anthology
Format: Dramatizations depicting the crucial moments that affect the lives of ordinary people.
Host: Bert Lytell.
Regular Performers: Jay Jostyn, Helen Choate.
Length: 15 minutes.
Network: NBC.
First Broadcast: 1938.

Best of All

Type: Music
Host: Robert Merrill.
Vocalist: Elizabeth Doubleday.
Announcer: Kenneth Banghart.
Orchestra: Skitch Henderson.
Length: 60 minutes.
Network: NBC.
First Broadcast: 1954.

Betty and Bob

Type: Serial
Format: The dramatic story of marrieds Betty and Bob Drake.

Cast:		
Betty Drake		Elizabeth Reller
		Betty Churchill
		Alice Hill
		Arlene Francis
		Edith Davis
		Mercedes McCambridge
	Bob Drake	Don Ameche
		Les Tremayne
		Spencer Bentley
		Carl Frank
		J. Anthony Hughes
		Van Heflin
Mae Drake, Bob's mother		Edith Davis
		Dorothy Shideler
Carl Grainger, their friend		Herbert Nelson
Ethel Grainger,		

Betty and Bob. Don Ameche and Betty Churchill.

Betty and Bob. Arlene Francis and Van Heflin.

Carl's wife	Eleanor Dowling
Al Bishop	Ned Weaver
Peter Standish	Francis X. Bushman
Marcia	Betty Winkler
Kathy Stone	Eloise Kummer
Tony Harker	Don Briggs

Length: 15 minutes.
Network: NBC.
First Broadcast: 1932.

Betty Boop Fables

Type: Children
Format: The comic misadventures of Betty Boop, the cartoon character created by Max Fleischer.

Cast:	
Betty Boop	Mae Questel
Freddie Frog	Red Pepper Sam William Costello

Music: Victor Erwin.
Length: 15 minutes.
First Broadcast: 1930s.

Betty Clarke Sings

Type: Musical Variety
Hostess: Betty Clarke.
Announcer: Don Lowe.
Music: Veryle Mills (harp), Frank Bantor (novachord), La La Porta (guitar).
Length: 15 minutes.
Network: ABC.
First Broadcast: 1949.

The Betty Crocker Magazine of the Air

Type: Women's
Format: Cooking tips, recipes, fashion ideas, household hints, and related information for housewives.
Hostess: Betty Crocker (portrayed by Zella Layne).
Announcer: Win Elliot.
Sponsor: General Foods.
Length: 20 minutes.

Betty Boop Fables. Mae Questel.

Network: ABC.
First Broadcast: 1947.

Betty Moore's Triangle Club

Type: Women's
Format: Decorating ideas, household hints, cooking and related information for housewives.
Hostess, portraying Betty Moore: Margaret MacDonald.
Regulars: Johnny Thompson, George Gann.
Music: Dahl Gable.
Length: 15 minutes.
Network: NBC Blue.
First Broadcast: 1943.

Beulah

Type: Comedy
Format: The misadventures of Beulah, Negro maid to the well-to-do Henderson family. Became the basis for a television series of the same title.

Cast:	Beulah	Marlin Hurt
		Bob Corley
		Hattie McDaniel
		Louise Beavers
		Lillian Randolph
	Harry Henderson, Beulah's employer	Hugh Studebaker
		Jess Kirkpatrick
	Alice Henderson, his wife	Mary Jane Croft
		Lois Corbett
	Donnie Henderson, their son	Henry Blair
		Sammy Ogg
	Oriole, Beulah's girlfriend	Ruby Dandridge
		Amanda Randolph
		Butterfly McQueen
	Bill Jackson, Beulah's boyfriend	Marlin Hurt
		Ernest Whitman

Vocalists: Eileen Wilson, Penny Piper, Carol Stewart.
Announcer: Hank Weaver, Marvin Miller, Ken Niles, Johnny Jacobs.
Orchestra: Buzz Adlam, Albert Sack, Gordon Kibbee.
Sponsor: Tums.
Length: 15 and 30 minute versions.
Network: CBS (1945) ABC (1947).
First Broadcast: 1945 (ended in 1953).

The Bickersons

Type: Comedy
Format: Incidents in the lives of John and Blanche Bickerson, a quarrelsome husband and wife. The series focused on their never-ending verbal battle as Blanche struggled to correct John's shortcomings.

Cast:	John Bickerson	Don Ameche
		Lew Porter
	Blanche Bickerson	Frances Langford
		Marsha Hunt
	Amos, Blanche's brother	Danny Thomas

Also: Lurene Tuttle, Lou Lubin, Benny
  Rubin, John Brown.
Announcer: John Holbrook.
Orchestra: Tony Romano.
Length: 30 minutes.
Network: CBS.
First Broadcast: 1947.

The Big Break

Type: Variety
Format: Performances by undiscovered
  professional talent.
Host: Eddie Dowling.
Announcer: David Ross.
Orchestra: Ray Bloch.
Length: 30 minutes.
Network: CBS.
First Broadcast: 1947.

Big City Serenade

Type: Musical Variety (broadcast from
  Chicago)
Host: Skip Farrell.
Regular: Henry Cooke.
Orchestra: Joseph Gallichio.
Length: 30 minutes.
Network: NBC.
First Broadcast: 1951.

The Big Guy

Type: Crime Drama
Format: The series dealt with the investi-
  gations of a hard-hitting private detec-
  tive.
Starring: John Calvin as the private detec-
  tive.
Also Cast: David Anderson, Dennis
  Alexander.
Length: 30 minutes.
Network: NBC.
First Broadcast: 1950.

The Big Hand

Type: Anthology
Format: Dramatizations of adventure stories.

Orchestra: Rex Maupin.
Length: 30 minutes.
Network: ABC.
First Broadcast: 1951.

The Big 'n' Little Club

Type: Children
Format: Songs, stories, and varied enter-
  tainment for children.
Host: Dick Collier.
Featured: Phil Cramer.
Length: 30 minutes.
Network: ABC.
First Broadcast: 1949.

The Big Show

Type: Variety
Format: Performances by celebrities.
Hostess: Tallulah Bankhead.
Announcer: Ed Herlihy.
Orchestra: Meredith Wilson.
Sponsor: Reynolds Aluminum, Chester-
  field cigarettes, Anacin, Dentyne.
Length: 90 minutes.
Network: NBC.
First Broadcast: 1950.

Big Sister

Type: Serial
Format: Dramatic incidents in the lives of
  two married sisters, Ruth Evans Wayne
  and Sue Evans Miller.
Cast: Ruth Evans
       Wayne   Ruth Chatterton
                      Nancy Marshall
                      Alice Frost
                      Marjorie Ander-
                        son
                      Mercedes
                        McCambridge
                      Grace Matthews
Sue Evans Miller   Helen Lewis
                      Haila Stoddard
                      Dorothy McGuire

The Big Show. Left to right: Guests Joan Davis, Mindy Carson, and Margaret Truman, with hostess Tallulah Bankhead.

	Peggy Conklin
	Fran Carden
Dr. John Wayne, Ruth's husband	Martin Gabel
	Paul McGrath
	Staats Cotsworth
Jerry Miller, Sue's husband	Ned Weaver
Michael West	Richard Kollmar
	Joseph Julian
Doris Monet	Joan Tompkins
Dr. Reed Bannister	Berry Koreger
	Ian Martin
	Arnold Moss
	David Gothard
Diane Ramsey	Elspeth Eric
Elsa Banning	Erin O'Brien Moore
Ernest Banning	Horace Braham

Roger Allen	Carl Benton Reid
Nurse Burton	Vera Allen
Dr. Seabrook	Everett Sloane

Also, various roles: Ed Begley, Ann Shepherd.

Announcer: Jim Ameche, Hugh Conover.

Organist: Richard Leibert.

Orchestra: William Meeder.

Sponsor: Ivory Soap, Spic and Span, Rinso.

Program Opening:

Announcer: Rinso presents "Big Sister" (over clock chimes), Yes, there's the clock in Glen Falls Town Hall telling us it's time for Rinso's story of "Big Sister," brought to you by the new soapy rich Rinso, R. . .I. . .N. . .S. . .O.

Length: 15 minutes.

Network: CBS.

First Broadcast: 1936.

Big Story

Type: Drama
Format: Dramatizations of headline-making newspaper stories.
Host-Narrator: Robert Sloane.
Announcer: Ernest Chappell.
Orchestra: Vladimir Selinsky.
Length: 30 minutes.
Network: NBC.
First Broadcast: 1947.

The Big Talent Hunt

Type: Variety
Format: Performances by unusual professional talent.
Host: Jim Backus.
Announcer: Ted Brown.
Orchestra: Emerson Buckley.

Length: 25 minutes.
Network: Mutual.
First Broadcast: 1948.

Big Town

Type: Crime Drama
Format: The exploits of Steve Wilson, a reporter for the *Illustrated Press*, a crusading newspaper in Big Town. Became the basis for a television series of the same title.
Cast: Steve Wilson   Edward G. Robinson
                          Edward Pawley
                          Walter Greaza
      Lorelei Kilbourne
      the society
      editor   Claire Trevor
                          Ona Munson

Big Town. Edward G. Robinson and Ona Munson.

	Fran Carlon
Inspector	
Callahan	Dwight Weist
Dusty Miller, the	
photographer	Lawson Zerbe
	Casey Allen
Eddie, the cab-	
driver	Ted de Corsia
D.A. Miller	Gale Gordon
Miss Foster	Helen Brown
The newsboy who	
shouts "Get	
your *Illu-*	
strated Press"	Bobby Winkler
	Michael O'Day

Narrator: Dwight Weist.
Announcer: Ken Niles.
Organist: John Gart.
Orchestra: Leith Stevens.
Length: 30 minutes.
Network: CBS (1937), NBC (1948).
First Broadcast: 1937.

The Bill Goodwin Show

Type: Variety
Host: Bill Goodwin.
Regulars: Peggy Knudsen, Shirley Mitchell, Jim Backus, Elvia Allman, Norene Gamel, Mary Jane Croft, The Girlfriends.
Orchestra: Jeff Alexander.
Length: 30 minutes.
Network: CBS.
First Broadcast: 1947.

The Billie Burke Show

Type: Comedy
Format: The comic escapades of a young woman.

Cast: Billie	Billie Burke
Her brother	Earle Ross
Her maid	Lillian Randolph
Banker Guthrie,	
Billie's romantic	
interest	Marvin Miller
Colonel Fitt,	
another suitor	Marvin Miller

Announcer: Tom Dickson, Marvin Miller.

Length: 30 minutes.
Network: CBS.
First Broadcast: 1944.

Billy and Betty

Type: Children's
Format: The story of Billy and Betty White, a brother and sister who constantly found themselves involved in daring adventures.

Cast: Billy White	Jimmy McCallion
Betty White	Audrey Egan
Melvin Castle-	
bury, their	
friend	Elliott Reid

Announcer: Kelvin Keech.
Length: 15 minutes.
Network: NBC.
First Broadcast: 1935.

The Bing Crosby Show

Type: Variety
Host: Bing Crosby.
Regulars: Connee Boswell, Rosemary Clooney, Peggy Lee, Bob Burns, Jud Conlon's Rhythmaires, The Red Nichols Combo, Skitch Henderson, The Buddy Cole Trio.
Announcer: Ken Carpenter, Glenn Riggs.
Orchestra: John Scott Trotter.
Sponsor: General Electric, Philco, Chesterfield.
Length: 30 and 25 minute versions.
Network: NBC (later CBS).
First Broadcast: 1931 (ended in 1962).

Biographies In Sound

Type: Anthology
Format: Interviews with and sketches of famous people. Guests narrated.
Producer: Joseph Meyers.
Orchestra: Leith Stevens.
Length: 60 and 25 minute versions.
Network: NBC.
First Broadcast: 1955 (ended in 1957).

The Bing Crosby Show. Guest Bob Hope and Bing Crosby.

The Bishop and the Gargoyle

Type: Crime Drama
Format: Retiring from his duties as a servant of God and interested in crime, a Bishop joins the parole board of Sing Sing State Prison. There he meets the Gargoyle, a convict he befriends and later reforms. The Gargoyle, upon completing his sentence, joins forces with the Bishop; the series depicted their battle against the sinister forces of evil.
Cast: The Bishop   Richard Gordon
      The Gargoyle   Milton Herman
                       Ken Lynch
Length: 30 minutes.
Network: Blue.
First Broadcast: 1936.

The Black Book

Type: Anthology
Format: Mystery presentations.
Narrator: Paul Frees.
Dramatic Cast: Paul Frees, John Dehner.

Announcer: Clarence Cassill.
Orchestra: Leith Stevens.
Length: 15 minutes.
Network: CBS.
First Broadcast: 1952.

The Black Castle

Type: Anthology
Format: Chilling dramatizations of people trapped in unexpected and dangerous situations.
Starring: Don Douglas (as all characters, including the host, the Wizard of the Black Castle).
Program Opening:
Announcer (over eerie sound effects): Now, up these steps to the iron-studded oaken door which yawns wide on rusted hinges, bidding us enter. (Over music): Music, do you hear it? Wait. It is well to stop, for here is the wizard of the Black Castle.
Wizard: There you are, back again, I see. Well, welcome, come in, come in. You'll be overjoyed at the tale I have for you tonight.
Length: 15 minutes.
Network: Mutual.
First Broadcast: 1943.

The Black Hood

Type: Crime Drama
Format: The crime-busting exploits of Kip Burland, a rookie cop who acquired magical powers by wearing a specially developed black hood.
Cast: Kip Burland,
        the Black Hood   Scott Douglas
        The girl reporter   Marjorie Cramer
Program Opening:
Announcer: The Black Hood.
Voice: Criminals beware! The Black Hood is everywhere.
Black Hood: I, The Black Hood, do solemnly swear that neither threats nor bribes nor bullets nor death itself shall keep me from fulfilling my vow to erase crime from the face of the earth!

Length: 15 minutes.
Network: Mutual.
First Broadcast: 1943.

The Black Museum

Type: Anthology
Format: Dramatizations based on Scotland Yard's Black Museum, a collection of murder weapons associated with London's most bizarre and baffling crimes. Each drama centered on one of the weapons and how it was used to commit a crime. Produced in England.
Host-Narrator (portraying the curator): Harvey Hayes (when broadcast under the title "Whitehall 1212"); Orson Welles.
Length: 30 minutes.
Network: Mutual.
First Broadcast: 1952. Originally titled "Whitehall 1212," which was aired in 1951.

Black Night

Type: Musical Variety
Format: A nocturnal jaunt to Chicago's points of interest, with narration and music.
Host: Don Dowd.
Vocalist: Carolyn Gilbert, Loretta Poynton.
Orchestra: Rex Maupin.
Length: 30 minutes.
Network: ABC.
First Broadcast: 1950.

Blackstone Plantation

Type: Variety
Hosts: Frank Crumit, Julia Sanderson.
Regulars: Santos Ortega, Ted de Corsia, Don Rodrigo, Don Escondido.
Length: 30 minutes.
Network: CBS.
First Broadcast: 1929.

Blackstone, the Magic Detective

Type: Adventure
Format: The exploits of Harry Blackstone, a former stage magician, as he used his show business experience to help people in distress. Very loosely patterned after the real life of Harry Blackstone.
Starring: Ed Jerome as Harry Blackstone.
Announcer: Alan Kent.
Music: William Meader.
Program Opening:
Announcer: The Magic Detective, starring the world's greatest living magician, Blackstone...Right after the story Blackstone will explain tricks that you yourself can perform and reveal the guarded secrets of the world's greatest living magician.
Length: 15 minutes.
First Broadcast: 1940s.

Blind Date

Type: Game
Format One: Competing were selected soldiers and/or sailors from the studio audience, each of whom vied for a blind date with a glamorous film actress (a guest). A dramatic sketch, performed by the cast, was stopped prior to its conclusion. Each of the male contestants, previously supplied with a comedy blackout line, related it to complete the sketch. The applause of the studio audience determined the winner, who received a date with the guest actress. This format, broadcast during World War II, featured a segment wherein a mother's letter to her serviceman son was read and relayed via shortwave.
Hostess: Frances Scully.
Dramatic Cast: Connie Haines, Mercedes McCambridge, Lizzie Tish (a comic female impersonator).
Vocalists: The Bryant Sisters.
Music: The Melodates Orchestra.
Length: 25 minutes.
Network: NBC.
First Broadcast: 1942.
Format Two: Six servicemen, selected

from the studio audience, tried to persuade three glamorous girls into accepting a blind date with them. The men and women were on stage separated from each other by a screen. Each male had to telephone a girl and, within a time limit, try to clinch a date. Each girl talked to two boys and selected the one she felt was the most romantic. Each of the three couples received a sponsored evening at a New York supper club. Became the basis for a television series of the same title.

Hostess: Arlene Francis.
Announcer: Tiny Ruffner.
Orchestra: Arnold Johnson.
Length: 30 minutes.
Network: ABC.
First Broadcast: 1943.

Bloch Party

Type: Musical Variety
Host: Ray Bloch.
Vocalist: Judy Lynn.
Chorus: Russ Emery.
Announcer: Martin Sweeney.
Orchestra: Ray Bloch.
Length: 60 minutes.
Network: CBS.
First Broadcast: 1951.

Blondie

Type: Comedy
Format: Events in the lives of the Bumstead family: Dagwood, a bumbling architect struggling to cope with life, Blondie, his attractive, but scatterbrained wife, and their children Alexander and Cookie. Based on the comic strip by Chic Young. Also the basis for a movie and television series of the same title.
Cast: Blondie

Blondie. Penny Singleton.

Bumstead	Penny Singleton
	Alice White
	Patricia Van
	Cleve
	Ann Rutherford
Dagwood Bumstead	Arthur Lake
Alexander (Baby Dumpling) Bumstead, their son	Leone Ledoux
	Larry Sims
	Jeffrey Silver
	Tommy Cook
Cookie Bumstead, their daughter	Marlene Ames
	Joan Rae
	Norma Jean Nilsson
Julius C. Dithers, Dagwood's boss	Hanley Stafford
	Arthur Q. Bryan
Cora Dithers, his wife	Elvia Allman
Herb Woodley, Dagwood's neighbor	Hal Peary
	Frank Nelson
Alvin Fuddle, Alexander's friend	Dix Davis
Mr. Fuddle,	

Alvin's father   Arthur Q. Bryan
                  Harry Lang
Harriet, Blondie's
  friend   Mary Jane Croft
Announcer: Bill Goodwin, Howard Petrie.
Orchestra: Harry Lubin, Billy Artzt.
Sponsor: Camel cigarettes.
Program Opening:
Announcer: Uh-uh-uh, don't touch that dial
  listen to
Dagwood: B-l-o-o-o-n-d-i-e-e-e!
Announcer: Yes folks, it's another half
  hour of fun with Blondie and Dagwood.
Length: 30 minutes.
Network: CBS.
First Broadcast: 1939.

The Blue Beetle

Type: Crime Drama
Format: The exploits of Dan Garrett, a
  rookie patrolman who, by wearing bullet-
  proof blue chain mail, transformed him-
  self into the mysterious Blue Beetle, a
  daring crusader for justice.
Starring Frank Lovejoy as Dan Garrett, the
  Blue Beetle.
Length: 15 minutes.
Syndicated.
First Broadcast: 1938.

Blue Ribbon Music Time

Type: Musical Variety
Hostess: Georgia Gibbs.
Announcer: Jimmy Wallington.
Orchestra: David Rose.
Sponsor: Pabst Blue Ribbon Beer.
Length: 30 minutes.
Network: NBC.
First Broadcast: 1947.

Blue Ribbon Time

Type: Musical Variety
Host: Kenny Baker.
Announcer: Ken Niles.

Orchestra/Chorus: Robert Armbruster.
Sponsor: Pabst Blue Ribbon Beer.
Length: 30 minutes.
Network: CBS.
First Broadcast: 1944.

Blue Ribbon Town

Type: Comedy-Variety
Starring: Groucho Marx, Virginia O'Brien,
  Donald Dickson, Kenny Baker.
Orchestra: Robert Armbruster.
Sponsor: Pabst Blue Ribbon Beer.
Length: 30 minutes.
Network: CBS.
First Broadcast: 1943.

Bluegrass Brevities

Type: Country/Western Musical Variety
Host: Chuck Hurton.
Announcer: Alan Jackson.
Orchestra: Robert Hutsell.
Length: 15 minutes.
Network: CBS.
First Broadcast: 1939.

The Bob and Ray Show

Type: Comedy
Format: Various skits satirizing everyday
  life.
Hosts: Bob Elliott, Ray Goulding.
Announcer: Jack Costello.
Organist: Rosa Rio.
Music: The Paul Taubman Trio.
Length: 15, 30, and 60 minute versions.
Network: NBC. Originally aired locally
  over station WHDH in Boston.
First Broadcast: 1948 (over WHDH), 1951
  (NBC). Also titled: "Matinee with Bob and
  Ray" and "Pick and Play with Bob and
  Ray," This title (NBC, 1953) featured a
  quiz segment wherein a contestant, se-
  lected from the studio audience, first
  chose a number and then attempted to
  answer a question associated with it.

Players received prizes whether they answered correctly or not, but strove to acquire the most correct answers to win a jackpot of merchandise gifts.

The Bob Burns Show

Type: Comedy
Format: Comic tales of a man called the Arkansas Traveler.
Starring: Bob Burns as the Arkansas Traveler.
Regulars: Shirley Ross, Ann Thomas, Doug Gourlay, Carry Allen.
Orchestra: Gordon Jenkins, Billy Artzt.
Length: 25 and 30 minute versions.
Network: CBS (1941), NBC (1944).
First Broadcast: 1941.

The Bob Crosby Show

Type: Musical Variety
Host: Johnny Mercer.
Starring: Bob Crosby.
Vocalists: Kay Starr, Bob Haggart, Eileen Wilson, The Pied Pipers.
Announcer: Les Tremayne, John Lund.
Music: The Bob Cats.
Length: 30 minutes.
Network: CBS (1939), NBC (1943).
First Broadcast: 1939.

Bob Hawk's Quixie Doodle Contest

See title: "Quixie Doodle."

The Bob Hawk Show

Type: Quiz
Format: Selected members of the studio audience competed in a series of question and answer rounds in return for cash prizes.
Host: Bob Hawk.
Regulars: Charles Stark, Art Gentry.
Announcer: Dennis James.
Orchestra: Peter Van Steeden.

Length: 30 minutes.
Network: CBS (1945), NBC (1947).
First Broadcast: 1945.

The Bob Hope Show

Type: Comedy
Format: Music, songs, monologues, and comedy sketches.
Cast: Bob Hope — Himself
Professor Colonna — Jerry Colonna
Vera Vague, the man-chasing girl — Barbara Jo Allen
Brenda, a society girl — Blanche Stewart
Cobina, a society girl — Elvia Allman
Miriam, the sponsor's pitch girl — Trudy Erwin
Honey Chile, the Southern Belle — Patricia Wilder, Claire Hazel
Also: Frank Fontaine, Irene Ryan.
Vocalists: Doris Day, Judy Garland, Gloria Jean, Bill Farrell, Frances Langford, The Six Hits and a Miss Vocal Group.
Announcer: Wendell Niles, Larry Keating, Bill Goodwin, Hy Averback, Art Baker.
Orchestra: Al Goodman, Red Nichols, Skinnay Ennis, Les Brown.
Sponsor: Pepsodent.
Length: 30 minutes.
Network: NBC.
First Broadcast: 1934.

The Bob Smith Show

Type: Variety
Host: Bob Smith.
Regulars: Clark Dennis, The Honeydreamers.
Orchestra: Bobbie Nicholson.
Length: 30 minutes.
Network: CBS.
First Broadcast: 1954.

Bobby Benson's Adventures

Type: Western
Format: The adventures of Bobby Benson, a twelve-year-old boy who operated and struggled to protect the B-Bar-B Ranch (also called the H-Bar-O Ranch when sponsored by H-O Oats.)

Cast:

Bobby Benson	Richard Wanamaker
	Ivan Curry
	Billy Halop
Tex Mason, the foreman	Herb Rice
	Neil O'Malley
	Charles Irving
	Al Hodge
	Tex Ritter
Polly Armstead	Florence Halop
Windy Wales, the handyman	Don Knotts
Harska, the Indian	Craig McDonnell
The Chinese cook	Herb Rice
Aunt Lilly	Larraine Pankow

Announcer: Bob Emmerick, Andre Baruch, Carl Warren, Carl Caruso.
Program Opening:
Announcer: Here they come. They're riding fast and they're riding hard. It's time for excitement and adventure in the modern west with Bobby Benson and the B-Bar-B riders. And out in front, astride his golden palomino Amigo, it's the cowboy kid himself, Bobby Benson.
Bobby: B-Bar-Beeeeeeee.
Length: 30 minutes.
Network: CBS (1932), NBC (1947), Mutual (1949).
First Broadcast: 1932.
Note: Also known as "B-Bar-B Ranch," and "Songs of the B-Bar-B."

The Bobby Doyle Show

Type: Musical Variety
Host: Bobby Doyle.
Featured: The Honey Dreamers Quintet.
Announcer: Jack Lester.

Orchestra: Harry Kogen.
Length: 15 minutes.
Network: NBC.
First Broadcast: 1947.

Bold Venture

Type: Adventure
Format: Background: Havana. The exploits of Slate Shannon and Sailor Duval, the owner-operators of a boat and hotel called the Bold Venture. Became the basis for a television series of the same title.

Cast:

Slate Shannon	Humphrey Bogart
Sailor Duval	Lauren Bacall

Orchestra: David Rose.
Program Opening:
Announcer: Bold Venture! Adventure intrigue, mystery, romance; starring Humphrey Bogart and Lauren Bacall together in the salty setting of tropical Havana and the mysterious islands of the Caribbean. Bold Venture!
Length: 30 minutes.
Syndicated.
First Broadcast: 1951.

Boston Blackie

Type: Crime Drama
Format: The exploits of Boston Blackie, a private detective working out of New York. Became the basis for a television series of the same title.

Cast:

Boston Blackie	Richard Kollmar
Mary Wesley, his girlfriend	Lesley Woods
	Jan Miner
Inspector Faraday	Richard Lane
	Maurice Tarplin
	Frank Orth

Announcer: Larry Elliott, Harlow Wilcox.
Organist: Hank Sylvern.
Sponsor: R & H Beer.
Program Opening:
Announcer: And now meet Richard Kollmar as Boston Blackie, enemy to

those who make him an enemy, friend to those who have no friends.

Length: 30 minutes.
Network: NBC (1944), Mutual (1945).
First Broadcast: 1944.

The Boston Pops Orchestra

Type: Musical Variety
Host: Arthur Fiedler.
Announcer: Ben Grauer.
Orchestra: The Boston Pops.
Length: 60 minutes.
Network: NBC.
First Broadcast: 1951.

The Botany Song Shop

Type: Musical Variety
Hostess: Ginny Simms.
Announcer: Harry Von Zell.
Music: The Buddy Cole Trio.
Sponsor: Botany Mills.
Length: 15 minutes.
Network: ABC.
First Broadcast: 1950.

Bouquet For You

Type: Musical Variety
Hostess: Patti Clayton.
Regulars: Billy Williams, Louise King, Billy Leach.
Announcer: Lee Vines, Franklyn MacCormack.
Orchestra: Howard Smith, Caesar Petrillo.
Length: 30 minutes.
Network: CBS.
First Broadcast: 1946.

Box 13

Type: Adventure
Format: The exploits of Dan Holliday, a newspaper writer who will "do anything and go anywhere" to aid people in need.

(The title was derived from the number on his mailbox — 13).

Cast: Dan Holliday   Alan Ladd
Suzy, his assistant   Sylvia Picker
Length: 30 minutes.
Syndicated.
First Broadcast: 1948.

Brave Tomorrow

Type: Serial
Format: The dramatic story of the Lambert family. Their story of love and courage was designed to show that from today's defeats we build our brave tomorrows.

Cast: Hal Lambert   Raymond Edward Johnson
                                Roger DeKoven
        Louise Lambert   Jeanette Dowling
        Jean Lambert   Nancy Douglas
                                Flora Campbell
        Marty Lambert   Jone Allison
                                Andree Wallace
Also: Ginger Jones, Frank Lovejoy, Carl Eastman, House Jameson, Myra McCormick, Margaret MacDonald, Paul Stewart.
Announcer: Ed Herlihy.
Music: William Meader.
Length: 15 minutes.
Network: NBC.
First Broadcast: 1943.

Break the Bank

Type: Quiz
Format: A series of question and answer rounds. Each correct response earned five dollars; players continued until defeated by two incorrect responses, or until they broke the bank by answering eight straight questions for the top prize. Each player who was defeated forfeited his earnings, which were deposited in the bank to a maximum of $1,000. Became the basis for a television series of the same title.

Host: John Reed King, Johnny Olsen, Bert
    Parks, Bud Collyer.
Announcer: Bud Collyer, Win Elliot.
Orchestra: Hank Sylvern, Peter Van Stee-
    den.
Organist: Lew White.
Length: 30 minutes.
Network: Mutual.
First Broadcast: 1945.

Breakfast at Sardi's

Type: Variety
Host: Tom Breneman.
Announcer: Carl Pierce.
Length: 30 minutes.
Network: NBC Blue.
First Broadcast: 1943.

The Breakfast Club

Type: Variety. Became the basis for a
    television series of the same title.
Host: Don McNeill.
Regulars: Fran Allison (as Aunt Fanny),
    Sam Cowling, Bill Thompson, Jack
    Owens, Janette Davis, Johnny Johnston,
    Jim and Marian Jordan (as Fibber McGee
    and Molly), Russell Pratt, Edna O'Dell,
    Annette King, Ilene Woods, Johnny Des-
    mond, Clark Dennis, Marion Mann, Gale
    Page, The Cadets, The Three Romeos,
    The Vagabonds, The Merry Macs.
Announcer: Charles Irving, Don Dowd,
    Durward Kirby, Bob McKee, Bob Mur-
    phy, Frank Ferguson, Ken Nordine.
Orchestra: Walter Blaufuss, Harry Kogen,
    Rex Maupin, Joseph Gallichio, Eddie Bal-
    lantine.
Length: 60 minutes.
Network: NBC (later ABC).
First Broadcast: 1933.

Breakfast in Hollywood

Type: Variety
Host: Arch Presby, Tommy Breneman,

Brenda Curtis. Agnes Moorehead.

    Garry Moore, Jack McElroy.
Regulars: Jack Coy, Johnny Montgall.
Announcer: John Nelson, Carl Pierce.
Orchestra: Gaylord Carter.
Length: 30 minutes.
Network: NBC (1942), ABC (1948).
First Broadcast: 1942.

Brenda Curtis

Type: Serial
Format: The story of Brenda Curtis, a bril-
    liant actress who forsakes her career to
    devote her time to her husband, Jim, a
    lawyer, and to establish a home and a
    new life.
Cast: Brenda Curtis   Vicki Vola
        Jim Curtis   Michael
                Fitzmaurice
                Hugh Marlowe

        Myra Belden,
        Brenda's friend   Helen Choate
        Brenda's mother   Agnes
                Moorehead

Length: 15 minutes.
Network: CBS.
First Broadcast: 1939.

Brenthouse

Type: Serial
Format: The story of Portia Brent, a widow who inherited Brenthouse, a book publishing company, from her late husband. The series followed her experiences as she attempted to cope with the problems of raising three children and running a publishing firm.

Cast: Portia Brent   Hedda Hopper
                        Georgia Backus
                        Kathleen Fitz
        Jane Brent, her
          daughter   Florence Baker
        Nancy Brent, her
          daughter   Lurene Tuttle
        Peter Brent,
          her son   Ernest Carlson
                        Larry Nunn
        Martha Dudley   Margaret
                          Brayton
        Lance Dudley   Wally Maher
        Philip West   Ben Alexander
        Steve Dirk   Al Cameron
        Gabrielle Faure   Anne Stone
        Nora Mawson   Jane Morgan
        Daphne Royce   Naomi Stevens
        Dr. Norfolk   Gavin Gordon

Length: 30 minutes.
Network: NBC Blue.
First Broadcast: 1938.

Bride and Groom

Type: Weddings
Format: Couples were married before the microphones, and later showered with gifts. Became the basis for a television series of the same title.
Host: John Nelson.
Announcer: Jack McElroy.
Length: 30 minutes.
Network: ABC.
First Broadcast: 1945

Bright Horizon

Type: Serial
Format: The story of Michael West — outwardly soft-hearted, and idealistic, inwardly a man filled with hard, bitter disillusionment. A spin-off from "Big Sister" in which the Michael West character was heard; Alice Frost, as Ruth Wayne, appeared briefly to establish the new series.

Cast: Michael West   Joseph Julian
                        Richard Kollmar
        Carol West   Sammie Hill
                        Joan Alexander
        Larry   Frank Lovejoy
        Margaret
          McCarey   Lesley Woods
        Bobby   Ronald Liss
        Barbara   Renee Terry
        Keith Richards   Lon Clark
        Lily   Alice Goodkin
        Bonnie   Audrey Totter
        Charles McCarey   Richard Keith

Also: Will Geer, Santos Ortega, Chester Stratton, Jackie Grimes.
Announcer: Marjorie Anderson.
Organist: John Gart.
Length: 15 minutes.
Network: CBS.
First Broadcast: 1941.

Bright Star

Type: Comedy-Drama
Format: The story centered around the adventures of a newspaper reporter for the *Hillsdale Morning Star*.

Cast: Susan, the
          reporter   Irene Dunne
        George, the
          editor   Fred MacMurray

Announcer: Harry Von Zell.
Length: 15 minutes.
Network: NBC.
First Broadcast: 1952.

The Brighter Day

Type: Serial

Format: The dramatic story of the Dennis family, residents of the town of Three Rivers.

Cast: Liz Dennis   Margaret Draper
                               Grace Matthews
         Richard Dennis   Bill Smith
         Althea Dennis   Jay Meredith
         Barbara Dennis   Lorna Lynn
         Grayling Dennis   Billy Redfield
         Patsy   Pat Hosley
         Sandra Talbot   Ann Hilary
         Cliff   John Larkin

Narrator: Ron Rawson.
Announcer: Bill Rogers, Len Sterling.
Organist: William Meeder.

Program Opening:

Announcer: The Brighter Day. Our years are as the falling leaves. We live, we love, we dream, and then we go. But somehow we keep hoping, don't we, that our dreams come true on that Brighter Day?

Length: 15 minutes.
Network: NBC (1948), CBS (1949).
First Broadcast: 1948.

Bring 'Em Back Alive

Type: Adventure
Format: The exploits of jungle adventurer, Frank Buck.
Starring: Frank Buck as himself.
Length: 15 minutes.
Network: Mutual.
First Broadcast: 1930s.

Bringing Up Father

Type: Comedy
Format: The misadventures of the Jiggs family. Based on the comic strip by George McManus.

Cast: Jiggs, the
           husband   Neil O'Malley
         Maggie, his wife   Agnes
                              Moorehead
         Nora, their
           daughter   Helen Shields
         Dinty Moore   Craig McDonnell
         The store

manager   Morgan Farley
Orchestra: Merle Kendrick.
Length: 30 minutes.
Network: NBC.
First Broadcast: 1941.

Broadway Matinee

Type: Musical Variety
Host: Jim Ameche.
Regulars: Ronald Graham, Patsy Garrett.
Orchestra: Allen Roth.
Length: 25 minutes.
Network: CBS.
First Broadcast: 1944.

Broadway Is My Beat

Type: Mystery
Format: The story of Danny Clover, a New York police detective assigned to the Broadway beat. The series dealt with crime, criminals, and the difficulty of living in a large city.

Cast: Danny Clover
           (later named
           Anthony Ross)   Larry Thor
         Sgt. Muggowen   Jack Kruschen
         Sgt. Tarlagita   Charles Calvert

Orchestra: Robert Stringer, Wilbur Hatch.
Length: 30 minutes.
Network: CBS.
First Broadcast: 1949.

Brownstone Theatre

Type: Anthology
Format: Adaptations of plays and stories popular at the turn of the century.
Host-Narrator: Clayton Hamilton.
Regular Performers: Jackson Beck. Gertrude Warner, Neil Hamilton.
Music: Sylvan Levin.
Length: 30 minutes.
Network: Mutual.
First Broadcast: 1945.

Buck Private and His Girl

Type: Romantic Drama
Format: The story of Steve Mason, a young draftee, and his sweetheart, Anne, and their romance, which is shattered by World War II.
Cast: Pvt. Steve Mason   Myron
                                  McCormick
       Anne   Anne Seymour
Also: Joan Banks, Alexander Kirkland, Tom Powers, Don McLaughlin.
Length: 15 minutes.
Network: NBC.
First Broadcast: 1941.

Buck Rogers in the 25th Century

Type: Science Fiction Adventure
Format: In Pittsburgh, in 1919, Buck Rogers, a young Air Corps veteran, begins surveying the lower levels of an abandoned mine. When the crumbling timbers give way, the roof from behind him caves in. Unable to escape, he is rendered unconscious by a peculiar gas that places him in a state of suspended animation.

As the earth shifts, fresh air enters the mine and awakens Buck. Emerging from the cave, he finds himself standing in the midst of a vast forest. Meeting Lieutenant Wilma Deering of the Space General's staff, he discovers that it is the year 2430 and the place is no longer Pittsburgh, but Niagara, America's capital. Stories depicted Buck's attempts to aid Wilma and the scientific genius, Dr. Huer, in their battle against evil, particularly Killer Kane, a madman seeking to control the world. Based on the comic strip conceived by John F. Dille.

Cast: Buck Rogers   Matt Crowley
                        Curtis Arnall
                        John Larkin

       Lt. Wilma
       Deering   Adele Ronson
                        Virginia Vass
       Dr. Huer   Edgar Stehle

Buck Rogers in the 25th Century. Matt Crowley in costume for his role as Buck Rogers.

       George "Buddy"
       Wade, Buck's
       ward   Ronald Liss
       Killer Kane   Bill Shelley
                        Arthur Vinton

       Ardala, a
       villainess   Elaine Melchoir
Announcer: Fred Uttal, Paul Douglas, Kenny Williams.
Sponsor: Popsicle Ice Cream Bars, Cocomalt.
Program Opening:
Announcer: Buck Rogers in the 25th Century ... Buck Rogers, who was held in suspended animation for five hundred years is now adventuring in the amazing world of the 25th Century. By turning a little dial to project us ahead in time we are able to be with Buck and his friends in the wonderful world of the future ...
Length: 15 and 30 minute versions.
Network: CBS (1931), Mutual (1939).
First Broadcast: 1931.

Bud Barton

See Title: "The Barton Family."

The Buddy Clark Show

Type: Musical Variety
Host: Buddy Clark.
Regulars: Nan Wynn, Anne Elstner, Ted de Corsia.
Orchestra: Leith Stevens, Frank Novak.
Length: 30 and 15 minute versions.
Network: CBS. (later Mutual).
First Broadcast: 1938.

Buddy Clark's Summer Colony

Type: Musical Revue
Host: Buddy Clark.
Regulars: Hildegarde, Fray and Brag-grate.
Orchestra: Leith Stevens.
Length: 30 minutes.
Network: CBS.
First Broadcast: 1939.

Bulldog Drummond

See title: "The Adventures of Bulldog Drummond."

Burl Ives Coffee Club

Type: Variety
Format: Popular and semi-classical songs and music.
Host: Burl Ives.
Regulars: Juan Arvizi, Genevieve Rowe, The Deltha Rhythm Boys.
Announcer: Hugh Brundige.
Orchestra: Walter Gross.
Length: 30 and 15 minute versions.
Network: CBS (1941), Mutual (1946).
First Broadcast: 1941.

Burns and Allen

See title: "The George Burns and Gracie Allen Show."

"The Buster Brown Gang."

See title: "The Smilin' Ed McConnell Show."

The Busy Mr. Bingle

Type: Comedy
Format: The misadventures of Mr. Bingle, a scatterbrained inventor and owner of the Bingle Pin Company.
Cast: Mr. Bingle   John Brown
The sales manager   Jackson Beck
The telephone operator   Ethel Owen
Mrs. Bingle, Bingle's absent-minded wife   Elizabeth Moran
Length: 30 minutes.
Network: Mutual.
First Broadcast: 1943.

By Kathleen Norris

Type: Anthology
Format: Dramatizations of stories by Kathleen Norris.
Hostess-Narrator: Kathleen Norris (portrayed by Ethel Everett).
Cast: Arlene Blackburn, House Jameson, Mary Cecil, Santos Ortega, Lawson Zerbe, Mildred Baker, Florence Malone, Betty Garde, Effie Palmer.
Announcer: Dwight Weist.
Length: 15 minutes.
Network: CBS.
First Broadcast: 1939.

By Popular Demand

Type: Musical Variety
Host: Bud Collyer.
Regulars: Mary Small, Harry Babbitt.
Announcer: Bud Collyer.
Orchestra: Ray Bloch.

Length: 30 minutes.
Network: Mutual.
First Broadcast: 1945.

Cabin B-13

Type: Anthology
Format: Mystery presentations related by Dr. Fabian, a ship physician who resides in Cabin B-13.
Starring: Arnold Moss as Dr. Fabian.
Narrator: Arnold Moss.
Music: Merle Kendrick.
Length: 30 minutes.
Network: CBS.
First Broadcast: 1948.

Cafe Istanbul

Type: Adventure
Format One: The series centered around the sultry Mlle. Madou, a cabaret performer in the Far East, and her involvement with international spies, murderers, and the Secret Police.
Cast: Mlle. Madou   Marlene Dietrich
        The American   Ken Lynch
        The Cop   Arnold Moss
Format Two: The change found Marlene Dietrich as Mlle. Madou, a sultry song siren and owner of a night club in San Francisco, who weaves dramatic tales of love, adventure and intrigue.
Starring: Marlene   Dietrich   as   Mlle. Madou.
Orchestra: Ralph Norman.
Length: 30 minutes.
Network: ABC.
First Broadcast: 1952.

Calamity Jane

Type: Drama
Format: A tongue-in-cheek portrayal of a conniving reporter and her attempts to expose racketeers.
Cast: Calamity Jane   Agnes
                           Moorehead

Her grandfather,
        the publisher   Dan Wolfe
Also: Cathy Lewis, Bill Johnstone.
Announcer: Ken Niles.
Length: 30 minutes.
Network: CBS.
First Broadcast: 1946.

California Caravan

Type: Anthology
Format: Dramatizations based on the legends stemming from the gold rush of 1849.
Cast: Virginia Gregg, Michael Hayes, Herb Vigran, John McGovern, Paul Frees, Bob Shennon, Bob Purcell.
Announcer: Fort Pearson.
Length: 30 minutes.
Network: Mutual.
First Broadcast: 1949.

Call for Music

See title: "Dinah Shore."

Call Me Freedom

Type: Anthology
Format: Dramatizations based on the ideals and principles of America's heritage. Produced in cooperation with the Freedom Foundation at Valley Forge.
Narrator: Nelson Olmsted.
Length: 30 minutes.
Network: ABC.
First Broadcast: 1953.

Call the Police

Type: Crime Drama
Format: An insight into the world of policemen as told through the experiences of Bill Grant, a college-bred, retired W.W. II Marine, now a police captain.
Cast: Bill Grant   Joseph Julian

George Petrie
His assistant   Amzie Strickland
The sergeant   Robert Dryden
Announcer: Jay Simms, Hugh James.
Length: 30 minutes.
Network: NBC.
First Broadcast: 1947.

The Callahans

Type: Variety
Format: Varied situations set against the background of a Broadway theatrical house.
Cast: Ma Callahan   Elsa Mae Gordon
        Pa Callahan   Arthur Hill
        Penelope Calla-
        han, their
        daughter   Florence Halop
Also: Ed Latimer, Donald Bain, Joe Latham, Betty Walker, Ethel Owen, Jack Arthur.
Announcer: Ted Campbell.
Orchestra: Jerry Sears, Van Alexander.
Length: 30 minutes.
Syndicated.
First Broadcast: 1944.

Calling All Detectives

Type: Mystery-Quiz
Format: A dramatization was enacted by varying casts. The crime guide, Robin, then pinpointed specific clues. As the story reached its climax, it was interrupted and five minutes of air time relinquished to the local stations carrying the program. Local announcers then telephoned listeners selected from post card entries. Based on the clues given by Robin, the listener had to identify the culprit. Once the five minutes had elapsed, the local stations rejoined the network and the story concluded. Listeners who correctly uncovered the culprit received war bonds as a prize, the amount varying with the local stations. At WGN in Chicago, for example a $100 bond was awarded for a correct response,

a $25 bond for an incorrect answer.
Host: Vincent Pelletier as Robin.
Organist: Dick Platt.
Length: 30 minutes.
Network: Mutual.
First Broadcast: 1945.

Calling America

Type: Musical Variety
Host-Commentator: Arthur Hale.
Regulars: Drew Pearson, Robert Allen, Gracie Barrie, The Tune-twisters.
Orchestra: Erno Rapee.
Length: 30 minutes.
Network: Mutual.
First Broadcast: 1939.

Camel Caravan

Type: Musical Variety
Host: Vaughn Monroe.
Announcer: Wayne Nelson, Joe King.
Vocalist: Sally Sweetheart.
Orchestra: Sauter-Finnegan, Vaughn Monroe.
Sponsor: Camel cigarettes.
Length: 30 minutes.
Network: CBS.
First Broadcast: 1951.

Camel Presents Harry Savoy

Type: Musical Variety
Host: Harry Savoy.
Regulars: Benay Venuta, Paula Kelly and the Modernaires.
Orchestra: Peter Van Steeden.
Sponsor: Camel cigarettes.
Length: 30 minutes.
Network: NBC.
First Broadcast: 1944.

Campana Serenade

Type: Variety
Host: Dick Powell.

Regulars: Martha Tilton, The Music Maids.
Announcer: Henry Chorles.
Orchestra: Lud Gluskin, Matty Malneck.
Sponsor: Campana makeup.
Program Opening:
Announcer: Campana Serenade, coast-to-coast, from Hollywood, starring Dick Powell, with Martha Tilton, and Lud Gluskin's orchestra. Presented by Campana, the makers of Solitare, the new cake makeup.
Length: 30 minutes.
Network: NBC.
First Broadcast: 1945.

Campbell Playhouse

See title: "The Mercury Theatre on the Air."

Can You Top This?

Type: Game
Format: A joke, sent in by a listener (who received $10) was related to the studio audience, whose applause was registered on a laugh meter. The three regular panelists each had to relate a joke in the same category, the object being to beat the listener's score. Each failure added five dollars to the listener's prize, to a total limit of $25. Became the basis for a television series of the same title.
Host: Ward Wilson.
Joke Teller: Peter Donald.
Panelists: Senator Edward Ford, Harry Hershfield, Joe Laurie, Jr.
Announcer: Charles Stark.
Sponsor: Par soft drink, Kirkman's Soap Flakes and Complexion Soap, The Colgate-Palmolive Company.
Length: 30 minutes.
Network: Mutual.
First Broadcast: 1940.

Candid Microphone

Type: Comedy

Format: The forerunner of TV's long-running "Candid Camera." The program used hidden microphones to record the response of unsuspecting individuals caught in pre-arranged situations.
Host: Allen Funt, Lamont Johnson.
Narrator: Don Hellenback.
Announcer: Ken Roberts.
Orchestra: Bernie Green.
Sponsor: Philip Morris cigarettes.
Length: 30 minutes.
Network: ABC (1947), CBS (1950).
First Broadcast: 1947.

Candy Matson, YUkon 2-8209

Type: Crime Drama
Format: The cases of Candy Matson, a beautiful female private detective working out of San Francisco.
Starring: Natalie Masters as Candy Matson.
Length: 30 minutes.
Network: NBC.
First Broadcast: 1950.

Canteen Girl

Type: Variety
Format: Sentimental ballads, dramatic monologues, and music set against the background of the Stage Door Canteen, a New York night club.
Hostess: Phyllis Jean Creare.
Length: 15 minutes.
Network: NBC.
First Broadcast: 1942.

Captain Flagg and Sergeant Quirt

Type: Comedy
Format: The misadventures of two bickering Marines: Captain Flagg and Sergeant Quirt.
Cast: Captain Flagg   Victor McLaglen

Sergeant Quirt	Edmund Lowe
The Major General	John Smith
The General's wife	Gloria Jones

Orchestra: Lou Kosloff.
Length: 30 minutes.
Network: NBC.
First Broadcast: 1941.

Captain Midnight

Type: Adventure
Format: The story of a private citizen who devoted his life to fighting crime. Named "Captain Midnight" for his daring air tactics during World War I, Captain Albright commands the Secret Squadron, a government organization designed to combat evil. Assisted by Chuck Ramsey, Ichabod Mudd, and Joyce Ryan, he battles the sinister forces of evil.

Cast: Captain Midnight	Ed Prentiss
	Bill Bouchey
	Paul Barnes
Chuck Ramsey	Bill Rose
	Jack Bivens
Ichabod "Ichy" Mudd	Hugh Studebaker
	Sherman Marks
Joyce Ryan	Angeline Orr
Ivan Shark, Midnight's nemesis	Boris Aplon
Fury Shark, Ivan's daughter	Rene Rodier
	Sharon Grainger

Announcer: Pierre Andre, Don Gordon, Tom Moore.
Sponsor: Skelly Oil Company, Ovaltine.
Program Opening:
Voice: Captain Midnight.
Announcer: Yes, Captain Midnight, brought to you every day, Monday through Friday, by the makers of Ovaltine, America's favorite food drink.
Length: 15 minutes.

Syndicated (1939), Mutual (1940).
First Broadcast: 1939.

Captain Stubby and the Buccaneers

Type: Variety
Host: Tom Foute.
Regulars: Tony Walberg, Sonny Fleming, Jerry Richards, Tiny Stokes.
Announcer: John Dalton.
Orchestra: Phil Davis.
Length: 15 minutes.
Syndicated.
First Broadcast: 1946.

The Career of Alice Blair

Type: Serial
Format: The struggles of a young career woman in New York City.

Cast: Alice Blair	Martha Scott
	Betty Moran

Also: Joseph Cotten.
Length: 15 minutes.
Network: Mutual.
First Broadcast: 1940.

Caricatures in Rhythm

Type: Musical Variety
Host: Harry Reser.
Regulars: Dorothy Rochelle, Barry McKinley, The Tune Twisters.
Orchestra: Harry Reser.
Length: 30 minutes.
Network: NBC.
First Broadcast: 1938.

Carl Hohengarten's Orchestra

Type: Musical Variety
Host: Carl Hohengarten.
Regulars: Tod Hunter, David McCall, Tommy Bartlett.
Orchestra: Carl Hohengarten.
Length: 25 minutes.

Network: CBS.
First Broadcast: 1939.

Carle Comes Calling

Type: Musical Variety
Host: Frankie Carle.
Regulars: Marjorie Hughes, Gregg Lawrence, The Starlighters.
Orchestra: Frankie Carle.
Length: 30 minutes.

The Carmen Miranda Show

Type: Musical Revue
Hostess: Carmen Miranda.
Regulars: Judy Ellington, The Rodgers Sisters.
Announcer: LeRoy Miller.
Orchestra: Nat Shilkert, Charles Barnett.
Length: 60 minutes.
Network: NBC.
First Broadcast: 1939.

The Carnation Contented Hour

Type: Musical Variety
Host: Tony Marvin.
Regulars: Jo Stafford, Buddy Clark, The Ken Lane Singers.
Announcer: Vincent Pelletier, Jimmy Wallington.
Orchestra: Percy Faith, Victor Young.
Sponsor: The Carnation Milk Company.
Length: 30 minutes.
Network: NBC (1931), CBS (1950).
First Broadcast: 1931.

The Carnation Family Party

Type: Variety-Game
Format: Interviews with people who had to prove or disprove certain facts about themselves.
Host: Jay Stewart.
Announcer: Larry Thor.
Sponsor: The Carnation Milk Company.
Length: 30 minutes.

Network: CBS.
First Broadcast: 1950.

Carnival with Bernie West

Type: Variety
Host: Bernie West.
Regulars: Lynn Collier, Johnny Morgan, Art Kahl, Pat Hosley, Flora MacMichaels, Billy Greene, Grace Valentine.
Announcer: Bob Sherry.
Orchestra: Henry Levine.
Length: 30 minutes.
Network: NBC.
First Broadcast: 1946.

Carolina Calling

Type: Country/Western Musical Variety
Host: Grady Cole.
Regulars: Fred Kirby, Claude Casey, Whitey and Hogan, The Swanee River Boys, The Johnson Family, Harry Blair, Howard Turner, The Briarhoppers.
Length: 30 minutes.
Network: CBS.
First Broadcast: 1946.

Carolina Hayride

Type: Country/Western Musical Variety
Host: Arthur Smith.
Regulars: Claude Casey, Larry Walker, The Tennessee Ramblers, Whitey and Hogan, The Southland Jubilee Singers, The Briarhoppers, Ma Johnson's Family.
Length: 30 minutes.
Network: CBS.
First Broadcast: 1944.

Caroline's Golden Store

Type: Comedy
Format: The series depicted comic incidents in the lives of Caroline, the proprietor of a small town general store, and

the people who frequented it.
Starring: Caroline Ellis as Caroline.
Customers: Jack Brinkley, Frank Behrens, Barbara Winthrop, Joan Kay, Cliff Carl, Ginger Jones, Guila Adams, Harriette Widmer.
Announcer: Franklin MacCormack.
Length: 15 minutes.
Network: NBC.
First Broadcast: 1939.

Carson Robinson's Buckaroos

Type: Country/Western Musical Variety
Host: Carson Robinson.
Announcer: Jack Costello.
Music: Bill, John, and Pearl Mitchell.
Length: 30 minutes.
Network: NBC.
First Broadcast: 1938.

The Carters of Elm Street

Type: Serial
Format: The dramatic story of the Carter family.

Cast:	
Mara Carter, the mother	Virginia Payne
Jeff Carter, the father	Vic Smith
Mildred Carter Randolph, their married daughter	Virginia "Ginger" Jones
Bunny Carter, their youngest daughter	Ann Russell
Jess Carter, their son	William Rose
Sidney Randolph, Mildred's husband	Herbert Nelson
Mattie Belle, the Carter's housekeeper	Harriette Widmer

Sponsor: Ovaltine.
Length: 15 minutes.

Network: NBC.
First Broadcast: 1939.

Carton of Smiles

Type: Musical Variety
Host: Henny Youngman.
Vocalist: Carol Bruce.
Announcer: Tom Shirley.
Orchestra: Eddy Howard.
Sponsor: Raleigh cigarettes.
Length: 30 minutes.
Network: NBC.
First Broadcast: 1944.

Casa Cugat

See title: "Xavier Cugat."

The Case Book of Gregory Hood

Type: Crime Drama
Format: The exploits of Gregory Hood, a gentleman detective working out of San Francisco.

Cast:	
Gregory Hood	Gale Gordon
	Elliott Lewis
	Jackson Beck
	Paul McGrath
	Martin Gabel
	George Petrie
Sandy, his sidekick	Bill Johnstone

Announcer: Harry Baslett.
Music: Dean Fossler.
Length: 30 minutes.
Network: Mutual (1946), ABC (1949).
First Broadcast: 1946.

Casey, Crime Photographer

Type: Crime Drama
Format: The exploits of Casey, a photographer for the *Morning Express*, a crusading newspaper. Became the basis for the television series of the same title.

Cast: Casey   Matt Crowley
                        Staats Cotsworth

       Anne Williams,
         his girlfriend Jone Allison
                        Alice Reinheart
                        Betty Furness
                        Lesley Woods
                        Jan Miner

       Ethelbert, the
         bartender in
         the Blue Note
         Cafe   John Gibson
       Police Captain
         Logan   Jackson Beck
                        Bernard Lenrow
Announcer: Tony Marvin, Bob Hite, Ken
    Roberts.
The Blue Note Cafe Pianist: Juan Fernan-
    dez, Herman Chittison, Teddy Wilson.
Organist: Lew White.
Orchestra: Archie Bleyer.
Program Opening:
Announcer: Good evening, this is Ken
    Roberts inviting you to listen to another
    adventure of "Casey, Crime Photo-
    grapher," ace cameraman who covers the
    crime news of a great city. Our adventure
    for tonight: "Thunderbolt."
Length: 30 minutes.
Network: CBS.
First Broadcast: 1943. Also known as
    "Flash Gun Casey."

The Cass Daley Show

Type: Comedy
Format: The misadventures of Cass Daley,
    a well-intentioned small town girl who
    tries to help others out, but only succeeds
    in causing unwanted trouble.
Cast: Cass Daley   Herself
       Her father   Fred Howard
       Her mother   Lurene Tuttle
Announcer: Arch Presby.
Orchestra: Robert Armbruster.
Length: 30 minutes.
Network: CBS.
First Broadcast: 1950.

Catch Me If You Can

Type: Quiz
Format: Two contestants compete: the
    Climber and the Challenger. A question is
    read by the host and the Climber receives
    the first chance to answer. If the oppo-
    nent believes the wrong answer was
    given, he challenges by attempting to
    give the correct response. If his challenge
    is successful, he defeats the Climber and
    moves to the first rung of a ladder. He
    then becomes the Climber and a new
    Challenger is brought on. If, however, the
    Climber gave a correct response, he
    moves up one rung on the ladder. The
    first player to reach the top rung (The
    Golden Door) receives the opportunity to
    unravel a mystery sentence for prizes.
Host: Bill Cullen.
Announcer: George Bryan.
Length: 30 minutes.
Network: CBS.
First Broadcast: 1948.

Cavalcade of America

Type: Anthology.
Format: Dramatizations depicting the
    struggles endured by the people who
    helped to shape America.
Narrator: Gabriel Heatter.
Featured Performer: Thomas Chalmers.
Announcer: Bud Collyer.
Orchestra: Donald Voorhees.
Organist: Rosa Rio.
Sponsor: The DuPont Corporation.
Length: 30 minutes.
Network: CBS (1938), NBC (1945).
First Broadcast: 1938.

The CBS Radio Mystery Theatre

Type: Anthology
Format: Mystery presentations.

Host-Narrator: E.G. Marshall.

Creator-Producer: Himan Brown.

Included:

The Impossible Is True. The story of a girl who fears that there is a horrible curse of death on her and her family.

Starring: Ann Williams, Earl Hammond.

Crossfire. A cabbie suddenly finds himself involved in a crossfire between two rival gangs when his fare, a jeweler, becomes involved in a murder.

Starring: Russell Horton, Ann Williams, Earl Hammond, Court Benson.

Wise Child. While vacationing, a married couple find an abandoned baby which, after much discussion, they decide to keep and raise as their own. As the weeks pass, the baby, who is seemingly healthy, doesn't grow — but the husband suddenly acquires the ability to read minds, an ability he uses to advance his position in life. Exactly who or what is the baby, where it came from, or what happened the night it was abandoned (during a fierce thunderstorm in an area reputed to be radioactive) was not explained; it was suggested that on that night a higher intelligence possessed the baby.

Starring: Ralph Bell, Ann Williams, Jackson Beck.

Ghost in the Well. The story concerns an artist, who, after painting the portrait of a girl he envisions, suddenly finds himself face to face with her spirit and involved in her plight as she attempts to prove who murdered her in 1799.

Starring: Tony Roberts, Patricia Elliott, Court Benson, Williams Griffis.

Program Opening:

Host: The CBS Radio Mystery Theatre presents (over a squeaking door that is opening)... Come in, welcome I'm E.G. Marshall... (an introduction to the evening's presentation is then given)

Program Closing:

Host: This is E.G. Marshall inviting you to return to our Mystery Theatre for another adventure in the macabre. Until next time, pleasant dreams (the squeaking door closes).

Length: 52 minutes.

Network: CBS (syndicated in areas where it was not picked up by a CBS station).

First Broadcast: 1974.

Ceiling Unlimited

Type: Musical Variety

Host: Joseph Cotten.

Vocalist: Nan Wynn.

Announcer: Pat McGeehan.

Orchestra: Wilbur Hatch.

Length: 30 minutes.

Network: CBS.

First Broadcast: 1943.

Central City

Type: Drama

Format: The series, based in Central City, an industrial complex of fifty thousand people, focused on a "typical" family and related dramatic incidents in their lives.

Cast:	
Commentator	Tom Powers
The father	Frank Wilcox
The mother	Selena Royle
The daughter	Eleanor Phelps
Her fiance	Van Heflin
Her rejected finance	Myron McCormick

Also: Everett Sloane, John McBryde, Elspeth Eric, Harry Bellaver.

Length: 15 minutes.

Network: NBC.

First Broadcast: 1938.

Challenge of the Yukon

See title: "Sergeant Preston of the Yukon."

The Chamber Music Society of Lower Basin Street

Type: Musical Variety
Host: Milton Cross, Gene Hamilton, Jane Pickens, Orson Bean.
Regulars: Dinah Shore, Jack McCarthy, Henry Levine, Diane Courtney, Lena Horne.
Orchestra: Paul LaValle, Henry Levine.
Program Opening:
Announcer: Four-thirty Sunday afternoon in New York and the R.C.A. building now stands up straight and respectfully removes its hat as we tune in on another concert by the no doubt world renowned Chamber Music Society of Lower Basin Street, whose members have gathered here to read from the classics of the three B's—Barrelhouse, Boogie Woogie, and the Blues.
Length: 30 minutes.
Network: Blue (1940-1944), NBC (1950-1952).
First Broadcast: 1940.

Chance of a Lifetime

Type: Quiz
Format: Four players competed. As a series of letters appeared on an electronic board, players were permitted to choose three each. During this process a bell or buzzer sounded. If the bell was heard, the player in the process of selecting his letters received a luxury gift; if a buzzer sounded, a less expensive gift was awarded. Following this segment, players were given a last opportunity to increase their winnings by pitting everything in a ten-second race against time. If, within that time, a player was able to choose a bell-associated letter from the board, he won; if not, he lost everything.
Host: John Reed King.
Assistant: Janice Ford.
Announcer: Ken Roberts.
Length: 30 minutes.
Network: ABC.
First Broadcast: 1949.

Chandu, the Magician

Type: Adventure
Format: The exploits of Frank Chandler, an American secret agent who used supernatural powers, acquired from a Hindu Yogi, to combat evil. Chandler was known in the secret places of the Far East as Chandu, the Magician.

Cast:

Frank Chandler/ Chandu	Gayne Whitman Tom Collins
Dorothy Regeant, his widowed sister, living in San Francisco	Margaret MacDonald Irene Tedrow
Bob Regeant, her son	Bob Bixby Lee Miller
Betty Regeant, her daughter	Betty Webb Joy Terry
Princess Nadji, Chandler's romantic interest	Veola Vonn
Roxor, Chandler's enemy	Luis Van Rooten

Announcer: Howard Culver.
Program Opening:
Sound Effect: A large gong sounding.
Announcer: (over music): Chandu, the Magician. Good evening ladies and gentlemen. The makers of White King Granulated Soap present for your enjoyment tonight and every weekday evening at this time Chandu, the Magician. Listen and you will travel to strange lands, you will thrill to high adventure, romance, and mystery... There are many tales told on radio, but only one Chandu; there are many soaps on your grocer's counter, but none like White King... Now let the play begin...
Program Closing:
Announcer: We pause before we say good evening, to suggest that you and your family listen to Chandu every weekday evening at this time. Travel with us to strange places and far away lands, into

the mystery and intrigue of Egypt and the Near East. And of course we like to have you use the soap we make, White King Granulated Soap... So, on your radio remember Chandu, the Magician ... and at your grocer's remember White King Granulated Soap... Goodnight.

Sponsor: White King Soap.

Length—Network-First   Broadcast: 15 minutes, Mutual, 1932-1936; 30 minutes, Mutual, 1948-1949; 30 minutes, ABC, 1949-1950.

Chaplain Jim

Type: Drama

Format: The experiences of a chaplain during World War II.

Cast: Chaplain Jim   John Lund
                                 Don MacLaughlin

Announcer: George Ansbro, Vinton Hayworth.

Length: 30 minutes.

Network: Blue.

First Broadcast: 1942.

The Charles Boyer Show

Type: Anthology

Format: Dramatic presentations.

Host: Charles Boyer (portraying a nightclubbing Parisian who earns his keep by spinning yarns for visiting novelists).

Length: 30 minutes.

Network: NBC.

First Broadcast: 1950.

Charlie and Jessie

Type: Comedy

Format: The misadventures of marrieds Charlie (a salesman for Bissell, Cartwright, Emerson, and Spillwork) and his wife Jessie.

Cast: Charlie   Donald Cook
        Jessie   Diane Bourbon
                             Florence Lake

Announcer: Nelson Case.

Length: 15 minutes.

Network: CBS.

First Broadcast: 1940.

Charlie Chan

Type: Mystery

Format: The exploits of famed Oriental detective Charlie Chan, a master investigator who incorporated scientific knowledge and deductive reasoning as he attempted to solve baffling crimes. Based on the books by Earl Derr Biggers.

Cast: Charlie Chan   Walter Connolly
                             (1932)
                             Ed Begley
                             (1944-1947)
                             Santos Ortega
                             (1947-1948)
                             William Rees
                             (1950)

        Lee Chan, his
        Number One
        Son   Leon Janney
                             (1944-1948)
                             Rodney Jacobs
                             (1950)

Announcer: Dorian St. George.

Organist: Lew White.

Sponsor: Lever Brothers; Pharmaco, Inc.

Program Opening:

Announcer: Right now, sit back, relax and listen to the greatest Oriental detective of all time, the incomparable Charlie Chan... in a new and exciting series. Join this famous detective of fiction, films, and radio as he combines the wisdom of the East with the science of the West in a dramatic chapter from the adventures of Charlie Chan.

Length: 15 and 25 minute versions.

Network-First   Broadcast: NBC   (1932-1933), Mutual (1937-1938), Mutual (1944-1946), as "The Adventures of Charlie Chan," ABC (1945-1947), Mutual (1947-1948), Syndicated (1950).

The Charlie Ruggles Show

Type: Comedy-Variety
Starring: Charlie Ruggles.
Vocalist: Linda Ware.
Length: 30 minutes.
Syndicated.
First Broadcast: 1944.

Charlie Wild, Private Detective

Type: Crime Drama
Format: The investigations of private detective Charlie Wild.
Cast: Charlie Wild   George Petrie
      McCoy, his
        assistant   Peter Hobbs
Announcer: Bill Rogers.
Length: 30 minutes.
Network: CBS.
First Broadcast: 1950.

The Charlotte Greenwood Show

Type: Comedy-Drama
Format: The story of Charlotte Greenwood, a cub reporter on a small town newspaper. The series underlined her one ambition: to venture on to Hollywood and become an actress.
Cast: Charlotte Green-
        wood   Herself
      The city editor   John Brown
Also: Harry Bartell, Will Wright, Ed McDonald, Veola Vonn.
Vocalists: The Richard Davis Chorus.
Announcer: Wendell Niles.
Orchestra: Charles Hathaway.
Length: 30 minutes.
Network: Blue.
First Broadcast: 1944.

The Chase

Type: Anthology
Format: Dramatizations based on the theory that at one time or another every person is either the hunter or the hunted —physically or mentally. Varying casts and stories.

Length: 30 minutes.
Network: NBC.
First Broadcast: 1952.

The Chesterfield Supper Club

Type: Musical Variety
Sponsor: Chesterfield cigarettes.
Format One:
Host: Martin Block.
Vocalists: Perry Como, Jimmy Savo, Mary Ashworth, The Satisfiers.
Orchestra: Ted Steele.
Length: 15 minutes.
Network: NBC.
First Broadcast: 1944.
Format Two:
Host: Tex Beneke.
Vocalist: Garry Stevens, Eddie Hubbard.
Orchestra: Glenn Miller.
Length: 15 minutes.
Network: NBC.
First Broadcast: 1947.
Format Three:
Host (Monday, Wednesday, Friday): Perry Como.
Vocalists: The Fontaine Sisters.
Announcer: Tom Reddy.
Orchestra: Mitchell Ayres.
Hostess (Tuesday): Jo Stafford.
Announcer: Tom Reddy.
Orchestra: Paul Weston.
Hostess (Thursday): Peggy Lee.
Featured: The King Cole Trio.
Announcer: Tom Reddy.
Orchestra: Dave Barbour.
Length: 15 minutes.
Network: NBC.
First Broadcast: 1948.

Chesterfield Time

Type: Musical Variety
Host: Martin Block.
Vocalists: Johnny Johnston, Monica Lewis.
Orchestra: Paul Baron.
Sponsor: Chesterfield cigarettes.
Length: 15 minutes.
Network: CBS.
First Broadcast: 1944.

The Chicago Theatre of the Air

Type: Variety
Host: Lee Bennett.
Baritones: Bruce Foote, Thomas L. Thomas, Earl Willkie.
Soprano: Nancy Carr.
Tenor: Attelio Baggiore.
Contralto: Ruth Slater.
Regulars: Donald Graham, Lawrence Lane, Cal McCormick, The WGN Chorus.
Dramatic Cast: Marvin Miller, Olan Soule, Betty Lou Gerson, Betty Winkler, Fran Carlon, Bret Morrison, Kay Westfall, Les Tremayne, Bob Jellison.
Announcer: John Weigle, Marvin Miller.
Chorus: Robert Trendler.
Music: The WGN Orchestra.
Length: 60 minutes.
Network: Mutual (from WGN in Chicago).
First Broadcast: 1939.

Chick Carter, Boy Detective

Type: Crime Drama
Format: The cases of Chick Carter, the a-dopted son of Nick Carter, world famous detective. A spin-off from "Nick Carter, Master Detective."
Cast: Chick Carter   Bill Lipton
                                     Leon Janney

      Sue, his
        assistant   Jean McCoy
                                     Joanne McCoy
      Tex, their friend   Gilbert Mack
Program Opening:
Announcer (over telegraph sounds):   Mutual to Y...O...U. Sending. Are you ready?
Voice: Y...O...U to Mutual, go ahead.
Announcer: Then listen to the adventures of Chick Carter, Boy Detective.
Length: 15 minutes.
Network: Mutual.
First Broadcast: 1943.

Chicken Every Sunday

Type: Comedy
Format: The antics of the residents of a Tucson boarding house.
Starring: Billie Burke, Harry Von Zell.
Orchestra: David Baskerville.
Length: 30 minutes.
Network: NBC.
First Broadcast: 1949.

Choose a Song Partner

Type: Musical Variety
Host: Don Moreland.
Vocalist: Beryl Vaughn.
Organist: Adele Scott.
Length: 15 minutes.
Network: ABC.
First Broadcast: 1948.

Choose Up Sides

Type: Quiz
Format: Two teams of experts answer questions submitted by listeners, who received ten dollars if theirs was chosen. The winning team received $50.
Host: Henry McLemore.
Length: 30 minutes.
Network: CBS.
First Broadcast: 1940.

The Choraliers

Type: Musical Variety
Host: Eugene Lowell (manager of the vocal group The Choraliers).
Announcer: Frank Knight.
Length: 30 minutes.
Network: CBS.
First Broadcast: 1950.

Christopher London

Type: Crime Drama
Format: The cases of Christopher London, a private detective who will "go anywhere and do anything" for a price. Based on the character created by Erle Stanley Gardner.
Starring Glenn Ford as Christopher London.

Length: 30 minutes.
Network: NBC.
First Broadcast: 1950.

The Christopher Lynch Show

Type: Musical Variety
Host: Christopher Lynch.
Orchestra: Emerson Buckley.
Length: 10 minutes.
Network: Mutual.
First Broadcast: 1953.

Christopher Wells

See title: "The Adventures of Christopher Wells."

Cimarron Tavern

Type: Western
Format: Depicted incidents in the lives of the people who frequented the Grand Hotelish, a tavern in Cimarron, Oklahoma during the 1800s.
Cast: Star Travis   Paul Conrad
        Joe Barton   Chester Stratton
Also: Ethel Everett, Stephen Courtleigh, Ronald Liss, Tony Burger, Neil O'Malley, Carl Emory.
Announcer: Bob Hite.
Length: 15 minutes.
Network: CBS.
First Broadcast: 1945.

Cinderella, Inc.

Type: Quiz
Format: Four housewives, selected from areas around the country, were brought to New York City, housed in lavish quarters, served breakfast in bed, escorted to a night club, attired in expensive clothes—in short, pampered from head to toe. After these experiences, each housewife related her impressions, feel-

ings, and thoughts to listeners.
Host: Bob Dixon.
Announcer: Tony Marvin.
Length: 30 minutes.
Network: CBS.
First Broadcast: 1940.

The Cinnamon Bear

Type: Children's
Format: The series centered on the adventures of Paddy O'Cinnamon (the Cinnamon Bear) and Judy and Jimmy Barton, as they embarked on a journey through Maybe Land, seeking to find the Silver Star for their Christmas tree—a star that was stolen by the Crazy Quilt Dragon. Usually broadcast during the Christmas season.
Cast: The Cinnamon
        Bear   Buddy Duncan
        Judy Barton   Barbara Jean
                            Wong
        Judy's mother   Verna Felton
        Santa Claus   Lou Merrill
Narrator: Bud Heistand.
Various Roles: Hanley Stafford, Gale Gordon, Joseph Kearns, Elvia Allman, Frank Nelson, Slim Pickens, Martha Wentworth.
Songs: The Paul Taylor Quartet.
Music: Felix Mills.
Length: 15 minutes.
Syndicated.
First Broadcast: 1937.

The Cisco Kid

Type: Western
Format: The exploits of O.Henry's famous Robin Hood of the Old West, the Cisco Kid, and his sidekick Pan Pancho.
Cast: The Cisco Kid   Jackson Beck
                            Jack Mather
        Pan Pancho   Louis Sorin
                            Harry Lang
                            Mel Blanc
Also: Vicki Vola, Bryna Raeburn, Mark

Chicken Every Sunday. Harry Von Zell.

Smith, Jean Ellyn.
Announcer: Marvin Miller, Michael Rye.
Length: 30 minutes.
Network: WOR (local New York, 1942), Mutual 1943.
First Broadcast: 1942.

City Hospital

Type: Anthology
Format: Medical dramatizations. Became the basis for a television series of the same title.
Cast: The Doctor   Santos Ortega
        The Nurse   Anne Burr
Announcer: John Cannon.
Length: 30 minutes.
Network: CBS.
First Broadcast: 1951.

Clara, Lu, and Em

Type: Serial
Format: A gossip session wherein three housewives who shared the same residence got together, either in the kitchen or backyard, and exchanged talk. The original format, which aired in 1931, dealt with the gossip of three spinsters; the housewives format was first incorporated in 1942.
Cast: Clara   Louise Starkey
                       Fran Allison
        Lu   Isabel Carothers
                       Isobel Beroy-
                          helmer
                       Dorothy Day
        Em   Helen King
                          Mitchell
                       Harriet Allyn
Announcer: Don David.
Music: Lou Webb.
Length: 15 minutes.
Network: Blue (1931), Syndicated (1946).
First Broadcast: 1931.

Claudia and David

Type: Serial
Format: The dramatic story of the Naughtons, David, an architect, and his naive eighteen-year-old wife, Claudia. Episodes focused on Claudia's struggles to cut the apron strings that bound her to her mother, and adjust to marriage. Became the basis for a television series of the same title.
Cast: Claudia Naugh-
          ton   Patricia Ryan
                       Katherine Bard
        David Naughton Richard Kollmar
                       Paul Crabtree
        Mrs. Brown,
          Claudia's
          mother   Jane Seymour
                       Peggy Allenby
        David's mother Irene Hubbard
Announcer: Charles Stark, Joe King.
Orchestra: Peter Van Steeden.
Length: 30 and 15 minute versions.
Network: CBS (1941), Syndicated (1947).
First Broadcast: 1941.

The Cliché Club

Type: Quiz
Format: A scrambled phrase, submitted by a listener, was related to a panel to be unscrambled and corrected. Failure on their part resulted in a prize for the listener.
Host: Walter Keirnan.
Panelists: Carol Lynn Gilmer, Agnes Rogers, Edward Hill.
Announcer: Les Griffith.
Length: 30 minutes.
Network: NBC.
First Broadcast: 1950.

The Clicquot Club Eskimos

Type: Musical Variety
Host: Harry Reser.
Regulars: Raymond Knight, Merle Johnson, Jimmy Brierly, Everett Clark, Virginia Hauer.
Announcer: Phil Carlin.
Orchestra: Harry Reser.
Sponsor: Clicquot Club Beverages.
Length: 30 minutes.
Network: NBC (1926), Syndicated (1951).
First Broadcast: 1926.

Cloak and Dagger

Type: Anthology
Format: Dramatizations based on the files of the Office of Strategic Services.
Cast: The O.S.S. Agent Joseph Julian.
Also: Raymond Edward Johnson, Ross Martin, Berry Kroeger, Karl Weber.
Length: 30 minutes.
Network: NBC.
First Broadcast: 1950.

The Clock

Type: Anthology
Format: Dramatizations revolving around the central theme of man vs. time. The narrator, posing as Father time, introduced the story and commented about the effects of time on the people involved.
Narrator: Gene Kirby.
Announcer: Bill Cargo.
Orchestra: Bernard Green.
Length: 30 minutes.
Network: ABC.
First Broadcast: 1946.

Club 15

Type: Musical Variety
Format One:
Host: Bob Crosby.
Regulars: The Andrews Sisters, Margaret Whiting, Patti Clayton, The Modernaires.
Announcer: Del Sharbutt.
Orchestra: Jerry Gray.
Length: 15 minutes.
Network: CBS.
First Broadcast: 1947.
Format Two:
Host (Monday, Wednesday, Friday): Bob Crosby.
Regulars: The Andrews Sisters.
Announcer: Jerry Gray.
Host (Tuesday, Thursday): Jo Stafford.
Regulars: The Modernaires.
Announcer: Del Sharbutt.
Orchestra: Jerry Gray.
Length: 15 minutes.
Network: CBS.
First Broadcast: 1950.
Format Three:
Host: Bob Crosby.
Regulars: Giselle MacKenzie, Jo Stafford, The Modernaires.
Announcer: Del Sharbutt.
Orchestra: Jerry Gray.
Length: 15 minutes.
Network: CBS.
First Broadcast: 1951.

Club Matinee

Type: Variety
Host: Ransom Sherman, Garry Moore, Durward Kirby.

Vocalists: Johnny Johnston, Clark Dennis, Evelyn Lynne, Phil Shukin, The Three Romeos, The Escorts and Betty.

Also: Bill Short, a bass player.

Announcer: Durward Kirby.

Orchestra: Rex Maupin.

Length: 60 minutes.

Network: NBC Blue.

First Broadcast: 1937 (ended in 1942). "Club Matinee" was actually an afternoon extension (4-5 p.m., E.T.) of "The Breakfast Club" (which see) with many of the same cast appearing from time to time.

The Clyde Beatty Show

Type: Adventure

Format: Dramatizations based on incidents in the life of animal trainer Clyde Beatty as he attempted to trap animals on behalf of the Cole Brothers-Ringling Brothers, Barnum and Bailey Circus.

Host-Narrator-Star: Clyde Beatty.

Announcer: Larry Thor.

Length: 30 minutes.

Network: Mutual.

First Broadcast: 1950.

Coast-to-Coast On a Bus

Type: Children's

Format: Each Sunday morning, a bus-load of children rode the White Rabbit Lines to some locale. While enroute, the talented cast of juveniles sang, danced, and acted in skits.

Host: Milton Cross.

The Lady Next Door: Madge Tucker.

Music: Walter Fleischer.

Creator-Producer-Director-Writer: Madge Tucker.

Length: 60 minutes.

First Broadcast: 1927 (ended in the late 30s). Originally titled "The Children's Hour."

The Cobbs

Type: Comedy

Format: The saga of a humble husband and his understanding wife.

Cast: Mr. Cobb   William Demarest
      Mrs. Cobb   Hope Emerson

Length: 30 minutes.

Network: CBS.

First Broadcast: 1954.

The Coca Cola Summer Show

Type: Musical Variety

Host: Roger Pryor.

Regulars: Nestor Chayres, Los Ponchos.

Orchestra: Charles Lichter.

Sponsor: Coca-Cola.

Length: 30 minutes.

Network: CBS.

First Broadcast: 1948.

Cohen and the Detective

Type: Detective Comedy

Starring: Patsy Flick, Nat Cantor, Charme Allen, John Brown.

Music: Joe Rines.

Length: 25 mintues.

Network: Blue.

First Broadcast: 1943.

The Coke Club

Type: Musical Variety

Hostess: Leah Ray.

Regulars: Morton Downey, The Coke Club Quartet.

Announcer: David Ross.

Orchestra: Jimmy Lytell.

Sponsor: Coca Cola.

Program Opening:

Announcer: Yes friends, it's time for another transcribed session of The Coke Club which brings you the romantic voice of Morton Downey, with Leah Ray as your hostess, Jimmy Lytell and his or-

chestra, The Coke Club Quartet and yours truly, David Ross . . .
Length: 15 minutes.
Network: Mutual.
First Broadcast: 1946.

The Colgate Spotlight

Type: Variety
Format: Performances by undiscovered professional talent.
Host: Ed East.
Announcer: Jeff Spartin.
Orchestra: Charles Hathaway.
Sponsor: Colgate Products.
Length: 30 minutes.
Network: CBS.
First Broadcast: 1941.

College Quiz Bowl

Type: Quiz
Format: The forerunner of TV's "G.E. College Bowl." Two teams of college students competed in a question and answer session. Winning teams received a $500 college grant; losers were awarded various individual prizes.
Host: Allen Ludden.
Announcer: Roger Tuttle.
Length: 30 minutes.
Network: NBC.
First Broadcast: 1953.

Colonel Humphrey Flack

Type: Comedy
Format: The story of two modern-day Robin Hoods: Humphrey Flack, a retired colonel, and his companion, Uthas P. (Patsy) Garvey. With larceny in their minds and charity in their hearts, they traveled throughout the world and, through imaginative deceptions, conned the confidence men in their attempts to assist

the needy. Became the basis for the television series of the same title.
Cast: Colonel Humphrey Flack   Wendell Holmes
        Uthas P. Garvey   Frank Maxwell
Announcer: Dick Dudley.
Length: 30 minutes.
Network: NBC.
First Broadcast: 1947.

Colonel Stoopnagle and Budd

Type: Comedy
Format: The misadventures of a fast-talking colonel who constantly gave advice but took little himself. Also known as "The Colonel," "Stoopnagle and Budd," and "The Gloom Chasers."
Cast: Colonel Lemuel
        Q. Stoopnagle   F. Chase Taylor
        Budd, his straight
        man   Wilbur   Budd
                            Hulick
        Erasmus Bumfil-
        dorfer   Louis Sain
        Quackenbush   John Gibson
Also: Mary Wickes, Amanda Randolph, Joan Banks, Margaret Arlen, Elaine Howard, Harry Clark, Alice Frost, Jeri Sullivan, Florence Halop, Hope Emerson, Eddie Green.
Vocalist: Gogo DeLys.
Chorus: Bobby Tucker.
Orchestra: Archie Bleyer, Donald Voorhees, Paul Baron, Peter Van Steeden.
Length: 15 and 30 minute versions.
Network: NBC (1943), CBS (1944).
First Broadcast: 1943.

Columbia Presents Corwin

Type: Anthology
Format: Dramatizations based on stories by Norman Corwin.
Writer-Producer-Director-Host: Norman Corwin.
Announcer: Roy Rowan.
Orchestra: Earl Robins.

Included:

Movie Primer. The first episode of the series presented a musical satire on Hollywood and the movie industry.

Starring: Everett Sloane, Frank Gallop, Minerva Pious, Peter Donald, Tony Marvin.

The Undecided. The story of a single molecule that almost upset the universe when it refused to combine with other elements.

Starring: Vincent Price, Groucho Marx, Robert Benchley, Keenan Wynn.

Length: 30 minutes.

Network: CBS.

First Broadcast: 1944.

Comedy By—

Type: Variety

Format: Performances by guest comedians.

Host: George Byron.

Regulars: The Eaton Boys, Howard and Shelton.

Orchestra: Bob Stanley.

Length: 30 minutes.

Network: Mutual.

First Broadcast: 1940.

Comedy Caravan

Type: Comedy-Variety

Starring: Jimmy Durante-Garry Moore.

Vocalist: Georgia Gibbs.

Orchestra: Roy Bargy.

Length: 30 minutes.

Network: NBC.

First Broadcast: 1943.

Comedy of Errors

Type: Quiz

Format: A short skit, which contained an error, was read to selected members of the studio audience. The first player to spot and correct the error won the round

and $5. Winners were the highest overall cash scorers.

Host: Jack Bailey.

Organist: Eddie Dunstedder.

Announcer: Fort Pearson.

Length: 25 minutes.

Network: Mutual.

First Broadcast: 1949.

Confession

Type: Anthology

Format: Dramatizations based on the files of various corrections departments throughout the country. The series was presented in cooperation with the California State Department of Corrections.

Starring: Paul Frees as Richard A. McGee, director of the California State Department of Corrections.

Music: J. Frederick Albech.

Length: 30 minutes.

Network: NBC.

First Broadcast: 1953.

Confidentially Yours

Type: Anthology

Format: Dramatizations based on the crime cases of Jack Lait, a reporter for the now defunct New York *Daily Mirror*.

Host-Narrator: Jack Lait.

Announcer: Bob Warren.

Orchestra: Jack Miller.

Length: 30 minutes.

Network: NBC.

First Broadcast: 1950.

Connee Boswell Presents

Type: Musical Variety

Hostess: Connee Boswell.

Regulars: Jack Pepper, Louis Jourdan, The Tympany Five.

Announcer: Jack McCarthy.

Orchestra: Paul Whiteman.

Length: 30 minutes.
Network: Blue.
First Broadcast: 1944.

The Constance Bennett Show

Type: Talk
Format: Topics of conversation of interest to women.
Hostess: Constance Bennett.
Announcer: George Ansbro.
Length: 15 minutes.
Network: ABC.
First Broadcast: 1945.

Coronet Quick Quiz

Type: Quiz
Format: The host related eight questions in rapid-fire succession, followed immediately by the answers. The purpose was for listeners to test their mental powers and abilities to answer questions rapidly.
Host: Charles Irving.
Announcer: Dan David.
Sponsor: Coronet Magazine.
Length: 5 minutes.
Network: Blue.
First Broadcast: 1944.

Coronet Story Theatre

Type: Anthology
Format: Dramatizations of stories appearing in *Coronet* Magazine.
Narrator: Marvin Miller.
Announcer: Vic Perrin.
Sponsor: *Coronet* Magazine, Kellogg's.
Length: 5 minutes.
Network: Blue (1944), ABC (1947).
First Broadcast: 1944.

Correction Please

Type: Quiz
Format: Selected members of the studio audience received ten dollars for bidding money. A multiple choice question was read and three answers appeared on a board, one of which was wrong. Contestant then bid for the opportunity to correct the error. If the highest bidding player corrected the statement he won ten times the bet amount. If he was incorrect, the best was deducted from his total.
Host: Jim McWilliams, Jay C. Flippen.
Orchestra: Jack Skilkret, Jerry Fears.
Length: 30 minutes.
Network: CBS (1943), NBC (1945).
First Broadcast: 1943.

Cosmo Tune Time

Type: Musical Variety
Host: Alan Kent.
Vocalists: The Four Chicks and a Chuck.
Orchestra: Henry Busse, Ernie Madriguera, Bernie Weissman.
Sponsor: Cosmopolitan Records.
Length: 30 minutes.
Network: Mutual.
First Broadcast: 1945.

The Coty Playgirl

Type: Variety
Hostess: Irene Bordoni, Adele Ronson.
Orchestra: Eugene Ormandy, Ray Noble.
Sponsor: Coty Cosmetics.
Length: 15 minutes.
Network: NBC.
First Broadcast: 1931.

Could Be

Type: Quiz
Format: Couples celebrating various occasions (e.g., a wedding anniversary) were the contestants. Players were first com-

ically interviewed, then competed in the quiz segment: a sound effect, which could be one of three things, was played. The orchestra then played a musical clue to help the players. If the couple identified the sound effect they received a cash prize—what could be gotten by dipping one hand into a treasure chest of money.
Host: Horace Heidt.
Orchestra: Horace Heidt.
Length: 30 minutes.
Network: NBC.
First Broadcast: 1939.

The Count of Monte Cristo

Type: Adventure
Format: Falsely accused of bearing treasonable information, Edmond Dantes is convicted and sentenced to life imprisonment in the Chateau d' If. Learning of a buried treasure from his cellmate, he digs his way out, escapes, and retreats to the island of Monte Cristo. Uncovering the treasure, he establishes himself as a mysterious and powerful figure for justice. Stories related his battle against the forces of corruption in 18th century France. Based on the story by Alexandre Dumas; also served as the basis for a television series of the same title.
Cast: Edmond Dantes   Carleton Young
       Rene Michon   Parley Baer
       Dante's romantic
         interest   Ann Stone
Announcer: Charles Arlington.
Music: Dean Fassler.
Length: 30 minutes.
Network: Mutual.
First Broadcast: 1946.

Counterspy

Type: Adventure
Format: The exploits of David Harding, U.S. Government counterspy during World War II. Became the basis for a television series of the same title.

Cast: David Harding   House Jameson
                          Don MacLaughlin
       Peters, his
         assistant   Mandel Kramer
Announcer: Bob Shepherd, Roger Krupp.
Program Opening:
Announcer: The Blue Network presents "Counterspy." Germany has its Gestapo, Italy its Zobra, and Japan its Black Dragon. But matched against all of these secret enemy agents are Uncle Sam's highly trained counter spies. Visualize ace counterspy of them all as David Harding.
Length: 30 minutes.
Network: Blue.
First Broadcast: 1942.

County Fair

Type: Audience participation
Format: Set against the background of a fairgrounds, contestants competed in various stunt contests in return for cash prizes.
Host: Win Elliot, Jack Bailey, Jack Barry.
Assistant: Lee Vines, Larry Keating.
Orchestra: Bill Gale.
Length: 30 minutes.
Network: CBS.
First Broadcast: 1945.

County Seat

Type: Serial
Format: Events in the lives of the people of a small town as seen through the eyes of Doc Hackett, the proprietor of a corner drugstore.
Cast: Doc Hackett   Ray Collins
       Sarah Whipple   Charme Allen
       Jerry Whipple   Cliff Carpenter
Length: 15 minutes.
Network: CBS.
First Broadcast: 1938.

The Couple Next Door

Type: Comedy
Format: The mishaps of a trouble-prone husband and wife.
Starring: Peg Lynch and Alan Bunce.
Length: 15 minutes.
Network: CBS.
First Broadcast: 1958 (ended in 1960).

The Coty Playgirl. Adele Ronson.

Cousin Willie

Type: Comedy
Format: The story of a husband, his wife, and a well-meaning cousin who comes for a visit and decides to stay.
Cast:

Cousin Willie	Bill Idelson
The husband	Marvin Miller
His wife	Patricia Dunlap
Their daughter	Dawn Bender
Their son	Stuffy Singer

Also: Patte Chapman, Bob Sweeney, Frank Nelson.
Announcer: Jimmy Wallington.

Orchestra: Robert Armbruster.
Length: 30 minutes.
Network: NBC.
First Broadcast: 1953.

Cracraft Electric Orchestra

Type: Musical Variety
Host: Andre Monici.
Vocalists: Connie Crandell, Arthur Tubertine, Don Lamont.
Orchestra: Tom Adrian Cracraft.
Length: 30 minutes.
Network: NBC.
First Broadcast: 1939.

Creeps By Night

Type: Anthology
Format: Varied mystery presentations enacted by a regular cast.
Host-Narrator: Boris Karloff.
Cast: Edmund Green, Everett Sloane, Abby Lewis, Gregory Morton.
Length: 30 minutes.
Network: Blue.
First Broadcast: 1944.

The Creightons Are Coming

Type: Comedy
Format: Events in the lives of the Creightons: Christopher, a sculptor, his wife Serena, a mystery novelist, and their children Victor and Crottie.
Cast:

Christopher Creighton	John Griggs
Serena Creighton	Ethel Owen
Victor Creighton	Norman Tokar
Crottie Creighton	Sammie Hill

Orchestra: Joseph Stopak.

Length: 30 minutes.
Network: NBC.
First Broadcast: 1942.

Crime and Peter Chambers

Type: Crime Drama
Format: The cases of private detective Peter Chambers.
Starring: Dane Clark as Peter Chambers.
Length: 25 minutes.
Network: NBC.
First Broadcast: 1954.

The Crime Cases of Warden Lawes

Type: Crime Drama
Format: Dramatizations based on the files of Lewis E. Lawes, warden of Sing Sing Prison.
Starring: Lewis E. Lawes as himself.
Announcer: Cy Harrice.
Orchestra: Burt Burham.
Length: 15 minutes.
Network: Mutual.
First Broadcast: 1946.

Crime Classics

Type: Anthology
Format: Dramatizations of true crime stories as related by Thomas Hyland, a connoiseur of crime.
Host-Narrator: Lou Merrill (as Thomas Hyland).
Regular Cast: Mary Jane Croft, Herb Butterfield, Sam Edwards, Ben Wright, Tudor Owen, Georgia Ellis, Bill Johnstone.
Orchestra: Bernard Herrmann.
Length: 30 minutes.
Network: CBS.
First Broadcast: 1953.

Crime Club

Type: Anthology
Format: Dramatizations based on stories appearing in *Crime Club* books. Varying casts and stories.
Program Opening:
Sound effect: Telephone ringing; receiver being picked up.
Voice: Hello, I hope I haven't kept you waiting. Yes, this is the Crime Club. I'm the librarian. "Dead Men Control?" Yes, we have that Crime Club story for you. Come right over.
Sound effect: Doorbell rings; door opens.
Voice: Ah, you're here, good. Take the easy chair by the window. Comfortable? The book is on the shelf, here it is ... let's look at it under the reading lamp ... (from this point on the story would begin).
Length: 30 minutes.
Network: Mutual.
First Broadcast: 1946.

Crime Doctor

Type: Crime Drama
Format: The story of a doctor, Benjamin Ordway, and his attempts to solve baffling crimes.
Cast: Dr. Benjamin
          Ordway   Ray Collins
                              House Jameson
                              Everett Sloane
                              John McIntire
          D.A. Miller   Edgar Stehli
          Inspector Rose   Walter Greaza
Announcer: Charles O'Connor.
Orchestra: Ray Bloch.
Length: 30 minutes.
Network: CBS.
First Broadcast: 1940.

The Crime Files of Flamond

Type: Crime Drama
Format: The cases of Flamond, a master private detective who used psychological methods to battle crime.
Cast: Flamond   Everett Clark
His secretary   Muriel Bremmer
Announcer: Bob Cunningham.
Length: 30 minutes.
Network: Mutual.
First Broadcast: 1953.

Crime Is My Pastime

Type: Anthology
Format: Varied mystery presentations enacted by a cast of regulars.
Cast: Gerald Mohr, Rod O'Connor.
Orchestra: Len Salve.
Length: 15 minutes.
Network: Mutual.
First Broadcast: 1945.

A Crime Letter From Dan Dodge

Type: Crime Drama
Format: The program, which detailed the investigations of private detective Dan Dodge, unfolded through a series of flashbacks as Dodge dictated a crime letter to his secretary relating the facts of a recent case.
Cast: Dan Dodge   Myron McCormick
His secretary   Shirley Eggleston
Length: 30 minutes.
Network: ABC.
First Broadcast: 1952.

Criminal Casebook

Type: Crime Drama
Format: Tales of criminals. Episodes began with a rough sketch of the crime and then delved into the facts that brought about and concluded it.
Cast: Donald Hastings, John Sylvester, Betty Garde, Mitzi Gould, Frances Lafferty, Santos Ortega, Bill Keene, Jimmy Blaine.
Announcer: Nelson Case.
Orchestra: John Gart.
Length: 30 minutes.
Network: ABC.
First Broadcast: 1948.

Crooked Square

Type: Anthology
Format: Varied mystery presentations enacted by a regular cast.
Cast: Roger DeKoven, Santos Ortega, Ethel Owen, Eddie Nugent, Larry Haines, Peggy Stanley.
Announcer: Tiny Ruffner.
Orchestra: Henry Sylvern.
Length: 15 minutes.
Network: Mutual.
First Broadcast: 1945.

The Cuckoo Hour

Type: Comedy
Host: Raymond Knight (as Ambrose J. Weems, the M.C. of radio station KUKU).
Regulars: Adelina Thompson (as Mrs. George Pennyfeather), Jack Arthur, Mary McCoy.
Announcer: Ward Wilson.
Orchestra: Robert Armbruster.
Length: 15 minutes.
Network: NBC.
First Broadcast: 1930.

The Curley Bradley Show

Type: Country/Western Musical Variety
Host: Curley Bradley.
Featured: The T-M-B Bar Ranch Boys.

Announcer: Franklyn Mac Cormack.
Length: 15 minutes.
Network: Mutual.
First Broadcast: 1949.

Cast: Daddy — Craig McDonnell
Rollo, his son — George Ward
Donald Hughes
Length: 15 minutes.
Network: Mutual.
First Broadcast: 1932.

Curley Bradley—The Singing Marshal

Type: Western
Format: Western dramatizations that detailed the exploits of U.S. Marshal Curley Bradley. Stories stressed more story and less gunplay.
Starring: Curley Bradley as himself.
Narrator: Don Gordon.
Length: 30 minutes.
Network: Mutual.
First Broadcast: 1950.

Curt Massey Time

Type: Musical Variety
Host: Curt Massey.
Vocalists: Martha Tilton, The Dinning Sisters, Marian Morgan, The Cheerleaders.
Announcer: Charles Lyon, Jack Narz.
Orchestra: Jack Fascinato, Billy Liebert.
Length: 15 minutes.
Network: CBS.
First Broadcast: 1943.

Daddy and Rollo

Type: Comedy
Format: A comedy dialogue between an inquisitive ten-year-old boy and his often bewildered father.

Daily Dilemmas

Type: Quiz
Format: A dilemma, as faced by nearly everyone in everyday life, was enacted. A selected studio audience member was then brought on stage, placed opposite a jury of studio audience members, and asked to identify the object of the dramatized dilemma. The jury's decision —whether they approved or disapproved of his answer—determined the player's prize.
Host: Jack Barry.
Enacting Dilemmas: Cecil Roy.
Length: 30 minutes.
Network: Mutual.
First Broadcast: 1946.

The Damon Runyon Theatre

Type: Anthology
Format: Dramatizations based on Damon Runyon's stories of the characters of old New York's underworld.
Narrator: John Brown as Broadway.
Included:
Butch Minds the Baby. The story of four thieves and the complications that ensued when, as they were planning to rob a safe, one member was left to take care of an infant.

Starring: John Brown, Sheldon Leonard, Herb Vigran, Jay Novello.

Breach of Promise. The misadventures of two bumbling underworld figures as they attempted to retrieve a client's love letters to a former girlfriend.

Starring: Herb Vigran, Willard Waterman.

Length: 30 minutes.

Syndicated.

First Broadcast: 1944.

Dan Harding's Wife

Type: Serial

Format: The dramatic story of Rhoda Harding and her struggles to cope with life after the death of her husband Dan.

Cast:
Rhoda Harding	Isabel Randolph
Dean Harding	Merrill Fugit
Donna Harding	Loretta Poynton
Arnie	Carl Hanson
Penny Latham	Alice Goodkin
Ralph Fraser	Herb Nelson
Eva Foster	Tommye Birch
Mrs. Graham	Judith Lowry
Jack Garland	Willard Farnum

Also, various roles: Templeton Fox, Cliff Soubier.

Announcer: Les Griffith.

Length: 15 minutes.

Network: NBC.

First Broadcast: 1936.

Danger, Dr. Danfield

Type: Crime Drama

Format: The cases of Dr. Daniel Danfield, a criminal psychologist.

Cast:
Dr. Daniel Danfield	Michael Dunne (later known as Steve Dunne)
Rusty Fairfax, his secretary	JoAnne Johnson

Length: 30 minutes.

Network: ABC.

First Broadcast: 1949.

Danger Is My Business

Type: Interview-Drama

Format: Interviews with people involved with hazardous occupations.

Host-Announcer: Jay Simms.

Length: 15 minutes.

Network: Mutual.

First Broadcast: 1940s.

Dangerous Assignment

Type: Adventure

Format: The exploits of Steve Mitchell, an international trouble shooter who investigated and solved crimes on behalf of the U.S. Government. Became the basis for a TV series of the same title.

Starring: Brian Donlevy as Steve Mitchell.

Program Opening:

Announcer: Baghdad, Martinique, Singapore, and all the places of the world where danger and intrigue walk hand in hand, there you will find Steve Mitchell on another Dangerous Assignment.

Length: 30 minutes.

Network: NBC.

First Broadcast: 1950.

Dangerously Yours

Type: Anthology

Format: Adventure dramatizations geared to women.

Host-Narrator (The Voice of Adventure):
  Martin Gabel.
Dramatic Cast: Victor Jory, Gertrude
  Warner.
Orchestra: Mark Warnow.
Network: CBS.
First Broadcast: 1944.

The Danny Kaye Show

Type: Variety
Host: Danny Kaye.
Regulars: Lionel Stander, Eve Arden,
  Joan Edwards, Butterfly McQueen,
  Everett Sloane, Goodman Ace, Kenny
  Delmar, Jim Backus, Everett Clark, The
  Four Clubmen.
Announcer: Dick Joy, Ken Niles.
Orchestra: Harry James, Lyn Murray,
  Harry Sosnik, David Terry.
Length: 30 minutes.
Network: CBS.
First Broadcast: 1945.

Danny O'Neal and His Guests

Type: Musical Variety
Host: Danny O'Neal
Regulars: Janette Davis, George Guest,
  Archie Robbins, The Song Spinners.
Announcer: Bill Cullen.
Orchestra: Archie Bleyer.
Length: 25 minutes.
Network: CBS.
First Broadcast: 1946.

The Danny O'Neal Show

Type: Variety
Host: Danny O'Neal
Vocalist: Lorna Lynn.

Orchestra: Ruby Newman.
Length: 15 minutes.
Network: CBS.
First Broadcast: 1945.

The Danny Thomas Show

Type: Variety
Host: Danny Thomas
Regulars: Marvin Miller, Hans Conried,
  Donelda Curry, Kathryn Card, Sid
  Ellstrom, Art Kahl, The Escorts and Bet-
  ty.
Announcer: Ben Gage.
Orchestra: Rex Maupin, Elliot Daniel and
  His All Girl Orchestra.
Length: 30 and 25 minute versions.
Network: Blue (1943), CBS (1948).
First Broadcast: 1943.

Dark Fantasy

Type: Anthology
Format: Dramatizations of people's en-
  counters with the world of the unknown.
Announcer: Keith Painton.
Length: 25 minutes.
Network: NBC.
First Broadcast: 1941.

A Date with Judy

Type: Comedy
Format: The misadventures of Judy
  Foster, an unpredictable teenage girl.
  Became the basis for a television series of
  the same title.

Cast: Judy Foster   Ann Gillis
                            Dellie Ellis
                            Louise Erickson

Melvyn Foster,
  her father,
  president of
  the Foster
  Can Company   Paul McGrath
                            Stanley Farrar
                            John Brown

Dora Foster,
  Judy's mother   Margaret
                              Brayton
                            Lois Corbett
                            Myra Marsh

Randolph Foster,
  Judy's brother   Dix Davis
                            Johnny
                              McGovern

Oogie Pringle,
  Judy's boy-
  friend   Harry Harvey
                            Dick Crenna

Mitzi, Judy's
  girlfriend   Mercedes
                              McCambridge
                            Georgia Backus

Mr. Pringle,
  Oogie's father   Fred Howard
Announcer: Bill Goodwin, Ken Niles, Marvin Miller, Ralph Langley.
Orchestra: Hal Gould, Thomas Peluse, Buzz Adlam.
Sponsor: Tums.
Program Opening:
Announcer: By transcription.
Song (sung by Oogie): I've got a date with Judy, a big date with Judy ... and Judy's got one with me.
Announcer: The American Broadcasting Company presents A Date with Judy starring Louise Erickson as Judy with John Brown as Father.
Length: 30 minutes.
Network: NBC (1941), ABC (1948).
First Broadcast: 1941.

A Date With Music

Type: Musical Variety
Featured: Sammy Liver.
Announcer: Allyn Edwards.
Orchestra: Doc Whipple.
Length: 15 minutes.
Syndicated.
First Broadcast: 1946.

Daughters of Uncle Sam

Type: Musical Variety
Hostess: Arlene Francis.
Regulars: Fannie Hurst, The Three Saluters, The Swing Patrol.
Orchestra: B. A. Rolfe.
Length: 30 minutes.
Network: NBC.
First Broadcast: 1942.

Dave Elman's Auction Gallery

Type: Auction
Format: Art or historical items are offered to the studio audience, then to home listeners who must respond with a bid within a specified time.
Host-Auctioneer: Dave Elman.
Length: 30 minutes.
Network: Mutual.
First Broadcast: 1945.

The Dave Garroway Show

Type: Variety
Host: Dave Garroway.
Regulars: Connie Russell, Jack Haskell, Charlie Andrews, Vivian Martin, June Christie, Jim Fleming.
Announcer: Jack Haskell.
Orchestra: Joseph Gallichio, Art Van Damme.
Length: 30 minutes.

Network: NBC.

First Broadcast: 1947. Also known as "Next, Dave Garroway," "Sunday with Garroway," "Dial Garroway," and "Reserved for Garroway." Became the basis for a television series of the same title.

David Harum

Type: Serial

Format: The life of David Harum, a small town banker.

Cast:

David Harum	Craig McDonnell
	Cameron Prud' Homme
Susan Wells	Peggy Allenby
	Gertrude Warner
	Joan Tompkins
Polly	Charme Allen
	Eva Condon
Elsie	Ethel Everett
John	Joseph Curtin
Clarissa	Marjorie Davies
	Claudia Morgan
James Benson	Bennett Kilpack
Charlie	Paul Stewart
Brian Wells	Philip Reed
	Ken Williams
Willy	Bill Redfield
Mark Carter	Paul Ford
Tess	Florence Lake

Announcer: Ford Bond.

Music: Stanley Davis.

Program Opening:

Announcer: We bring you the story that has thrilled America for generations; the true-to-life story of David Harum, the kindly little country philosopher who makes life worth living by helping those who need help and by outwitting those who are too clever and scheming in helping themselves.

Length: 15 minutes.

Network: NBC.

First Broadcast: 1936.

The David Rose Show

Type: Musical Variety

Host: David Rose.

Featured: Lee Simpkins.

Announcer: Fort Pearson.

Orchestra: David Rose.

Length: 30 minutes.

Network: CBS.

First Broadcast: 1950.

A Day in the Life of Dennis Day

Type: Comedy

Format: The series focused on the misadventures of Dennis Day, a well-meaning but trouble-prone young man.

Cast:

Dennis Day	Himself
Millie Anderson, his girlfriend	Betty Miles
	Barbara Eiler
	Sharon Douglas
Mr. Anderson, Millie's father	Francis Trout
Mrs. Anderson, Millie's mother	Bea Benaderet
Mr. Willoughby	John Brown

Also: Ken Carson as the sponsor's (Lustre Creme Shampoo) vocalist.

Announcer: Verne Smith, Frank Barton, Jimmy Wallington.

Orchestra: Charles Dant, Robert Armbruster.

Length: 30 minutes.

Network: NBC.

First Broadcast: 1946.

Deadline Drama

Type: Anthology

Format: A regular cast had to perform a drama based on a twenty-word situation, submitted by a listener, within a two-minute time limit. Listeners received a U.S. Savings Bond if their situation was chosen.

Cast: Bob White, Joan Banks, Irene Wicker, Frank Lovejoy.
Organist: Rosa Rio.
Length: 30 minutes.
Network: Blue.
First Broadcast: 1944.

Dear Margy, It's Murder

Type: Crime Drama
Format: Revolved around an American studying in England under the G.I. Bill and his attempts to help the Scotland Yard inspector he befriends solve crimes. The title was derived from letters sent home by the Vet to his girl friend Margy, in which he related his experiences.
Cast: The Vet   Mason Adams
       The Inspector   Ian Martin
Length: 25 minutes.
Network: Mutual.
First Broadcast: 1953.

Dear Mom

Type: Comedy
Format: The misadventures of Homer Stubbs, a private in boot camp just prior to World War II. The series unfolded as Homer wrote of his experiences to his mother (hence the title).
Cast: Pvt. Homer
         Stubbs   John Walsh
       Pvt. Ulysses
         Hink   Lou Krugman
       Sgt. Mike
         Monihan   Marvin Miller
       Cpl. Red Foster Dolph Nelson
Announcer: Tom Moore.
Sponsor: Wrigley's Gum.
Length: 25 minutes.
Network: CBS.
First Broadcast: 1941.

Dearest Mother

Type: Serial
Format: The series followed the experiences of Rita Morgan and her struggles to begin a new life in a big city. The title was derived from the fact that after a misunderstanding between Rita and her father, Rita impulsively decided to leave home; she promised, however, that no matter where she was or what her position, she would write to her mother.
Cast: Rita Morgan   Judith March
       Mrs. Morgan   Melba Lee
       Mr. Morgan   Fred Howard
Also: Chris Ford, Kay Miller, Harriet Linehan, Frank Mills.
Length: 15 minutes.
Syndicated.
First Broadcast: 1940.

Death Valley Days

Type: Anthology
Format: Western dramatizations set against the background of Death Valley. Became the basis for a television series of the same title.
Cast: The Old Ran-
         ger (Host)   Tim Frawley
                        George Rand
                        Harry Hum-
                          phrey
                        John MacBryde
       Sheriff Mark
         Chase   Robert Haag
       The Old Pros-
         pector   Harvey Hayes
       The Cowboy   John White
       Cousin Cassie   Olyn Landick
Announcer: George Hicks.
Orchestra: Joseph Bonime.
Sponsor: Boraxo.
Length: 30 minutes.
Network: Blue.
First Broadcast: 1930.

Note: In 1944 the series became "Death Valley Sheriff," below.

Death Valley Sheriff

Type: Western
Format: The exploits of Mark Chase, sheriff of Canyon County, California.
Cast: Sheriff Mark
 Chase — Robert Haag, Bob Warren, Donald Briggs
 Cassandra, his housekeeper — Olyn Landick
Length: 25 minutes.
Network: CBS.
First Broadcast: 1944.

December Bride

Type: Comedy
Format: The trials and tribulations of Ruth and Matt Henshaw, a couple married eight years, and the life and romantic misadventures of Lily Ruskin, Ruth's mother, a widow who lives with them. Became the basis for a television series of the same title.
Cast: Lily Ruskin — Spring Byington
 Ruth Henshaw — Doris Singleton
 Matt Henshaw — Hal March
Also: John Brown, Alan Reed, Hans Conried.
Orchestra: Wilbur Hatch.
Length: 30 minutes.
Network: CBS.
First Broadcast: 1952.

Defense Attorney

Type: Drama
Format: The exploits of a successful female attorney.
Starring: Mercedes McCambridge as the attorney.
Length: 30 minutes.
Network: ABC.
First Broadcast: 1951.

Destiny's Trails

Type: Anthology
Format: Dramatizations of two of James Fenimore Cooper's Leather stocking tales: *Deerslayer* and *The Last of the Mohicans*.
Cast: Stacy Harris, Kay Loring, Lesley Woods, Frank Lovejoy, Jerry Macy, Alfred Shirley, Gertrude Warner, Jean Gillespie, Joseph Julian, Ogden Miles, Craig McDonnell, Joe Boland.
Length: 15 minutes.
Syndicated.
First Broadcast: 1945 (ran for 39 weeks).

Detect and Collect

Type: Quiz
Format: Clues, relating to an article concealed behind a curtain, were related to members of the studio audience. The player who was able to identify the article received $25 or less depending on the number of clues given.
Hosts: Wendy Barrie and Fred Uttal, Lew Lehr.
Announcer: Fred Uttal.
Orchestra: Ted Rapf.
Length: 30 minutes.
Network: CBS.
First Broadcast: 1945.

Detect and Collect

Type: Quiz
Format: A musical selection was play-

ed, followed by other tunes. In between each of the selections, snatches of the original tune were inserted. If listener (post card selection) could detect the number of times the original tune was played, he won a war bond.

Host: Vincent Lopez.
Regulars: Judy Lang, Terry Allen.
Announcer: Norman Brokenshire.
Orchestra: Robert Stanley.
Length: 30 minutes.
Network: Mutual.
First Broadcast: 1945.

Dick Cole

See Title "The Adventures of Dick Cole."

The Dick Robertson Show

Type: Musical Variety
Host: Dick Robertson.
Orchestra: Dick Robertson.
Length: 15 minutes.
Network: Mutual.
First Broadcast: 1940.

Dick Tracy

Type: Crime Drama
Format: The exploits of famed police detective Dick Tracy. Based on the comic strip created by Chester Gould.

Cast:	Dick Tracy	Ned Weaver
		Matt Crowley
		Barry Thompson
	Junior Tracy	Andy Donnelly
		Walter Kinsella
		Jackie Kelk
	Police Chief	
	Brandon	Howard Smith
	Tess Trueheart	Helen Lewis
	Pat Patton	Walter Kinsella

Narrator: Don Gardiner.
Announcer: George Gunn, Dan Seymour, Ed Herlihy, Tom Reddy, Don Gardiner.
Music: Ray Carter.
Sponsor: Quaker Puffed Wheat, Tootsie Roll Candy.
Program Opening:
Announcer: And now, Dick Tracy!
Tracy: This is Dick Tracy on (name of episode; such as) "The Case of the Broken Window." Stand by for action. Let's go men.
Announcer: Yes, it's Dick Tracy, protector of law and order.
Length: 15 minutes; a half-hour version appeared in 1946.
Network-First Broadcast: Mutual (1935-1937), NBC (1937-1939), Blue (1943-1944), ABC (1944-1948).

Dimension X

See title: "X Minus One."

The Dinah Shore Show

Type: Musical Variety
Hostess: Dinah Shore.
Regulars: The Joe Lilly Singers.
Announcer: Harry Von Zell, Jack Rourke.
Orchestra: Paul LaValle, Robert Emmett Dolan, Johnny Mercer.
Length: 15 and 30 minute versions.
Network: NBC (1939-1944), CBS (1948).
First Broadcast: 1939. Also known as "Birdseye Open House" (when under the sponsorship of Birdseye) and "Call for Music." Became the basis for a series of television programs with the same title.

Doc, Duke, and the Colonel

Type: Comedy
Format: An exchange of comedy dialogue between Doc, a retired veterinarian, his friend Duke, and a Southern colonel.

| Cast: | Doc | Jess Pugh |
| | Duke | Clarence Hart-zell |

The Colonel   Cliff Soubier
Length: 15 minutes.
Network: NBC.
First Broadcast: 1945.

Doc Hopkins and His Country Boys

Type: Country/Western Musical Variety
Host: Doc Hopkins.
Orchestra: Doc Hopkins.
Length: 15 minutes.
Syndicated.
First Broadcast: 1945.

The Doctor's Wife

Type: Serial
Format: The drama of a doctor's life as
   seen through the eyes of his wife. The
   doctor conducted his practice from an of-
   fice on Elm Street in a suburban New
   York town.
Cast: The Doctor   Dan Curtis
        His wife   Patricia Wheel
        Their maid   Margaret Hamil-
                            ton
        The doctor's
           brother   George Hill
Announcer: Bob Schaerry.
Length: 15 minutes.
Network: ABC.
First Broadcast: 1952.

Dollar a Minute

Type: Audience participation
Format: A unusual concept wherein any-
   one with a gripe or with a desire to
   display his talent paid for air time at the
   rate of a dollar a minute.
Host: Bill Goodwin.
Music: The Elliot T. Daniel Trio.
Length: 30 minutes.
Network: CBS.
First Broadcast: 1950.

The Doris Day Show. Doris Day (shown here in a 1964 pose).

The Don Ameche Show

Type: Variety
Host: Don Ameche.
Regulars: Pinky Lee, Joanell James.
Announcer: Truman Bradley, Marvin Mil-
   ler.
Orchestra: Joe Lilley.
Sponsor: Drene Shampoo.
Length: 30 minutes.
Network: NBC.
First Broadcast: 1946.

Don Winslow of the Navy

Type: Adventure Serial
Format: The exploits of Don Winslow, a
   Naval Intelligence agent.
Cast: Commander Don
           Winslow   Bob Gilbert
                            Raymond Ed-
                            ward Johnson

Red Pennington,
  his aide   Edward Davison
                  John Gibson
Mercedes Colby,
  his girlfriend   Lenore Kingston
                  Betty Lou Gerson
                  Gertrude Warner
Also: Jone Allison, Ted deCorsia, William Pringle.
Length: 15 minutes.
Network: Blue (1937), NBC (1944).

The Doris Day Show

Type: Musical Variety
Hostess: Doris Day.
Announcer: Johnny Jacobs, Roy Rowan.
Length: 25 minutes.
Network: CBS.
First Broadcast: 1952.

Dorsey Drive

Type: Musical Variety
Host: Tommy Dorsey.
Regulars: Stuart Foster, Freddy Martin, Ziggy Elman.
Orchestra: Tommy Dorsey.
Length: 30 minutes.
Network: NBC.
First Broadcast: 1946.

Dorothy Dix on the Air

Type: Advice
Format: An advice to the lovelorn column.
Hostess: Dorothy Dix.
Featured: Nancy Prescott.
Announcer: Joe Ripley.
Length: 15 minutes.
Network: ABC.
First Broadcast: 1949.

The Dorothy Gordon Show

Type: Variety
Hostess: Dorothy Gordon.

Announcer: Henry Morgan.
Length: 15 minutes.
First Broadcast: 1938.

The Dorothy Lamour Show

Type: Variety
Hostess: Dorothy Lamour.
Vocalists: The Crew Chiefs Quartet.
Orchestra: Henry Russell.
Sponsor: Sealtest products.
Length: 30 minutes.
Network: NBC.
First Broadcast: 1948 (ended in 1949). Also known as "The Sealtest Variety Show."

Double Or Nothing

Type: Quiz
Format: Selected players chose a category of questions on which they were quizzed. When the player earned ten dollars he could either quit or risk another question in an attempt to double it. Forty dollars was the maximum a player could win; an incorrect response forfeited his earnings.
Host: Walker Compton, Todd Russell, Walter O'Keefe, John Reed King.
Announcer: Fred Cole, Murray Wagner.
Sponsor: Feenamint and Chooz.
Length: 30 minutes.
Network: Mutual (1940), CBS (1947).
First Broadcast: 1940.

Dough Re Mi

Type: Quiz
Format: Members of the studio audience competed in a game designed to test their musical knowledge. The first player to correctly identify a myster song received a cash prize.
Hostess: Hope Emerson.
Announcer: Radcliffe Hall.

Orchestra: Paul LaValle.
Length: 30 minutes.
Network: NBC.
First Broadcast: 1942.

Down You Go

Type: Game
Format: Four regular panelists competed. The host presented a cryptic clue
representing a popular slogan, quotation,
or phrase, indicated by a line of dashes,
one per letter, on a large board. Players
each received one free guess. If the
phrase was not identified, each panelist
suggested a letter of the alphabet. If an
incorrect letter was given, that player
was disqualified from the round and
forfeited five dollars to the listener who
sent in the phrase. Based on the television program of the same title.
Host: Dr. Bergen Evans
Panelists: Carmelita Pope, Fran Coughlin,
Toni Gilman, Robert Breen.
Vocalist: Katie Carnes.
Music: The Starnotes
Length: 30 minutes.
Network: Mutual.
First Broadcast: 1952.

Dr. Christian

Type: Medical Drama
Format: The story of Dr. Paul Christian
and the infinite problems faced by a doc-
tor in the small town of River's End.
Became the basis for a television series of
the same title.
Cast: Dr. Paul
        Christian   Jean Hersholt
        Judy Price,
        his nurse   Lurene Tuttle
                           Rosemary
                             DeCamp
                           Kathleen Fitz
Announcer: Art Gilmore.
Length: 30 minutes.
Network: CBS.
First Broadcast: 1937.

Dr. Gino's Musicale

Type: Dixieland Music
Host: Gene Hamilton.
Announcer: Gene Hamilton.
Orchestra: Henry Levine.
Length: 30 minutes.
Network: ABC.
First Broadcast: 1950.

Dr. I.Q.

Type: Quiz
Format: Members of the studio audience,
chosen by announcers, were asked questions by Dr. I.Q., the mental banker, in
return for silver dollars. Became the basis
for a television series of the same title.
Hosts: Lew Valentine, Garry Moore, Gene
Kemper, Jimmy McClain, Stanley
Vainrib, Bert Igou, Bob Richardson,
Robert Enoch.
Announcer: Allan C. Anthony.
Program Opening:
Announcer: Presenting Dr. I.Q. Mars In-
corporated, makers of America's most en-
joyable candy bars, brings you another
half-hour of fun with your genial master
of wit and information, Dr. I.Q., the men-
tal banker.
Length: 30 minutes.
Network: NBC.
First Broadcast: 1939.

Dr. I.Q., Jr.

Type: Quiz
Format: A children's version of the adult
game; see previous title for information
Host: Lew Valentine.
Announcer: Allan C. Anthony.
Length: 30 minutes.
Network: NBC.
First Broadcast: 1948.

Dr. Paul

Type: Drama

Dr. Christian. Photo taken May 19, 1947. Pictured are stars Jean Hersholt (second from left) and Rosemary DeCamp (third from right). Second from right is series producer Dorothy B. McCann; director John Wilkenson is standing on the far right behind Miss McCann. The four remaining people are the winners of a script-writing contest held that year.

Format: The story of a small town doctor and his ambitious and scheming wife, who wants him to leave and establish a fancy practice in New York City. The series stressed love and service to humanity.

Cast: Dr. Paul   Russell Thorson
        His wife   Peggy Webber

Also: Janet Logan, Gloria Gordon, Vic Perrin, Sam Edwards, Jean Olivet, Bob Holton, Willard Waterman, Henry Blair.

Length: 15 minutes.
Network: NBC.
First Broadcast: 1949.

Dr. Six Gun

Type: Western
Format: The story of Dr. Ray Matson and the problems faced by a doctor on the frontier of the late 1800s.

Cast: Dr. Ray Matson   Karl Weber
        His gypsy cohort   Bill Griffis

Length: 30 minutes.
Network: NBC.
First Broadcast: 1954.

Dr. Standish, Medical Examiner

Type: Mystery
Format: The cases of Dr. Peter Standish, a medical examiner.

Cast: Dr. Peter
        Standish   Gary Merrill
        The Homicide
        Inspector   Eric Dressler
        Peter's assistant Audrey Christie

Announcer: Lee Vines.
Length: 30 minutes.
Network: CBS.
First Broadcast: 1948.

Dragnet

Type: Crime Drama
Format: Realistic dramatizations based on the files of the Los Angeles Police Department. Became the basis for a television series of the same title.
Cast:

Sgt. Joe Friday	Jack Webb
Officer Ben Romero, his partner	Barton Yarborough
The Police Chief	Richard Boone
Officer Frank Smith, Joe's partner, later episodes	Ben Alexander

Also: Raymond Burr, Harry Morgan.
Announcer: George Fenneman, Hal Gibney.
Music: Walter Schumann.
Sponsor: Chesterfield cigarettes; Fatima cigarettes.
Length: 30 minutes.
Network: NBC.
First Broadcast: 1949.

Dreamboat

Type: Musical Variety
Hostess: Doris Drew.
Regulars: Tom Casey, Jack Lester, Bill Snary.
Orchestra: Rex Maupin.
Length: 30 minutes.
Network: ABC.
First Broadcast: 1951.

Duffy's Tavern

Type: Comedy
Format: The misadventures and dealings of Archie, a con artist who operated and managed Duffy's Tavern, a run-down restaurant bar on Third Avenue in New York City, for the never-seen Mr. Duffy.

Duffy's Tavern. Left to right: Ed Gardner and guests Frances Langford and Jon Hall.

Became the basis for the television series of the same title.
Cast:

Archie	Ed Gardner
Miss Duffy, Duffy's daughter	Shirley Booth
	Florence Halop
	Gloria Erlanger
	Florence Robinson
	Sandra Gould
	Hazel Shermet
Clifton Finnegan, Archie's friend	Charlie Cantor
Eddie, the waiter	Eddie Green
	Ed "Fats" Pichon
Wilfred, Finnegan's brother	Dick Van Patten
Clancy, the neighborhood cop	Alan Reed

Vocalists: Benay Venuta, Bob Graham, Helen Wark, Tito Guizar, Johnny Johnston, The Jack Kirby Chorus.
Announcers: Rod O'Connor, Jay Stewart, Tiny Ruffner, Jimmy Wallington, Marvin Miller, Perry Ward, Alan Reed.
Orchestra: Matty Malneck, Jack Kirby, Joe Venuti.
Sponsor: Vitalis Hair Tonic, Trushay Hand

Lotion, Minit-Rub, Sal Hapatica, Blatz Beer.

Program Opening:

Announcer: It's Wednesday night so we take you now to Duffy's Tavern, with our guest for tonight, Garry Moore, and starring Archie himself, Ed Gardner. Duffy's Tavern is brought to you by Bristol Myers, makers of Trushay for softer, lovelier hands, and Vitalis for well-groomed hair . . .

Program Closing:

Announcer: It's time now to leave Duffy's Tavern for this evening. So let's meet here again at this same time next Wednesday when our guest will be Miss Olga San Juan. Until next Wednesday then, this is Rod O'Connor reminding you that for well-groomed hair remember Vitalis, and for softer, lovelier hands remember Trushay. Each Wednesday Bristol Myers brings you Duffy's Tavern and Mr. District Attorney, which follows immediately over most of these stations.

Length: 30 minutes.
Network: CBS (1941), NBC (1942).
First Broadcast: 1941.

The Duke of Paducah and Opry Songs

Type: Country-Western Musical Variety
Host: Whitey Ford (as the Duke of Paducah).
Regulars: George Morgan, Annie Lou.
Announcer: Jud Collins.
Music: The Moon Mullian Band.
Length: 30 minutes.
Network: NBC.
First Broadcast: 1952.

The Dunninger Show

Type: Variety
Format: Demonstrations of the art of mind reading.
Host: Joseph Dunninger.
Regulars: Bill Slater, Marilyn Day, The Andy Love Vocal group.
Announcer: Don Lowe, Roger Krupp.

Orchestra: Mitchell Ayres.
Length: 30 minutes.
Network: Blue (1943), NBC (1945).
First Broadcast: 1943.

The Earl Wilson Show

Type: Gossip
Format: A transformation of Earl Wilson's *New York Post* Broadway column from the newspapers to the airwaves.
Host: Earl Wilson.
Assistant: Paul Douglas.
Length: 15 minutes.
Network: Mutual.
First Broadcast: 1945.

Earn Your Vacation

Type: Game
Format: A question, "Where on earth would you like to go and why" was posed to the studio audience. Those with the best responses received the opportunity to win an all-expense-paid vacation to their desired place. The player selected a subject category and answered questions of ascending difficulty within four plateaus, each plateau representing a segment of the vacation. Became the basis for the television series of the same title.
Host: Jay C. Flippen, Steve Allen.
Announcer: Johnny Jacobs.
Length: 30 minutes.
Network: CBS.
First Broadcast: 1949.

Easy Aces

Type: Comedy
Format: Events in the lives of the Aces; Jane, the Dumb Dora type, and Goodman, her husband, the recipient of her unpredictable antics. Became the basis for a television series of the same title.
Cast: Goodman Ace   Himself
      Jane Ace   Herself

Marge, their boarder	Mary Hunter
Laura, their maid	Helene Dumas
Betty, Jane's friend	Ethel Blume

Also: Leon Janney, Eric Dressler, Florence Robinson, Everett Sloane, Frank Butler.

Announcer: Ford Bond, Ken Roberts.

Vocalists: The Ken Christy Chorus.

Orchestra: Ken Christy, Morris Surdin.

Sponsor: Rinso, Lipton Tea, Lifebuoy soap, Anacin.

Program Opening:

Announcer (over music theme): Once again the strains of Manhattan Serenade introduce Easy Aces, radio's distinctive laugh novelty.

Length: 15 and 30 minute versions.

Network-First Broadcast: Local Missouri (1930), NBC (1931-1945), Syndicated (1945), CBS (1948). In 1944 the series was also known as "Mr. Ace and Jane."

Easy Money

Type: Mystery

Format: The cases of a magician turned private detective. The series spot-lighted his use of magic to apprehend criminals.

Starring: Willard Waterman as The Magician.

Announcer: George Stone.

Music: Lou Webb.

Length: 30 minutes.

Network: Mutual.

First Broadcast: 1946.

Ed East and Polly

Type: Talk-Variety

Hosts: Ed East, Polly East.

Regulars: Lee Sullivan, Doug Browning Bob Hamilton.

Length: 30 minutes.

Network: Blue.

First Broadcast: 1943.

The Ed Sullivan Show

Type: Variety. Became the basis for TV's "Toast of the Town."

Host: Ed Sullivan.

Regulars: Adele Gerard, Lynne Gardner, Terry Allen.

Announcer: Harry Von Zell, David Ross.

Orchestra: Will Bradley.

Length: 30 minutes.

Network: CBS.

First Broadcast: 1931.

The Ed Wynn Show

Type: Comedy

Host: Ed Wynn.

Announcer: Graham McNamee.

Orchestra: Eddie Duchin, Mark Warnow.

Sponsor: Texaco Fire Chief Gasoline.

Program Opening:

Announcer: For speed, power, action, Texaco Fire Chief, the gasoline that's bought by more tourists than any other brand .... Texaco service stations and dealers in our 48 states present for your entertainment Eddie Duchin and his music, Graham McNamee, and Ed Wynn, the Fire Chief ...

Length: 30 minutes.

Network: NBC.

First Broadcast: 1931 (under the title "The Fire Chief").

The Eddie Albert Show

Type: Variety

Host: Eddie Albert

Regulars: Barbara Eiler, Earle Ross, Joe Crambly, Conni Crowder.

Orchestra: Basil Adlam.

Length: 30 minutes.

Network: NBC.

First Broadcast: 1947.

The Eddie Bracken Show

Type: Comedy-Variety
Host: Eddie Bracken
Regulars: Ann Rutherford, William Dema-
rest, Janet Waldo, Ruth Perrott, Shirley
Booth.
Announcer: John   Wald,   Jimmy   Wall-
ington.
Orchestra: Lee Harlin.
Length: 30 minutes.
Network: NBC (1945), CBS (1946).
First Broadcast: 1945.

The Eddie Cantor Show. Eddie Cantor and Deanna
Durbin.

The Eddie Cantor Show

Type: Variety
Format: Varied mixture of music, songs,
and comedy sketches.
Cast: Host   Eddie Cantor
       The Mad
         Russian   Bert Gordon
       Mademoiselle
         Fifi   Veola Vonn
       Parkyakarkas   Harry Einstein

       Mr. Guffy   Sidney Fields
Regulars: Shirley Dinsdale (ventriloquist;
her   dummy;   Judy   Splinters),   Dave
Rubinoff "and his magic violin"), Alan
Reed, Nan Rae, Maude Davis, John
Brown, Lionel Stander, Frank Nelson,
The Sportsmen Quartet.
Vocalists: Dinah Shore, Deanna Durbin,
Nora Martin, Margaret Whiting, Bobby
Breen.
Announcer: Walter Woolfe King, Harry
Von Zell, Jimmy Wallington.
Orchestra: Cookie Fairchild, George Stoll,
Louis Gress, Jacques Renard, Bobby
Sherwood.
Program Opening:
Announcer: Pabst Blue Ribbon Beer, the
finest beer served anywhere Presents—
Chorus: The Eddie Cantor Pabst Blue Rib-
bon Show.
Announcer: With   our   guest   star   Dan
Dailey, our weekly guest Dinah Shore,
The Sportsmen, Cookie Fairchild's Or-
chestra, Alan Reed, Frank Nelson, yours
truly Harry Von Zell, and starring your
man Friday, Eddie Cantor . . .
Length-Network-First Broadcast: 60 min-
utes, NBC, 1931-1935 (also known as "The
Chase and Sanborn Hour"), 30 minutes,
CBS, 1935-1939 (also known as "The Eddie Cantor Pabst Blue Ribbon Show"), 30
minutes, NBC, 1940-1949.

Eddie Condon's Jazz Concert

Type: Jazz Music
Host: Eddie Condon.
Regulars: Bobby   Hackett,   Miff   Mole,
Pee Wee Russell, Max Kominsky, Billy
Butterfield, James P. Johnson, Hot Lips
Paige, Gene Schroeder, Bob Casey, Joe
Grasso, Liza Morrow, Rex Stuart, Sonny
Greer, Jonah Jones, Willie Smith, Tony
Mottola, Gene Krupa, Joe Marsala, Mug-
gsy Spanier.
Orchestra: Eddie Condon.
Length: 30 minutes.
Network: NBC.
First Broadcast: 1944.

The Eddie Duchin Show

Type: Variety
Host: Eddie Duchin.
Regulars: Nan Wynn, Jimmy Shields, Tony Russell, Durelle Alexander, The Tune Twisters, The Mullins Sisters.
Announcer: Frank Waldecker.
Length: 30 and 15 minute versions.
Network: NBC (1938), ABC (1947).
First Broadcast: 1938.

The Eddy Arnold Show

Type: Variety
Host: Eddy Arnold.
Regulars: Marvin Hughes, Joan Hager, Dorothy Dillard, Anita Kerr.
Announcer: Bill Allen.
Length: 30 minutes.
Network: CBS.
First Broadcast: 1956.

The Edgar Bergen and Charlie McCarthy Show

Type: Comedy-Variety
Host: Edgar Bergen (ventriloquist; dummies: Charlie McCarthy, Mortimer Snerd, Effie Klinker).
Cast:

Pasquale	Don Ameche
Charlie's school principal	Norman Field
Vera Vague, the vocalist	Barbara Jo Allen
Ersel Twing	Pat Patrick
Prof. Carp	Richard Haydn

Regulars: Carol Richards, Gary Crosby, Jack Kirkwood, June Kilgore, Donald Dixon, The King Sisters, Eddie Mayehoff, Jim Backus, The Stroud Twins, Jack Kirkwood.
Frequent Guest: W.C. Fields.
Featured Sketch: "The Bickersons." The story of a quarrelsome husband and wife, with Don Ameche as John Bickerson and Marsha Hunt (later Frances Langford) as Blanche Bickerson.
Announcer: Ken Carpenter, Ben Alexander, Bill Goodwin, Bill Baldwin, Howard Petrie.
Orchestra: Robert Armbruster, Ray Noble.
Sponsor: Chase and Sanborn Coffee.
Program Opening:
Announcer: The makers of instant Chase and Sanborn Coffee present The Edgar Bergen and Charlie McCarthy Show. This is Ken Carpenter, ladies and gentlemen, greeting you from Hollywood, California on behalf of Edgar Bergen, Charlie McCarthy, Mortimer Snerd, Don Ameche and Marsha Hunt and the Bickersons . . . Ray Noble and his Orchestra, and Pat Patrick as Ersel Twing . . .
Length: 30, 60, and 55 minute versions.
Network: NBC (later CBS).
First Broadcast: 1936.

Edith Adam's Future

Type: Serial
Format: The trials and tribulations of Edith Adams, a woman married thirty-five years, and her struggles in handling minor household crises.
Cast:

Edith Adams	Della Louise Orton
Her husband	Joseph Harding
Their daughter	Mary Louise Lantz
Edith's friend	Dolores Dahl

Announcer: John Adams.
Length: 15 minutes.
Network: Mutual.
First Broadcast: 1941.

The Edward Everett Horton Show

Type: Variety
Format: Comedy sketches tailored to Horton's techniques.
Host: Edward Everett Horton.
Announcer: Les Tremayne.
Orchestra: Raymond Paige.
Length: 30 minutes.

The Edgar Bergen and Charlie McCarthy Show. Edgar Bergen (center) with dummies Charlie McCarthy (left) and Mortimer Snerd.

Network: NBC.
First Broadcast: 1945.

The Eileen Barton Show

Type: Musical Variety
Hostess: Eileen Barton.
Announcer: Joe King.
Music: The Alvy West Combo.
Length: 15 minutes.
Network: CBS.
First Broadcast: 1954.

The Eileen Farrell Show

Type: Classical Music
Hostess: Eileen Farrel (soprano).
Announcer: Stewart Young.
Music: The CBS Symphony Orchestra under the direction of Charles Litcher.
Length: 30 minutes.
Network: CBS.
First Broadcast: 1946.

The Edgar Bergen and Charlie McCarthy Show. Left to right: Edgar Bergen, Charlie McCarthy, and W.C. Fields. (The photo depicts the feud that existed between Fields and McCarthy.)

The Edgar Bergen and Charlie McCarthy Show. Left to right: Guest Jack Benny, Charlie McCarthy, and Edgar Bergen.

The Electric Hour

Type: Musical Variety
Host: Nelson Eddy.
Announcer: Frank Graham.
Orchestra-Chorus: Robert Armbruster.
Sponsor: The Electric Light and Power Company.
Length: 30 minutes.
Network: CBS.
First Broadcast: 1943.

Ellery Queen

See Title: "The Adventures of Ellery Queen."

Elsa Maxwell's Party Line

Type: Gossip
Hostess: Elsa Maxwell.
Length: 15 minutes.
Network: Mutual.
First Broadcast: 1945.

Emily Post

Type: Advice
Format: An over-the-air session of responses to listeners' questions.
Hostess: Emily Post.
Length: 30 minutes.
Network: NBC.
First Broadcast: 1938.

Encore

Type: Musical Variety
Host: Robert Merrill.
Regulars: Marguerite Piazza, The Ray Charles Chorus.
Announcer: Kenneth Banghart.
Orchestra: Meredith Wilson.

Length: 30 minutes.
Network: NBC.
First Broadcast: 1952.

Endorsed By Dorsey

Type: Musical Variety
Format: A series of broadcasts filling in for Tommy Dorsey (who was on the road at the time).
Host: Emerson Buckley.
Regulars: Vera Holly, Buddy Merino, Bert Howell, The Holidays, The Chitterson Trio, The Clark Sisters.
Orchestra: Sy Oliver.
Length: 30 minutes.
Network: Mutual
First Broadcast: 1946 (March 27 to October 18, 1946).

Escape

Type: Anthology
Format: High Adventure dramatizations. Became the basis for a television series of the same title.
Narrator: William Conrad, Paul Frees.
Frequently Cast: William Conrad, Paul Frees, John Dehner, Charles McGraw, Ben Wright.
Announcer: Jack McCoy, Elliott Lewis.
Music: Cy Feuer.
Program Opening:
Announcer: We offer you Escape, designed to free you from the four walls of today for a half-hour of high adventure.
Included:
Plunder of the Sun. The story of an amateur detective and his attempts to transport the map to a fortune in ancient Inca gold across South America.
Starring: Paul Frees, Gerald Mohr.
The Birds. Based on Daphne DuMaurier's story about a British coastal community that is attacked by murderous birds.

Starring: Ben Wright.

Violent Night. The story of an American plantation owner's attempts to escape through the treacherous jungle from a dictator seeking to kill him.

Starring: William Conrad.

Length: 30 minutes.

Network: CBS.

First Broadcast: 1947.

Escape With Me

Type: Anthology

Format: Romantic, escapist dramatizations.

Hostess-Narrator: Kathi Norris.

Length: 30 minutes.

Network: ABC.

First Broadcast: 1952.

Ethel and Albert

Type: Comedy

Format: A comedy dialogue between marrieds Ethel and Albert Arbuckle, residents of the town of Sandy Harbor. Became the basis for the television series of the same title.

Cast: Ethel Arbuckle   Peg Lynch
        Albert Arbuckle   Alan Bunce
        Baby Susie, their
          daughter   Madeleine Pierce

Announcer: Don Lowe, George Ansbro, Fred Cole, Cy Harrice, Herb Sheldon, Glenn Riggs.

Orchestra: Ralph Norman.

Organists: Rosa Rio, Lew White, Dolph Gobel.

Length: 15 minutes.

Network: ABC.

First Broadcast: 1944.

The Ethel Merman Show

Type: Comedy

Format: The series, set against a show business background, was about a Broadway star (Ethel Merman), her friend (Allen Drake), and a floor mop tycoon (Arthur Q. Bryan), the backer of the show.

Starring: Ethel Merman.

Also: Allen Drake, Arthur Q. Bryan, Leon Janney, Ethel Brouniny, Charles Webster, Santos Ortega.

Producer-Director: Kenneth MacGregor.

Sponsor: Lysol.

Length: 30 minutes.

Network: CBS (1935), NBC (1949).

First Broadcast: 1935. Originally titled "Rhythm at Eight" (it aired Sunday nights at 8 p.m.).

The Eve Young Show

Type: Musical Variety

Hostess: Eve Young.

Announcer: Don Pardo.

Orchestra: Norman Cloutier, Milt Katims.

Length: 15 minutes.

Network: NBC.

First Broadcast: 1951.

The Evelyn Pasen Show

Type: Classical music

Hostess: Evelyn Pasen (a twenty-year-old Met soprano).

Announcer: Sidney Berry.

Music: Bernard Herrmann and the Columbia Concert Orchestra.

Length: 30 minutes.

Network: CBS.

First Broadcast: 1945.

Evelyn Winters

See title: "The Strange Romance of Evelyn Winters."

Ever Since Eve

Type: Serial

Format: Varying story lines and casts depicting women's successful or unsuccessful attempts to procure a man; a saga of a lonely woman's search for love.

Narrator: Keith Morgan.
Length: 15 minutes.
Network: ABC.
First Broadcast: 1954.

Everybody Wins

Type: Quiz
Format: Called for members of the studio audience to answer questions in return for cash prizes.
Host: Phil Baker.
Announcer: Ken Roberts.
Length: 30 minutes.
Network: CBS.
First Broadcast: 1948.

Everything for the Boys

Type: Musical Variety
Format: Entertainment geared to servicemen.
Host: Dick Haymes.
Vocalist: Helen Forrest.
Orchestra: Gordon Jenkins.
Length: 30 minutes.
Network: NBC.
First Broadcast: 1944.

Exploring the Unknown

Type: Anthology
Format: Featured stories of "science at work, searching for knowledge that will shape your future." Guests appeared in varying dramatizations.
Sponsor: Revere Copper and Brass Company.
Producer: Sherman H. Dryer.
Length: 30 minutes.
Network: Mutual (1945-1947), ABC (1947-1948).
First Broadcast: 1945.

The Fabulous Dr. Tweedy

Type: Comedy
Format: The misadventures of Dr. Tweedy, a professor at Potts College, a girls' school.
Starring: Frank Morgan as Dr. Tweedy.
Also: Nana Bryant, Eddie Green.
Announcer: Bud Heistand.
Orchestra: Elliot Daniel.
Length: 30 minutes.
Network: NBC.
First Broadcast: 1946.

The Falcon

Type: Mystery
Format: The exploits of Michael Waring, a daring crusader for justice, known and feared by criminals as the Falcon. Also known as "The Adventures of the Falcon." Became the basis for the television series of the same title.
Cast: Michael Waring James Meighan
Les Damon
Berry Kroeger
Les Tremayne
George Petrie
Nancy, his girl-
friend/assistant Joan Banks
Elspeth Eric
Announcer: Russ Dunbar, Ed Herlihy.
Organist: Bob Hamilton.
Orchestra: Emerson Buckley, Harry Sosnik.
Sponsor: Gem Razors and Blades.
Program Opening:
Announcer (over sounds of a ticking clock): Avoid five o'clock shadow.
Voice: Use Gem blades ...
Announcer: Gem Razors and Gem Blades present The Adventures of the Falcon.
Sound effect: Phone rings; receiver is picked up.
The Falcon: Hello, yes this is The Falcon (from this point on the story would begin).
Length: 30 minutes.

Network: Blue (1943), Mutual (1945), NBC (1950).
First Broadcast: 1943.

Falstaff's Fables

Type: Children's
Format: Parodies on classic children's stories.
Starring: Alan Reed, Sr., and Alan Reed, Jr.
Announcer: Dick Tufeld.
Length: 5 minutes.
Network: ABC.
First Broadcast: 1949.

Fame and Fortune

Type: Variety
Format: The series spotlighted the work of amateur songwriters. Winners, determined by studio audience applause, received $100.
Starring: Frank Sinatra, Connie Haynes.
Length: 30 minutes.
Network: NBC.
First Broadcast: 1940.

The Family Hour

Type: Classical music
Commentator: Deems Taylor.
Regulars: Gladys Swarthout, Ross Graham, Jack Smart, The Al Goodman Chorus.
Orchestra: Al Goodman.
Length: 45 minutes.
Network: CBS.
First Broadcast: 1941.

Family Skeleton

Type: Serial
Format: The dramatic story of Sarah Ann Spencer.
Starring: Mercedes McCambridge as Sarah Ann Spencer.
Also: Russell Thorson, John Dehner, Jeanette Nolan, Forrest Lewis, Marvin Miller, Marilyn Steiner, Herb Vigran.
Length: 15 minutes.
Network: CBS.
First Broadcast: 1953 (June 8, 1953 to March 5, 1954).

Famous Jury Trials

Type: Drama
Format: Dramatizations of actual courtroom cases. Became the basis for a television series with the same title.
Starring: Maurice Franklin as the Judge.
Narrator: Roger DeKoven, DeWitt McBride.
Announcer: Peter Grant, Roger Krupp, Hugh James.
Length: 30 minutes.
Network: NBC (1933), Mutual (1936).
First Broadcast: 1933.

Fannie Hurst Presents

Type: Anthology
Format: Dramatizations of stories by Fannie Hurst.
Hostess-Narrator: Fannie Hurst.
Length: 30 minutes.
Network: Blue.
First Broadcast: 1944.

Fashion Discoveries

Type: Women's
Host: Wynn Price.
Regulars: Ruth Hopkins, Peggy Read.
Length: 30 minutes.
Network: NBC.
First Broadcast: 1941.

The Fat Man

Type: Crime Drama

Format: The investigations of Brad Runyon, an overweight private detective created by Dashiell Hammett.
Cast: Brad Runyon   J. Scott Smart
       Lila North, his
         secretary   Mary Patton
       Sergeant O'Hara   Ed Begley
Orchestra: Bernard Green.
Program Opening:
Woman's Voice: There he goes, into that drugstore. He's stepping on the scales (a coin is heard dropping into the machine). Weight 237 pounds; (a card is heard dropping) fortune: danger. Whoooo is it?
Man's Voice: The Fat Man.
Length: 30 minutes.
Network: ABC.
First Broadcast: 1946.

Father Knows Best

Type: Comedy
Format: Events in the lives of the Anderson Family: Jim, an insurance salesman, his wife Margaret, and their children Betty, Bud, and Kathy. Basis for the television series of the same title.
Cast: Jim Anderson   Robert Young
       Margaret
         Anderson   June Whitley
       Betty Anderson   Rhoda Williams
       Bud Anderson   Ted Donaldson
       Kathy Anderson   Norma Jean
                           Nilson
       Elizabeth Smith,
         their neighbor Eleanor Audley
       Hector Smith,
         her husband   Herb Vigran
       Billy Smith,
         their son   Sam Edwards
Announcer: Marvin Miller, Bill Forman.
Music: Roy Bargy.
Sponsor: Post cereals.
Length: 30 minutes.
Network: NBC.
First Broadcast: 1949.

Faultless Starch Time

Type: Musical Variety
Host: Bob Atcher.

Hostess: Mary Jane Johnson.
Announcer: Franklyn Ferguson.
Music: The Caesar Giovannini Combo.
Sponsor: Faultless Starch.
Length: 15 minutes.
Network: ABC.
First Broadcast: 1948.

Favorite Story

Type: Anthology
Format: Dramatizations based on stories chosen by guest stars.
Host: Ronald Colman.
Musical Director: Claude Sweetern, Robert Mitchell.
Length: 30 minutes.
Syndicated.
First Broadcast: 1947.

The F.B.I. in Peace and War

Type: Crime Drama
Format: Dramatizations based on the files of the Federal Bureau of Investigation.
Starring: Martin Blaine as Adam Sheppard, the F.B.I. field agent.
Announcer: Warren Sweeney, Len Sterling.
Music: Vladimir Selinsky.
Length: 25 minutes.
Network: CBS.

The Fanny Brice Show

Type: Comedy
Format: The antics of a teenage girl named Irma.
Cast: Irma   Fanny Brice
       Irma's father   Hanley Stafford
       The postman   Danny Thomas
Orchestra: Carmen Dragon.
Length: 30 minutes.
Network: CBS.
First Broadcast: 1944.

Fibber McGee and Molly. Front: Jim and Marian Jordan. Back: Bill Thompson (Wallace Wimple) and Arthur Q. Bryan (Doc Gamble).

Fibber McGee and Molly

Type: Comedy
Format: There was no story line; situations arose when people entered the McGee home at 79 Wistful Vista and found themselves involved in various dilemmas.
Cast: Fibber McGee   Jim Jordan
       Molly McGee   Marian Jordan
       Throckmorton
         P. Gildersleeve,
         their friend   Hal Peary
       Doc Gamble   Arthur Q. Bryan
       Mayor LaTrivia   Gale Gordon
       Wallace Wimple,
         the henpecked
         husband   Bill Thompson
       The Old Timer   Cliff Arquette
                          Bill Thompson

       Teeny, the girl
         nextdoor   Marian Jordan
       Beulah, the maid   Marlin Hurt
       Sis, the little girl   Marian Jordan
       Mrs. Weary-
         bottom   Marian Jordan

       Mr. Williams
         (Foggy), the
         weatherman   Gale Gordon
       Uncle Dennis   Bill Thompson
                          Ranson Sherman
       Lena, the maid   Gene Carroll
Also: Jess Kirkpatrick.
Vocalists: The Kingsmen Quartet.
Announcer: Harlow Wilcox.
Orchestra: Bill Mills, Ted Weems.
Sponsor: Johnson Wax, Pet Milk, Alka-Seltzer.
Announcer: The makers of Johnson's wax products present Jim and Marian Jordan as Fibber McGee and Molly with Bill Thompson, Gale Gordon, Arthur Q. Bryan, Jess Kirkpatrick, and me, Harlow Wilcox.
Length: 30 minutes.
Network: NBC.
First Broadcast: 1934 (ended in 1952; became the basis for a 1959 television series of the same title).

51 East 51st

Type: Musical Variety
Format: Variety acts set against the background of the mythical Manhattan Cafe' located at 51 East 51st Street.
Host: Kay Thompson.
Regulars: Everett Sloane, Erik Rhodes, Lionel Stander.
Orchestra: Archie Bleyer.
Length: 30 minutes.
Network: CBS.
First Broadcast: 1941.

Finders Keepers

Type: Quiz
Format: Members of the studio audience competed. A dramatic cast first enacted a scene containing an error. The first player to spot and correct the mistake won the round and a cash prize.
Host: Bob Sherry, Happy Felton.
Dramatic Cast: Julie Conway, Florence Halop, Lee Brady, Arthur Elmes.

Orchestra: Irving Miller, Jerry Jerome.
Length: 30 minutes.
Network: NBC.
First Broadcast: 1944.

The First Hundred Years

Type: Comedy
Format: The trials and tribulations of a young married couple.
Cast: The husband   Sam Edwards
      The wife   Barbara Eiler
Also: Joseph Kearns, Myra Marsh, Bea Benaderet, Earle Ross.
Announcer: Owen James.
Length: 30 minutes.
Network: ABC.
First Broadcast: 1949.

First Nighter

Type: Anthology
Format: Dramatic and comedy presentations of three-act plays.
Host: (Mr. First Nighter): Charles P. Hughes, Bret Morrison, Marvin Miller, Don Briggs, Ed Prentiss.
Regular Performers: Don Ameche, Olan Soule, Betty Lou Gerson, Rye Billsbury, June Meredith, Barbara Luddy, Les Tremayne, Bob Jellison.
Announcer: Larry Keating, Rye Billsbury, Vincent Pelletier.
Orchestra: Eric Sagerquist, Frank Worth, Caesar Petrillo.
Sponsor: Campana's Solitaire Make-up and Campana Balm.
Program Opening:
Mr. First Nighter: Theatre time; Broadway is buzzing with excitement and eagerly awaiting to welcome an opening night performance at the Little Theatre off Times Square. And we have a crowd of onlookers and autograph fans on hand at the entrance to greet the celebrities who always attend the premiere on the Great White Way. So let's not miss a minute of the excitement... (From this point on, we would accompany Mr. First Nighter to his special seat in the theater

First Nighter. Co-stars Barbara Luddy and Les Tremayne. The photo, dated July 14, 1937, is the first picture ever taken of Luddy and Tremayne together.

and then listen to the evening's story.)
Length: 30 and 25 minute versions.
Network: NBC (1929), CBS (1940), Mutual (1943).
First Broadcast: 1929.

Fish Pond

Type: Quiz
Format: Players chosen from the studio audience were designated as fish. Each fish then performed a routine (monologue, song, etc.) and awaited the verdict of the "fish pond" judges (the studio audience). If the judges approved of the performance, the fish was reeled in and the player received a prize; if the judges disapproved, the fish was thrown back (lost).
Host: Win Elliot.
Regulars: Dorian St. George, Jack McCarthy, John Keller, Eddie Willis, Leon Weber.
Length: 30 minutes.
Network: Blue.
First Broadcast: 1944.

First Nighter. Left to right: Bob Jellison, Olan Soulé, Barbara Luddy, Rye Billsbury.

Five Minute Mysteries

Type: Anthology
Format: Varied mystery presentations enacted by a regular cast.
Cast: Frank Lovejoy, Jackson Beck, Ian MacAllister, Abby Lewis, Timmy Hyler, Michael Fitzmaurice, Staats Cotsworth.
Organist: Rosa Rio.
Length: 5 minutes.
Syndicated.
First Broadcast: 1946.

Flash Gordon

Type: Science Fiction Adventure
Format: The exploits of Flash Gordon, the resourceful son of a famous scientist, as he strove to maintain peace throughout the universe. Based on the comic strip created by Alex Raymond.

Cast: Flash Gordon   Gale Gordon
                                      James Meighan
          Dr. Zarkoff, the
            brilliant Earth
            scientist   Maurice Franklin
          Ming the Merci-
            less, the evil
            ruler of the
            plant Mongo   Bruno Wick
Length: 15 minutes.
Network: Mutual.
First Broadcast: 1935.

The Fleischman's Yeast Hour

Type: Variety
Host: Rudy Vallee.
Announcer: Graham McNamee.
Orchestra: The Connecticut Yankees.
Sponsor: Fleischman's Yeast.
Length: 60 minutes.
Network: NBC.
First Broadcast: 1935 (ended in 1939).

The Flying Patrol

Type: Adventure
Format: Dramatizations based on the exploits of the Coast Guard Air Corps.
Cast: The Coast Guard
    Chief   Hugh Rowlands
    His girlfriend   Sharon Grainger
Coast Guards: Sidney Ellstrom, Bob Guilbert, Cliff Soubier.
Also: Norma Jean Ross, Mary Frances Desmond, Kay Campbell, Pat Murphy, Willard Farnum.
Length: 15 minutes.
Network: NBC.
First Broadcast: 1941.

The Ford Show

Type: Variety
Host: Lawrence Brooks.
Orchestra/Chorus: Robert Russell Bennett.
Sponsor: Ford Motor Company.
Length: 30 minutes.
Network: NBC.
First Broadcast: 1945.

The Ford Summer Hour

Type: Variety
Host: James Melton.
Regulars: Francis White, Audrey Marsh, The Dixie Eight.
Orchestra: Donald Voorhees.
Sponsor: The Ford Motor Company.
Length: 60 minutes.
Network: CBS.
First Broadcast: 1939.

The Ford Summer Hour

Type: Variety
Host: Meredith Wilson.
Regulars: Jane Pickens, Gordon Gifford, Linton Wells, Paul Wing, Bud Mitchell.
Vocalists/Music: The Ford Orchestra and Chorus.
Sponsor: The Ford Motor Company.
Length: 60 minutes.
Network: CBS.
First Broadcast: 1941.

The Ford Sunday Evening Hour

Type: Classical Music
Hosts: John Charles Thomas, Lawrence Tibbett.
Regulars: Sir Thomas Beecham, W.J. Cameron.
Orchestra: Eugene Ormandy; The Detroit Symphony Orchestra.
Sponsor: The Ford Motor Company.
Length: 60 minutes.
Network: CBS.
First Broadcast: 1933.

Ford Theatre

Type: Anthology
Format: Dramatic and comedy presentations.
Announcer: Nelson Case.
Music: Cy Feuer.
Sponsor: The Ford Motor Company.
Included:
Anna Christie. The romance between a beautiful girl with a sexually checkered past and a rough dock worker.
Starring: Ingrid Bergman, Broderick Crawford, John Quaylen.
The Horn Blows at Midnight. The story of a man who dreams he is an angel who has been sent to destroy sinful Earth.
Starring: Jack Benny, Claude Rains, Mercedes McCambridge, Hans Conried.
Length: 60 minutes.
Network: NBC.
First Broadcast: 1947.

Foreign Assignment

Type: Adventure
Format: The exploits of a daring foreign correspondent.
Cast: The Foreign
    Correspondent   Bartlett Robinson
                      Maurice Wells

	Jay Jostyn
His beautiful assistant	Vicki Vola

Narrator: Joseph Julian.
Orchestra: Henry Sylvern.
Length: 30 minutes.
Network: Mutual.
First Broadcast: 1943.

Forever Ernest

Type: Comedy
Format: The misadventures of a bumbling
  young man.

Cast: Ernest	Jackie Coogan
His girl friend	Lurene Tuttle
Their Friend	Arthur Q. Bryan

Announcer: Dick Joy.
Orchestra: Billy May.
Length: 30 minutes.
Network: CBS.
First Broadcast: 1946.

Forever Tops

Type: Musical Variety
Chorus: Eugene Baird.
Orchestra: Paul Whiteman.
Length: 25 minutes.
Network: ABC.
First Broadcast: 1946.

Fort Laramie

Type: Western
Format: The exploits of Lee Quince, the
  captain of a cavalry troop stationed at
  Fort Laramie, Wyoming, during the late
  1800s.

Cast: Captain Lee Quince	Raymond Burr
Sgt. Goerss	Vic Perrin
Lt. Seiberts	Harry Bartell
Major Daggett	Jack Moyles

Music: Amerigo Moreno.
Announcer: Dan Cubberly.
Program Opening:

Announcer: Fort Laramie, starring Raymond Burr as Captain Lee Quince, specially transcribed tales of the dark and tragic ground of the wild frontier. The saga of fighting men who rode the rim of empire and the dramatic story of Lee Quince, captain of cavalry.

Length: 30 minutes.
Network: CBS.
First Broadcast: 1955.

The Frank Fontaine Show

Type: Variety
Host: Frank Fontaine.
Regulars: Helen O'Connell, Mary Jane Croft.
Announcer: Harry Von Zell.
Orchestra: Lud Gluskin.
Length: 30 minutes.
Network: CBS.
First Broadcast: 1952.

Frank Merriwell

See title: "The Adventures of Frank Merriwell."

Frank Race

See title: "The Adventures of Frank Race."

The Frank Ray Show

Type: Musical Variety
Host: Frank Ray.
Orchestra: Harry Salter.
Length: 30 minutes.
Network: NBC.
First Broadcast: 1941.

The Frank Sinatra Show

See title: "Songs by Sinatra."

The Fred Allen Show. Fred Allen.

The Frankie Laine Show

Type: Musical Variety
Host: Frankie Laine.
Announcer: Stuart Metz.
Orchestra: Freddie Martin.
Length: 30 minutes.
Network: CBS.
First Broadcast: 1951.

The Fred Allen Show

Type: Comedy-Variety
Host: Fred Allen.
Regulars: Portland Hoffa Allen, Kenny Baker, Wynn Murray, Ned Sparks, Charlie Cantor, Alan Reed, Larry Elliott, Eileen Douglas, John Brown, Jack Smith, Shirley Booth, Walter Tetley.
"Allen's Alley" Cast:*

Fred Allen	Himself
Titus Moody	Parker Fennelly
Senator Beauregard Claghorn	Kenny Delmar
Mrs. Pansy	

Nussbaum	Minerva Pious
Ajax Cassidy	Peter Donald

Vocalists: The Hugh Martin Singers, the John Brown Chorus, The Al Goodman Chorus. The Merry Macs, The Lyn Murray Chorus, The DeMarco Sisters, The Town Hall Quartet, Hi-Lo Jack and a Dame.
Announcer: Harry Von Zell, Jimmy Wallington, Kenny Delmar.
Orchestra: Peter Van Steeden, Al Goodman, Lou Katzman, Lennie Hayton.
Sponsor: Hellmann's Mayonnaise, Ipana and Sal Hepatica, Blue Bonnett Margarine, Tender Leaf Tea, Shefford's Cheese, Ford Motor Company, V-8 Vegetable Juice, Texaco gasoline.
Length: 60 minutes (1932-1942), 30 minutes (1942-1949).
Network: CBS (1932), NBC (1938), CBS (1940).
First Broadcast: 1932 (October 23, 1932 to June 26, 1949). The series was also titled "The Linit Show," "The Salad Bowl Revue," "The Hour of Smiles," "Town Hall Tonight," and "Texaco Star Theatre."
*The "Allen's Alley" segment found Fred strolling down an alley to drop in on some friends. Other features included "Town Hall News of the Week," and "The Mighty Allen Art Players."

The Fred Astaire Show

Type: Variety
Host: Fred Astaire.
Orchestra: Johnny Green.
Length: 15 minutes.
Network: NBC.
First Broadcast: 1936.

The Fred Brady Show

Type: Variety
Host: Fred Brady.
Regulars: Martha Tilton, Joe DiRita, Charlie Kimper, Lou Lubin, Shirley Mitchell.
Orchestra: Gordon Jenkins.
Length: 30 minutes.

Network: NBC.
First Broadcast: 1943.

The Fred Keating Show

Type: Variety
Host: Fred Keating.
Regulars: Martha Tilton, Murray Mar-
    cellino, Sally Rand, Bobby Sherwood,
    George Jay, Peter Lind Hayes.
Announcer: Gary Breckner.
Orchestra: Leon Leonardi.
Length: 30 minutes.
Syndicated.
First Broadcast: 1940.

The Fred Waring Show

Type: Musical Variety
Host: Fred Waring.
Regulars: Murray Kane, Hal Kanner,
    Lydia Perrone, Donna Dae, Patsy Gar-
    rett, Stuart Churchill, Gordon Goodman,
    Poley McClintock, The Twin Trio, The
    Fred Waring Glee Club, Honey and the
    Bees, The Three Girl Friends, Les Paul,
    Ruth Cottingham, Virginia Morley, Kay
    Thompson, Tom Waring.
Announcer: David Ross, Bob Considine,
    Paul Douglas.
Orchestra: Fred Waring.
Length: 15 and 30 minute versions.
Network: NBC.
First Broadcast: 1938.

The Freddy Martin Show

Type: Variety
Host: Freddy Martin.
Regulars: Johnny Corcoron, Bill Curtis,
    The Martin Men.
Orchestra: Freddy Martin.
Length: 30 minutes.
Network: CBS.
First Broadcast: 1954.

Free for All

Type: Variety
Starring: Bill Grey, Betty Randall, Bob
    Stanley.
Orchestra: Steve Shultz and his Katzen-
    jammers.
Length: 30 minutes.
Network: Mutual.
First Broadcast: 1943.

The Fresh Up Show

Type: Variety
Host: Barry Grant.
Regulars: Annette Warren, Walter Kin-
    sella (as the Irish policeman), Artie Elmer,
    Jim Backus, Lee Brady, Hildegarde Holli-
    day.
Announcer: Jerry Lawrence.
Orchestra-Chorus: David Terry.
Sponsor: 7-Up.
Length: 30 minutes.
Network: Mutual.
First Broadcast: 1945.

Friendship Ranch

Type: Children's
Format: Country and Western entertain-
    ment acts, set against the background of
    a bunkhouse, for children.
Starring: Don Parker, Jack Vincent, Mar-
    gie Hammer, Ronald Smith, Nancy Gon-
    zales, Marilyn Gusten, Billy Daniels, The
    Warner Singers.
Announcer: Tex Antoine.
Length: 30 minutes.
Network: NBC.
First Broadcast: 1944.

Front Page Farrell

Type: Drama
Format: The story of David Farrell, a re-

porter for the *Daily Eagle*, a crusading New York newspaper.

Cast: David Farrell   Richard Widmark
           Carleton Young
           Staats Cotsworth

Sally Farrell,
his wife   Betty Garde
        Virginia Dwyer
        Florence Williams

Mrs. Howard,
Sally's mother   Ethel Intropide
        Evelyn Varden

Lt. Carpenter
N.Y.P.D.   Robert Donley

Announcer: Bill Bond, James Fleming.
Organist: Rosa Rio, Ann Leax.
Sponsor: Kriptin decongestant, Aerowax, Bisodol Mints.
Program Opening:
Announcer: We now present the exciting, unforgettable radio drama, Front Page Farrell, the story of a crack newspaperman and his wife. The story of David and Sally Farrell. Today David is covering the story which he calls "The Blinding Light Murder Case."
Length: 15 minutes.
Network: Mutual.
First Broadcast: 1941.

Frontier Gentleman

Type: Western
Format: The story of Jonathan B. Kendall, an English journalist who traveled throughout the American West of the 1880s to report the stories for the *London Times*.
Starring: John Dehner as Jonathan B. Kendall.
Music Conductor: Wilbur Hatch.
Music Composer: Jerry Goldsmith.
Program Opening:
Announcer: Frontier Gentleman. Here with an Englishman's account of life and death in the West. As a reporter for the *London Times*, he writes his colorful and unusual stories; but as a man with a gun he lives and becomes part of the violent years in the new territories. Now, starring John Dehner, this is the story of Jonathan B. Kendall, Frontier Gentleman.
Length: 30 minutes.
Network: CBS.
First Broadcast: 1958 (February 2, 1958 to November 16, 1958).

Frontier Town

Type: Western
Format: The exploits of Chad Remington, a lawyer in a ruthless frontier town of a century ago.
Starring: Jeff Chandler as Chad Remington.
Length: 30 minutes.
Syndicated.
First Broadcast: 1952.

Fu Manchu

See title: "The Shadow of Fu Manchu."

Fun For All

Type: Variety
Format: Comedy skits, music, and game contests for prizes.
Hosts: Arlene Francis, Bill Cullen.
Organist: Bert German, Abe Goldman.
Length: 30 minutes.
Network: CBS.
First Broadcast: 1952.

Fun in Print

Type: Quiz

Format: Pitted selected members of the studio audience against professional writers in a series of question and answer rounds.
Host: Sigmund Spaeth.
Length: 30 minutes.
Network: CBS.
First Broadcast: 1940.

The Galen Drake Show

Type: Variety
Host: Galen Drake.
Regulars: Betty Johnson, Stuart Foster, The Three Beaus and a Peep.
Announcer: Olin Tice.
Orchestra: Bernard Leighton.
Length: 60 minutes.
Network: CBS.
First Broadcast: 1954.

Game Parade

Type: Quiz
Format: Five children competed in a series of educational question and answer rounds.
Host: Arthur Elmer.
Assistant: Renee Terry.
Length: 30 minutes.
Network: Blue.
First Broadcast: 1943.

Gangbusters

Type: Crime Drama
Format: Dramatizations of actual case histories of the operations of law enforcement agents in their battle against the underworld.
Host-Announcer: Charles Stark, Frank Gallop, Don Gardiner, Roger Forster.
Narrator: Phillips H. Lord, John C. Hilley, Dean Carlton, Louis J. Valentine, Col. Norman Schwartzkopf, plus a guest law-enforcement official for each episode.
Program Opening:

Announcer: Sloans Liniment presents Gangbusters. At war, marching against the underworld from coast-to-coast. Gangbusters, Police, the G-Men, our government agents marching toward the underworld.
Length: 30 minutes.
Network: CBS.
First Broadcast: 1935.

The Gary Crosby Show

Type: Variety
Host: Gary Crosby.
Orchestra: Buddy Bergen.
Length: 30 minutes.
Network: CBS.
First Broadcast: 1955.

The Garry Moore-Jimmy Durante Show

See Title: "The Jimmy Durante-Garry Moore Show."

The Garry Moore Show

Type: Variety
Host: Garry Moore.
Regulars: Eileen Wood, Irving Miller, Ken Carson.
Announcer: Bill Wendell.
Orchestra: Howard Petrie.
Length: 60 minutes.
Network: CBS.
First Broadcast: 1949.

Gaslight Gaysters

Type: Musical Variety
Starring: Beatrice Kay, Michael O'Shea, Sally Sweetland.
Orchestra: Charles "Bud" Dant.
Length: 30 minutes.
Network: NBC.
First Broadcast: 1944.

Gasoline Alley

Type: Drama

Format: Adapted from the comic strip by Frank King, the series dramatized incidents in the life of Skeezix, a mechanic in a gasoline station.

Cast: Skeezix   Jimmy McCallion
                           Bill Idelson
                           Bill Lipton

       Nina Clock, his
         girlfriend   Janice Gilbert
                           Jean Gillespie

       Wumple, Skee-
         zix's boss   Cliff Soubier
       Ling Wee, the
         Chinese waiter   Junius Matthews
       Auntie Blossom   Irna Phillips

Length: 15 minutes.

Network: NBC.

First Broadcast: 1941.

Gateway to Hollywood

Type: Variety

Format: Two undiscovered hopefuls performed a playlet with an established celebrity. Thirteen such couples competed over a thirteen-week period and the couple whose performance was judged outstanding received a contract with RKO Radio Pictures.

Host: John L. Lasky.

Announcer: Ken Niles.

Orchestra: Wilbur Hatch.

Length: 30 minutes.

Network: CBS.

First Broadcast: 1939.

The Gay Mrs. Featherstone

Type: Comedy

Format: The misadventures of Mrs. Featherstone, a well-meaning mother-in-law. Living with her daughter and son-in-law, she feels the need to remedy domestic problems, but finds her intentions backfiring and situations worsening. Her attempts to undo the damage comprised the heart of the series.

Cast: Mrs. Feather-
         stone   Billie Burke
       Her daughter   Florence Lake
       Her son-in-law   John Brown

Announcer: Marvin Miller.

Orchestra: Eddy Howard.

Sponsor: Raleigh cigarettes.

Length: 30 minutes.

Network: NBC.

First Broadcast: 1945.

Gay Nineties Revue

Type: Variety

Format: Music, songs, and comedy skits set against the background of the Granada, an 1890s-style night club in New York.

Cast: Host-Club
         Proprietor   Jack Norworth
       Broadway Harry   Frank Lovejoy
       Danny Donovan   Jack Arthur

Regulars: Genevieve Rowe, Beatrice Kay, Ed Latimer, Joe Howard, Don Costello, Billy Greene, The Clubman, The Elm City Four.

Announcer: John Reed King.

Orchestra: Ray Bloch.

Length: 60 minutes.

Network: CBS.

First Broadcast: 1939.

Gene Autry's Melody Ranch

Type: Western Variety

Format: Music, songs, and playlets set against the background of the Double M Ranch.

Host: Gene Autry.

Regulars: Pat Buttram, Frank Mahoney. Scotty Harrell, Jim Boles, Tyler McVey, Nancy Mason, The Pinafors, The Johnny Bond Trio, The King Sisters, The Cass Country Boys.

Announcer: Lou Crosby.

Orchestra: Paul Sills.

Sponsor: Wrigley's Doublemint Chewing Gum.
Length: 15 and 30 minute versions.
Network: CBS.
First Broadcast: 1940.

The General Electric Theatre

Type: Anthology
Format: Dramatic presentations.
Announcer: Ken Carpenter.
Orchestra: Wilbur Hatch.
Sponsor: General Electric.
Length: 30 minutes.
Network: CBS.
First Broadcast: 1953.

Gentleman Adventurer

See title: "Special Agent."

The George Burns and Gracie Allen Show

Type: Comedy-Variety
Format: Comedy sketches, songs, and routines. Became the basis for a television series of the same title.
Starring: George Burns and Gracie Allen.
Cast: The Happy
Postman	Mel Blanc
Tootsie	Elvia Allman
Muriel	Sara Berner
Waldo	Dick Crenna

Regulars: Margaret Brayton, Clarence Nash, Jimmy Cash, Han Conried, Bill Baldwin, Tony Martin, Dick Ryan, Edith Evans, Frank Parker, Gale Gordon, Henry Blair, The Les Paul Trio.
Announcer: Ted Husing, Bill Goodwin, Toby Reed, Harry Von Zell, Truman Bradley, Jimmy Wallington.
Orchestra: Jacques Renard, Ray Noble, Paul Whiteman, Meredith Wilson.
Length: 30 minutes.
Network: CBS (later NBC).
First Broadcast: 1931. Also titled "Maxwell House Coffee Time."

The George Burns and Gracie Allen Show. An early 1930s photo of George Burns and Gracie Allen.

George Jessel Salutes

Type: Variety
Format: Tributes to servicemen's clubs.
Host: George Jessel.
Vocalists: Tony Bovaar, Shirley Haimer, John Steele.
Orchestra: Paul Whiteman.
Length: 30 minutes.
Network: ABC.
First Broadcast: 1953.

The George Jessel Show

Type: Variety
Host: George Jessel.
Regulars: Mary Small, Ernest Chappell, Sam Carlson.
Orchestra: Dick Himber.
Length: 30 minutes.
Network: Mutual.
First Broadcast: 1937.

The George O'Hanlon Show

Type: Comedy

The George Burns and Gracie Allen Show. George Burns and Gracie Allen in a late 40s pose.

Format: The story of a not-too-bright husband, his patient wife, his chiseling best friend, and his overbearing boss.

Cast: The husband   George O'Hanlon
His wife   Lurene Tuttle
The friend   Cliff Young
The boss   Alan Reed

Orchestra: Harry Zimmerman.
Length: 30 minutes.
Network: Mutual.
First Broadcast: 1948.

Get Rich Quick

Type: Quiz
Format: Following a dramatic skit, the host placed a telephone call to a listener. If the listener could identify the person, place, or thing represented by the skit, he won $25.
Host: Johnny Olsen.
Announcer: Jimmy Blaine.
Length: 30 minutes.
Network: ABC.
First Broadcast: 1948.

Gibbs and Finney, General Delivery

Type: Comedy
Format: The story of Gideon Gibbs and Asa Finney, two friends who opened a livery stable in New England with the advent of the gas and rubber shortage during World War II.

Cast: Gideon Gibbs   Parker Fennelly
Asa Finney   Arthur Allen
The Widow   Ethel Owen
The Printer   Roy Fant

Vocalists: Walter Scanlon, Paul Parks.
Length: 15 minutes.
Network: Blue.
First Broadcast: 1942.

The Ginny Simms Show

Type: Musical Variety
Hostess: Ginny Simms.
Announcer: Don Wilson.
Orchestra: Frank DeVol.
Length: 30 minutes.
Network: CBS.
First Broadcast: 1945.

Ginny Simms Song Book

Type: Musical Variety
Hostess: Ginny Simms.
Announcer: Frank Graham.
Music: The Buddy Cole Trio.
Length: 15 minutes.
Network: ABC.
First Broadcast: 1950.

The George Burns and Gracie Allen Show. Harry Von Zell, George's long-time announcer, with Marie Wilson ("My Friend Irma").

Girl Alone

Type: Serial
Format: The dramatic story of Patricia Rogers.
Cast:

Patricia Rogers	Betty Winkler
Alice Warner	Joan Winters
Scoop Curtis	Don Briggs
	Pat Murphy
	Arthur Jacobson
Stormy Curtis	June Travis
Scott Webb	Henry Hunter
Virginia	Laurette Fillbrandt
John Knight	Les Damon
	Karl Weber
	Syd Simons
Helen Adams	Betty Lou Gerson
Stella Moore	Janet Logan
Leo Warner	Willard Waterman
	Ted Maxwell
Kate	Kathryn Card
Clara	Hope Summers

Length: 15 minutes.
Network: NBC.
First Broadcast: 1935.

Girl from Paris

Type: Musical Variety
Hostess: Jane Morgan.
Orchestra: Andrew Ackers.
Length: 15 minutes.
Network: NBC.
First Broadcast: 1951.
Note: Series title was derived from Miss Morgan's trip to Paris at the time.

Girl Alone. Betty Winkler.

Give and Take

Type: Game
Format: Members of the studio audience selected one of several prizes, then competed in a series of question and answer rounds to win it.
Host: John Reed King.
Announcer: Jim Brown.
Length: 30 minutes.
Network: CBS.
First Broadcast: 1951.

Glamour Manor

Type: Variety
Host: Kenny Baker.

Regulars: Cliff Arquette, Lurene Tuttle, Bea Benaderet, Tyler McVey, John McIntyre, Jack Bailey, Hal Stevens, Barbara Eiler.
Announcer: Terry O'Sullivan.
Orchestra: Charles Hale.
Length: 30 minutes.
Network: Blue.
First Broadcast: 1944.

The Gloomchasers

Type: Variety
Host: Allen Courtney.
Regulars: Red Dave, Eleanor Sherry.
Orchestra: Lea Freaudberg.
Length: 30 minutes.
Network: Mutual.
First Broadcast: 1939.

Gloria Carroll Entertains

Type: Musical Variety
Hostess: Gloria Carroll.
Music: The Three Embers.
Length: 15 minutes.
Syndicated.
First Broadcast: 1947.

Go for the House

Type: Game
Format: Seven couples competed in a series of seven question and answer rounds. At the end of each round, the lowest scoring couple was disqualified; the remaining couples each received household furnishings and the opportunity to quit with what they had already won or risk the loss of everything on the next round. If players correctly answered the questions in all seven categories they won a small by-a-waterfall cottage.
Host: John Reed King.
Announcer: Doug Browning.
Organist: George Benninger.
Length: 30 minutes.

Network: ABC.
First Broadcast: 1948.

The Gold and Silver Minstrels

Type: Musical Variety
Host: Roland Winters.
Regulars: Jimmy Carroll, Betty Mulliner, Happy Jim Parsons, The Gold and Silver Quartet and Trio.
Announcer: Ted Brown.
Orchestra: Ray Bloch.
Length: 30 minutes.
Network: Mutual.
First Broadcast: 1946.

The Goldbergs

Type: Comedy-Drama
Format: The story of a poor Jewish family living in the Bronx. Became the basis for a television series of the same title.

Cast:	
Molly Goldberg	Gertrude Berg
Jake Goldberg, her husband	James R. Waters
Rosalie Goldberg, their daughter	Roslyn Siber
Sammy Goldberg, their son	Alfred Ryder
	Everett Sloane
Uncle David, Molly's father's brother	Menasha Skulnik
	Eli Mintz
Seymour Fingerhood	Arnold Stang
	Eddie Firestone, Jr.
Mr. Fowler, the handyman	Bruno Wick
Uncle Carlo	Tito Vuolo
Jane Brown	Joan Tetzel

Program Opening:
Molly: Yoo hoo, is anybody ...
Announcer: There's Molly folks, that means your friends the Goldbergs are here.
Length: 15 minutes.
Network: Blue.

First Broadcast: 1929 (under title "Rise of the Goldbergs").

Good Listening

Type: Quiz
Format: Called for contestants to answer questions based on a medley of vocal clues that were constantly interrupted by plants in the studio audience. A player won money ($3, $6, or $9) based on how many questions he could answer that were related to the interrupted songs.
Host: Lionel Kaye.
Vocalists: The Three Chances.
Orchestra: Van Alexander.
Length: 30 minutes.
Network: CBS.
First Broadcast: 1943.

Good News

Type: Musical Variety
Host: Dick Powell.
Vocalist: Mary Martin.
Orchestra: Meredith Wilson.
Length: 30 minutes.
Network: NBC.
First Broadcast: 1939.

The Goon Show

Type: Comedy
Format: British series about a group of goons, people "of inarticulate language with one-cell brains who think in the fourth dimension," who are anti-everything and whose sole purpose is first to destroy the British Empire, then the rest of the world. Every known effect that broadcasting can offer was used to present the stories—all of which revolved around one Netty Seagoon, a man of many occupations, yet completely naive and stupid. His exploits in the absurd world of dimwitted, absolutely unbelievable buffoons is the basis of the series.
Principal Characters: Netty Seagoon (Peter Sellers), Eccles, the idiot (Spike Milligan); Moriarity (Harry Secombe); Major Bloodknock, Indian Army, retired (Harry Secombe); Bluebottle, the character who always reads the stage directions in his script (Harry Secombe), Min and Henry (Harry Secombe, Spike Milligan).
Announcer: Wallace Greenslade.
Vocalist: Max Geldry.
Orchestra: Wally Stark.
Also: The Ray Ellington Quartet.
Length: 30 minutes.
Network: NBC.
First Broadcast: 1955.

The Gordon MacRae Show

Type: Musical Variety
Host: Gordon MacRae.
Vocalists: Sheila Stevens, Marian Bell.
Announcer: Dan Seymour.
Orchestra: Archie Bleyer, Johnny Guarneri.
Length: 15 minutes.
Network: CBS.
First Broadcast: 1945.

The Gracie Fields Show

Type: Variety
Hostess: Gracie Fields (a British comedienne).
Regulars: Bob Burns, The Spartan Quartet, Don Hancock.
Announcer: Bill Goodwin.
Orchestra: Harry Sosnik, Lou Bring, Carl Hoffman.
Length: 5 minutes (1942), 15 minutes (1943), 30 minutes (1944).
Network: Blue (1942), Mutual (1943), NBC (1944).
First Broadcast: 1942.

Gramps

Type: Comedy
Format: The story of a small town newspaper editor, his wife, their two children,

and how trouble begins when Gramps, a well-meaning old codger who has a knack for innocently starting trouble, comes for a visit and decides to stay.

Cast: Gramps   Edgar Stehli
       The husband   Craig McDonnell
       His wife   Anne Seymour
       Their daughter   Joan Lazer
       Their son   Edwin Bruce
Length: 30 minutes.
Network: NBC.
First Broadcast: 1947.

Granby's Green Acres

Type: Comedy
Format: The story of John Granby, an es-asperated bank clerk who decided to get away from it all and begin life as a farmer. The series spotlighted his adventures as he attempted to cope with the problems associated with operating a broken-down farm. Basis for the television series "Green Acres."

Cast: John Granby   Gale Gordon
       Iris Granby,
         his wife   Bea Benaderet
       Their daughter   Louise Erickson
       Eb, their
         hired man   Parley Baer
Orchestra: Opie Cates.
Length: 30 minutes.
Network: CBS.
First Broadcast: 1950.

Grand Central Station

Type: Anthology
Format: Human interest stories about people whose lives are affected by contact with Grand Central Station in New York City.
Narrator: Jack Arthur, John Reed King, Alexander Scourby.
Announcer: George Baxter, Ken Roberts, Tom Shirley.

Organist: Lew White.
Sponsor: Pillsbury Sno-Sheen Flour.
Program Opening:
Announcer: Pillsbury Sno-Sheen Cake Flour brings you Grand Central Station. As a bullet seeks its target, shining rails in every part of our great country are aimed at Grand Central Station, heart of the nation's greatest city. Drawn by the magnetic force of the fantastic metropolis, day and night great trains rush toward the Hudson River, sweep down its eastern bank for one hundred and forty miles, flash briefly by the long red row of tenement houses south of 125 Street, dive with a roar into a two and one-half mile tunnel which burrows between the glitter and swank of Park Avenue. And then—Grand Central Station, crossroads of a million private lives, gigantic stage on which are played a thousand dramas daily.
Length: 25 and 15 minute versions.
Network: NBC (1937), CBS (1944), ABC (1956).
First Broadcast: 1937.

Grand Hotel

Type: Anthology
Format: Dramatizations in the lives of the people staying at Grand Hotel. Based on the novel by Vicki Baum.
The Telephone Operator (opened each show): Betty Winkler, Luise Barclay.
Regulars: Don Ameche, Anne Seymour, Jim Ameche, Betty Lou Gerson, Les Tremayne, Henry Hunter, Charles Eggleston, Henry Drew, Jean David.
Announcer: Vincent Pelletier.
Organist: Dave Bacal.
Length: 30 minutes.
Network: Blue (1933), CBS (1940).
First Broadcast: 1933.

Grand Marquee

Type: Anthology
Format: Dramatic and comedy presentations.

Grand Central Station. A cast enacting a performance. Left side of microphone: Bill Johnstone, Hugh Marlowe; right side: Roger DeKoven, Gloria Stokowski.

Regular Performers: Jim Ameche, Olan Soulé, Beryl Vaughn.

Announcer: George Stone.

Orchestra: Joseph Gallichio.

Included:

Half a Dog. The story concerned a man's attempts to get a dog—the heir to an estate—to like him.

Starring: Jim Ameche.

Hex Marks the Spot. The manager of a baseball team tries to overcome the problems of a superstitious pitcher and owner.

Starring: Olan Soulé.

Hold It Please. A prima donna vows to get even with the newspaper photographer who published unfavorable pictures of her.

Starring: Beryl Vaughn, Jim Ameche.

Length: 30 minutes.

Network: NBC.

First Broadcast: 1946.

The Grand Ole Opry

Type: Country-Western Musical Variety

Host: George D. Hay

Regulars: Whitey Ford, Minnie Pearl, Dave Macon, Bill Monroe, Rod Brasfield, Roy Acuff, Ernest Tubb, Gene Autry, Granpa Jones, Robert Lunn, Pee-wee King, The Smoky Mountain Boys, The Delmore Brothers, The Hossier Hot-Shots.

Announcer: Dave Stone, Louie Buck.

Length: 30 minutes.

Network: NBC.

First Broadcast: 1925.

Grand Slam

Type: Quiz
Format: Using the basis of the game of Bridge, the program offered a $100 Savings Bond for any contestant who could answer five questions in a row. If, at any time during the questioning, the contestant responded incorrectly, he was disqualified and the listener who submitted the questions won $5.
Hostess: Irene Beasley.
Assistant-Announcer: Dwight Weist.
Length: 30 minutes.
Network: CBS.
First Broadcast: 1943.

The Gray Gordon Show

Type: Musical Variety
Host: Gray Gordon.
Regulars: Shirley Lane, Cliff Bradden, The Lane Sisters.
Orchestra: Gray Gordon.
Length: 30 minutes.
Network: NBC.
First Broadcast: 1938.

The Great Adventure

Type: Anthology
Format: Dramatizations of America's development through the progress of science and industry.
Narrator: Westbrook Van Voorhis.
Length: 30 minutes.
Network: ABC.
First Broadcast: 1951.

The Great Day

Type: Game
Format: Selected servicemen related a story why $100 should be awarded to him. The most impressive story, as determined by studio audience applause, earned the serviceman the $100.

Host: John Reed King.
Length: 30 minutes.
Network: Mutual.
First Broadcast: 1952.

The Great Gildersleeve

Type: Comedy
Format: The home and working life of Throckmorton P. "The Great" Gildersleeve, water commissioner in the town of Summerfield, and the bachelor uncle of two children, Marjorie and Leroy Forrester. Became the basis for the television series of the same title.

Cast:
Throckmorton P. Gildersleeve	Hal Peary Willard Waterman
Marjorie Forrester*	Lurene Tuttle Marylee Robb
Leroy Forrester	Walter Tetley
Birdie Lee Coggins, the maid	Lillian Randolph
Judge Hooker, Gildersleeve's nemesis	Earle Ross
Peavey, the druggist	Richard Legrand Forrest Lewis
Floyd, the barber	Arthur Q. Bryan
Leila Ransom, the Southern Belle	Shirley Mitchell
Rumson Bullard, Gildersleeve's neighbor	Gale Gordon
Kathryn Milford, Gildersleeve's romantic interest	Cathy Lewis
Bronco Thompson (married Marjorie in later episodes)	Dick Crenna

Announcer: Harlow Wilcox, John Wald, John Laing, Ken Carpenter, John Easton.
Orchestra: Jack Meakin, Claude Sweetern, Robert Armbruster.
Sponsor: Johnson's Wax; The Kraft Foods Company.

The Great Gildersleeve. Center, then left to right: Hal Peary (Gildersleeve), Lurene Tuttle (Marjorie), Lillian Randolph (Birdie), and Walter Tetley (Leroy.)

Length: 30 minutes.
Network: NBC.
First Broadcast: 1941.
*Originally in 1941, Evelyn Forrester.

Great Gunns

Type: Comedy
Format: The trials and tribulations of the Gunns, a former stage family.
Cast: Chris Gunn, the
husband   Bret Morrison
Veronica Gunn,
his wife   Barbara Luddy
Buster Gunn,
their son   Bob Jellison
Pop Gunn,
Chris' father   Phil Lord
Moe, their agent   Marvin Miller

Gloomy, their
butler   Marvin Miller
Lorson Snells,
the producer   Marvin Miller
Announcer: Marvin Miller.
Orchestra: Harold Stokes.
Length: 30 minutes.
Network: Mutual.
First Broadcast: 1941.

The Great Merlini

Type: Crime Drama
Format: The story of the Great Merlini, a crusading necromancer who made a hobby of exposing fake seances.
Starring: Chester Morris as The Great Merlini.

The Great Gildersleeve. Later cast leads: Willard Waterman (center), Marylee Robb (left), and Walter Tetley (right).

Length: 30 minutes.
Network: NBC.
First Broadcast: 1950.

The Green Hornet

Type: Crime Drama
Format: After building the *Daily Sentinel* into one of America's greatest newspapers, editor Dan Reid turns over the management to his playboy bachelor son, Britt, hoping the responsibility will mature him, and secretly hires ex-cop Mike Axford to watch over Britt's activities. Instilled with his father's goals, Britt, like his great-grand-uncle, John Reid (The Lone Ranger), undertakes a crusade to protect the rights and lives of decent citizens. Adopting the guise of the Green Hornet (the symbol of the insect that is most deadly when aroused) he establishes a base in an abandoned building and reveals his true identity to Kato, his Oriental houseboy. Considered criminal and wanted by the police, The Green Hornet and Kato avenge crimes as semi-fugitives, always disappearing before the authorities take over.

Cast: Britt Reid/The
        Green Hornet   Al Hodge
                            Bob Hall
                            Jack McCarthy
        Kato   Raymond
                             Hayashi
                            Rollon Parker
                            Michael Tolan
        Lenore Case
        ("Casey"),
        Britt's Secre-
        tary   Lee Allman
        Mike Axford   Jim Irwin
                            Gil Shea
        Ed Lowry, a
        reporter   Jack Petruzzi
Announcer: Charles Woods, Bob Hite, Mike Wallace, Hal Neal.
Program Opening:
Announcer: The Green Hornet. He hunts the biggest of all game, public enemies that even the G-Men cannot reach. The Green Hornet. With his faithful valet, Kato, Britt Reid, daring young publisher, matches wits with the underworld, risking his life that criminals and racketeers, within the law, may feel its weight by the sting of The Green Hornet. Ride with Britt Reid as he races toward another thrilling adventure as The Green Hornet rides again.
Length: 30 minutes.
Network: Mutual.
First Broadcast: 1938.

The Green Lama

Type: Crime Drama
Format: The story of Jethro DuMont, a daring crime fighter known as The Green Lama, who uses amazing secret powers to battle evil. DuMont, a wealthy young American, acquired his special powers after ten years of study in Tibet. Because of his great wisdom—to devote his life to fighting crime—and powers of concentration, he became The Green Lama; green because it is one of the six sacred colors of Tibet and the symbol for justice.

Cast: Jethro DuMont   Paul Frees
     Toku, his
        assistant   Ben Wright
Announcer: Larry Thor.
Music: Richard Aurandt.
Program Opening:
Announcer: Time now for another exciting adventure from the files of Jethro DuMont. Jethro DuMont, a wealthy young American who, after ten years in Tibet, returned as The Green Lama to amaze the world with his amazing powers in his single-handed fight against injustice and crime.
Length: 30 minutes.
Network: CBS.
First Broadcast: 1949.

Green Valley, U.S.A

Type: Serial
Format: Dramatic incidents in the lives of the people of Green Valley, a small, rural town.
Narrator: Santos   Ortega,   Henry   M. Neeley.
Cast: Alan Devitt, Elspeth Eric, Richard Widmark, Gilbert Mack, Frank Behrens, Ann Shepherd, Ed Begley.
Orchestra: Emery Deutsch.
Length: 25 and 30 minute versions.
Network: CBS (1942), Mutual (1944).
First Broadcast: 1942.

The Groucho Marx Show

Type: Variety
Host: Groucho Marx.
Regulars: Donald   Dickson,   Virginia O'Brien.
Orchestra-Chorus: Robert Armbruster.
Length: 30 minutes.
Network: CBS.
First Broadcast: 1943.

Guess Where

Type: Quiz
Format: A dramatization, depicting a specific place, was enacted. Players who were able to identify the subject of the drama received a cash prize.
Hostess: June Walker.
Regulars: Charles Cantor, Jack Johnson, Wilbur Budd Hulick.
Length: 30 minutes.
Network: Mutual.
First Broadcast: 1939.

Guiding Light

Type: Serial
Format: The dramatic story of Dr. John Ruthledge, a minister in a small town. The series later focused on the lives of the Bauer family. Became the basis for a television series of the same title.

Cast:	
Rev. John Ruthledge	Arthur Peterson
Mary Ruthledge	Sarajane Wells
	Mercedes McCambridge
Trudy Bauer	Laurette Fillbrandt
Bill Bauer	Lyle Sudrow
Meta Bauer	Jone Allison
Ned Holden	Ed Prentiss
Peggy	Jane Webb
Phyllis Gordon	Sharon Grainger
Sister Lillian	Annette Harper
Rose	Ruth Bailey
	Charlotte Manson
Iris Marsh	Betty Arnold
Charlotte Brandon	Betty Lou Gerson
Charles Matthews	Hugh Studebaker
Julie Collins	Mary Lansing
Norma Greenman	Eloise Kummer
Edward Greenman	Ken Griffin

Announcer: Bud Collyer, Herbert Allen, Chet Kingsbury.
Sponsor: Proctor and Gamble
Length: 15 minutes.
Network: (NBC (1937), CBS (1947).
First Broadcast: 1937.

The Gulf Screen Guild Theatre

Type: Anthology

Format: Radio adaptations of well-known motion pictures. The actors donated their work, and the money that they would ordinarily have received was given to the motion picture relief fund to help build a home for retired actors.

Host: Roger Pryor.

Regular Performers: Fred Allen, Robert Benchley, John Charles Thomas.

Announcer: Harry Von Zell, Claude Easton.

Music: Oscar Bradley and the Gulf Orchestra.

Program Opening:

Announcer: The Gulf Screen Guild Theatre. Your host, the director of the stars' own theatre, Roger Pryor.

Pryor: Good evening, everyone. Your neighborhood good Gulf dealer and the Gulf Oil Company welcome you once again to the Gulf Screen Guild Theatre...

Included:

The Strawberry Blonde. Two turn-of-the century men try to outdo each other to win the hand of the town beauty.

Starring: James Cagney, Olivia deHavilland, Jack Carson.

Mr. Jinx Goes to Sea. A young man joins the Navy despite the fact that his family is jinxed when it comes to the sea.

Starring: Bing Crosby, Jean Parker, Andy Devine.

If Only She Could Cook. A man and a woman pose as a butler and cook to relieve their financial burdens.

Starring: Humphrey Bogart, Alice Faye, Herbert Marshall.

Length: 30 minutes.

Network: CBS.

First Broadcast: 1939.

Gunsmoke

Type: Western

Format: The dramatic story of Matt Dillon, a U.S. Marshal, as he attempted to maintain law and order in Dodge City, Kansas during the late 1800s. Became the

Gunsmoke. William Conrad in costume as Marshal Matt Dillon.

basis for the television series of the same title.

Cast:
Matt Dillon	William Conrad
Chester Proudfoot, his deputy	Parley Baer
Kitty Russell, the owner of the saloon	Georgia Ellis
Doc Adams, the town physician	Howard McNear

Announcer: George Walsh, George Fenneman.

Music: Rex Koury.

Sponsor: L & M cigarettes; Kellogg's cereals.

Program Opening:

Announcer: Gunsmoke, starring William Conrad. The fictionalized story of the violence that moved west with young America and the story of a man who moved with it.

Dillon: I'm that man, Matt Dillon, United States Marshal, the first man they look for and the last man they want to meet.

Length: 30 minutes.

Network: CBS.

First Broadcast: 1954.

Guy Lombardo Time

Type: Musical Variety
Host: Guy Lombardo.
Regulars: Kenny Gardner, Bill Flannigan, Mindy Carson, Don Rodney, Rose Marie, Billy Leach, Ogden Nash.
Announcer: Andre Baruch, Z.A. Riggs, David Ross.
Orchestra: Guy Lombardo.
Length: 30 minutes.
Network-First Broadcast: CBS (1938), Blue (1944), Syndicated (1947), CBS (1950).

The Hal McIntyre Show

Type: Musical Variety
Host: Hal McIntyre
Regulars: Ruth Gaynor, Al Noble, Johnny Turnbull.
Orchestra: Hal McIntyre.
Length: 30 minutes.
Network: Blue.
First Broadcast: 1945.

The Hal Peary Show—Honest Harold

Type: Comedy
Format: The misadventures of "Honest" Harold Hemp, the host of "The Homemaker" program over radio station KHJP in the town of Melrose Springs. Created by Hal Peary.
Cast: "Honest" Harold
    Hemp   Hal Peary
    Mrs. Hemp,
    his mother   Jane Morgan
    Marvin,
    his nephew   Sammy Ogg
    Gloria, the station
    switchboard
    operator   Gloria Holliday
    Doc Yak Yak,
    Harold's friend   Joseph Kearns
    Peter the
    policeman   Parley Baer
    Miss Turner,
    the school
    teacher   June Witley
Announcer: Bob Lemond.

Orchestra: Jack Meakin.
Length: 30 minutes.
Network: CBS.
First Broadcast: 1950.

Hallmark Playhouse

Type: Anthology
Format: Dramatic presentations. Basis for the TV series, "Hallmark Hall of Fame."
Host-Narrator: James Hilton.
Announcer: Frank Gast.
Music: Lyn Murray.
Sponsor: Hallmark Cards.
Included:
Elmer the Great. The story of a baseball pitcher with amazing abilities.
Starring: Bob Hope, Jeff Chandler.
Random Harvest. James Hilton's story of an amnesiac veteran who marries his sweetheart, then disappears on an overnight trip.
Starring: Joan Fontaine.
Cimarron. The Edna Ferber novel about a woman who helps settle the Oklahoma territory during the 1800s.
Starring: Irene Dunne.
Morning Glory. A stage-struck girl's efforts to break into show business.
Starring: Elizabeth Taylor, Gerald Mohr.
Goodbye, Mr. Chips. Hilton's tale of a gentle, captivating English school teacher.
Starring: Ronald Colman.
Length: 30 minutes.
Network: CBS.
First Broadcast: 1948.

Halls of Fantasy

Type: Anthology
Format: Supernatural tales in which the Prince of Darkness often triumphed.
Organist: Harold Turner.
Length: 30 minutes.
Network: Mutual.
First Broadcast: 1953.

The Halls of Ivy

Type: Comedy

Format: Stories related the incidents that befall the mythical Ivy college, its students and faculty. Became the basis for the television series of the same title.

Cast:

Dr. William Hall, the president	Ronald Colman
Victoria Hall, his wife	Benita Hume
Penny, their maid	Gloria Gordon
Professor Warren	Arthur Q. Bryan
Professor Heathcliff	Alan Reed
Mr. Meriwether	Willard Waterman
Clarence Wellman	Herb Butterfield

Announcer: Ken Carpenter.
Orchestra: Henry Russell.
Program Opening:
Song: Oh, we love the Halls of Ivy that surround us here today . . .
Announcer: Welcome again to Ivy, Ivy College that is, in the town of Ivy, U.S.A. Starring Mr. and Mrs. Ronald Colman. . .
Length: 30 minutes.
Network: NBC.
First Broadcast: 1949.

Hannibal Cobb

Type: Crime Drama
Format: The cases of private detective Hannibal Cobb.
Cast: Hannibal Cobb   Santos Ortega
Announcer: Les Griffith.
Organist: Rosa Rio.
Length: 30 minutes.
Network: ABC.
First Broadcast: 1949.

Hap Hazard

Type: Comedy
Format: Comedy sketches interwoven around Crestfallen Manor, a rustic hotel with numerous problems.
Cast: Hap Hazard, the proprietor   Ransom Sherman

Mr. Pittaway, his assistant	Cliff Soubier
Waitress	Elmira Roessler
Waitress	Mary Patton
Cyclone, the handyman	Ray Grant

Vocalist: Edna O'Dell.
Announcer: Durward Kirby, Ben Gage.
Orchestra: Billy Mills, Gordon Jenkins.
Length: 30 minutes.
Network: NBC.
First Broadcast: 1941.

The Happiness Boys

Type: Variety
Starring: Billy Jones and Ernie Hare, the Happiness Boys.
Orchestra: Ben Selvin.
Length: 15 and 30 minute versions.
First Broadcast: 1921. Also titled: "The Best Foods Boys" (for Best Foods products), "The Interwoven Pair" (when sponsored by Interwoven Socks), and "The Tasty Breadwinners" (under the sponsorship of Tastyeast Bakers).

The Happy Gang

Type: Variety
Host: Bert Pearl.
Regulars: Eddie Allen, Cliff McKay, Jimmy McNamara, Kathleen Stakes, Hugh Bartlett, Joe Nios, Bob Semly, Blain Mothe.
Length: 30 minutes.
Syndicated.
First Broadcast: First heard in the U.S. in 1946. Originally a local Canadian series, first broadcast in 1937.

Happy Island

Type: Comedy
Format: The series focused on life in the mythical paradise of Happy Island.
Starring: Ed Wynn as King Bubbles.

Regulars: Evelyn Knight, Jerry Wayne, Hope Emerson, Craig McDonnell, Jackson Beck, Ron Rawson, Lorna Lynn, Rolfe Sedan, Amy Sedell, Natalie Core, Winifred Hoeney.
Orchestra: Mark Warnow.
Length: 30 minutes.
Network: Blue.
First Broadcast: 1944.

Happy Jack Turner

Type: Variety
Host: Jack Turner.
Music: Jack Turner (provided his own piano backing).
Length: 15 minutes.
Network: NBC.
First Broadcast: 1941.

Happy Jim Parsons

Type: Variety
Host: Jim Parsons.
Announcer: Irving Kaufman.
Length: 15 minutes.
Network: NBC.
First Broadcast: 1940.

The Hardy Family

Type: Comedy
Format: The trials and tribulations of the Hardy family. Based on the motion picture series.
Cast:

Andy Hardy, the son	Mickey Rooney
Judge Hardy, his father	Lewis Stone
Mrs. Hardy, his mother	Fay Holden
Beasey, Andy's friend	Dick Crenna
Andy's romantic interest	Judy Garland

Program Opening:
Announcer: We are proud to present The Hardy Family, based on the famous Metro-Goldwyn-Mayer motion picture

series, which brought them to life to millions and reflected the common joys and tribulations of the average American family. And now here are the same great stars in the parts they created on the screen — Lewis Stone, Mickey Rooney, and Fay Holden — the Hardy Family.
Length: 30 minutes.
Syndicated.
First Broadcast: 1949.

Harold Teen

Type: Comedy
Format: The misadventures of Harold Teen, the young adolescent comic strip character created by Carl Ed.
Cast:

Harold Teen	Charles Flynn
	Willard Farnum
	Eddie Firestone, Jr.
Shadow, his friend	Bob Jellison
Lillums, his girlfriend	Loretta Poynton
	Eunice Yankee
Mr. Teen, Harold's father	
	Willard Waterman
Cynthia, Harold's other girlfriend	Beryl Vaughn
Josie, a friend	Rosemary Garbell
Beezie Jenks, a friend	Marvin Miller
Mr. Jenks, Beezie's father	Jack Spencer

Length: 30 minutes.
Network: Mutual.
First Broadcast: 1941.

Harry James and His Orchestra

Type: Musical Variety
Host: Harry James.
Regulars: Kitty Kallen, Buddy DeVito.
Orchestra: Harry James.

Length: 30 minutes.
Network: CBS.
First Broadcast: 1945.

The Harry Savoy Show

Type: Variety
Host: Harry Savoy.
Regulars: Vera Holly, The Murphy Sisters
   Trio.
Orchestra: John Gart.
Length: 30 minutes.
Network: Mutual.
First Broadcast: 1946.

Harvest of Stars

Type: Musical Variety
Host: Raymond Massey, James Melton.
Announcer: Don Hancock.
Orchestra: Howard Barlow, Frank Black.
Sponsor: International Harvester.
Length: 30 minutes.
Network: NBC.
First Broadcast: 1941.

Harvey and Dell

Type: Serial
Format: Dramatic incidents in the lives of
   a three-member family.
Cast: Harvey, the
         father   Dwight Meade
       Dell, his wife   Doris Meade
       Dorothy, their
         daughter   Dorothy Meade
Length: 15 minutes.
Network: CBS.
First Broadcast: 1942.

Hashknife Hartley

Type: Western
Format: The exploits of two happy-go-
   lucky cowboys: Hashknife Hartley and
   his side-kick, Sleepy Stevens.
Cast: Hashknife Hart-
         ley   Frank Martin
       Sleepy Stevens   Barton
                          Yarborough

Prologue-Epilogue Narration: W.C. Tuttle.
Announcer: Don McCall.
Orchestra: Harry Zimmerman.
Length: 30 minutes.
Network: Mutual.
First Broadcast: 1950.

The Haunting Hour

Type: Anthology
Format: Suspense-adventure   dramatiza-
   tions.
Program Opening:
Announcer: No! No! Stay where you are!
   Do not break the stillness of this moment!
   For this is a time of mystery, a time when
   the imagination is free and moves swiftly.
   This is The Haunting Hour!
Length: 30 minutes.
Syndicated.
First Broadcast: 1946.

Have Gun—Will Travel

Type: Western
Format: The exploits of Paladin, a former
   army officer turned professional gunman
   who hired his guns and experience to people unable to protect themselves. Paladin
   operated from the Hotel Carlton in San
   Francisco, 1875, and had a calling card
   that read "Have Gun — Will Travel. Wire
   Paladin, San Francisco." The extreme
   popularity of the video series, which starred   Richard Boone, prompted this radio
   version.
Cast: Paladin   John Dehner
       Hey Boy, his
         servant   Ben Wright
       Hey Boy's
         girlfriend   Virginia Gregg
Announcer: Hugh Douglas.
Program Opening:
Announcer: Have Gun — Will Travel, star-
   ring Mr. John Dehner as Paladin. San
   Francisco, The Carlton Hotel, headquar-
   ters of the man called Paladin.
Length: 30 minutes.
Network: CBS.

First Broadcast: 1958 (November 23, 1958 to November 27, 1960).

Hawaii Calls

Type: Musical Variety
Host-Commentator: Webley Edwards.
Regulars: Danny Kinclair, Al Kealoha, Perry and His Singing Surfsiders.
Announcer: Jim Wahl.
Length: 30 minutes.
Network: Mutual.
First Broadcast: 1935.

Hawk Durango/Hawk Larabee

Type: Western
Format: The story of Hawk Durango (Hawk Larabee) a saloon owner. The series title switched from "Hawk Durango" to "Hawk Larabee" one year after its original premiere.
Cast: Hawk Durango   Elliott Lewis
         Hawk Larabee   Barton
                                 Yarborough
Announcer: James Matthews.
Orchestra: Wilbur Hatch.
Length: 30 minutes.
Network: CBS.
First Broadcast: 1946 (to 1947 as "Hawk Durango"); 1947 (to 1948 as "Hawk Larabee").

Hawthorne TBA (To Be Announced)

Type: Variety
Host: Jim Hawthorne.
Announcer: John Storm.
Orchestra: Robert Armbruster.
Length: 30 minutes.
Network: NBC.
First Broadcast: 1953.

Hear It Now

Type: Documentary
Format: The   series   replayed   famous

events previously heard on the air.
Host-Narrator: Edward R. Murrow.
Orchestra: Alfredo Antonini.
Length: 60 minutes.
Network: CBS.
First Broadcast: 1950.

Heart Throbs of the Hills

Type: Anthology-Variety
Format: An updated, transcribed version of "Hillbilly Heart-Throbs," which see. Like the original series, the new version presented dramatizations based on old folk songs.
Cast: Robert Strauss, Bella Allen, Robert Porterfield, Johnnie Rogers, Margaret Johnson, Travis Johnson.
Announcer: Kelvin Keech.
Music: The Hilltop Harmonizers.
Producer-Writer: Ethel Park Richardson.
Length: 15 minutes.
Network: NBC.
First Broadcast: 1939.

Heartbreak Theatre

Type: Anthology
Format: Stories of the Salvation Army and its role in our society.
Host: C.P. MacGregor, Marvin Miller.
Sponsor: The Salvation Army.
Length: 30 minutes.
Syndicated.
First Broadcast: 1956.

Hearthstone of the Death Squad

See title: "Mystery Theatre."

The Hedda Hopper Show

Type: Variety
Format: Celebrity interviews, editorial comments, comedy sketches.
Hostess: Hedda Hopper.

Orchestra: Frank Worth.
Length: 30 minutes.
Network: NBC.
First Broadcast: 1950.

Hedda Hopper's Hollywood

Type: Gossip
Hostess: Hedda Hopper.
Orchestra: Richard Aurandt.
Length: 15 minutes.
Network: NBC (1939), CBS (1944).
First Broadcast: 1939.

The Helen Hayes Theatre

Type: Anthology
Format: Dramatic presentations.
Hostess;   Helen Hayes.
Announcer: George Bryan.
Length: 30 minutes.
Network: Blue.
First Broadcast: 1935.

Helen Holden: Government Girl

Type: Drama
Format: The romance, intrigues, and adventures of Helen Holden, a U.S. government agent in Washington, D.C.
Cast: Helen Holden   Nancy Ordway
        Mary Holden, her
        aunt, a news-
        paper corre-
        spondent   Nell Fleming
        David, Helen's
        romantic
        interest   Robert Pollard
Announcer: Frank Blair.
Length: 15 minutes.
Network: Mutual.
First Broadcast: 1941.

Hello

Type: Musical Variety
Hostess: Louise King.
Orchestra: Joseph Gallichio.

Length: 15 minutes.
Network: NBC.
First Broadcast: 1943.

Hello, Peggy

Type: Serial
Format: The struggles of young marrieds Peggy and Ted Hopkins.
Cast: Peggy Hopkins   Eunice Howard
        Ted Hopkins   Alan Bunce
Length: 15 minutes.
Network: NBC.
First Broadcast: 1937.

A Helping Hand

Type: Anthology
Format: Dramatizations mirroring life.
Host: John J. Anthony.
Announcer: Don Hancock.
Organist: Elsie Thompson.
Length: 15 minutes
Network: CBS.
First Broadcast: 1941.

Helpmate

Type: Serial
Format: The dramatic story of three married couples: Linda and Steve Harper, Grace and Clyde Marshall, and Holly and George Emerson.
Cast: Linda Harper   Arlene Francis
                             Fern Parsons
        Steve Harper   Myron McCor-
                             mick
                             John Larkin
        Grace Marshall   Judith Evelyn
        Clyde Marshall   Karl Weber
        Holly Emerson   Beryl Vaughn
        George Emerson   Sidney Ellstrom
Length: 15 minutes.
Network: NBC.
First Broadcast: 1941.

The Henry Morgan Show

Type: Comedy-Variety
Cast: Henry Morgan   Himself

Gerard   Arnold Stang
Daphne   Alice Pearce
Gertrude   Madaline Lee
The athlete   Art Carney
Hortense   Florence Halop

Regulars: Lisa Kirk, Charles Irving, Minerva Pious, The Billy Williams Choir.

Announcer: Ben Grauer, Art Ballinger, Dan Seymour, Ed Herlihy, David Ross, Durward Kirby.

Orchestra: Bernie Green, Milton Katims.

Sponsor: Eversharp razor blades, Lifesavers candy, Shell gasoline, Adler Elevator Shoes, Lifebuoy soap, Ironized Yeast, Pall Mall cigarettes.

Length: 30 minutes.

Network: NBC (1945), ABC (1948), NBC (1949).

First Broadcast: 1945. Prior to his above series, Henry Morgan starred in "Here's Morgan (a.k.a. "Meet Mr. Morgan"), a six times a week, 15 minute variety outing in which he handled all roles. The series broadcast from 1940 to 1943, was basically local New York (over WOR) and sometimes aired over the full Mutual network.

Her Honor, Nancy James

Type: Serial
Format: The dramatic story of Nancy James, a woman judge.
Cast: Judge Nancy
      James   Barbara Weeks
      Richard Wharton,
      the mayor   Joseph Curtin
      Anthony Hale,
      the D.A.   Ned Weaver
      Evelyn Wharton,
      Richard's wife Kay Strozzi
Length: 15 minutes.
Network: CBS.
First Broadcast: 1938.

Herb Shriner Time

Type: Variety
Host: Herb Shriner.
Music: The Raymond Scott Quintet.

Length: 15 minutes.
Network: CBS.
First Broadcast: 1948 (ended in1949).

Hercule Poirot

Type: Crime Drama
Format: The cases of Hercule Poirot, the famous detective created by Agatha Christie.
Starring: Harold Huber as Hercule Poirot.
Length: 30 minutes.
Network: Mutual.
First Broadcast: 1945.

Here Comes Elmer

Type: Comedy
Format: The misadventures of Elmer Blurt, the super salesman who never seemed to be able to sell anything. See also "Al Pearce and His Gang."
Cast: Elmer Blurt   Al Pearce
      The switchboard
      operator at the
      Puny Plaza Hotel (she set Elmer up with
      temporary
      lodging)   Arlene Harris
Vocalists: The Smart Set.
Announcer: Wendell Niles.
Orchestra: Mickey Sillette.
Length: 30 minutes.
Network: CBS.
First Broadcast: 1944.

Here's Howe

Type: Human Interest
Format: A discussion of strange facts.
Host: Pete Howe.
Length: 15 minutes.
Network: Mutual.
First Broadcast: 1945.

Here's to Romance

Type: Variety
Host: Buddy Clark.

Announcer: Jim Ameche.
Orchestra/Chorus: David Broekman.
Length: 25 minutes.
Network: Blue.
First Broadcast: 1943.

Here's to You

Type: Musical Variety
Host: Phil Hanna.
Vocalists: Betty Brewer and Her Boy
    Friends.
Announcer: Durward Kirby.
Orchestra: Phil Davis.
Length: 15 minutes.
Network: CBS.
First Broadcast: 1947.

Hidden Stars

Type: Musical Variety
Host: Orrin Tucker.
Regulars: Bonnie Baker, Jack Bartell.
Music: The Bobby Guardi Quartet.
Length: 30 minutes.
Network: NBC.
First Broadcast: 1940.

High Adventure

Type: Anthology
Format: Dramatizations of the experi-
    ences of ordinary people projected into
    unusual circumstances.
Host-Narrator: Henry Norell, George San-
    ders.
Announcer: Phil Tonkin.
Orchestra: Jim Boles.
Length: 30 minutes.
Network: Mutual.
First Broadcast: 1947.

Highway Patrol

Type: Crime Drama
Format: The exploits of two state troopers
    Corporal Steve Taylor and his assistant

Mike Gallager.
Cast: Cpl. Steve Taylor   Michael Fitz-
                                    maurice
    Mike Gallager   John McGovern
Length: 15 minutes.
Network: Mutual.
First Broadcast: 1943.

Highways in Melody

Type: Musical Variety
Host-Commentator: Roland Winters.
Vocalist: Dorothy Kirsten.
Chorus: Ken Christy.
Announcer: Ford Bond.
Orchestra: Paul LaValle.
Length: 30 minutes.
Network: NBC.
First Broadcast: 1944.

Hilda Hope, M.D.

Type: Drama
Format: The dramatic story of Hilda Hope,
    a dedicated female physician.
Starring: Selena Royle as Hilda Hope.
Also: Richard Gordon, Ann Shepherd,
    House Jameson, Vera Allen.
Organist: Charles Paul.
Length: 15 minutes.
Network: NBC.
First Broadcast: 1939.

Hildegarde

Type: Variety
Hostess: Hildegarde Loretta Sell.
Announcer: Radcliffe Hall.
Orchestra: Bob Grant.
Length: 30 minutes.
Network: NBC.
First Broadcast: 1943.

Hillbilly Heart-Throbs

Type: Anthology-Variety
Format: The series presented dramatiza-
    tions, in song and story, based on old folk

Hillbilly Heart-Throbs. A very rare photograph of Ethel Park Richardson.

songs. During its last season on the air, the series presented "hillbilly" adaptations of Shakespeare's stories.

Cast: Ethel Park Richardson, Curtis Arnall, Anne Elstner, Agnes Moorehead, Bud Collyer, Brian Donlevy, Ray Collins, Billy Halop, Florence Halop.
Vocalists: Frank Luther, Carson Robinson, The Vass Family.
Producer-Writer: Ethel Park Richardson.
Length: 15 minutes.
Network: NBC.
First Broadcast: 1933 (May 23, 1933 to October 27, 1938). Also titled: "Heart Throbs of the Hills" (1934), and "Dreams of Long Ago" (1935). See also: "Heart Throbs of the Hills," for a later version of the series.

Hilltop House

Type: Serial
Format: The story of Bess Johnson, matron of an orphanage in the town of Glendale. The series stressed her struggles to choose between love and her career of raising other women's children. See

also: "The Story of Bess Johnson," the spin-off series.

Cast: Bess Johnson   Herself
         Julie Erickson   Grace Matthews
                               Jan Miner
         Jean Adair   Janice Gilbert
         Jerry Adair   Jim Donnelly
         Grace Doblen   Vera Allen
         Dr. Clark   Carleton Young
                               Spencer Bentley
         Jeffrey Barton   John Moore
         Thelma   Irene Hubbard
         Stella   Estelle Levy
         Pixie   Jeanne Elkins
         Linda   Dorothy Lowell
         Tulip   Gee Gee James
Organist: Chet Kingsbury.
Length: 15 minutes.
Network: CBS and Mutual.
First Broadcast: 1937.

His Honor, the Barber

Type: Comedy
Format: The story of a small-town judge who operates a barber shop on the side. His attempts to help people comprised the core of the series.
Cast: Judge Fitz   Barry Fitzgerald
         The Sheriff   Leo Cleary
Townspeople: Barbara Fuller, William Greene, Dawn Bender.
Announcer: Frank Martin.
Orchestra: Opie Cates.
Length: 30 minutes.
Network: NBC.
First Broadcast: 1945.

The Hoagy Carmichael Show

Type: Musical Variety
Host: Hoagy Carmichael.
Regulars: Shirlee Turner, Buddy Cole, Phil Stevens.
Announcer: Bob Lemond.
Orchestra: Hoagy Carmichael.
Length: 15 minutes.
Network: CBS.
First Broadcast: 1946.

Hobby Lobby

Type: Hobbies
Format: The program spotlighted the unusual hobbies of ordinary people. The title was derived from a segment wherein a guest celebrity appeared to "lobby his hobby." Became the basis for a television series of the same title.
Host: Dave Elman.
Announcer: Harry Von Zell, Allan Kent.
Orchestra: Harry Salter, Ted Rapf, Harry Sosnik.
Length: 30 minutes.
Network: NBC.
First Broadcast: 1937.

Hogan's Daughter

Type: Comedy
Format: The story of a patient father and his attempts to cope with his slightly dizzy daughter.
Cast: Pop Hogan   Everett Sloane
       His daughter   Shirley Booth
Also: Betty Garde, Howard Smith.
Orchestra: Bernard Green.
Length: 30 minutes.
Network: NBC.
First Broadcast: 1949.

Holiday for Music

Type: Musical Variety
Hostess: Kitty Kallen.
Featured: Curt Massey.
Orchestra: David Rose.
Length: 30 minutes.
Network: CBS.
First Broadcast: 1946.

Holland Housewife

Type: Variety
Hostess: Merle Oberon.
Regulars: Don McNeill, Bob Jellison, Ed Prentiss, Curt Roberts, Sharon Lee Smith, Hilda Graham.

Announcer: Verne Smith.
Orchestra: Benny Goodman.
Sponsor: Holland Furnaces.
Length: 30 minutes.
Network: NBC.
First Broadcast: 1941.

Hollywood Airport

Type: Anthology
Format: Dramatizations, set against the background of Hollywood Airport, of stories appearing in *Photoplay* magazine.
Host-Narrator-Star: Joe Jeigesen (appearing as Cal York, a *Photoplay* columnist).
Announcer: Dorian St. George.
Length: 30 minutes.
Network: ABC.
First Broadcast: 1954.

Hollywood Calling

Type: Quiz
Format: The program tested listeners' knowledge of film personalities. Following a clue related over the air, the host telephoned a listener. If he identified the personality by the clue, he won a prize.
Host: George Murphy.
Length: 60 minutes.
Network: NBC.
First Broadcast: 1949.

Hollywood Hotel

Type: Anthology
Format: Dramatic presentations.
Hosts: Dick Powell, Fred MacMurray, Herbert Marshall, William Powell.
Hostess: Louella Parsons.
The Telephone Operator: Duane Thompson.
Announcer: Ken Niles.
Orchestra: Raymond Paige, Ted Fiorito.
Length: 30 minutes.
Network: CBS.
First Broadcast: 1934.

Hollywood Jackpot

Type: Game
Format: Involved players in various game contests in return for merchandise prizes.
Host: Kenny Delmar.
Announcer: Bill Cullen.
Length: 30 minutes.
Network: CBS.
First Broadcast: 1946.

Hollywood Love Story

Type: Anthology
Format: Fictional romances based on stories appearing in *Photoplay* magazine.
Host: Alexander Scourby.
Length: 30 minutes.
Network: NBC.
First Broadcast: 1951.

Hollywood Playhouse

Type: Anthology
Format: Dramatic presentations.
Hosts: Charles Boyer, Jim Ameche, Gale Page, Tyrone Power, Herbert Marshall.
Music: Harry Sosnik.
Length: 30 minutes.
Network: Blue.
First Broadcast: 1937.

Hollywood Mystery Time

Type: Anthology
Format: Varied dramatizations featuring a cast of regular performers.
Cast: Carleton Young, Gloria Blondell.
Announcer: Jim Doyle.
Orchestra: Ernest Gill.
Length: 30 minutes.
Network: Blue.
First Broadcast: 1944.

Hollywood Open House

Type: Variety
Host: Enric Madriquera.

Regulars: Jerry Cooper, Patricia Gilmore, Harry Cool.
Announcer: Jim Ameche.
Orchestra: Enric Madriquera, Ray Bloch.
Length: 30 minutes.
Syndicated.
First Broadcast: 1946.

Hollywood Squares

Type: Variety
Host: Mickey Rooney.
Regulars: Buddy Cole, Dave Barry, Barbara Fuller, Julie Wilson.
Announcer: Bob Lemond.
Orchestra: Lud Gluskin.
Length: 30 minutes.
Network: CBS.
First Broadcast: 1948.

Hollywood Star Showcase

Type: Anthology
Format: Dramatic presentations.
Host-Narrator: Herb Rowlinson.
Announcer: Norman Brokenshire.
Orchestra: Jeff Alexander.
Length: 30 minutes.
Network: CBS.
First Broadcast: 1950.

Hollywood Theatre

Type: Anthology
Format: Dramatic presentations.
Host-Announcer: Don Wilson.
Music: Jeff Alexander.
Length: 30 minutes.
Network: NBC.
First Broadcast: 1951.

Hollywood Whispers

Type: Gossip
Host: George Fisher.
Length: 15 minutes.
Network: Mutual.
First Broadcast: 1941.

Home of the Brave

Type: Serial
Format: The story of a boyish telephone lineman (Joe), and Casino, the girl he loves, but who doesn't love him. Set in the town of New Chance, Colorado.

Cast: Joe   Tom Tully
                           Ed Latimer
        Casino   Jeanette Nolan
                           Sammie Hill
        Neil Davison   Richard Widmark
                           Vincent Donehue
        Lois Davisson   Jone Allison
        Spencer Howard   Alan Bunce
        Patrick Mulvaney   Ted de Corsia
        Doc Gordon   Ed Latimer
Organist: Charles Paul.
Length: 15 minutes.
Network: CBS.
First Broadcast: 1941.

Home Folks

Type: Variety
Host: Owen Bradley.
Regulars: Ernest Tubb, The Beasley Sisters, The Aunt Jemima Quartet.
Sponsor: The Quaker Oats Company.
Length: 15 minutes.
Network: CBS.
First Broadcast: 1952.

Home Town, Unincorporated

Type: Variety
Format: An entertainment session set against the background of a fictional locale populated by 498 people. Also known as "Showboat."
Host: Cliff Soubier (as Captain Barney Barnett).
Regulars: Virginia Verrill, Van Dyne, Marlin Hurt, Hugh Studebaker, Dick Todd.
Orchestra: Robert Trendler, Robert Strong.
Length: 30 minutes.
Network: NBC (broadcast on 19 Southern stations only).
First Broadcast: 1939.

Honest Harold

See title: "The Hal Peary Show — Honest Harold."

Honeymoon in New York

Type: Interview
Format: An engaged couple, brought before the microphones, was interviewed and asked to relate various aspects of their lives in return for prizes.
Host: Durward Kirby.
Vocalist: Joy Hodges.
Orchestra: Jerry Jerome.
Length: 25 minutes.
Network: NBC.
First Broadcast: 1946.

Hoofbeats

Type: Western
Format: The exploits of cowboy star Buck Jones.
Starring: Buck Jones as himself.
Announcer: The Old Wrangler (as identified).
Sponsor: Post Grape Nuts Flakes.
Program Opening:
Announcer: Hoofbeats, Howdy folks, you'll be mighty glad to hear, I reckon, that the makers of Grape Nuts Flakes, that's America's most famous cereal in flake form, are gonna bring you America's most famous cowboy, hard ridin' hard hittin', hard to beat, everybody's favorite, Buck Jones.
Length: 15 minutes.
Syndicated.
First Broadcast: 1937.

Hook 'n' Ladder Follies

Type: Country-Western Musical Variety
Starring: Ralph Dumke as Captain Walt.
Regulars: Carson Robinson, Ed Durlocker, Budd Hulick, The Song Spinners.
Orchestra: Frank Novak.
Length: 30 minutes
Network: NBC.
First Broadcast: 1943.

Hop Harrigan

Type: Adventure
Format: The exploits of Hop Harrigan, an
air ace, and his pal, Tinker.
Cast: Hop Harrigan   Chester Stratton
                                Albert Aley
      Gale Nolan, his
        his girlfriend   Mitzi Gould
      Tinker, his
        mechanic   Ken Lynch
                                Jackson Beck
Announcer: Glenn Riggs.
Sponsor: The Air Training Corps of Amer-
ica.
Program Opening:
Announcer: Presenting Hop Harrigan,
America's ace of the airwaves... Coming
in for another transcribed episode in the
adventures of Hop Harrigan.
Length: 30 minutes.
Network: Blue.
First Broadcast: 1942.

Hopalong Cassidy

Type: Western
Format: The exploits of cattle rancher
Hopalong Cassidy and his side-kick Cal-
ifornia. (Hopalong's ranch: The Bar 20).
Cast: Hopalong
      Cassidy   William Boyd
      California   Andy Clyde
Music: Albert Glasser.
Program Opening:
Announcer: With action and suspense out
of the Old West comes the most famous
hero of them all, Hopalong Cassidy, starring William Boyd. The ring of the silver
spurs heralds the most amazing man ever
to ride the prairies of the early West,
Hopalong Cassidy. The same Hoppy you
cheer in motion pictures and the same
California you've laughed at a million
times. Raw courage and quick shooting
have built a legend around this famous
hero. Hopalong is a name to be feared,
respected, and admired, for this great
cowboy rides the trails of adventure and
excitement. William Boyd as Hopalong
Cassidy and Andy Clyde as California.

Length: 30 minutes.
Network: Mutual.
First Broadcast: 1949.

The Horace Heidt Show

Type: Musical Variety
Host: Horace Heidt.
Regulars: Henry Russell, Fred Lowery,
Bob Matthews.
Orchestra: Horace Heidt.
Length: 30 minutes.
Network: Blue.
First Broadcast: 1944.

Horatio Hornblower

Type: Adventure
Format: A British-produced series about
Captain Horatio Hornblower's adven-
tures at sea. In service with the Royal
Navy, he sails and fights somewhere in
the Baltic Sea. Based on the novel by C.S.
Forester.
Starring: Michael Redgrave as Horatio
Hornblower.
Orchestra: Sidney Torch.
Length: 30 minutes.
Network: CBS.
First Broadcast: 1952.

Hot Copy

Type: Drama
Format: The story of Patricia Murphy, a
syndicated newspaper columnist and re-
porter.
Cast: Patricia Murphy   Eloise Kummer
                                    Fern Parsons
      The office boy   Hugh Rowlands
Orchestra: Roy Shield.
Length: 30 minutes.
Network: NBC.
First Broadcast: 1941.

The Hotpoint Holiday Hour

Type: Anthology
Format: Dramatic presentations.
Host-Narrator: Mel Ferrer.
Announcer: Marvin Miller.
Sponsor: Hotpoint appliances.
Length: 60 minutes.
Network: CBS.
First Broadcast: 1950.

The House Beside the Road

Type: Variety
Format: The series dealt with "the poi-
gnant, homey little tales of the simple
kindness of Ma and Pa."
Cast: Ma   Vivia Ogden
        Pa   William Adams
        Evelyn Dale   Mary Smith
        Aunt Julie   Ethel Park
                      Richardson
        David Minor   Warren Colston
Also: Anne Elstner, Ruth Russell, Jackie
Kelk, Walter Tetley, Laddie Seaman,
Fannie Mae Baldridge.
Length: 30 minutes.
Network: CBS.
First Broadcast: 1932 (ended in 1934). Also
known as "The Wayside Cottage."

A House in the Country

Type: Drama
Format: The trials and tribulations of a
young suburban couple newly relocated
from the city.
Cast: Joan, the wife   Frances Chaney
                         Joan Banks
                         Patsy Campbell
        Bruce, her
        husband   John Raby
                         Lyle Sudrow
        Sam, their friend Parker Fennelly
        The handyman   Sam Poletchek
                         Ed Latimer
        The shopkeeper   Ray Knight
        The telephone
        operator   Abby Lewis
Announcer: Bud Collyer, Hugh James.

Orchestra: John Gart.
Length: 15 and 30 minute versions.
Network: NBC (1941), Syndicated (1946).
First Broadcast: 1941.

House of Glass

Type: Comedy
Format: Concerned the activities at a
Catskill Mountain resort hotel owned and
operated by Barney Glass. Created by
Gertrude Berg.
Cast: Barney Glass   Joseph Buloff
        Sophie, the cook Gertrude Berg
        The waitress   Ann Thomas
Music: Milton Katims.
Length: 25 minutes.
Network: NBC.
First Broadcast: 1953.

The House of Mystery

Type: Anthology
Format: Mystery presentations for chil-
dren.
Host—Narrator: John Griggs as Roger
Elliott, The Mystery Man.
Program Opening:
Announcer: This is The House of Mystery
Host: Good evening. This is Roger Elliott,
otherwise known as The Mystery Man,
welcoming you to another story-telling
session here at The House of Mystery.
Length: 30 minutes.
Network: Mutual.
First Broadcast: 1944.

The House on Q Street

Type: Drama
Format: The series, set in a large boarding house on Q Street in Washington,
D.C., depicted society as seen through the
eyes of its occupants: the housekeeper, an
ex-Senator, his daughter, a Russian ex-
Countess (still devoted to the Soviet
cause), a British army officer, and a U.S.
educated Chinese Embassy representa-
tive.

House of Glass. Gertrude Berg (left) and Ann Thomas.

Cast: The housekeeper   Jessie Royce
                                    Landis
          The Senator   Douglas C. Holm
          His daughter   Celeste Holm
          The Russian
             Countess   Adelaide Klein
          The British army
             officer   Eric Dressler
          The Chinese
             representative   Ed Begley
Also: Cameron Andrews, Stanley Bell,
   Donald Bain.
Length: 25 minutes.
Network: Blue.
First Broadcast: 1943.

House Party

Type: Variety. Became the basis for a tele-
   vision series of the same title.
Host: Art Linkletter.
Announcer: Jack Slattery, Larrie Harper.

Music: The Muzzy Marcellino Trio.
Sponsor: General Electric.
Length: 30 minutes.
Network: CBS.
First Broadcast: 1944.

The Howard Miller Show

Type: Variety
Host: Howard Miller.
Announcer: Ed Joyce.
Length: 15 minutes.
Network: CBS.
First Broadcast: 1955.

How'm I Doin'?

Type: Quiz
Format: Called for two contestants, each
   of whom received $30, to answer three

questions posed to them by the host. Each correct answer added $10 to a player's score; an incorrect response deducted $10. Players were defeated when they ran out of money; winners kept what they had earned.
Host: Bob Hawk.
Announcer: Bert Parks.
Orchestra: Vaughn Monroe.
Length: 30 minutes.
Network: NBC.
First Broadcast: 1942.

How's the Family?

Type: Game
Format: A question and answer session wherein married couples competed for merchandise prizes.
Host: Marshall Kent.
Announcer: Pierre Andre.
Length: 30 minutes.
Network: Mutual.
First Broadcast: 1953.

How To

Type: Discussion
Format: An edited version of the television soundtrack. A person with a problem was brought on stage. The host and panelists then attempted to resolve the difficulty.
Host: Roger Price.
Panelists: Anita Martell, Leonard Stern, Stapley Adams.
Announcer: Bob Lemond.
Length: 30 minutes.
Network: CBS.
First Broadcast: 1951.

Howdy Doody

Type: Children's
Format: An audio version of the television soundtrack. The series depicted the efforts of a circus troup to perform in the town of Doodyville against the wishes of Phineas T. Bluster, the old man opposed to people having fun.

Cast: Buffalo Bob
Smith,
the host — Bob Smith
Clarabell Hornblow, the clown — Bob Nicholson
Princess Summer-Fall Winter-Spring — Judy Tyler
Puppets:
Howdy Doody, the red-haired, freckle-faced boy — Bob Smith
Phineas T. Bluster — Dayton Allen
Dilly Dally — Bill LeCornec
The Flubadub, the main circus attraction — Dayton Allen
Music: Edward Kean.
Length: 60 minutes.
Network: NBC.
First Broadcast: 1951.

Howie Wing

Type: Adventure
Format: The exploits of Howie Wing, a young air ace, as he battled evil.
Cast: Howie Wing — William Janney
Donna Cavendish, his girlfriend — Mary Parker
Captain Harvey — Neil O'Malley
Length: 15 minutes.
Network: CBS.
First Broadcast: 1938.

Hy Gardner Calling

Type: Gossip
Host: Hy Gardner.
Length: 15 minutes.
Network: NBC.
First Broadcast: 1952.

I Deal in Crime

Type: Crime Drama
Format: The cases of private detective Ross Dolan.

Starring: William Gargan as Ross Dolan.
Announcer: Dresser Dahlstead.
Music: Skitch Henderson.
Length: 30 minutes.
Network: ABC.
First Broadcast: 1946.

I Fly Anything

Type: Adventure
Format: The exploits of Dockery Crane, a free lance pilot who undertook any assignment—as long as it netted money and adventure.
Starring: Dick Haymes as Dockery Crane.
Announcer: Jay Arlen.
Orchestra: Rex Maupin.
Length: 30 minutes.
Network: ABC.
First Broadcast: 1950.

I Love a Mystery

Type: Adventure
Format: The exploits of Doc Long, Jack Packard, and Reggie York, three daring globetrotters who, after meeting in an Oriental prison and escaping the bombing of Shanghai, joined forces and vowed to roam the world and battle evil. (Doc, Jack, and Reggie operated the A-1 Detective Agency.)

Cast:	Doc Long	Barton Yarborough
		Jim Boles
	Jack Packard	Michael Raffetto
		Russell Thorson
		Jay Novello
		John McIntire
	Reggie York	Walter Paterson
		Tony Randall
	Gerry Booker, their secretary	Gloria Blondell

Program Opening:
Announcer: The makers of Fleishman's Yeast present I Love a Mystery... I Love a Mystery, presenting the latest adventures of Jack, Doc, and Reggie, specialists in crime and adventure, now following the Chinese pirate map of P. Wy Ling...

Length: 15 and 30 minute versions.
Network: NBC Red, NBC Blue, CBS.
First Broadcast: 1939. In 1948 the series was revived for one day when Carlton E. Morse, the creator, presented an adventure with Doc, Jack, and Reggie over the program "I Love Adventure." A television version of the series appeared on NBC on July 23, 1973. The two hour "I Love a Mystery" pilot film, which was filmed in 1966, but never sold, starred David Hartman as Doc, Les Crane as Jack, and Hagan Beggs as Reggie.

I Love Adventure

Type: Anthology
Format: Adventure presentations.
Host-Announcer: Dresser Dahlstead.
Organist: Rex Koury.
Length: 30 minutes.
Syndicated.
First Broadcast: 1948.

I Love Lucy

Type: Comedy
Format: The trials and tribulations of married life as depicted through the hectic experiences of the Ricardos: Ricky, an orchestra leader at the Tropicana Club, and his scatterbrained wife, Lucy. A simulcast of the television series of the same title.

Cast:	Lucy Ricardo	Lucille Ball
	Ricky Ricardo	Desi Arnaz
	Fred Mertz, their landlord	William Frawley
	Ethel Mertz, Fred's wife	Vivian Vance

Announcer: Johnny Jacobs.
Music: Wilbur Hatch.
Length: 30 minutes.
Network: CBS.
First Broadcast: 1952.

I Was a Communist for the F.B.I.

Type: Drama

Format: The story of Matt Cevetic, a man who for nine years acted as a member of a Communist cell in the U.S. while reporting regularly to the F.B.I. on cell operations.
Starring: Dana Andrews as Matt Cevetic.
Length: 30 minutes.
Syndicated.
First Broadcast: 1952.

Ice Box Follies

Type: Variety
Host: Wendell Niles.
Regulars: Don Prindle, Gale Robbins, Mel Blanc.
Announcer: Harlow Wilcox.
Orchestra: Billy Mills.
Length: 30 minutes.
Network: ABC.
First Broadcast: 1945.

Ilka Chase's Penthouse Party

Type: Musical Variety
Hostess: Ilka Chase.
Regulars: Yvette Harris, Elizabeth Huston, Judith Anderson.
Orchestra: Paul Barton.
Length: 30 minutes.
Network: CBS.
First Broadcast: 1941.

I'll Find My Way

Type: Serial
Format: The story of a small-town girl with ambitions of becoming an actress. Her ambitions, however, were hindered by her father's failing newspaper which sidetracked her as she attempted to save it.
Cast: The girl   Phyllis Jeanne
        Her father   Jack Preston
        The printer   Arch Schmidt
        The doctor   Leonard Sherer
        The city intruder Billy Kenton
Length: 15 minutes.
Network: Mutual.
First Broadcast: 1941.

Imperial Time

Type: Musical Variety
Hostess: Mary Small.
Vocalists: The Boy Friends.
Announcer: Dan Seymour.
Orchestra: Phil Wall.
Sponsor: Imperial margarine.
Length: 15 minutes.
Network: Mutual.
First Broadcast: 1941.

Information Please

Type: Quiz
Format: Tested a panel's knowledge of various subjects. Questions were submitted by listeners who received money if they stumped the panel.
Host: Clifton Fadiman.
Panelists: Franklin P. Adams, John Kiernan, John Gunther, Oscar Levant, Milton Cross.
Announcer: Jay Jackson, Ben Grauer, Milton Cross, Don Baker, Ed Herlihy.
Music: Joe Kahn.
Sponsor: Canada Dry beverages.
Length: 30 minutes.
Network: NBC.
First Broadcast: 1938.

Inner Sanctum Mysteries

Type: Anthology
Format: Mystery-Suspense presentations.
Host: Raymond Edward Johnson, Paul McGrath, House Jameson.
Announcer: Dwight Weist, Ed Herlihy.
Orchestra: John Hicks.
Sponsor: Lipton Tea and Lipton soups, Carter's Little Liver Pills, Bromo-Seltzer, Palmolive Shave Cream.
Included:
Wailing Wall. After murdering his wife and burying her in the basement, a man finds his life haunted by the groans and moanings of her spirit.
Starring: Boris Karloff.
Death Across the Board. The story of a doctor who, after killing a man in self-

defense, finds he is a chess piece in a cleverly conceived plot using real people instead of chessmen.

Starring: Raymond Massey.

The Vengeful Corpse. A woman, burned as a witch in 17th Century Salem, returns to seek revenge.

Starring: Barbara Weeks, Karl Swenson.

Program Opening:

Announcer: Lipton Tea and Lipton Soups present Inner Sanctum Mysteries.

Sound Effect: A creaking door opening.

Host: Good evening friends of the Inner Sanctum. This is your host to welcome you in through the squeaking door for another half-hour of horror . . .

Length: 30 minutes.

Network: NBC Blue (1941), CBS (1943), ABC (1950).

First Broadcast: 1941.

Inspector Hearthstone of the Death Squad

See title: "Mystery Theatre."

Inspector Mark Saber

See title: "Mystery Theatre."

Inspector Thorne

Type: Crime Drama

Format: The cases of police Inspector Thorne.

Cast: Inspector Thorne   Karl Weber
       Sergeant Muggin   Danny Ocko

Length: 30 minutes.

Network: NBC.

First Broadcast: 1951.

Into the Light

Type: Serial

Format: The series depicted the hatred between two brothers and the healing influence of a young woman's love.

Cast: Tanya, the
       young woman   Margo
       The first brother   Peter Donald
       The second
       brother   Martin Wolfson
       Emily   Mitzi Gould
       Ma Owen   Chassie Allen
       Mr. Kriss   Morris Carnovsky

Also: Peter Capell, Margaret Foster.

Length: 15 minutes.

Network: NBC.

First Broadcast: 1941.

The Irene Rich Theatre

Type: Anthology

Format: Dramatic presentations.

Hostess: Irene Rich.

Announcer: Ed Herlihy, Marvin Miller, Frank Goss.

Length: 30 minutes.

Network: Blue.

First Broadcast: 1933.

Island Venture

Type: Adventure

Format: The story of Gil Berry, an ex-Navy pilot turned owner of an air freight line in the South Pacific. His adventures, as he tried to maintain the line, were dramatized.

Cast: Gil Berry   Jerry Walter
       Trigger Brett,
       his partner   Hugh Rowlands
       Mendoza, the
       owner of a
       cargo line   Clare Boreum
       Chula, the island
       big shot   Willard Waterman
       Mendoza's daughter Jane Webb

Also: Ken Nordine, Norman Gottschalk, Jonathan Hale.

Length: 30 minutes.

Network: CBS.

First Broadcast: 1945.

It Happened in Hollywood

Type: Variety
Starring: John Conte, Martha Mears.
Also: Helen Troy (as the comic telephone operator).
Orchestra: Eddie Dunstedder.
Length: 15 minutes.
Network: CBS.
First Broadcast: 1939.

It Happens Every Day

Type: Interview
Format: Interviews with people with unusual stories to tell.
Hostess: Arlene Francis.
Announcer: Bill Cullen.
Length: 5 minutes.
Network: CBS.
First Broadcast: 1952.

It Pays to Be Ignorant

Type: Comedy-Quiz
Format: A contestant was interviewed, then picked a question from "The Dunce Cap." The question was read (e.g., "What kind of wood was in the old oaken bucket?") and the three "ignorant" panelists provided comic answers while evading the correct response. Prizes were awarded accordingly—basically for facing the panel. Became the basis for a television series of the same title.
Host: Tom Howard.
Panelists: George Shelton, Lulu McConnell, Harry McNaughton.
Vocal Group: The Esquires.
Closing Theme Vocal: Al Madru.
Announcer: Richard Stark, Ken Roberts.
Musical Director: Tom Howard, Jr.
Orchestra: Doc Novak.
Program Opening:
Host: Why do people eat garlic?
Panelist: So you can find them in the dark.
Host: Correct. Pay that man eight dollars. How do you make anti-freeze?
Panelist: Hide her pajamas.
Host: Correct. Pay that man nine dollars because—
Announcer: It Pays to Be Ignorant, a zany half-hour with those masters of insanity, Harry McNaughton, George Shelton, and Lulu McConnell, and featuring Doc Novak's orchestra ... And now here's the man who proves It Pays to Be Ignorant, Tom Howard ...
Length: 30 minutes.
Network: CBS (1942; originally local New York over WOR, also in 1942).
First Broadcast: 1942.

It Takes a Woman

Type: Anthology
Format: Capsule dramas depicting women in a sentimental but heroic light.
Hostess-Narrator: Frankie Burke (portraying Frances Scott).
Length: 5 minutes.
Syndicated.
First Broadcast: 1945.

It's a Living

Type: Human Interest
Format: Interviews with people who have strange or unusual jobs.
Host: Ben Alexander.
Length: 30 minutes.
Network: Mutual.
First Broadcast: 1948.

It's Always Albert

Type: Comedy
Format: The problems of Albert, a would-be composer who was unable to find work.
Cast: Albert   Arnold Stang
       His brother   Jan Murray
       His girlfriend   Pert Kelton
Announcer: George Bryan.
Orchestra: Jack Miller.
Length: 30 minutes.
Network: CBS.
First Broadcast: 1948.

It's Higgins, Sir

Type: Comedy
Format: The story of an average middle-class American family that inherited, in addition to a rare and expensive silver set, a butler named Higgins from a titled British relative. The series focused on the attempts of the English butler to adjust to life in America and to his new employers, and of the family to adjust to having a butler. Became the basis for the "Our Man Higgins" television series.
Cast: Higgins   Harry McNaughton
        The father   Vinton Hayworth
        His wife   Peggy Allenby
        Their daughter Pat Hosley
        Their daughter Denise Alexander
        Their son   Charles Nevil
Also: Ethel Wilson, Adelaide Klein.
Length: 30 minutes.
Network: NBC.
First Broadcast: 1951.

It's the Barrys

Type: Comedy
Format: Events in the lives of the Barry family: Jack, a bumbling husband, Marcia, his level-headed wife, and Jeff, their son.
Cast: Jack Barry   Himself
        Marcia Barry   Marcia Van Dyke (Mrs. Barry)
        Jeff Barry   Himself
Length: 15 minutes.
Network: NBC.
First Broadcast: 1953.

It's Up To You

Type: Quiz
Format: Two players were assigned a task (e.g., reciting "Mary Had a Little Lamb," or talking himself out of a traffic ticket) that each had to perform to the best of his ability. The winner, chosen by studio audience applause, received merchandise prizes.

Host: Dale Baxter.
Length: 30 minutes.
Network: NBC.
First Broadcast: 1939.

Jack and Cliff

Type: Variety
Format: Songs, music, and comedy sketches that revolved around Jack Pearl's Baron Munchausen (a teller of tall tales) character. See Also: "The Jack Pearl Show."
Hosts: Jack Pearl, Cliff Hall.
Regulars: Ann Thomas, Dick Karlan, Johnny Gibson, Hazel Shermet, Florence Mac-Michael, Byrna Raeburn, Craig McDonnell, Joe O'Brien, Bernie Gould, Eve Young, The Jack Allison Quartet.
Announcer: Bob Sherry.
Orchestra: Milton Katims.
Length: 30 minutes.
Network: NBC.
First Broadcast: 1948.

Jack Armstrong, the All-American Boy

Type: Adventure Serial
Format: The exploits of Jack Armstrong, his friends Billy and Betty Fairfield, and their Uncle Jim.
Cast: Jack Armstrong   John Terrell
                         Jim Ameche
                         Stanley Harris
                         Charles Flynn
                         Michael Rye
        Billy Fairfield Murray McLean
                         John Gannon
                         Roland Butterfield
                         Milton Guion
                         Dick York
        Betty Fairfield Ann Shepherd
                         Sarajane Wells
                         Loretta Poynton
                         Patricia Dunlap
        Uncle Jim Fairfield   James Goss

Vic Hardy (re-
placed Jim and
Betty in 1946),
a crime inves-
tigator   Ken Griffin
Coach Hardy, the
athletic coach
at Hudson High
School   Arthur Van Slyke
                   Olan Soule
Announcer: Ed Prentiss, David Owen,
Tom Shirley, Truman Bradley, Paul
Douglas, Bob McKee.
Sponsor: Wheaties cereal.
Program Opening:
Announcer: Wheaties, breakfast of cham-
pions, brings you the thrilling adventures
of Jack Armstrong, the All-American
Boy.
Length: 15 and 30 minute versions.
Network: CBS.
First Broadcast: 1933.

The Jack Benny Program

Type: Comedy-Variety. Became the basis
for a television series of the same title.
Cast: Jack Benny   Himself
        Mary, Jack's girl-
           friend   Mary Livingstone
                          (Mrs. Benny)
        Rochester, Jack's
           valet   Eddie Anderson
        Dennis Day, vocal-
           ist   Himself
        Don Wilson, an-
           nouncer   Himself
        Phil Harris, Jack's
           friend   Himself
        Mabel, the tele-
           phone operator Sara Berner
        Gertrude, the tele-
           phone operator Bea Benaderet
        Professor Le-
           Blanc, Jack's
           violin teacher Mel Blanc
        Schlepperman   Sam Hearn
        Sounds of Jack's
           Maxwell car   Mel Blanc
        T. Wimley, the
           sound man   Mel Blanc

The train an-
   nouncer   Mel Blanc
Kitzel, the Jewish
   foil   Artie Auerbach
Regulars: Frank Nelson, Sheldon Leon-
ard, Kenny Baker, The Sportsmen Quar-
tet.
Announcer: George Hicks, Paul Douglas,
Kenny Delmar, Don Wilson.
Orchestra: George Olsen, Frank Black,
Johnny Green, Bob Crosby, Phil Harris.
Sponsor: Lucky Strike cigarettes; Jell-O.
Length: 30 minutes.
Network: CBS (1932), NBC (1939).
First Broadcast: 1932.

Jack Bundy's Carnival

Type: Musical Variety
Host: Jack Bundy.
Regulars: Monica Lewis, Bob Shepherd.
Orchestra: Bob Stanley.
Length: 30 minutes.
Network: Mutual.
First Broadcast: 1944.

The Jack Carson Show

Type: Variety
Format: Music, songs, and comedy sket-
ches.
Host: Jack Carson.
Regulars: Johnny Richards, Hanley Staf-
ford, Maxie Rosenbloom, The King
Sisters, Anita Ellis, Arthur Treacher,
Norma Jean Nilsson, Dave Willock, Mel
Blanc, Doris Drew, Tony Romano.
Announcer: Del Sharbutt, Bob Stewart,
Hy Averback.
Orchestra: Freddy Martin, Johnny Rich-
ards, Walter Gross, Roy Chamberlain.
Length: 30 minutes.
Network: CBS.
First Broadcast: 1943.

The Jack Coffey Show

Type: Musical Variety
Host: Jack Coffey.

Regulars: Beverly Blayne, Dick Kapi, Three Smart Girls.
Orchestra: Jack Coffey.
Length: 30 minutes.
Network: Blue.
First Broadcast: 1941.

The Jack Haley Show

Type: Variety
Host: Jack Haley.
Regulars: Virginia Verrill, Lucille Ball, Artie Auerbach.
Orchestra: Ted Fiorito.
Length: 30 minutes.
Network: CBS.
First Broadcast: 1938.

The Jack Kirkwood Show

Type: Variety
Format: Comedy, music, and songs set against the background of the Madhouse Little Theatre.
Host: Jack Kirkwood.
Regulars: Lillian Lee, Don Reid, Jean McKean, Jimmy Wallington, Lee Albert, Gene Lavalle.
Announcer: Jimmy Wallington, Steve Dunne.
Orchestra: Irving Miller.
Organist: Gaylord Carter, Lud Gluskin.
Length: 30 minutes.
Network: CBS.
First Broadcast: 1944.

Jack Oakie's College

Type: Comedy-Variety
Host: Jack Oakie.
Vocalist: Judy Garland.
Orchestra: Benny Goodman.
Sponsor: Camel cigarettes.
Length: 60 minutes.
Network: CBS.
First Broadcast: 1936 (December 29, 1936 to March 22, 1938).

The Jack Paar Show

Type: Variety
Host: Jack Paar.
Regulars: Florence Halop, Hans Conried, Martha Stewart, Trudy Erwin, The Page Cavanaugh Trio.
Announcer: Hy Averback.
Orchestra: Jerry Fielding.
Length: 30 minutes.
Network: NBC.
First Broadcast: 1947.

The Jack Pearl Show

Type: Comedy
Format: Featured the tall tales of one Baron Munchausen.
Cast: Baron Munchausen — Jack Pearl
Sharlie, the straight man — Cliff Hall
The slightly dizzy secretary — Mae Questel
Also: Charlie Hall, Brad Reynolds, Jean Merrill.
Announcer: Frank Gallop.
Orchestra: Morton Gould.
Sponsor: Raleigh and Kool cigarettes.
Length: 30 and 45 minute versions.
Network: Blue (1933), Mutual (1942).
First Broadcast: 1933. Also known as "The Raleigh and Kool Show." See also, "Jack and Cliff."

The Jack Pepper Show

Type: Musical Variety
Host: Jack Pepper.
Regulars: Jeri Sullivan, Sandra Gould, Art Carney, Dan Ochs, Jackson Beck, Mickey O'Day, The Murphy Sisters.
Announcer: Tip Corning.
Orchestra: Mitchell Ayres.
Length: 30 minutes.
Network: CBS.
First Broadcast: 1944.

The Jack Smith Show

Type: Variety
Host: "Whispering" Jack Smith.
Announcer: Dan Hancock.
Orchestra: Earl Sheldon.
Program Opening:
Jack (singing): Hello dear friends, hello . . .
Announcer: Hello Jack. Here's "Whispering" Jack Smith and his Whispering Strings once more bringing you his intimate melodies sung as only he can sing them. This electronically transcribed program by the one and only "Whispering" baritone is brought to you by Ironized Yeast, the new yeast, vitamin B, and iron tablet . . .
Length: 15 minutes.
Network: CBS.
First Broadcast: 1946.

The Jack Smith, Dinah Shore, Margaret Whiting Show

Type: Musical Variety
Host (Tuesday, Wednesday, and Thursday Evenings): Jack Smith, Dinah Shore.
Announcer: Bob Stevenson.
Orchestra: Frank DeVol.
Host (Monday and Friday evenings): Margaret Whiting.
Announcer: Bob Stevenson.
Orchestra: Frank DeVol.
Length: 15 minutes.
Network: CBS.
First Broadcast: 1950.

The Jackie Gleason—Les Tremayne Show

Type: Comedy-Variety
Hosts: Jackie Gleason, Les Tremayne.
Regulars: Andy Russell, Patsy Garrett.
Orchestra: Sylvan Levin.
Length: 30 minutes.
Network: NBC.
First Broadcast: 1944.

Jack's Place

Type: Variety
Host: Jack Gregson.
Vocalist: Mary Mayo.
Announcer: John Hicks.
Length: 85 minutes.
Network: CBS.
First Broadcast: 1953.

The Jailbusters

Type: Musical Variety
Hosts: The Jailbusters (Theodore Brooks, George McFadden, J.C. Ginyard, Orville Brooks, Everett Barkstable).
Length: 15 minutes.
Network: CBS.
First Broadcast: 1945.

The James and Pamela Mason Show

Type: Anthology
Format: Dramatic presentations.
Hosts-Performers: James and Pamela Mason.
Regular Performer: Lurene Tuttle.
Announcer: Frank Barton.
Orchestra: David Raksin.
Length: 30 minutes.
Network: NBC.
First Broadcast: 1949.

The James Melton Show

Type: Variety
Host: James Melton
Regulars: Joan Roberts, James Wallington.
Orchestra: Al Goodman.
Length: 30 minutes.
Network: CBS.
First Broadcast: 1943.

The Jan August Show

Type: Musical Variety
Hostess: Jan August.
Regulars: Monica Lewis, Chick Robertson, Tony Esper.
Announcer: Ken Roberts.
Music: Jan August (pianist).
Sponsor: Revere cameras.
Length: 15 minutes.
Network: CBS.
First Broadcast: 1947.

Jane Ace, Disc Jockey

Type: Music and Humor
Format: Jane Ace (of "Easy Aces") as a disc jockey, spinning records and relating light nonsense.
Starring: Jane Ace.
Announcer: Don Pardo.
Length: 30 minutes.
Network: NBC.
First Broadcast: 1951.

Jane Arden

Type: Serial
Format: The dramatic story of Jane Arden, a newspaper reporter for the *Bulletin.*
Cast: Jane Arden   Ruth Yorke
       Betty Harrison   Florence
                         Freeman
       Louise   Helene Dumas
       Jane's father   Richard Gordon
       Jane's mother   Betty Garde
       Jack Galloway   Howard Smith
Music: Howard Smith.
Length: 15 minutes.
Network: Blue.
First Broadcast: 1938.

The Jane Froman—Jan Pearce Show

Type: Musical Variety
Hosts: Jane Froman, Jan Pearce.

Orchestra: Ernie Rapee.
Length: 30 minutes.
Network: CBS.
First Broadcast: 1939.

The Jane Froman Show

Type: Variety
Hostess: Jane Froman.
Regulars: Hugh Herbert, Ted Husing.
Orchestra: Dick Himber.
Length: 30 minutes.
Network: CBS.
First Broadcast: 1938.

The Jane Pickens Show

Type: Musical Variety
Hostess: Jane Pickens.
Featured: Jack Kiltz.
Announcer: Robert Warren.
Orchestra/Chorus: Norman Cloutier.
Length: 30 minutes.
Network: NBC.
First Broadcast: 1948.

The Janette Davis Show

Type: Musical Variety
Hostess: Jeanette Davis.
Announcer: Lee Vines.
Orchestra: Archie Bleyer, Howard Smith.
Length: 15 minutes.
Network: ABC (1946), CBS (1948).
First Broadcast: 1946.

Jason and His Golden Fleece

Type: Adventure
Format: The exploits of Jason, a philosophic adventurer and owner of the Golden Fleece, a sixty-foot cabin cruiser.
Cast: Jason   Macdonald Carey
       Louis Dumont,
         his sidekick   William Conrad
Orchestra: Frank Worth.
Length: 30 minutes.

Network: NBC.
First Broadcast: 1952.

Jay Stewart's Fun Fair

Type: Audience participation
Format: Called for contestants to exhibit
their pets, submit to capsule interviews,
and compete in various quizzes for prizes.
Host: Jay Stewart.
Announcer: Lou Cook.
Length: 30 minutes.
Network: ABC.
First Broadcast: 1949.

The Jean Gablon Show

Type: Musical Variety
Hostess: Jean Gablon.
Orchestra: Paul Baron.
Length: 15 minutes.
Network: CBS.
First Broadcast: 1946.

Jeff Regan, Investigator

Type: Crime Drama
Format: The cases of Jeff Regan, a hard-
boiled private investigator. Regan car-
ried the nickname "The Lyon's Eye"
because his employer, the owner of the in-
vestigative agency, was named Ben Lyon.
Cast: Jeff Regan   Jack Webb
Ben Lyon   Marvin Miller
Announcer: Marvin Miller.
Length: 30 minutes.
Network: CBS.
First Broadcast: 1948.

The Jerry Cooper Show

Type: Musical Variety
Host: Jerry Cooper.
Regulars: The DeVore Sisters, The
Smoothies, The Eight Men.
Announcer: Jimmy Leonard.
Orchestra: William Stoees.

Length: 15 minutes.
Network: NBC.
First Broadcast: 1935.

The Jerry Lester Show

Type: Variety
Host: Jerry Lester.
Regulars: Diane Courtney, Ray Sinatra.
Announcer: Fred Uttal.
Length: 30 minutes.
Network: CBS.
First Broadcast: 1943.

The Jerry Wayne Show

Type: Musical Variety
Host: Jerry Wayne.
Regulars: Carole Candes, Hope Emerson,
Lorna Lynn, Craig McDonnell.
Announcer: Dan Seymour.
Chorus: Jeff Alexander.
Music: The Jeff Alexander Orchestra, The
Alvy West Band.
Length: 15 and 30 minute versions.
Network: Blue (1945), CBS (1948).
First Broadcast: 1945.

The Jim Backus Show

Type: Comedy-Variety
Host: Jim Backus.
Regulars: Dink Trout, Frances Robertson,
Jerry Hausner.
Announcer: Frank Graham.
Length: 30 minutes.
Network: Mutual.
First Broadcast: 1947.

The Jim Backus Vaudeville Show

Type: Variety
Host: Jim Backus.
Regulars: Mary Small, The Eight Balls
of Fire.
Orchestra: Jeff Alexander.
Length: 30 minutes.

Network: CBS.
First Broadcast: 1942.

Jimmy Carroll Sings

Type: Musical Variety
Host: Jimmy Carroll.
Vocalists: The Ken Christy Chorus.
Orchestra: Ted Dale.
Length: 15 minutes.
Network: CBS.
First Broadcast: 1945.

The Jimmy Dorsey Show

Type: Musical Variety
Host: Jimmy Dorsey.
Regulars: Claire Hogan, Kenny Martin.
Announcer: Bob Shipley.
Orchestra: Jimmy Dorsey.
Length: 30 minutes.
Network: CBS.
First Broadcast: 1950.

The Jimmy Durante—Garry Moore Show

Type: Comedy-Variety
Hosts: Jimmy Durante, Garry Moore.
Regulars: Jeri Sullivan, Elvia Allman (as Cuddles Bongschnook), Alan Young, Georgia Gibbs, Susan Ellis, Florence Hallop, Howard Petrie.
Announcer: Howard Petrie.
Orchestra: Xavier Cugat, Roy Bargy.
Length: 30 minutes.
Network: NBC.
First Broadcast: 1945. On alternate weeks the program was titled "The Garry Moore-Jimmy Durante Show"; in this manner both stars received equal billing.

The Jimmy Durante Show

Type: Comedy-Variety
Host: Jimmy Durante.
Regulars: Arthur Treacher, Barbara Jo Allen, Candy Candido, Florence Halop.

The Jimmy Durante-Garry Moore Show. Jimmy Durante (left) and Garry Moore.

Announcer: Howard Petrie.
Orchestra: Roy Bargy.
Sponsor: Rexall Products.
Program Opening:
Announcer: Good health to all from Rexall ... From Hollywood, The Jimmy Durante Show ... Yes, it's The Jimmy Durante Show with Arthur Treacher, Candy Candido, Roy Bargy and his Orchestra, yours truly Howard Petrie, and our special guest tonight, Bing Crosby ...
Length: 30 minutes.
Network: NBC.
First Broadcast: 1943.

The Jimmy Edmondson Show

Type: Variety
Host: Jimmy Edmondson (known as "Professor Backwards" as he spelled and pronounced words from end to start).
Regulars: Nanette Fabray, Juano Hernandez, Art Kahl, Florence MacMichael, Patricia Hosley, The Esquire Quartet.
Announcer: Bob Sherry.
Orchestra: Jerry Jerome.

The Jimmy Durante-Garry Moore Show. Left to right, beginning with the lower step: Director Phil Cohan, Musical Director Roy Bargy, Announcer Howard Petrie, Vocalist Georgia Gibbs, Garry Moore, guest Marlene Dietrich, Jimmy Durante, and regular Elvia Allman.

Length: 30 minutes.
Network: NBC.
First Broadcast: 1946.

Jimmy Gleason's Diner

Type: Comedy
Format: Set against the background of a film studio, the series presented the exchange of talk between Jimmy Gleason, the owner of a diner, and his customers.
Cast: Jimmy Gleason   Himself
     Lucille Gleason,
      his wife   Herself
Also: Willie Best, Joseph Kearns, Ken Christy.
Music: The ABC Staff Orchestra.
Length: 30 minutes.
Network: ABC.
First Broadcast: 1946.

The Jo Stafford Show

Type: Musical Variety
Hostess: Jo Stafford.
Vocalists: Clark Dennis, The Starlighters.
Announcers: Marvin Miller, Johnny Jacobs.
Music: The Page Cavanaugh Trio, The Paul Weston Orchestra.
Length: 15 and 25 minute versions.
Network: ABC (1948), CBS (1953).
First Broadcast: 1948.

The Joan Benoit Show

Type: Variety
Hostess: Joan Benoit.
Length: 15 minutes.
Network: NBC.
First Broadcast: 1941.

The Joan Brooks Show

Type: Musical Variety
Hostess: Joan Brooks.
Orchestra: Archie Bleyer.
Length: 15 minutes.
Network: CBS.
First Broadcast: 1945.

The Joan Davis Show

Type: Comedy
Format: The misadventures of the char-
acters who inhabit The Swanville Tea
Shop.
Starring: Joan Davis as Joan.
Also: Verna Felton, Andy Russell, Shirley
Mitchell.
Announcer: Harry Von Zell, Bob Lemond.
Orchestra: Paul Weston, Lud Guskin.
Length: 25 minutes.
Network: CBS.
First Broadcast: 1945.

Joe and Ethel Turp

Type: Comedy
Format: Adventures of the Turp Family.
Based on characters created by Damon
Runyon.

Cast: Joe Turp	Jackson Beck
Ethel Turp	Patsy Campbell
Uncle Ben	Jack Smart
Billy Oldham	Art Carney

Organist: Fred Fiebel.
Length: 15 minutes.
Network: CBS.
First Broadcast: 1943.

Joe and Mabel

Type: Comedy
Format: The romantic problems of two
young lovers: Joe, a cab driver who feels
he is not yet ready for marriage, and
Mabel, a manicurist, the girl who yearns
to become his wife. Became the basis for a
television series of the same title.

Cast:	Joe	Ted deCorsia
	Mabel	Ann Thomas
	Mike, Joe's	
	friend	Walter Kinsella
	Shoiman, Mabel's	
	brother	Jack Grimes
	Mabel's mother	Betty Garde
	The Flatbush	
	Siren	Jean Ellyn

Announcer: George Putnam.
Length: 30 minutes.
Network: NBC.
First Broadcast: 1941.

The Joe DiMaggio Show

Type: Children's
Format: Called for children to answer
sports related questions in return for
prizes.   Also   featured   were   short
dramatizations of the lives of professional
sports figures.
Host: Joe DiMaggio.
Regulars: Jack Barry, Adelaide Klein,
Leon Janney, Charles Irving, Jackson
Beck.
Announcer: Ted Brown.
Length: 30 minutes.
Network: ABC.
First Broadcast: 1949.

The Joe E. Brown Show

Type: Variety
Host: Joe E. Brown.
Regulars: Frank Gill, Bill Demming, Mar-
garet McCrae.
Orchestra: Harry Sosnik.
Length: 30 minutes.
Network: CBS.
First Broadcast: 1938.

Joe Palooka

Type: Comedy
Format: The story of heavyweight boxer
Joe Palooka, a clean-living, moral champ
ignorant of gambling, fixed fights, blonde

sirens, and night clubs. Based on the character created by Ham Fisher. Became the basis for a television series of the same title.

Cast: Joe Palooka — Norman Gottschalk
Teddy Bergman
Karl Swenson

Ann Howe, his girlfriend — Elmira Roessler
Elsie Hitz
Mary Jane Higby

Knobby Walsh, his manager — Frank Readick
Hal Lansing

Clyde, his trainer — Murray Forbes

Length: 15 minutes.
Syndicated.
First Broadcast: 1945.

The Joe Penner Show

Type: Comedy
Format: The adventures of Joe Penner, the black sheep member of the Park Avenue Penner family.
Cast: Joe Penner — Himself
Susabelle — Gay Seabrook
Joe's mother — Martha Wentworth
Gertrude — Margaret Brayton
Also: Dick Ryan, Russ Brown, Harriet Hilliard, Kenny Stevens, Jim Bannon, Harry Holcombe, Dick Merrill, Roy Atwell, Tommy Lane, Gene Austin.
Orchestra: Ozzie Nelson, Jacques Renard, Jimmy Grier.
Sponsor: Cocomalt, Word Bread.
Length: 30 minutes.
Network: CBS, later NBC Blue.
First Broadcast: 1933.

Joe Powers of Oakville

Type: Musical Variety
Host: Joe Powers.
Regulars: Julian Noa, David Anderson, Elizabeth Reller, Helen Shields, Richard Leonar.

Orchestra: George Sherman.
Length: 30 minutes.
Network: CBS.
First Broadcast: 1946.

The John Conte Show

Type: Musical Variety
Host: John Conte.
Music: The John Magnante Trio.
Length: 5 minutes.
Network: ABC.
First Broadcast: 1952.

The John Kirby Show

Type: Musical Variety
Host: John Kirby.
Regulars: Maxine Sullivan, The Golden Gate Quartet.
Orchestra: John Kirby.
Length: 30 minutes.
Network: CBS.
First Broadcast: 1940.

John Steele, Adventurer

Type: Anthology
Format: Adventure stories related by John Steele.
Orchestra: Sylvan Levin.
Length: 30 minutes.
Network: Mutual.
First Broadcast: 1950.

Johnny Desmond Goes to College

Type: Musical Variety
Format: Music and songs set against a college motif.
Host: Johnny Desmond.
Regulars: Doris Drew, The Four Vagabonds, The George Barnes Octet.
Orchestra: Rex Maupin.
Length: 30 minutes.
Network: ABC.
First Broadcast: 1950.

Johnny Dollar

See title: "Yours Truly, Johnny Dollar."

Johnny Fletcher

Type: Crime Drama
Format: The cases of Johnny Fletcher, a
  quick-witted amateur sleuth.
Cast: Johnny Fletcher   Bill Goodwin
      Sam, his
        sidekick   Sheldon Leonard
Announcer: Owen James.
Orchestra: Buzz Adlam.
Length: 30 minutes.
Network: ABC.
First Broadcast: 1948.

The Johnny Green Show

Type: Variety
Format: Music and songs coupled with
  dramatic vignettes.
Host: Johnny Green.
Vocalist: Genevieve Rose.
Orchestra: Johnny Green.
Length: 30 minutes.
Network: CBS.
First Broadcast: 1939.

The Johnny Long Show

Type: Musical Variety
Host: Johnny Long.
Vocalist: Helen Young.
Orchestra: Johnny Long.
Length: 30 minutes.
Network: NBC.
First Broadcast: 1939.

Johnny Luzack of Notre Dame

Type: Drama
Format: Fictionalized yarns centered a-
  round Johnny Luzack, a former Notre
  Dame quarterback.
Cast: Johnny Luzack   Himself
      His side-kick   Ed Prentiss

Announcer: Boris Aplon.
Length: 30 minutes.
Network: ABC.
First Broadcast: 1949.

The Johnny Mack Brown Show

Type: Country Western Musical Variety
Host: Johnny Mack Brown.
Vocalist: Isleta Gayle.
Music: The Texas Rangers.
Length: 30 minutes.
Network: CBS.
First Broadcast: 1939. Also titled "Under
  Western Skies."

The Johnny Mercer Show

Type: Musical Variety
Host: Johnny Mercer.
Regulars: The Notables, The Roger
  Wayne Chorale.
Announcer: Johnny Jacobs.
Music: The Paul Smith Trio.
Length: 60 minutes.
Network: CBS.
First Broadcast: 1953.

Johnny Mercer's Music Shop

Type: Musical Variety
Host: Johnny Mercer.
Regulars: Jo Stafford, Ella Mae Morse,
  The Pied Pipers.
Announcer: Wendell Niles.
Orchestra: Paul Weston.
Length: 15 minutes.
Network: NBC.
First Broadcast: 1943.

The Johnny Morgan Show

Type: Comedy-Variety
Host: Johnny Morgan.
Regulars: Gloria Mann, Norman Broken-
  shire, Jack Arthur, Bill Keene, Walter
  Kinsella, The Smoothies.
Announcer: Jack Costello.

Length: 30 minutes.
Network: NBC.
First Broadcast: 1946.

Johnny Modero, Pier 23

Type: Drama
Format: The exploits of Johnny Modero, a detective working out of the San Francisco waterfront.
Starring: Jack Webb as Johnny Modero.
Orchestra: Harry Zimmerman.
Length: 30 minutes.
Network: Mutual.
First Broadcast: 1947.

Johnny Olsen's Luncheon Club

Type: Variety
Hosts: Johnny and Penny Olsen.
Announcer: Bob Maurer.
Organist: Al Greiner.
Length: 25 minutes.
Network: ABC.
First Broadcast: 1950.

Johnny Presents

Type: Variety
Format: Music and dramatic vignettes.
Host: Barry Wood.
Regulars: Cornelia Otis Skinner, Roland Young.
Announcer: Ken Roberts.
Orchestra/Chorus: Ray Bloch.
Featured Sketch: "William and Mary," which depicted the struggles of young marrieds.
Cast: William   Roland Young
          Mary   Cornelia Otis
                              Skinner
Sponsor: Philip Morris cigarettes. (The title was derived from the sponsor's living trademark, a shrill-voiced bellboy named Johnny, played by Johnny Roventini. At the beginning of each program Johnny would shout "Call for Philip Morrees," followed by announcer Ken Roberts stating "Johnny Presents.")

Length: 30 minutes.
Network: NBC.
First Broadcast: 1945.

The Johnson Family

Type: Drama
Format: The story of a Negro family with all parts being played by Jimmy Scribner.
Length: 15 minutes.
Network: Mutual.
First Broadcast: 1936.

Jonathan Trimble, Esquire

Type: Drama
Format: The story, set in a city of 60,000 people in 1905, focused on the life of Jonathan Trimble, the town newspaper publisher, a crotchety old conservative opposed to all the progress that was to follow.
Cast: Jonathan Trimble   Donald Crisp
                                      Gale Gordon
          Alice Trimble,.
             his wife   Irene Tedrow
          Mildred, their
             maid   Jean Gillespie
Also: Leora Thatcher, Roderick Thomas, Ruth Barnett, Earle Ross, Victor Rodman, Art Gilmore, Jack Mather.
Announcer: Tony LeFrano.
Music: Jack Meakin.
Length: 30 minutes.
Network: Mutal.
First Broadcast: 1946.

Jones and I

Type: Comedy
Format: The story of Sally Jones, an eighteen-year-old girl, and her unofficial fiancé, Jack Scott.
Cast: Sally Jones   Sammie Hill
          Jack Scott   Scott Fransworth
          Ned Scott, Jack's
             misguided
             uncle   Mason Adams
Also: Betty Philson, Jerry Tucker, John

Monks, Ann Thomas, Ethel Owen, Lorna Lynn, Amzie Strickland.
Organist: Charles Paul.
Length: 30 minutes.
Network: CBS.
First Broadcast: 1941.

Joyce Jordan, Girl Interne

Type: Serial
Format: The story of Joyce Jordan, a doctor who gave up a brilliant hospital career to begin a private practice in the small town of Preston. In later episodes the series dealt with Joyce's experiences in a large city hospital.

Cast: Joyce Jordan Rita Johnson
     Ann Shepherd
     Betty Winkler
     Elspeth Eric
     Gertrude Warner
     Fran Carlon
 Cassie, her
  housekeeper Ethel Owen
 Paul Sherwood Myron Mc-
     Cormick
 Dr. Hans Simons Lesley Woods
 Dr. Alan Webster Richard Widmark
 Dr. Tracy Irene Hubbard
Also: Bernard Lenrow, Arnold Moss.
Announcer: Ken Roberts.
Length: 15 minutes.
Network: CBS (1937-1948), ABC (1951).
First Broadcast: 1937.
Note: In 1941, the series title became "Joyce Jordan, M.D."

The Judge

Type: Crime Drama
Format: The story of a retired judge who drew on his long experience behind the bench to help track down criminals.
Cast: The Judge John Dehner
 The Police
  Lieutenant Larry Dobkin
Announcer: Dan Cubberly.
Music: Leith Stevens.
Length: 30 minutes.
Network: CBS.
First Broadcast: 1952.

Judy and Jane

Type: Serial
Format: The dramatic story of two girls.
Cast: Judy Marge Calvert
 Jane Donna Reade
 Joyce, their
  friend Ireene Wicker
 Dr. Bishop Marvin Miller
Announcer: Jack Blinkley.
Sponsor: Folger's Coffee.
Length: 15 minutes.
Network: Blue.
First Broadcast: 1932.

The Judy Canova Show

Type: Comedy
Format: Events in the life of Judy Canova, a country girl who moves to the big city to live with her aunt.
Cast: Judy Canova Herself
 Aggie, her aunt Ruth Perrott
     Verna Felton
 Pedro, the
  handyman Mel Blanc
 Geranium, the
  maid Ruby Dandridge
 Aggie's neighbor Gale Gordon
 Count Benchley
  Bostford,
  Aggie's friend Joseph Kearns
 Joe Crunchmiller,
  the cab driver Sheldon Leonard
Also: Elvia Allman, Hans Conried.
Announcer: Verne Smith, Ken Niles, Howard Petrie.
Orchestra: Opie Cates, Charles "Bud" Dant, Gordon Jenkins.
Length: 30 minutes.
Network: NBC.
First Broadcast: 1945.

Judy 'n' Jill 'n' Johnny

Type: Musical Variety
Starring: Susan Douglas (as Judy), Susan Thorne (as Jill) and Johnny Desmond (as Johnny).
Announcer: Bert Parks.
Orchestra: Casa Loma.

The Judy Canova Show. Judy Canova.

Length: 30 minutes.
Network: NBC.
First Broadcast: 1945.

Juke Box Jury

Type: Variety
Format: Guest celebrities rate the value of new or soon-to-be released songs. Became the basis of the television series "Peter Potter's Juke Box Jury."
Host: Peter Potter.
Announcer: Johnny Jacobs.
Length: 30 minutes.
Network: CBS.
First Broadcast: 1954.

The Julius La Rosa Show

Type: Musical Variety
Host: Julius La Rosa.
Vocalists: The Wanderers.
Orchestra: Russ Case.
Length: 10 minutes.
Network: CBS.
First Broadcast: 1953.

Jungle Jim

Type: Adventure
Format: Based on the comic strip by Alex Raymond, the series followed the exploits of Jungle Jim Bradley.
Cast: Jungle Jim
    Bradley   Matt Crowley
    Kolu, his
    companion   Juano Hernandez
    The female lead   Vicki Vola
Announcer: Glenn Riggs, Roger Krupp.
Sponsor: The Comic Weekly — Hearst Newspapers.
Length: 15 minutes.
Syndicated.
First Broadcast: The early 1940s.

Junior Miss

Type: Comedy
Format: The misadventures of Judy Graves, an unpredictable fifteen-year-old girl, who lives at 36 East 82nd Street, Manhattan.
Cast: Judy Graves   Shirley Temple
                     Barbara Whiting
    Lois Graves, her
    older sister   K.T. Stevens
                     Barbara Eiler
                     Peggy Knudsen
    Harry Graves,
    her father   Gale Gordon
                     Elliott Lewis
    Grace Graves,
    her mother   Sarah Selby
                     Margaret Lansing
    Hilda, their maid Myra Marsh
    Fluffy Adams,
    Judy's friend   Priscilla Lyon
                     Beverly Wills
Also: Gil Stratton, Jr.
Orchestra: Walter Schumann.
Program Opening:
Announcer: Presenting Junior Miss, brought to you transcribed; based on the delightful characters created by Sally Benson. With Gale Gordon as Harry Graves and starring Barbara Whiting.
Length: 30 minutes.
Network: CBS.
First Broadcast: 1948.

Just Easy

Type: Variety
Host: Jack Gregson.
Vocalist: Peggy Ann Ellis.
Orchestra: Bobby Hackett.
Length: 60 minutes.
Network: ABC.
First Broadcast: 1954.

Just Entertainment

Type: Country-Western Musical Variety
Host: Pat Buttram.
Regulars: Betty Martin, Jack Holloran.
Music: The Pat Buttram Band.
Length: 15 minutes.
Network: CBS.
First Broadcast: 1956.

Just Entertainment

Type: Variety
Host: Burgess Meredith.
Regulars: Mahalia Jackson, Gogi Grant, Lenny Colyer, The Four Lads.
Announcer: Joe Foss.
Orchestra: Caesar Petrillo.
Length: 25 minutes.
Network: CBS.
First Broadcast: 1956.

Just for You

Type: Variety
Host: Eddy Howard.
Announcer: Dick Noble.
Music: The Twelve Piece WMAQ Staff Orchestra.
Length: 60 minutes.
Network: NBC (from Chicago).
First Broadcast: 1954.

Just Neighbors

Type: Comedy
Format: Featured the philosophy of three neighbors.

Starring: Betty Caine, Helen Behmiller, Kathryn Card.
Length: 30 minutes.
Network: NBC.
First Broadcast: 1938.

Just Plain Bill

Type: Serial
Format: The story of Bill Davidson, the kindly barber of Hartville.

Cast:		
Bill Davidson	Arthur Hughes
Nancy Donovan, his married daughter	Ruth Russell
Kerry Donovan, Nancy's husband	James Meighan
Kathleen Chatton	Ara Gerald
Jonathan Hillery	Macdonald Carey
Shirley King	Audrey Egan
Reba Britton	Charlotte Lawrence
Margaret Burns	Elizabeth Day
Humphrey Fuller	Charles Egleston
Pearl Sutton	Ann Shepherd
John Britton	William Woodson

Announcer: Andre Baruch, Ed Herlihy, Roger Krupp.
Program Opening:
Announcer: Now to the many friends who wait for him we present Just Plain Bill, barber of Hartville. The story of a man who might be living right next door to you; the real-life story of people just like people we all know.
Length: 15 minutes.
Network: CBS.
First Broadcast: 1932.

Juvenile Jury

Type: Children
Format: A panel of five children answered questions, submitted by listeners or guests concerning problems faced by children. Became the basis for the television series of the same title.
Host: Jack Barry.

Just Plain Bill. Left to right: , Ruth Russell, Ara Gerald, Arthur Hughes.

Announcer: John Scott.
Sponsor: Gaines Dog Food.
Length: 30 minutes.
Network: Mutual.
First Broadcast: 1946.

The Kaiser Traveler

Type: Variety
Host: Burl Ives.
Announcer: Cy Harrice.
Sponsor: Kaiser Aluminum.
Length: 15 minutes.
Network: ABC.
First Broadcast: 1949.

Kate Hopkins, Angel of Mercy

Type: Serial

Format: The story of Kate Hopkins, an angel of mercy in the town of Forest Hills in the Sleeping Elephant Mountains.

Cast: Kate Hopkins,
a widow   Helen Lewis
                           Margaret
                           MacDonald

Tom Hopkins,
her son   Ned Weaver
                           Bud Collyer

Robert Atwood,
her friend   Raymond
                           Edward
                           Johnson

Jessie Atwood,
Robert's wife   Constance Collier

Length: 15 minutes.
Syndicated (1939), CBS (1940).
First Broadcast: 1939.

The Kate Smith Show. Kate Smith with guest Babe Ruth.

The Kate Smith Show

Type: Variety
Hostess: Kate Smith.
Regulars: Arthur Allen, Parker Fennelly, Ted Collins, The Ted Straeter Chorus, Johnny Williams and the Smart Set.
Announcer: Andre Baruch, Ted Collins.
Orchestra: Jack Miller.
Length: 60 and 15 minute versions.
Network: CBS (1936). Also known as "Kate Smith Speaks," "The A&P Bandwagon," and "The Kate Smith Hour."

The Kathy Godfrey Show

Type: Variety
Hostess: Kathy Godfrey.
Announcer: Bob Hite.
Orchestra: Norman Leyden.
Length: 25 minutes.
Network: CBS.
First Broadcast: 1955.

Katie's Daughter

Type: Serial
Format: The series revolved around life in the theatrical world.

Cast: Grace Cooper, Martin Blaine, Marie Geyer, Kenneth Banghart.
Announcer: Kenneth Banghart.
Sponsor: Manhattan Soap.
Length: 15 minutes.
Network: NBC.
First Broadcast: 1947.

Kay Kyser's Kollege of Musical Knowledge

Type: Variety Quiz
Format: Musical numbers were interspersed with a quiz segment, against a college format. Contestants competed in tests of musical knowledge divided into midterms and final exams. The professor (host) led the orchestra in a selection that the player had to identify. If he was correct he won a prize; if he was unable to answer the question, the correct response was relayed by the studio audience (students). Became the basis for the television series of the same title.
Host: Kay Kyser.
Regulars: Ish Kabibble, Phil Harris, Diane Templeton, Georgia Carroll, Don Leslee, Harry Babbitt, Shirley Mitchell, Ginny Simms, Diane Templeton, Sully Mason. The King Sisters, The Campus Kids, The Town Criers.
Announcer: John Heistand, Verne Smith.
Orchestra: Kay Kyser.
Length: 30 minutes.
Network: NBC.
First Broadcast: 1938.

Keeping Up With Rosemary

Type: Drama
Format: The trials and tribulations of a female magazine reporter.

Cast:
Rosemary	Fay Wray
The managing editor	Sydney Smith
Rosemary's father	Henry M. Neeley
Rosemary's mother	Ruth McDevitt
Rosemary's brother	Raymond Ives

The Kate Smith Hour. Left to right: Kate Smith,
Jo Stafford (guest), Jack Miller, and Lou Costello
(guest).

Rosemary's ro-
  mantic interest   Ben Lockwood
The editor's
  assistant   Joseph Julian
Also: Brad Baker.
Orchestra: Joseph Stopak.
Length: 30 minutes.
Network: NBC.
First Broadcast: 1942.

Keeping Up With Wigglesworth

Type: Comedy
Format: Events in the hectic life of Snuffy
  Wigglesworth.
Starring: Jack Ayres as Snuffy Wiggles-
  worth.
Also: Floyd Buckley, Eunice Howard, Bill
  Adams, Anthony Rivers, Marilyn Er-
  skine, Charles Miller.
Announcer: Matt Crowley.
Music: Lloyd Shaffer.
Length: 15 minutes.

Syndicated.
First Broadcast: 1945.

Keepsakes

Type: Variety
Format: Nostalgic songs and musical num-
  bers.
Hostess: Dorothy Kristen.
Announcer: Mack Harrell.
Orchestra-Chorus: Harry Sosnik.
Length: 30 minutes.
Network: Blue.
First Broadcast: 1943.

Kelly's Courthouse

Type: Quiz
Format: Selected members of the studio
  audience competed. A six-minute
  mystery vignette was performed and
  stopped prior to its conclusion (the reveal-

ing of the culprit). Three musical clues were then provided to help contestants solve the mystery. The first player to correctly uncover the culprit received a $25 war bond. If a player gave an incorrect response, a gun shot was heard and that player was disqualified.

Host: Fred Uttal.
Cast: Roger Krupp, Phyllis Clarke, Roc Rogers, Don Douglas, Sanford Bichart, John Aulicino, Bryna Raeburn.
Announcer: Dan Seymour.
Organist: Henry Sylvern.
Orchestra: Joseph Stopak.
Length: 30 minutes.
Network: Blue.
First Broadcast: 1944.

The Ken Banghart Show

Type: Variety
Host: Ken Banghart.
Vocalist: Arthur Gray.
Announcer: Jack Costello.
Length: 15 minutes.
Network: NBC.
First Broadcast: 1947.

The King Cole Trio

Type: Musical Variety
Host: Ted Pearson.
Starring: The King Cole Trio.
Length: 15 minutes.
Network: NBC.
First Broadcast: 1946.

The King's Men

Type: Musical Variety
Starring: Ken Darby, Bud Lynn, Rod Robinson, Jan Dobson.
Announcer: Harlow Wilcox.
Orchestra: Elliot Daniel.
Length: 30 minutes.
Network: NBC.
First Broadcast: 1949.

King's Row

Type: Serial
Format: The dramatic story of Parris Mitchell, a doctor in the town of King's Row. Based on the novel by Henry Bellamann.
Cast: Dr. Parris
Mitchell   Francis DeSales
Randy   Charlotte Manson
Elsie Mitchell   Charlotte Holland
Fulmer Green   Jim Boles
Announcer: John McDougall.
Music: Burt Buhrman.
Length: 15 minutes.
Network: CBS.
First Broadcast: 1951.

Kiss and Make Up

Type: Game
Format: Married couples, situated in a staged courtroom, were brought before the bench and asked to air their grievances. A panel of studio audience members decided which mate was at fault. The penalty: kiss and make up.
Host-Judge: Milton Berle.
Vocalists: The Murphy Sisters.
Orchestra: Harry Salter.
Length: 30 minutes.
Network: CBS.
First Broadcast: 1946.

Kitty Foyle

Type: Serial
Format: A first-person account of the life and loves of Kitty Foyle (flashbacks recall her reminiscences). Based on the novel by Christopher Morley. Became the basis for a television series of the same title.
Cast: Kitty Foyle   Julie Stevens
Kitty's father   Mark Smith
The Foyles' maid   Amanda
                    Randolph
Kitty's romantic
interest   Victor Thorley
Announcer: Mel Allen.

The Kraft Music Hall. Penny Singleton in a 1937 pose when she made her radio debut on "The Kraft Music Hall." At the time she used her real name, Dorothy McNulty; she became the blonde Penny Singleton in 1938 (see "Blondie" for photo).

Length: 15 minutes.
Network: CBS.
First Broadcast: 1942.

Knickerbocker Playhouse

Type: Anthology
Format: Dramatic presentations.
Host-Narrator: Elliott Lewis.
Featured Performer: Betty Winkler.
Orchestra: Carl Hohengarten.
Length: 30 minutes.
Network: CBS.
First Broadcast: 1939.

The Korn Kobblers

Type: Country-Western Musical Variety
Starring: Harry Turner, Charles Koening, Howard McElroy, Nels Loakso, Stan Frittle, Marty Gould.

Announcer: Alan Courtney.
Length: 15 minutes.
Syndicated.
First Broadcast: 1946.

The Kraft Music Hall

Type: Variety. Became the basis for a television series of the same title.
Host: Bing Crosby, Al Jolson, Nelson Eddy, Dorothy Kirsten.
Regulars: Bob Burns, Connee Boswell, Marty Martin, Jerry Lester, Victor Borge, The Charioteers, The Music Maids, Yuki, Marilyn Maxwell.
Announcer: Don Wilson, Ken Carpenter, Roger Krupp.
Orchestra: Jimmy Dorsey, John Scott Trotter, Lou Bring, Robert Armbruster.
Sponsor: Kraft Dairy Products.
Length: 60 minutes.
Network: NBC.
First Broadcast: 1934.

Ladies Be Seated

Type: Variety
Format: Games, music, and celebrity interviews.
Host: Jimmy Blaine, Johnny and Penny Olsen, Tom Moore.
Announcer: George Ansbro.
Music: The Buddy Weed Trio.
Length: 30 minutes.
Network: ABC.
First Broadcast: 1944.

Ladies Fair

Type: Variety
Format: Songs, games, and quizzes for the female listener.
Host: Tom Moore.
Announcer: Holland Engle, Don Gordon.
Organist: Porter Heaps, Herbert Foote.
Length: 30 minutes.
Network: Mutual.
First Broadcast: 1949.

The Lady Esther Screen Guild Playhouse. Pictured is Rosemary DeCamp, one of many performers to guest on this long-running program.

The Lady Esther Screen Guild Playhouse

Type: Anthology
Format: Radio adaptations of famous motion pictures.
Sponsor: Lady Esther Beauty Products.
Included:
Arsenic and Old Lace. The Broadway play about two elderly women who find pleasure in poisoning their male boarders.
Starring: Boris Karloff, Eddie Albert.
High Sierra. The story of an escaped convict who decides to pull one last job.
Starring: Humphrey Bogart, Ida Lupino.
Gildersleeve's Bad Day. The misadventures that befall the Great Gildersleeve when he is summoned for jury duty.
Starring: Harold Peary, Lillian Randolph, Walter Tetley, Richard Legrand.
The Paleface. The story of Painless Potter, a dentist who travels West to find new clients — and becomes involved with Indians and outlaws.
Starring: Bob Hope, Jane Russell.
Length: 30 minutes.

Network: NBC.
First Broadcast: 1941. In 1952 the series title became "Stars in the Air."

Land of the Lost

Type: Children's
Format: The story of two children, Isabel and Billy, and their adventures with Red Lantern, a talking fish whom they befriended and with whom they traveled beneath the sea seeking their lost toys. (The Magic Seaweed enabled Isabel and Billy to breathe beneath the water.)
Cast: Red Lantern   Junius Matthews
                        Art Carney
         Isabel   Betty Jane Tyler
         Billy   Raymond Ives
Also: Dolores Gillis, Walter Vaughn, Floyd Buckley.
Narrator: Isabel Manning Hewson, who told the story as if she were a child sharing the adventure with her brother.
Announcer: Michael Fitzmaurice.
Vocalist: Peggy Marshall.
Length: 30 minutes.
Network: Blue (1943), ABC (1945).
First Broadcast: 1943.

The Lanny Ross Show

Type: Musical Variety
Host: Lanny Ross.
Regulars: Evelyn Knight, Louise Carlyle.
Announcer: Jean Paul King, Jimmy Blaine, John Scott, Nelson Case.
Music: The Buddy Weed Trio, The Al Fannell Trio, The Herman Chittison Trio, The Will Lorin Orchestra.
Length: 30 and 15 minute versions.
Network: CBS (1939), Mutual (1950).
First Broadcast: 1939.

The Larry Carr Show

Type: Musical Variety
Host: Larry Carr.
Announcer: John Tillman.
Orchestra: Howard Smith.

Length: 15 minutes.
Network: CBS.
First Broadcast: 1946.

Lassie

Type: Adventure
Format: The story focused on the adventures of a collie named Lassie. Became the basis for a television series of the same title.
Voice of Lassie: Lassie.
Lassie's Trainer: Rudd Weatherwax.
Other Dog Imitations: Earl Keen.
Announcer: Charles Lyon.
Organist: John Duffy.
Sponsor: Red Heart Dog Food.
Program Opening:
Announcer: From   Hollywood . . . Three Flavor Red Heart, America's favorite dog food   presents   Metro-Goldwyn-Mayer's favorite motion picture star, Lassie.
Length: 15 minutes.
Network: ABC.
First Broadcast: 1947.

The Laugh and Swing Club

Type: Variety.
Format: Music, songs, and sketches.
Host: Morey Amsterdam.
Regulars: Mabel Todd, Del Casino, Henry Morgan.
Orchestra: Van Alexander.
Length: 30 minutes.
Network: Mutual.
First Broadcast: 1946.

The Lawrence Welk High Life Revue

Type: Musical Variety.
Host: Ted Brown.
Regulars: Helen Ramsey, Dick Hall, Roy Waldrum.
Orchestra: Lawrence Welk.
Sponsor: Miller High Life Beer.
Length: 30 minutes.
Network: ABC.
First Broadcast: 1949.

Lawyer Q

Type: Quiz.
Format: An actual criminal case was reenacted. Practicing lawyers appeared following the dramatization and presented a capsule summary to a jury of twelve studio audience members. Those jurors whose verdict followed that in the original case split a cash jackpot.
Host: Karl Swenson.
Cast: Ronny Liss, Joseph Julian, Eleanor Audley, Neil O'Malley.
Announcer: Dennis James.
Length: 30 minutes.
Network: Mutual.
First Broadcast: 1947.

Lawyer Tucker

Type: Comedy
Format: The story of Dan Tucker, an attorney with a big heart and his own idea as to how the law should be administered. The series focused on the bickering that resulted when he and his liberal-minded junior partner clashed over a case.
Cast: Dan Tucker   Parker Fennelly
        The junior
        partner   Maurice Wells
        Dan's sister/
        housekeeper   Mae Shutts
Also: Arthur   Anderson,   Ted   Osborne, Cameron Andrews.
Length: 30 minutes.
Network: CBS.
First Broadcast: 1947.

Leave It to Joan

See title: "The Joan Davis Show."

Leave It to Mike

Type: Comedy
Format: The misadventures of Mike McNally.
Cast: Mike McNally   Walter Kinsella
        Dinny, his girl-
        friend   Joan Alexander

Mr. Berkeley, his
employer — Jerry Macy
Mrs. Berkeley — Hope Emerson
Length: 30 minutes.
Network: Mutual.
First Broadcast: 1945.

Leave It to the Girls

Type: Advice
Format: A panel of females answer listeners' questions. Became the basis for a television series of the same title.
Moderator: Elissa Landi, Dorothy Kilgallen, Paula Stone, Maggi McNellis.
Panelists: Constance Bennett, Robin Chandler, Eloise McElhone, Hedda Hopper.
Announcer: Andre Baruch.
Length: 25 minutes.
Network: Mutual.
First Broadcast: 1945.

Lefty

Type: Comedy
Format: The antics of a southpaw pitcher named Lefty.
Cast: Lefty — Jack Albertson
The society
reporter — Joan Alexander
Lefty's secretary — Maxine Stuart
Length: 30 minutes.
Network: CBS.
First Broadcast: 1946.

Leonidas Witherall

See title: "The Adventures of Leonidas Witherall."

The Les Paul and Mary Ford Show

Type: Variety
Hosts: Les Paul and Mary Ford.
Regulars: Bob and Eileen Pollard.
Length: 10 minutes.
Network: Mutual.
First Broadcast: 1955.

Let George Do It

Type: Drama
Format: The cases of George Valentine, a hard-boiled private detective. His newspaper ads read: "If the job's too tough for you, you've got a job for me..."
Cast: George Valentine — Bob Bailey
Brooksie, his
secretary — Virginia Gregg
Length: 30 minutes.
Syndicated.
First Broadcast: 1950.

Let's Be Charming

Type: Variety
Hosts: Julia Sanderson, Pat Barnes.
Music: Jack Shilkret, John Gart.
Length: 15 minutes.
Network: Mutual.
First Broadcast: 1943.

Let's Be Crazy

Type: Variety
Hosts: Dale Evans, Tom Moore.
Orchestra: Caesar Petrillo.
Length: 30 minutes.
Network: CBS.
First Broadcast: 1940.

Let's Dance, America

Type: Musical Variety
Host: Fred Robbins.
Orchestra: Tex Beneke, Skitch Henderson.
Length: 30 minutes.
Network: CBS.
First Broadcast: 1948.

Let's Laugh and Get Acquainted

Type: Interview.
Format: Couples chosen from the studio audience appeared on stage and discussed various topics with the host. The couples received prizes for participating.
Host: Jack Gregson.

Announcer: Don Stanley, Hal Gibney.
Length: 30 minutes.
Network: NBC.
First Broadcast: 1946.

Let's Play Reporter

Type: Quiz.
Format: A contestant chosen from the studio audience took on the role of a newspaper reporter. A story submitted by a listener was told to the reporter by the host. Following the story, the reporter was asked to relate certain facts of the story. Each correct response earned the reporter one dollar.
Hostess: Frances Scott.
Assistants: James L. Kilgallen, Bob Denton.
Orchestra: Jack Martin.
Length: 30 minutes.
Network: NBC.
First Broadcast: 1943.

Let's Pretend

Type: Children
Format: Dramatizations of fairy tales.
Adult Performers: Harry Swan, Bill Adams, Marilyn Erskine, Miriam Wolfe (who usually portrayed a witch.)
Child Performers: (Varied greatly from year to year; listed is the cast from 1939): Albert Aley, Vivian Block, Jack Grimes, Estelle Levy, Betty Jane Tyler, Patricia Ryan, Jimmy Lydon, Jackie Jordan, Patricia Reardan, Kenneth Darby.
Orchestra: Maurice Brown.
Sponsor: Cream of Wheat.
Length: 30 minutes.
Network: CBS.
First Broadcast: 1930 (series ended in 1954). Originally titled "The Adventures of Helen and Mary" from 1930 to 1934.

Let's Talk Hollywood

Type: Quiz.
Format: Celebrity guests attempted to answer questions submitted by listeners.

Listeners whose questions stumped the guests received an R.C.A. television set as a prize.
Host: George Murphy.
Announcer: Hy Averback.
Length: 30 minutes.
Network: NBC.
First Broadcast: 1948.

Let Yourself Go

Type: Variety
Host: Milton Berle.
Regulars: Connie Russell, Joe Besser.
Announcer: Ken Roberts.
Orchestra: Jacques Renard, Ray Bloch.
Sponsor: Eversharp pens and pencils.
Program Opening:
Announcer: Yes, Let Yourself Go, starring Milton Berle with Ray Bloch and his orchestra, Connie Russell, and Joe Besser. Presented by Eversharp, would's leading manufacturer of fountain pens, repeater pencils, lead and desk sets...And now, here's the entertainment you've been waiting for, here's the fellow who let himself go and became Ziegfeld's biggest folly — Milton Berle...
Length: 30 minutes.
Network: NBC Blue.
First Broadcast: 1944.

The Liberace Show

Type: Musical Variety.
Host: Liberace.
Orchestra: George Liberace.
Length: 30 minutes.
Syndicated.
First Broadcast: 1954.

Life Begins

Type: Serial
Format: The dramatic story of Martha Webster.
Cast: Martha Webster   Bess Johnson
       Winfield Craig   Carleton Young
       Virginia Craig   Toni Gilman
       Richard Craig   Jimmy Donnelly

Life Can Be Beautiful. Left to right: Ralph Locke, Alice Reinheart, and John Holbrook.

Lucy Craig   Betty Philson
Dick Young   Donald Cook
Holly   Margaret Mac-
                    Donald
Also: Floyd Buckley, Eleanor Phelps, Jeanette Nolan, Everett Sloane.
Announcer: Ken Roberts.
Length: 15 minutes.
Network: CBS.
First Broadcast: 1940.

Life Begins at 80

Type: Discussion
Format: A panel of elderly people discussed various aspects of life. Became the basis for a television series of the same title.
Host: Jack Barry.
Announcer: Dan McCullough.
Length: 30 minutes.
Network: Mutual.
First Broadcast: 1948.

Life Can Be Beautiful

Type: Serial
Format: The story dramatized incidents in the lives of the people of a small town.
Cast: Carol Conrad   Alice Reinheart
                            Teri Keane
       David Solomon   Ralph Locke
       Barry Markham   Richard Kollmar
                            Dick Nelson

       Stephen Hamil-
         ton   Earl Larrimore
                          John Holbrook
       Nellie   Ethel Owen
                          Agnes
                            Moorehead
       Al Douglas   Humphrey Davis
       Logan Smith   Bud Collyer
       Maybelle Owens   Ruth Yorke
       Nurse Kimball   Peggy Allenby
       Muriel Kellogg   Ruth Weston
       Rita Yates   Mitzi Gould
Announcer: Ed Herlihy, Ralph Edwards, Ron Rawson, Bob Dixon, Don Hancock.

Organist: Herschel Leucke.

Program Opening:

Announcer: John Ruskin wrote this: "Whenever money is the principal object of life it is both got ill and spent ill and does harm in both getting and spending. When getting and spending happiness is our aim, Life Can Be Beautiful." Life Can Be Beautiful is an inspiring message of faith drawn from life, written by Carl Bixby and Don Becker and brought to you by Spic and Span. No soap, no other cleaner, nothing in America cleans painted walls, woodwork, and linoleum like Spic and Span.

Length: 15 minutes.

Network: CBS.

First Broadcast: 1938.

A Life in Your Hands

Type: Drama

Format: The story of Jonathan Kegg, a wealthy retired lawyer who devoted his time to impartially cross-examining witnesses during criminal proceedings when justice was threatened.

Cast: Jonathan Kegg   Ned LeFevre
                                     Lee Bowman
                                     Carlton KaDell

Narrator: Myron Wallace, Carlton KaDell.

Announcer: Ken Nordine.

Length: 30 minutes.

Network: NBC.

First Broadcast: 1949.

The Life of Irene Castle

Type: Serial

Format: Serialized stories based on the life of Irene Castle, "the best dressed woman in America." `

Starring: Irene Rich.

Sponsor: Formfit Bras.

Length: 15 minutes.

Syndicated.

First Broadcast: 1931.

The Life of Mary Sothern

Type: Serial

Format: The dramatic story of Mary Sothern.

Cast: Mary Sothern   Linda Carlon
                                     Minabelle Abbott
                                     Betty Caine
          Danny Stratford   Jack Zoller
                                     Joseph Julian
                                     Leon Janney
          Phyllis Stratford   Florence Golden
          Alice Sanders   Bess McCammon

Announcer: Ken Roberts.

Length: 15 minutes.

Network: Mutual.

First Broadcast: 1936.

The Life of Mortimer Meek

See title: "Meet Mr. Meek."

The Life of Riley

Type: Comedy

Format: The life of Chester A. Riley, a not-too-bright husband, his wife Peg, and their children Babs and Junior. Became the basis for a television series of the same title.

Cast: Chester A. Riley   Lionel Stander
                                     William Bendix
          Peg Riley   Grace Coppin
                                     Paula Winslow
                                     Georgia Backus
          Barbara "Babs"
            Riley   Peggy Conklin
                                     Sharon Douglas
                                     Barbara Eiler
          Chester Riley, Jr.
            (Junior)   Jack Grimes
                                     Scotty Beckett
                                     Conrad Binyon
                                     Tommy Cook
          Jim Gillis, their
            neighbor   John Brown
          Olive "Honeybee"
            Gillis, Jim's
            wife   Shirley Mitchell

Digby "Digger"
O'Dell, the under-
taker   John Brown
Waldo Binney, Ril-
ey's neighbor   Dink Trout
Announcer: Jimmy Wallington, Ken Car-
penter, Ken Niles.
Orchestra: Lou Kosloff.
Sponsor: Prell Shampoo.
Length: 30 minutes.
Network: NBC.
First Broadcast: 1941.

Life with Charlotte

Type: Variety
Format: Music, songs, and comedy sket-
ches set against the background of the
Greenwood Boarding House in Washing-
ton, D.C.
Hostess: Charlotte Greenwood.
Regulars: Arthur Q. Bryan, Shirley Mitch-
ell.
Vocalists: Three Hits and a Miss.
Orchestra: Matty Malneck.
Length: 30 minutes.
Network: NBC.
First Broadcast: 1944.

Life with Luigi

Type: Comedy
Format: The story of Luigi Basco, antique
dealer, an immigrant brought to Chicago
from Italy by his friend Pasquale, the
owner of Pasquale's Spaghetti Palace.
Stories related Luigi's attempts to adjust
to his new homeland and his struggles to
evade Pasquale's endless attempts to
marry him to his overweight daughter
Rosa. Episodes opened and closed with
Luigi writing a letter to his Mama Basco
in Italy. Became the basis for a television
series of the same title.
Cast: Luigi Basco   J. Carrol Naish
Pasquale   Alan Reed
Rosa   Jody Gilbert
Miss Spaulding,
Luigi's night
school teacher   Mary Shipp

Horowitz, Luigi's
friend   Joe Forte
Schultz, Luigi's
friend   Hans Conried
Peterson, Luigi's
friend   Ken Peters
Announcer: Charles Lyon, Bob Lemond.
Orchestra: Lud Gluskin.
Program Opening:
Announcer: ...we invite you to Chicago's
Little Italy for a new comedy, Life with
Luigi, the story of an immigrant, created
by Cy Howard and starring J. Carrol
Naish.
Length: 30 minutes.
Network: CBS.
First Broadcast: 1948.

Lights Out

Type: Anthology
Format: Suspense tales of the occult and
the supernatural. Became the basis for a
television series of the same title.
Announcer: George Stone, Bob Lemond.
Orchestra: Leith Stevens.
Program Opening:
Announcer: This is the witching hour. It
is the hour when dogs howl and evil is let
lose on a sleeping world. Want to hear
about it? Then turn out your lights!
Length: 15 minutes.
Network: NBC (later CBS, then ABC).
First Broadcast: 1942.

L'il Abner

Type: Comedy
Format: Based on Al Capp's comic strip,
the series followed the lives of hillbillies
in the village of Dogpatch.
Cast: L'il Abner   John Hodiak
Daisy Mae   Laurette Fill-
brandt
Mammy Yokum   Hazel Dopheide
Pappy Yokum   Clarence Hartzell
Announcer: Durward Kirby.
Length: 15 minutes.
Network: NBC.
First Broadcast: 1939.

Lincoln Highway

Type: Anthology
Format: Dramatizations of supposedly true stories that occurred along U.S. Route 30.
Host-Narrator: John McIntire.
Music: Jack Arthur.
Length: 30 minutes.
Network: NBC.
First Broadcast: 1940.

Linda's First Love

Type: Serial
Format: The dramatic story of Linda, a girl who worked in a department store and whose first love, for a rich society playboy, was threatened by her mother, who disapproved and sought to break up their romance.
Cast: Linda   Arline Blackburn
Danny Grogan,
     her boyfriend   Karl Swenson
Linda's mother   Mary Jane Higby
Announcer: Andre Baruch.
Sponsor: The Kroger Grocery and Baking Company.
Program Opening:
Announcer: The Kroger Grocery and Baking Company brings you, transcribed, Linda's First Love, the true-to-life story of a young girl; a girl in love with the world about us and in love with the wealthy young Kenneth Woodruff. She is a shop girl; he is a young society man. The romance is frowned upon by Linda's friends and family and Linda faces the world with her dream of happiness alone.
Length: 15 minutes.
First Broadcast: 1940.

The Line-up

Type: Crime Drama
Format: The investigations of Lt. Ben Guthrie and Sergeants Matt Grebb and Peter Carter, plainclothes detectives with the San Francisco Police Department. Became the basis for a television series of the same title.
Cast: Lt. Ben Guthrie   Bill Johnstone
Sgt. Matt Grebb   Joseph Kearns
Sgt. Peter Carter John McIntire
Announcer: Dan Cubberly.
Orchestra: Eddie Dunstedder.
Length: 30 minutes.
Network: CBS.
First Broadcast: 1950.

Listen to a Love Song

Type: Musical Variety
Host: Tony Martin.
Announcer: Jimmy Wallington.
Orchestra/Chorus: Al Sack.
Length: 30 minutes.
Network: CBS.
First Broadcast: 1946.

Listening Post

Type: Anthology
Format: Dramatizations of stories from the *Saturday Evening Post*.
Host-Narrator: Bud Collyer.
Length: 30 minutes.
Network: ABC.
First Broadcast: 1944.

Little Old Hollywood

Type: Talk-Music
Host: Ben Alexander.
Featured: Gogo DeLys.
Orchestra: Gordon Jenkins.
Length: 30 minutes.
Network: NBC.
First Broadcast: 1940.

Little Orphan Annie

Type: Adventure Serial
Format: The story followed the adventures of an orphan girl and her dog. Based on the comic strip by Harold Gray.
Cast: Little Orphan
     Annie   Shirley Bell
                    Janice Gilbert

Daddy Warbucks	Stanley Andrews
	Boris Aplon
Sandy, the dog	Brad Barker
Joe Corntassle,	
Annie's chum	Allan Baruck
Aha, the Chinese	
cook	Olan Soulé

Announcer: Pierre Andre.
Sponsor: Ovaltine.
Length: 15 minutes.
Network: Blue.
First Broadcast: 1931.

Live Like a Millionaire

Type: Variety
Format: Called for children to introduce their talented parents. The most talented parents, as determined by studio audience applause, received prizes. Became the basis for a television series of the same title.
Host: Jack McCoy.
Announcer: John Nelson.
Orchestra: Ivan Ditmars.
Length: 30 minutes.
Network: NBC.
First Broadcast: 1950.

The Lives of Harry Lime

Type: Adventure
Format: The story of Harry Lime, an international rogue and confidence man. Based on the movie "The Third Man."; later a television series titled "The Third Man."
Starring: Orson Welles as Harry Lime.
Music: Anton Karas.
Length: 30 minutes.
Syndicated.
First Broadcast: 1951.

Lone Journey

Type: Serial
Format: The difficulties of Wolfe Bennett, a Chicago businessman who left his urban way of life for a ranch in the Judith Mountain area of Montana.

Cast:	Wolfe Bennett	Les Damon
		Reese Taylor
		Staats Cotsworth
		Henry Hunter
	Nita Bennett,	
	his wife	Betty Winkler
		Claudia Morgan
		Betty Ruth Smith
		Eloise Kummer
		Olive Deering
		Charlotte Holland
	Port	Vinton Hayworth
	Matron	Lesley Woods
	Nita's aunt	Polly Rowles
	Wolfe's mother	Nancy Osgood
	Cecily Andrews	Dorothy Lovell
	Cullen Andrews	James Meighan
	Jim Matthews	John Gibson
	Jesse King	Bess McCammon
	Kyle King	Geraldine Kay

Also: Delores Gillis, Joan Alexander, Ginelle Gibbs, Minerva Pious, Marilyn Monk.
Narrator: Charles Woods.
Announcer: Durward Kirby, Nelson Case, Henry Morgan, Richard Stark.
Length: 15 minutes.
Network: NBC (1940-1943), ABC (1946).
First Broadcast: 1940.

The Lone Ranger

Type: Western
Format: Trailing the notorious Butch Cavendish Hole-in-the-Wall Gang, a group of six Texas Rangers stop as they approach the canyon passage to Bryant's Gap. Their scout, who is secretly working for Butch, returns and informs Captain Dan Reid that the passage is clear. Riding in, the Rangers are led into a trap and downed by the Cavendish Gang. Believing that all are dead, the gang rides off.
Later that afternoon, Tonto, an Indian riding through the canyon, finds the lone survivor, John Reid, the captain's brother. Regaining consciousness, Reid learns of his fate and recalls Tonto, an Indian he had befriended years go, the childhood com-

panion who called him "Kemo Sabe" (translated as both "Trusted Scout" and "Faithful Friend").

To convince Cavendish that all the Rangers had been killed, Tonto digs six graves— the sixth marked with the name John Reid—to conceal the fact that one ranger had lived to avenge the others—The Lone Ranger.

At Tonto's suggestion, Reid fashions a mask from his brother's black vest and, posing as an outlaw, he tracks down and apprehends the Cavendish gang.

Bearing the trademark of the silver bullet, The Lone Ranger and Tonto rode the Western plains of the 19th century striving to maintain law and order in a wild and lawless era. Became the basis for the television series of the same title.

Cast: John Reid, The

Long Ranger	George Seaton
	Jack Deeds
	Earl Graser
	Brace Beemer
	John Todd
	Jim Jewell
Tonto	John Todd
Dan Reid, John's	
nephew	Ernie Stanley
	James Lipton
	Dick Beals
Butch Cavendish	Jay Michael
Thunder Martin,	
the ranch	
owner	Paul Hughes

Announcer-Narrator: Brace Beemer, Harold Golder, Charles Woods, Bob Hite, Fred Foy.

Sponsor: Wheaties and Cheerios cereals.

Program Opening:

Ranger: Hi Yo Silver, Awaaaayyyyy!

Announcer: A fiery horse with the speed of light, a cloud of dust, and a hearty Hi Yo Silver, The Lone Ranger. When the Western United States were first opened to settlers, the promise of easy wealth brought both honest men and criminals to the new territory. Both found that wealth could only be purchased by hard work and the criminals returned to their old habits. The masked rider of the Plains fought them tirelessly, however, astride his great horse Silver. He rode the length and breadth of seven states in the cause of justice and in time he brought law and order to the lawless frontier. Return with us now to those thrilling days when the West was young and adventure lay at the end of every trail. The Lone Ranger rides again!

Length: 30 minutes.

Network: Mutual.

First Broadcast: 1930.

The Lone Wolf

Type: Crime Drama

Format: The exploits of Michael Lanyard, a private detective known as The Lone Wolf. Based on characters created by Louis Vance. Became the basis for a television series of the same title.

Cast: Michael Lanyard   Walter Coy
                                    Gerald Mohr

Length: 30 minutes.

Network: Mutual.

First Broadcast: 1948.

Lonely Women

Type: Serial

Format: The series, set in the Towers women's hotel during World War II, stressed the feelings of loneliness experienced by several women whose men were off to war.

Cast:	
Judith Clark	Barbara Luddy
Judith Evans	Eileen Palmer
Marilyn Lari-	
more	Bett Lou Gerson
Peggy	Harriette Widmer
Geroge Bartlett	Reese Taylor
Helen	Florence Brower
Nora	Nanette Sargent
Jack Crandall	Les Tremayne
Bertha Schultz	Patricia Dunlap
Bertha's mother	Virginia Payne
Bertha's father	Murray Forbes

Also: Viola Berwick, Norma Jean Race.

Announcer: Fort Pearson, Marvin Miller.

Organist: Bernice Yanoiek.
Length: 15 minutes.
Network: Blue.
First Broadcast: 1942.

The Lonesome Girl

Type: Men
Format: An unusual program geared to the male audience. The title character, who was anonymous and wore a mask when playing the role, talked with as seductive a voice as had been heard on radio. She treated her entire audience as one and rambled on with chatter in an intimate vein, directed to her male listeners. Her soft, mellow tones suggested that she could be looked upon as either a lover, friend, or companion. "The Lonesome Girl" opened the program and immediately played up the sex motif; the program itself was interspersed with talk and music.
Length: 15 minutes.
Network: Mutual.
First Broadcast: 1950.

The Longines Symphonette

Type: Music
Host: Frank Knight.
Announcer: Frank Knight.
Orchestra: Mishel Piastro.
Sponsor: The Longines-Wittnauer Watch Company.
Length: 30 minutes.
Network: CBS.
First Broadcast: 1948.

Look Your Best

Type: Women
Format: Beauty tips and advice.
Host: Richard Willis.
Announcer: Bill Shipley.
Length: 30 minutes.
Network: CBS.
First Broadcast: 1950.

Lora Lawton

Type: Serial
Format: The dramatic story of Lora Lawton, housekeeper to Peter Carver, a shipbuilder in Washington, D.C.

Cast:	Lora Lawton	Joan Tompkins
		Jan Miner
	Peter Carver	James Meighan
		Ned Weaver
	May Case, Peter's secretary	Ethel Wilson
	Helene Hudson	Fran Carlon
	Octavia	Carol Summers
	Gail Carver	Marilyn Erskine
		Charita Bauer
	Clyde Houston	James Van Dyke
	Rex Lawton	Lawson Zerbe
	Iris Houston	Elaine Kent
	Russ	Walter Greaza

Also: Gertrude Warner, Staats Cotsworth, Michael Fitzmaurice, Spencer Bentley, Sammie Hill, Helen Shields.
Announcer: Ford Bond.
Organist: Ted Steele.
Length: 15 minutes.
Network: NBC.
First Broadcast: 1943.

Lorenzo Jones

Type: Comedy Serial
Format: The story of Lorenzo Jones, a garage mechanic who spent most of his time inventing seemingly useless gadgets.

Cast:	Lorenzo Jones	Karl Swenson
	Belle Jones, his wife	Betty Garde
		Lucille Wall
	Abby Matson, their friend	Jean McCoy
	Sandy Matson, Abby's husband	Joseph Julian
	Jim Barker, Lorenzo's employer	John Brown
	Irma Barker, Jim's wife	Nancy Sheridan
		Mary Wickes
		Grace Keddy

Lorenzo Jones. Left to right: Lucille Wall, Elliott
Reid, Karl Swenson, and Colleen Ward.

Nick   Elliott Reid
Judy   Colleen Ward
Margaret   Ann Shepherd
Angus   Art Carney

Announcer: Don Lowe.
Organist: Rosa Rio, Ann Leaf.
Sponsor: Phillips Milk of Magnesia, Dreft.
Program Opening:
Announcer: Now smile awhile with Loren-
    zo Jones and his wife Belle. We all know
    couples like loveable and practical Loren-
    zo Jones and his dedicated wife Belle.
    Lorenzo's inventions have made him a
    character to the town, but not to Belle
    who loves him. Their struggle for secur-
    ity is anybody's story, but somehow with
    Lorenzo it has made more smiles than
    tears.
Length: 15 minutes.

Network: NBC.
First Broadcast: 1937.

The Louella Parsons Show

Type: Gossip
Hostess: Louella Parsons.
Announcer: Marvin Miller, Verne Smith.
Length: 15 and 5 minute versons.
Network: ABC (1946), CBS (1951).
First Broadcast: 1946.

The Louise Florea Show

Type: Musical Variety
Hostess: Louise Florea.
Organist: Jessie Crawford.

The Louella Parsons Show. Louella Parsons.

Orchestra: Leopold Spitalny.
Length: 15 minutes.
Network: Blue.
First Broadcast: 1938.

Louise Massey and the Westerners

Type: Country-Western Musical Variety
Hostess: Louise Massey.
Co-Hosts: Curt and Allen Massey.
Regulars: Mill Mable, Larry Wellington.
Music: The Westerners.
Length: 15 minutes.
Syndicated.
First Broadcast: 1945.

Love Notes

Type: Women
Format: Romantic poetry readings.
Host: Jerry Wayne.
Announcer: Ben Grauer.
Length: 5 minutes.
Syndicated.
First Broadcast: 1945.

Love Story Theatre

Type: Anthology
Format: Romantic dramatizations.
Host: Jim Ameche.
Orchestra: Sylvan Levin.
Length: 30 minutes.
Network: Mutual.
First Broadcast: 1946.

Lovely Lady

Type: Women
Format: Beauty tips and advice.
Host-Fashion Commenator: John Slanton.
Featured: Lester Harding.
Orchestra: Milton Shrednik.
Length: 30 minutes.
Network: NBC.
First Broadcast: 1940.

Lucky Stars

Type: Variety
Format: Performances by undiscovered, promising talent.

Host: Jack Kiltie.
Regulars: Marie Ragndahl, Bob Houston, Lynn Collier, The Smoothies.
Orchestra: Leopold Spitalny.
Length: 30 minutes.
Network: NBC.
First Broadcast: 1946.

Lulu and Johnny

Type: Variety
Hosts: Lulu Bates, Johnny Morgan.
Orchestra: Joe Rines.
Length: 15 minutes.
Network: Blue.
First Broadcast: 1943.

Lum and Abner

Type: Comedy
Format: The hectic adventures of Lum Edwards and Abner Peabody, proprietors of the Jot 'Em Down Store in Pine Ridge, Arkansas. Basis of a short-lived television series in 1949.
Cast: Lum Edwards   Chester Lauck
        Abner Peabody   Norris Goff
        Mose Muich, the
          barber   Andy Devine
Also: Zasu Pitts, Dink Trout, Edna Best.
Announcer: Del Sharbutt, Gene Hamilton, Wendell Niles, Roger Krupp, Lou Crosby, Gene Baker.
Orchestra: Opie Cates.
Organist (prior to 1949):   Sylvia Bock, Elsie Mae Emerson.
Sponsor: Frigidaire, Ford, Alka-Seltzer, One-A-Day Vitamins.
Length: 15 and 30 minute versions.
Network: NBC (then CBS, ABC, CBS, Mutual).
First Broadcast: 1931.

Luncheon at the Waldorf

Type: Variety
Format: Music and songs set against the background of the Empire Room of the Waldorf-Astoria Hotel in New York.

Hostess: Ilka Chase.
Featured: Frank Luther.
Announcer: Bert Parks.
Orchestra: Paul Baron.
Length: 30 minutes.
Network: NBC.
First Broadcast: 1940.

The Lux Radio Theatre

Type: Anthology
Format: Radio adaptations of well known Broadway plays and Hollywood motion pictures. Also titled "Lux Presents Hollywood." Became the basis for "The Lux Video Theatre" television series.
Hosts: Mark Hellinger, Cecil B. DeMille, William Keighley, William Keeley, Hal Wallace.
Substitute Host: Irving Cummings.
Announcer: Mel Ruick, John Milton Kennedy, Ken Carpenter.
Orchestra: Louis Silvers.
Sponsor: Lux.
Included:
The Farmer's Daughter. The story of an ingenuous and beautiful farm girl and the sophisticated politician whose life she changes.
Starring: Loretta Young, Joseph Cotten.
All About Eve. The story of an ambitious actress who will stop at nothing to reach the top.
Starring: Bette Davis, Anne Baxter, Gary Merrill.
Swanee River. A dramatization of the life, loves, and triumphs of Stephen Foster.
Starring: Al Jolson, Dennis Morgan.
Wuthering Heights. The tragic love affair between two people in 18th Century England. Based on the book by Emily Bronte.
Starring: Ida Lupino, Basil Rathbone.
Length: 60 minutes.
Network: CBS.
First Broadcast: 1936.

Lyrics By Liza

Type: Musical Variety
Hostess: Liza Morrow.

Lum and Abner. Chester Lauck and Norris Goff in costume as Lum and Abner.

Orchestra: Jimmy Lytell.
Length: 25 minutes.
Network: NBC.
First Broadcast: 1943.

The McCoy

Type: Crime Drama
Format: The cases of Mike McCoy, a private detective working out of Los Angeles.
Cast: Mike McCoy   Howard Duff
      The Police Lieu-
        tenant   Sheldon Leonard
Length: 30 minutes.
Network: NBC.
First Broadcast: 1950.

McGarry and His Mouse

Type: Comedy
Format: The misadventures of a not-too-bright rookie sleuth, Dan McGarry, and his assistant, Kitty Archer, the Mouse.

Based on the comic strip by Matt Taylor in *This Week* magazine.
Cast: Dan McGarry   Roger Pryor
                        Wendell Corey
                        Ted de Corsia
      Kitty Archer   Shirley Mitchell
                        Peggy Conklin
                        Patsy Campbell
      Kitty's mother   Betty Garde
Announcer: Bert Parks.
Orchestra: Peter Van Steeden.
Length: 30 minutes.
Network: NBC.
First Broadcast: 1946.

Ma and Pa

Type: Comedy
Format: An exchange of comic dialogue between and elderly married couple.
Cast: Ma   Margaret Dee
      Pa   Parker Fennelly
Length: 15 minutes.
Network: CBS.
First Broadcast: 1936.

Ma Perkins. Virginia Payne in costume as Ma Perkins.

Ma Perkins

Type: Serial
Format: Events in the life of Ma Perkins, the owner of a lumberyard in Rushville Center, a woman who managed to travel widely, mend broken hearts, and counsel her family and loved ones.

Cast:		
Ma Perkins	Virginia Payne
Fay Perkins Henderson	Rita Ascot
	Marjorie Hannan
	Cheer Breston
	Laurette Fillbrandt
	Margaret Draper
John Perkins	Gilbert Faust
Shuffle Shober	Charles Egleston
	Edwin Wolfe
C. Pemberton Tooley	Fred Howard
	Forrest Lewis
Willie Fitz	Murray Forbes
Junior Fitz	Cecil Roy
	Arthur Young
	Bobby Ellis
Evey Perkins Fitz	Dora Johnson
	Laurette Fillbrandt
	Kay Campbell
Tom Wells	John Larkin
	Casey Allen
Frank Fenton	Barry Drew
	Dan Sutter
Burton Wiley	Les Tremayne
Deborah Matthews	Betty Hanna
Phineas Herringbone	Herb Butterfield
Flossie Herringbone	Angeline Orr
Jessica Herringbone	Beryl Vaughn
Tweetsie Heringbone	Elmira Roessler
Paulette Henderson	Nanette Sargent
	Judith Lockser
Gladys Pendleton	Virginia Payne
	Patricia Dunlap
	Helen Lewis
Rufus	Forrest Lewis

Announcer: Jack Brinkley, Dick Wells, Marvin Miller, Dan Donaldson.
Orchestra: Doc Whipple.
Sponsor: Oxydol.
Program Opening:
Announcer: Now everybody ready for Oxydol's own Ma Perkins, America's mother of the air. Brought to you by Procter and Gamble, makers of Oxydol.
Length: 15 minutes.
Network: NBC (later CBS).
First Broadcast: 1933 (December 4, 1933 to November 25, 1960). Originally aired over a local Cincinnati station, August — December, 1933.

Mad Masters

Type: Variety
Hosts: Monty Masters, Natalie Masters.
Regulars: Helen Kleeb, Henry Leff, Paul Waltre.

Orchestra: Tony Freeman.
Length: 30 minutes.
Network: NBC.
First Broadcast: 1947.

Magic Rhythm

Type: Musical Variety
Hostess: Betty Dorsey.
Vocalists: The Debonaires.
Announcer: Jack Block.
Length: 30 minutes.
Network: Mutual.
First Broadcast: 1948.

The Magnificent Montague

Type: Comedy
Format: The story of Edwin Montague, a once brilliant but now washed-up Shakespearean actor, reduced to hosting an insipid children's radio program.
Cast: Edwin Montague   Monty Woolley
Lily Montague,
   his wife   Anne Seymour
Agnes, their
   housekeeper   Pert Kelton
Length: 30 minutes.
Network: NBC.
First Broadcast: 1950.

The Mahalia Jackson Show

Type: Variety
Hostess: Mahalia Jackson.
Announcer: Hal Stark.
Music: The Jack Halloran Quartet.
Length: 25 minutes.
Network: CBS.
First Broadcast: 1954.

Main Street Music Hall

Type: Musical Variety
Host: Earl Wrightston, Russ Emery.
Vocalist: Nancy Evans.
Orchestra: Alfredo Antonini.

Length: 15 minutes.
Network: CBS.
First Broadcast: 1949.

Maisie

Type: Comedy
Format: The misadventures of Maisie Revere, the Good Samaritan secretary to Mr. Dorsey, a wealthy lawyer.
Cast: Maisie Revere   Ann Sothern
   Mr. Dorsey   John Brown
   Mike, Maisie's
      boyfriend   Wally Maher
Also: Elliott Lewis, Lurene Tuttle.
Announcer: Ken Niles.
Orchestra: Harry Zimmerman.
Sponsor: Eversharp.
Length: 30 minutes.
Network: CBS (1945-1947), Mutual (1947-1948), Syndicated (1949).
First Broadcast: 1945. The revised 1949 syndicated version found Maisie (Ann Sothern) as a smart aleck shop girl who always managed to "gum up the works" for herself and fellow employees by talking back to rich customers.

Major Bowes and His Original Amateur Hour

Type: Variety
Format: Performances by undiscovered talent. The series served as the basis for "The Ted Mack and the Original Amateur Hour" television series.
Host: Major Edward Bowes, Jay C. Flippin, Ted Mack.
Announcer: Graham McNamee, Jimmy Wallington, Norman Brokenshire, Ralph Edwards, Dan Seymour, Tony Marvin, Warren Sweeney, Don Hancock, Roy Greece.
Music: Lloyd Marx.
Sponsor: Chase and Sanborn Coffee.
Length: 30 and 60 minute versions.
Network: NBC (1934), CBS (1936), ABC (1948).
First Broadcast: 1934.

Major Bowes and His Original Amateur Hour. Major Bowes.

Major Bowes' Shower of Stars

Type: Variety
Format: Performances by undiscovered talent.
Host: Major Edward Bowes.
Regulars: Regina Resnick, Larry Elliott.
Orchestra: Morton Gould.
Length: 30 minutes.
Network: CBS.
First Broadcast: 1945.

Major Hoople

Type: Comedy
Format: The series focused on Major Amos Hoople, an overstuffed philosopher, and his wife Martha. Based on the comic strip "Our Boarding House" by Gene Ahern.
Cast: Major Amos
        Hoople   Arthur Q. Bryan
        Martha Hoople   Patsy Moran
        Alvin Hoople,
        Amos' nephew   Franklin Breese
        Tiffany Twiggs,
        the Hoople's
        boarder   Mel Blanc

Orchestra: Lou Bring, Walter Green.
Length: 30 minutes.
Network: Blue.
First Broadcast: 1942.

Major North, Army Intelligence

Type: Drama
Format: The exploits of Major Hugh North, a U.S. Army Intelligence agent. The series detailed his battle against Nazi-facist plottings against international security. Also known as "The Man from G-2."
Cast: Major Hugh
        North   Staats Cotsworth
        His girlfriend   Joan Alexander
Orchestra: Bernard Green.
Length: 30 minutes.
Network: Blue.
First Broadcast: 1945.

The Malcolm LaProde Show

Type: Variety
Host: Malcolm LaProde.
Organist: Lew White.
Length: 15 minutes.
Network: NBC.
First Broadcast: 1924.

Make Believe Town

Type: Anthology
Format: Dramatizations set against the background of Hollywood.
Hostess: Virginia Bruce.
Announcer: Johnny Jacobs.
Length: 30 minutes.
Network: CBS.
First Broadcast: 1949.

Make Mine Music

Type: Musical Variety
Hosts: Connie Russell, Billy Leach.
Orchestra: Caesar Petrillo.

Length: 30 minutes.
Network: CBS.
First Broadcast: 1948.

Man About Hollywood

Type: Variety
Format: Music, talk, interviews.
Host: George McCall.
Regulars: Maxine Beach, Sara Berner, Steve White, Linda Ware, Willie Desmond.
Orchestra: Wilbur Hatch.
Length: 30 minutes.
Network: CBS.
First Broadcast: 1939.

Man Against Crime

Type: Crime Drama
Format: The cases of Mike Barnett, an unarmed private detective working out of New York City. Became the basis for a television series of the same title.
Starring: Ralph Bellamy as Mike Barnett.
Length: 30 minutes.
Network: CBS.
First Broadcast: 1947.

The Man Behind the Gun

Type: Anthology
Format: Dramatizations of actual events that occurred in the U.S. Armed Forces. Varying casts.
Announcer-Narrator: Jackson Beck.
Music: Nathan Van Cleve.
Length: 30 minutes.
Network: CBS.
First Broadcast: 1943.

The Man Called X

Type: Adventure
Format: The exploits of Ken Thurston, an American Intelligence Agent who opera-

ted under the code name X. Became the basis for a television series of the same title.

Cast: Ken Thurston — Herbert Marshall
His girlfriend — Gee Gee Pearson
Pagan, his sidekick — Leon Belasco
Announcer: Wendell Niles.
Music: Felix Mills, Johnny Greene.
Length: 30 minutes.
Network: ABC (1944), NBC (1945).
First Broadcast: 1944.

The Man from G-2

See title: "Major North, Army Intelligence."

The Man from Homicide

Type: Crime Drama
Format: The exploits of Lou Dana, a hardboiled homicide detective.
Starring: Dan Duryea as Lt. Lou Dana.
Music: Basil Adlam.
Length: 30 minutes.
Network: ABC.
First Broadcast: 1950.

The Man I Married

Type: Serial
Format: The dramatic story of the Warings, Adam and Evelyn, a happily married couple.

Cast: Evelyn Waring — Vicki Vola
Gertrude Warner
Lesley Woods
Betty Winkler
Barbara Lee
Adam Waring — Van Heflin
Bud Collyer
Matt — Ethel Owen
Phineas Grant — Santos Ortega
Ella Hunt — Frances Carden
Shelly — Spencer Bentley
Ted Hunt — Jack Grimes
Frank — Arnold Moss

Florence   Betty Worth
Ed Spaulding   Raymond Edward
                  Johnson
Announcer: Del Sharbutt, Howard Petrie.
Length: 15 minutes.
Network: NBC (1939), CBS (1941).
First Broadcast: 1939.

A Man Called Jordan

See title: "Rocky Jordan."

The Man of Magic

Type: Variety
Format: Demonstrations on the art of mind reading.
Host: Felix Greenfield (a mind reader).
Assistant: Wendy Barrie.
Sponsor: Eichler's Beer.
Length: 30 minutes.
Network: Mutual.
First Broadcast: 1944.

Mandrake the Magician

Type: Adventure
Format: During the 12th Century, wizards carried on the secrets of ancient Egypt and the magic of ancient China. Sweeping the Western world, the hordes of Genghis Khan destroyed the wizards and their lore. The few who managed to survive established the College of Magic in a Tibetan Valley wherein the lore was preserved. Once a decade one youth was chosen and taught the ancient secrets.
The 20th Century: Brought to the college by his father, a former graduate who had only a few months to live, Mandrake was taught the ancient secrets by Theron, the Master of Magic.
Ten Years later Mandrake became greater than his master and, upon his release from the college, teamed with his servant Lothar. Stories depicted their battle against evil. Based on the comic strip char-

acters created by Lee Falk and Phil Davis. Became the basis for a television series of the same title.
Cast: Mandrake   Raymond Edward
                         Johnson
       Lothar   Juano Hernandez
       Narda   Francesca Lenni
Length: 15 minutes.
Network: Mutual.
First Broadcast: 1940.

Manhattan Merry-Go-Round

Type: Variety
Format: Presented music from imaginary night clubs in New York.
Singers: Dennis Ryan, Rachel Carlay, Glenn Cross, Conrad Thibault, Lucy Marlowe, The Jerry Mann Singers, The Men About Town.
Announcer: Ford Bond, Roger Krupp.
Orchestra: Victor Arden, Andy Sanella.
Program Opening:
Announcer: Here's the Manhattan Merry-Go-Round that brings you the bright side of life, that whirls you in the music to all the big night spots of New York town to hear the top songs of the week sung so clearly that you can understand every word and sing them yourself.
Length: 30 minutes.
Network: NBC.
First Broadcast: Early 1930s.

Manhattan Mother

Type: Serial
Format: The dramatic story of Patricia and Tony Locke, a middle-aged married couple.
Cast: Patricia Locke   Margaret Hillias
       Tony Locke   Dan Sutter
       Their daughter   Louise Fitch
       Her husband   Ken Griffin
Program Opening:
Announcer: Cities are made of steel and stone, but human hearts are of a different stuff. We give you Manhattan Mother.

Length: 15 minutes.
Network: CBS.
First Broadcast: 1939.

Manhunt

Type: Crime Drama
Format: The exploits of two detectives
and their battle against crime.
Cast: Detective   Maurice Tarplin
       Detective   Larry Haines
Length: 15 minutes.
Syndicated.
First Broadcast: 1945.

The March of Games

Type: Quiz
Format: Five children competed in an edu-
cational series of question and answer
rounds, in return for cash prizes.
Host: Anthony Ross.
Assistant: Sybil Trent.
Length: 30 minutes.
Network: CBS.
First Broadcast: 1939.

The March of Time

Type: Documentary
Format: Dramatizations of the people and
events that have shaped America and the
world.
Narrator: Ted Husing, Harry Von Zell,
Westbrook Van Voorhis.
Music: Howard Barlow, Mark Warnow,
Donald Voorhees.
Sponsor: Time Magazine.
Length: 30 minutes.
Network: CBS.
First Broadcast: 1931 (ended in 1945). Also
known as "The March of Time Through
the Years."

The Mario Lanza Show

Type: Variety
Host: Mario Lanza

Vocalist: Giselle MacKenzie.
Announcer: Bill Baldwin.
Orchestra: Ray Sinatra.
Length: 30 minutes.
Network: NBC.
First Broadcast: 1951.

Mark Trail

Type: Adventure
Format: The story of Mark Trail, a forest
ranger, as he battled to protect Nature
from the evils of man. Based on the comic
strip by Ed Dodd, the program stressed
the importance of protecting forests and
wild life.
Cast: Mark Trail   Matt Crowley
                           John Larkin
                           Staats Cotsworth

       Scotty, his part-
          ner   Ben Cooper
                           Ronald Liss

       Cherry, his girl-
          friend   Joyce Gordon
                           Amy Sidell
Announcer: Jackson Beck, Glenn Riggs.
Orchestra: John Gart.
Mark's St. Bernard dog: Andy.
Sponsor: Kellogg's cereals.
Program Opening:
Announcer: For more punch 'till lunch it's
Kellogg's Corn Flakes, and for more
thrilling adventures in the great outdoors
it's Mark Trail. Battling the raging ele-
ments, fighting the savage wilderness,
striking at the enemies of man and na-
ture, one man's name resounds from
snow-capped mountains down across the
sun-baked plains—Mark Trail—guardian
of the forests, protector of wildlife, champion of man and nature—Mark Trail.
Length: 30 and 15 minute versions.
Network: Mutual (1950), ABC (1951).
First Broadcast: 1950.

The Mark Warnow Show

Type: Musical Variety
Host: Mark Warnow.

Regulars: Lanny Ross, The Raymond Scott Quintet.
Announcer: Andre Baruch.
Commercial Spokesman (for Lucky Strike cigarettes): Speed Riggs.
Orchestra: Mark Warnow.
Length: 45 minutes.
Network: CBS.
First Broadcast: 1939.

The Marriage

Type: Comedy-Drama
Format: The life of the close-knit Marriott family: Ben, an attorney, his wife Liz, and their children Emily and Peter. Became the basis for a short-lived television series of the same title.
Cast:
Ben Marriott	Hume Cronyn
Liz Marriott	Jessica Tandy
Emily Marriott	Susan Strasberg
Peter Marriott	Malcolm Brodrick

Length: 30 minutes.
Network: NBC.
First Broadcast: 1953.

Marriage Club, Inc.

Type: Interview-Quiz
Format: Married couples discussed their domestic problems in return for merchandise prizes.
Host: Haven MacQuarrie.
Announcer: Nelson Case.
Length: 30 minutes.
Network: NBC (1939), CBS (1940).
First Broadcast: 1939.

Marriage for Two

Type: Serial
Format: The story of a romantic but wise girl's marriage to an affectionate but irresponsible young man.
Cast:
Vikki, the girl	Fran Lefferty
Roger, the boy	Staats Cotsworth
Vikki's mother	Evelyn Varden

Also: Marion Barney, Gertrude Warner.
Announcer: John Tillman.

Organist: Fred Feibel.
Length: 15 minutes.
Network: CBS.
First Broadcast: 1948.

Married for Life

Type: Human Interest
Format: Couples who were about to wed were interviewed. A short dramatization followed, relating how the couple met and fell in love. Following this, the couple was again interviewed, along with friends and relatives.
Host: Bill Slater.
Cast: Bryna Raeburn, Eleanor Shernon, Johnny Sylvester, Lawson Zerbe.
Announcer: Don Fredericks.
Length: 30 minutes.
Network: Mutual.
First Broadcast: 1946.

The Martin and Lewis Show

Type: Variety
Hosts: Dean Martin and Jerry Lewis.
Regulars: Florence MacMichael, The Skylarks.
Announcer: Jimmy Wallington, Johnny Jacobs.
Orchestra: Dick Stabile.
Length: 30 minutes.
Network: NBC.
First Broadcast: 1949.

Martin Kane, Private Eye

Type: Crime Drama
Format: The cases of Martin Kane, a private detective working out of New York City. Became the basis of a television series of the same title.
Cast:
Martin Kane	William Gargan
	Lloyd Nolan
Happy McMartin, his aide	Walter Kinsella
Sgt. Ross	Nicholas Saunders
The Police Captain	Frank M. Thomas

Announcer: Fred Uttal.
Length: 30 minutes.
Network: Mutual (1949), NBC (1951).
First Broadcast: 1949.

Marvin Miller, Storyteller

Type: Anthology
Format: Capsule dramatizations of famous
people who faced a crisis in their lives.
Host-Narrator-All Voices: Marvin Miller.
Length: 5 minutes.
Syndicated (1948), CBS (1958).
First Broadcast: 1948.

Mary and Bob's True Stories

Type: Anthology
Cast: Mary   Nora Stirling
                    Elizabeth Wragge
      Bob   William Brenton
                    Cecil Secrest
                    David Ross
                    Eddie Wragge
Announcer: Ted Husing, Paul Douglas.
Music: Howard Barlow.
Length: 30 minutes.
Network: CBS (1928), NBC Blue (1938).
First Broadcast: 1928.

The Mary Mercer Show

Type: Variety
Hostess: Mary Mercer.
Length: 5 minutes.
Network: CBS.
First Broadcast: 1943.

Matinee at Meadowbrook

Type: Musical Variety
Host: John Tillman.
Regulars: Jackson Wheeler, Helen Lewis,
Kay Little, Jerry Wayne, Frank Dailey,
Art Carney, Teddy Norman, Bernie
Gould, Chris Adams.

Orchestra: Bobby Byrne, Ray McKinley.
Length: 60 minutes.
Network: CBS.
First Broadcast: 1941.

Matinee in Rhythm

Type: Musical Variety
Hostess: Ruth Norcross.
Regulars: Vera Holly, Tiny Schwartz, The
Men of Note.
Announcer: Ed Reimers.
Orchestra: Bob Armstrong.
Length: 15 minutes.
Network: NBC.
First Broadcast: 1939.

Matinee with Bob and Ray

See title "Bob and Ray."

Maudie's Diary

Type: Comedy
Format: Events in the life of Maudie Mason, a fun-loving teenage girl. (The series
title was derived from the events Maudie
recorded in her diary.)
Cast: Maudie Mason   Mary Mason
                        Charita Bauer
                        Carol Smith
      Mr. Mason, her
        father   William John-
                          stone
      Mrs. Mason, her
        mother   Betty Garde
      Sylvia Mason, her
        sister   Marjorie Davis
      Davie Dillon, her
        romantic in-
          terest   Robert Walker
      Pauley, her friend Carol Smith
Announcer: W. Arthur Millet.
Orchestra: Elliott Jacoby.
Length: 30 minutes.
Network: CBS.
First Broadcast: 1941.

Mary and Bob's True Stories. Elizabeth and Eddie Wragge.

The Maxwell House Showboat

Type: Variety

Format One:

Format: Based on the famous Broadway and movie musical, "Showboat," the series, set on a "showboat traveling down river," featured performances by top variety stars.

Original Host (portraying Captain Barney): Charles Winniger. Frank McIntire replaced Winniger for a brief period.

Later Host: Lanny Ross, Jack Haley.

Cast: Aunt Marie, Barney's sister   Irene Hubbard
         Mammy   Hattie McDaniel

Vocalists: Annette Hanshaw, Lanny Ross, Virginia Verrill, Conrad Thibault, Mary Lou (Muriel Wilson).

Comics: Molasses 'n' January (later to become Pick and Pat).

Frequent Guest Star: Jessica Dragonette.

Announcer: Tiny Ruffner.

Orchestra: Al Goodman, Donald Voorhees, Gus Haenschen.

Sponsor: Maxwell House Coffee.

Length: 60 minutes.

Network: NBC.

First Broadcast: 1932 (ended in 1938).

Format Two:

Format: Same as Format One.

Host: Carlton Brickert as Captain Barnet Barnett.

Regulars: Marlin Hurt (as Beulah), Dick Todd, Virginia Verrill, Louise Massey and Her Westerners.

Sponsor: Maxwell House Coffee.

Length: 30 minutes.

Network: NBC Blue.

First Broadcast: 1940.

Mayor of the Town. Lionel Barrymore and Agnes
Moorehead.

Mayor of the Town

Type: Comedy
Format: The home and working life of the
mayor of the small town of Springdale.
Became the basis for a television series of
the same title.
Cast: The Mayor   Lionel Barrymore
Marilly, his house-
keeper   Agnes Moorehead
Butch, his
nephew   Conrad Binyon
Announcer: Frank Martin, Carlton Ka-
Dell
Orchestra: Bernard Katz, Frank Worth.
Length: 30 minutes.
Network: NBC (1942), ABC (1947).
First Broadcast: 1942.

Me and Janie

Type: Comedy

Format: The misadventures of a not-too-
bright, henpecked husband, his chatter-
ing changeable wife, and their precocious
son.
Cast: Janie, the wife   Lurene Tuttle
Her husband   George O'Hanlon
Their son   Jeffrey Silver
The boss   Willard
Waterman
Also: Hope Emerson, Marvin Miller.
Announcer: Ann Wilson.
Organist: Johnny Duffy.
Length: 30 minutes.
Network: NBC.
First Broadcast: 1949.

Meet Corliss Archer

Type: Comedy
Format: The activities of Corliss Archer, a
pretty, unpredictable teenage girl. Be-

came the basis for a television series of the same title.

Cast: Corliss Archer   Janet Waldo
                               Priscilla Lyon
                               Lugene Sanders
        Harry Archer, her
          father, a lawyer Fred Shields
                               Bob Bailey
        Janet Archer,
          her mother   Irene Tedrow
                               Helen Mack
        Dexter Franklin,
          her boyfriend   Sam Edwards
                               David Hughes
                               Irwin Lee
Also: Mary Jane Croft, Ken Christy.
Announcer: John Heistand, Del Sharbutt, Ken Carpenter, Jack Hartz.
Orchestra: Charles "Bud" Dant, Wilbur Hatch, Felix Mills.
Program Opening:
Announcer: And now, transcribed from Hollywood, we invite you to meet Corliss Archer, America's teenage sweetheart, featuring Sam Edwards, Fred Shields, Mary Jane Croft, and starring Janet Waldo.
Length: 30 minutes.
Network: CBS (1943), ABC (1950), CBS (1954).
First Broadcast: 1943.

Meet Me at Parky's

Type: Comedy-Variety
Format: Set against the background of a beanery, the series related the advice and witticisms of its owner, Nick Parkyakarkas, and the customers who frequented it.
Cast: Nick Parkyakar-
          kas   Harry Einstein
        The cashier   Joan Barton
Vocalists: Peggy Lee, Jane Rhodes, Dave Street, The Short Order Chorus, Patty Bolton, Betty Jane Rhodes.
Announcer: Art Gilmore.
Orchestra: Opie Cates.
Length: 30 minutes.
Network: NBC.
First Broadcast: 1945.

Meet Me in St. Louis

Type: Comedy
Format: A story of middle class domestic life in St. Louis. Based on the *New Yorker* magazine stories by Russell Beggs.
Cast: Esther Smith, the
          tomboyish girl   Peggy Ann
                               Garner
        Her sister   Brook Byron
        Glenn Smith, her
          father   Vinton Hayworth
        Anne Smith, her
          mother   Agnes Young
Also: Billy Redfield, Raymond Edward Johnson, Ethel Wilson, Jack Edwards.
Orchestra: Vladimir Selinsky.
Length: 30 minutes.
Network: NBC.
First Broadcast: 1950.

Meet Millie

Type: Comedy
Format: The trials and tribulations of Millie Bronson, a secretary who is secretly in love with her employer's son, Johnny Boone. Stories depicted her mother's attempts to spark a romance between the two. Became the basis for a television series of the same title with Elena Verdugo in the title role.
Cast: Millie Bronson   Audrey Totter
        Her mother   Florence Halop
        Johnny Boone   Bill Tracy
        J.R. Boone, Sr.,
          Johnny's
          father   Earle Ross
Announcer: Bob Lemond.
Orchestra: Irving Miller.
Length: 30 minutes.
Network: CBS.
First Broadcast: 1951 (ended in 1954).

Meet Miss Julia

Type: Drama
Format: The story of Miss Julia, a seventy-years-young, all-wise, motherly house-

keeper at a boarding house on Gramercy Park in New York City.

Starring: Josephine Holl as Miss Julia.
Length: 15 minutes.
Network: Mutual.
First Broadcast: 1940.

Meet Mr. McNutley

Type: Comedy
Format: Based on the television series of the same title, the program followed the misadventures of Ray McNutley, a professor of English at the all-girl Lynhaven College.
Cast: Prof. Ray
   McNutley Ray Milland
  Peggy McNutley,
   his wife Phyllis Avery
  Pete Thompson,
   their friend Gordon Jones
  Ruth Thompson,
   Pete's wife Jacqueline deWit
Also (various roles):   Joseph Kearns, Ken Christy, Mel Blanc, Joan Banks.
Announcer: Del Sharbutt.
Sponsor: General Electric.
Length: 30 minutes.
Network: CBS.
First Broadcast: 1953 (ended in 1954).

Meet Mr. Meek

Type: Comedy
Format: The troubles of Mortimer Meek, the bumbling head of a household. Also known as "The Adventures of Mr. Meek," "The Life of Mortimer Meek," and "Meet the Meeks."
Cast: Mortimer Meek Wilbur Budd
        Hulick
        Forrest Lewis
        Frank Readick
  Agatha Meek,
   his wife Adelaide Klein
        Fran Allison
  Peggy Meek,
   their daughter Doris Dudley
        Elmira Roessler

Louie, the brother-
  in-law Jack Smart
Mortimer's crony Ian McAllister
The maid (early
  episodes) Agnes Moorehead

The maid (later
  episodes) Ann Thomas
Announcer: Dan Seymour.
Length: 30 minutes.
Network: CBS.
First Broadcast: 1940.

Meet the Dixons

Type: Drama
Format: The trials and tribulations of Wesley Dixon, a newspaperman, and his wife Joan, as they struggled to survive on a scanty income.
Cast: Wesley Dixon Richard Widmark
  Joan Dixon Barbara Weeks
  Wesley's
   employer Charles Dingle
Length: 15 minutes.
Network: CBS.
First Broadcast: 1939.

Meet Your Lucky Partners

Type: Quiz
Format: A studio audience player was teamed with a home listener by telephone. Each correct response to a question, to a maximum of three, gained each player a prize.
Host: Paul Brenner.
Length: 30 minutes.
Network: Mutual.
First Broadcast: 1948.

Meet Your Match

Type: Quiz
Format: Two contestants chosen from the studio audience competed. The winner of a question and answer session received

money and the opportunity to select another player from the audience as his opponent. The one player who remained until a bell sounded the end of the competition was the overall winner and received a chance to earn additional money by answering the jackpot question, related by a masked character called the Baron. Became the basis for a very short-lived television series of the same title.
Hosts: Tom Moore, Jan Murray.
Length: 30 minutes.
Network: Mutual.
First Broadcast: 1949.

The Mel Blanc Show

Type: Comedy
Format: The series focused on the mishaps of Mel Blanc, the owner-operator of a "we can fix anything shop."
Cast: Mel Blanc   Himself
          Betty Colby, his
             girlfriend   Mary Jane Croft
          Betty's father   Joseph Kearns
          Betty's mother   Bea Benaderet
Also: Victor Miller, Hans Conried, Jim Backus, Earle Ross.
Orchestra: Bud Helstand.
Length: 25 minutes.
Network: CBS.
First Broadcast: 1946. Also known as "Mel Blanc's Fix-It-Shop."

The Mel Torme Show

Type: Musical Variety
Host: Mel Torme.
Announcer: John Reed King.
Music: The Walter Gross Quintet.
Length: 15 minutes.
Network: NBC.
First Broadcast: 1947.

Melachrino Musicale

Type: Musical Variety
Host: George Melachrino.

Announcer: Veryle Mills.
Orchestra: George Melachrino.
Length: 15 minutes.
Syndicated.
First Broadcast: 1954.

Melody and Madness

Type: Musical Variety
Host: Robert Benchley.
Vocalists: Dick Todd, Helen Forrest.
Orchestra: Artie Shaw.
Sponsor: Old Gold cigarettes.
Length: 30 minutes.
Network: CBS.
First Broadcast: 1939.

Melody Highway

Type: Musical Variety
Narrator: Milton Cross.
Regulars: Stuart Foster, Earl Wild.
Orchestra: Bernard Green.
Length: 30 minutes.
Network: ABC.
First Broadcast: 1952.

Melody Lane with Jerry Wayne

Type: Musical Variety
Host: Jerry Wayne
Regulars: Patti Clayton, Peter Donald.
Announcer: Peter Donald.
Orchestra: Jeff Alexander.
Length: 30 minutes.
Network: Mutual.
First Broadcast: 1945.

Melody Ranch

See title: "Gene Autry's Melody Ranch."

Melody Roundup

Type: Country-Western Musical Variety
Host: Andy Devine.

The Mercury Theatre on the Air. Here, Orson Welles (upper left with arms raised) directs the single most famous radio broadcast—"The War of the Worlds" (October 30, 1938), a drama about Mars invading Earth that seemed so real it caused a nationwide panic.

Regulars: Henry Russell, Sonny Spencer, Jim Doyle, Bob Nolan and the Sons of the Pioneers, The Range Singers.
Orchestra: Perry Botkin.
Length: 30 minutes.
Network and Date of First Broadcast unknown.

The Mercury Theatre on the Air

Type: Anthology
Format: Dramatic presentations.
Host: Orson Welles.
Featured: John Houseman.
Included:
The Hitchhiker. The story of a man whose cross-country motor trip suddenly turns to terror when he discovers he's being mysteriously followed by a hitchhiker — a man who is always one step ahead of him.

This 1946 story, often repeated in response to listeners' requests, also appeared as an episode of TV's "The Twilight Zone" in 1960. Strangely, a woman (played by Inger Stevens) was chosen to be the victim.
Starring: Orson Welles.
The Apple Tree. The story focused on a lonely man as he recalled his lost love.
Starring: Orson Welles, Agnes Moorehead.
Count Dracula. An Englishman's recounting of the terrifying Dracula legend.
Starring: Orson Welles.
Sherlock Holmes. An adaptation of Sir Arthur Conan Doyle's characters. The story pitted wit against wit as Holmes and Moriarity sought a set of valuable letters held by a beautiful woman.
Starring: Orson Welles (as Sherlock Holmes), Ray Collins (Dr. Watson).

Program Opening:

Announcer: The Columbia Network takes pride in presenting Orson Welles in The Mercury Theatre on the Air, dramatizing famous narratives by guest authors.

Length: 60 minutes.

Network: CBS.

First Broadcast: 1938. Also titled "The Mercury Summer Theatre," "Campbell Playhouse" (when under the sponsorship of the Campbell Soup Company), and "The Mercury Wonder Show" (during the 1940s, when Welles took the show on tour to contribute to the war effort).

The Meredith Wilson—John Nesbitt Show

Type: Variety

Format: Music, coupled with stories from John Nesbitt's "Passing Parade." The 1942 summer replacement for "Fibber McGee and Molly."

Host: John Nesbitt.

Orchestra: Meredith Wilson.

Length: 30 minutes.

Network: NBC.

First Broadcast: 1942.

The Merry Life of Mary Christmas

Type: Comedy

Format: Hectic events in the life of Mary Christmas, a Hollywood gossip columnist.

Cast: Mary Christmas   Mary Astor
        Her husband   Paul Marlon

Also: Frank Martin, Howard Dinsdale, Jerry Epstein.

Length: 25 minutes.

Network: CBS.

First Broadcast: 1945.

The Meyer Davis Orchestra

Type: Variety

Host: Larry Higgin.

Announcer: Larry Higgin.

Orchestra: Meyer Davis.

Length: 30 minutes.

Network: Mutual.

First Broadcast: 1954.

The M-G-M Theatre of the Air

Type: Anthology

Format: Radio adaptations of M-G-M film scripts.

Host: Howard Dietz.

Music: Joel Herron.

Length: 60 minutes.

Network: Mutual.

First Broadcast: 1952.

Michael and Kitty

Type: Comedy-Mystery

Format: The investigations of an amateur detective and his wife.

Cast: Michael   John Gibson
        Kitty   Elizabeth Reller

Length: 25 minutes.

Network: NBC.

First Broadcast: 1941.

Michael Shayne, Private Detective

See title: "The Adventures of Michael Shayne."

Midstream

Type: Serial

Format: The dramatic story of Julia and Charles Meredith, a middle-aged couple seeking a life of their own after devoting most of their lives to their children, now raising families of their own.

Cast: Julia Meredith   Betty Lou Gerson
                            Fern Parsons
        Charles Meredith   Hugh Studebaker
                            Russell Thorson
        Midge Meredith,
          their daughter-
          in-law   Mercedes Mc-
                            Cambridge
                            Sharon Grainger

Midstream. Betty Lou Gerson.

David Meredith,
  Midge's hus-
  band   Willard Farnum
Ruth Andrews   Connie Osgood
                   Annette Harper
Amy Bartlett   Josephine Gilbert
Meredith Conway   Lesley Woods
Sandy   Bob Jellison
Announcer: Gene Baker.
Length: 15 minutes.
Network: NBC.
First Broadcast: 1939.

The Mildred Bailey Revue

Type: Musical Variety
Hostess: Mildred Bailey.
Regulars: Red Norvo, Teddy Wilson.
Orchestra: Paul Baron.
Length: 30 minutes.
Network: CBS.
First Broadcast: 1944.

Mike Mallory

Type: Crime Drama
Format: The investigations of private detective Mike Mallory.
Starring: Steve Brodie as Mike Mallory.

Length: 30 minutes.
Network: ABC.
First Broadcast: 1953.

The Milt Herth Trio

Type: Musical Variety
Starring: King Johnson, Marty Jacoby, Ed Cooper.
Music: The Milt Herth Trio.
Length: 15 minutes.
Syndicated.
First Broadcast: 1946.

The Milton Berle Show

Type: Variety
Host: Milton Berle.
Regulars: Mary Shipp, Charles Irving, Roland Winters, Jack Gilford, Arnold Stang, Jackson Beck, Bert Gordon, Eileen Barton.
Announcer: Frank Gallop.
Orchestra: Ray Bloch.
Sponsor: Quaker Oats.
Length: 30 minutes.
Network: NBC.
First Broadcast: 1939.

The Mindy Carson Show

Type: Musical Variety
Hostess: Mindy Carson.
Announcer: Don Pardo.
Orchestra: Norman Cloutier, Russ Case.
Length: 15 minutes.
Network: CBS.
First Broadcast: 1949.

Mirth and Madness

Type: Variety
Starring: Jack Kirkwood, Herb Sheldon, Don Reid, Jean McKean, Lillian Lee, Tom Harris, Billy Grey.
Orchestra: Irving Miller, Jerry Jerome.
Length: 30 minutes.
Network: NBC.
First Broadcast: 1943.

Miss Hattie

Type: Serial
Format: The story of the Thompsons, a typical American family.
Cast: Hattie Thompson   Ethel Barrymore
    Hattie's husband   Eric Dressler
    Their son   Dick Van Patten
    Their daughter   Lois Wilson
Also: Warren Parker, John Gibson, Andree Wallace.
Announcer: Roland Winters.
Orchestra: Doc Whipple.
Length: 30 minutes.
Network: Blue.
First Broadcast: 1944.

Miss Meade's Children

Type: Serial
Format: The story of three motherless children who are sent to live with their aunt in Buffalo, New York.
Cast: Miss Meade   Margaret Ryan
    The children   Joan Barrett
             Lemond Scherer
             Arlene Brock
Orchestra: Dave Cheskin.
Length: 15 minutes.
Network: Mutual.
First Broadcast: 1942.

Miss Pinkerton, Inc.

Type: Drama
Format: A young lady attempts to run a detective agency she inherited from her uncle.
Starring: Joan Blondell as the young lady.
Also: Dick Powell, Gale Gordon, Hanley Stafford.
Length: 30 minutes.
Network: NBC.
First Broadcast: 1941.

Miss Switch the Witch

Type: Children's Comedy
Format: The misadventures of a bumbling witch.

Starring: Miriam Wolfe (as Miss Switch the Witch).
Length: 15 minutes.
Syndicated.
First Broadcast: Late 1950s.

Modern Romances

Type: Anthology
Format: Dramatizations of stories appearing in *Modern Romances* magazine.
Hostess-Narrator: Gertrude Warner, Kathi Norris, Eloise McElhone.
Announcer: Bob Sabin.
Organist: George Henniger.
Length: 30 and 15 minute versions.
Network: Blue (1936), ABC (1949).
First Broadcast: 1936.

The Mohawk Treasure Chest

Type: Musical Variety
Host: Ralph Kirberry.
Orchestra: Harold Levy.
Sponsor: Mohawk carpets.
Length: 15 minutes.
Network: NBC Red and Blue.
First Broadcast: 1934.

Molle Mystery Theatre

See title: "Mystery Theatre."

Mommie and the Men

Type: Serial
Format: The story of a woman and the four men in her life: her husband and her three children.
Cast: The mother   Elspeth Eric
    Her husband   Lon Clark
    Their children   Charles Muller
             Jackie Grimes
             Dolores Gillen
Also: Sid Ward, Richard Keith.
Announcer: Ron Rawson.
Music: Dick Liebert.
Length: 15 minutes.

Network: CBS (broadcast over 17 Eastern stations while "The Jack Kirkwood Show" aired elsewhere).
First Broadcast: 1945.

Monday Merry-Go-Round

Type: Musical Variety
Host: Phil Duay.
Regulars: Bea Wain, Evelyn McGregor, Alan Holt, Marion McManus, The Myer Rapport Chorus.
Announcer: Ford Bond.
Orchestra: Victor Arden.
Length: 15 minutes.
Network: NBC.
First Broadcast: 1941.

Money-Go-Round

Type: Quiz
Format: Called for studio audience members to answer questions based on vocal clues. Cash prizes were awarded for each correct response.
Host: Benay Venuta, Fred Uttal.
Vocalists: Larry and Ginger Duo.
Length: 30 minutes.
Network: Blue.
First Broadcast: 1944.

Moon Dreams

Type: Variety
Host-Narrator: Marvin Miller.
Vocalist: Warren White.
Orchestra: Del Castillo.
Length: 15 minutes.
Syndicated.
First Broadcast: 1946.

The Morton Downey Show

Type: Musical Variety
Host: Morton Downey.
Chorus: Carmen Mastren.
Announcer: Joe King.

Orchestra: Eddy Duchin, Carmen Mastren.
Length: 30 and 15 minute versions.
Network: NBC (1939), Mutual (1947).
First Broadcast: 1939.

Mother and Dad

Type: Variety
Format: Comedy dialogue, quotations, poems, and songs delivered by an elderly couple to friends who visited their home.
Cast: Mother   Effie Palmer
         Dad   Parker Fennelly
Organist: Tiny Renier.
Length: 15 minutes.
Network: CBS.
First Broadcast: 1947.

Mother Knows Best

Type: Variety
Format: Songs, quizzes, and games slanted to women.
Host: Warren Hull.
Assistant: Isabelle Beach.
Announcer: Ralph Paul.
Length: 30 minutes.
Network: Broadcast in the western United States over the Columbia Pacific Network (CBS). In the East, it aired only on WCBS, New York.
First Broadcast: Late 1940s.

Mother of Mine

Type: Serial
Format: Following the death of her husband, who left her in serious debt, a woman regretfully sold her home and moved in with her married son, the owner of a farm. The series focused on the struggles of the middle-aged woman, and the trials and tribulations of the young marrieds.
Cast: Mother Morrison Agnes Young
        John Morrison,
          her son   Donald Cook

Helen Morrison,
John's wife   Ruth Yorke
Anne Morrison,
John and Hel-
en's daughter   Patte Chapman
Pete Morrison,
their son   Jackie Kelk
Also: Betty Jane Tyler, Arthur Allen, Paul Nugent.
Announcer: Charles Stark
Length: 15 minutes.
Network: Blue.
First Broadcast: 1940.

Motor City Melody

Type: Musical Variety
Host: Cyril Wezemael.
Vocalists: The Don Large Choir.
Announcer: Bill McCullough, Orrin Kelly.
Orchestra: Samuel Benavie.
Length: 30 minutes.
Network: CBS.
First Broadcast: 1940.

Mouquin Inc., Presents . . .

Type: Musical Variety
Host: Louis F. Mouquin.
Orchestra: The Mouquin Salon Orchestra.
Length: 15 minutes.
First Broadcast: Early 1930s.

Movietown Radio Theatre

Type: Anthology
Format: Dramatic presentations.
Included:
Schizo-Schizo. The story of a reporter who attempts to interview a psychiatrist and is mistaken for—and treated like—a mental patient.
Starring: Jeanne Cagney.
Mulligan the Mighty. Set in the time of the American Revolution, the story followed the exploits of a diminutive tailor who risked his life to smuggle vital secrets to George Washington.

Starring: Jimmy Gleason.
To Love Again. A strange love story: night after night a woman dreams of a man whose every trait and feature she can visualize. As the dream becomes more and more clear, she meets the man of her dreams—a man who tells her that he has dreamed of her for years also.
Starring: Virginia Bruce.
Length: 30 minutes.
Syndicated.
First Broadcast: 1949.

The Moylan Sisters Show

Type: Musical Variety
Hostesses: Marianne and Peggy Joan Moylan.
Announcer: Don Lowe.
Piano Music: The Moylan Sisters, Morry Howard.
Length: 15 minutes.
Network: NBC.
First Broadcast: 1939.

Mr. Ace and Jane

See title: "Easy Aces."

Mr. Adams and Mrs. Eve

Type: Quiz
Format: Two teams of four, male vs. female, competed in a question and answer session wherein the highest scoring team received $50; the runner-ups won $25.
Host: Frank Crumit.
Hostess: Julia Sanderson.
Length: 30 minutes.
Network: CBS.
First Broadcast: 1942.

Mr. Aladdin

Type: Drama
Format: The story of Mr. Aladdin, a man

hired to solve crimes on the basis of his a-
bility to perform miracles.
Starring: Paul Frees as Mr. Aladdin.
Orchestra: Marlen Skiles.
Length: 30 minutes.
Network: CBS.
First Broadcast: 1951.

Mr. and Mrs. Blandings

Type: Comedy
Format: The trials and tribulations of Jim
and Muriel Blandings, a sophisticated city
couple who decided to move to the
country for some peace and quiet. Their
attempts to adjust to a much simpler way
of life were the focal point of the series.
Cast: Jim Blandings   Cary Grant
        Muriel Blandings   Betsy Drake
        The lawyer   Gale Gordon
Length: 30 minutes.
Network: NBC.
First Broadcast: 1951.

Mr. and Mrs. North

Type: Crime Drama
Format: The story of the Norths: Jerry,
a former private detective turned publisher, and his attractive, level-headed
wife Pamela, who accidentally stumbled
upon and involved Jerry in crimes. Based
on the characters created by Richard and
Frances Lockridge. Became the basis for
the television series of the same title.
Cast: Jerry North   Joseph Curtin
                            Richard Denning
        Pamela North   Alice Frost
                            Barbara Britton
        Detective Bill
          Weingand   Staats Cotsworth
                            Frank Lovejoy
                            Francis De Sales
        Sergeant Mullins   Walter Kinsella
        Susan, the North's
          niece   Betty Jane Tyler
        Mahatma
          McGloin,
          the driver   Mandel Kramer

Announcer: Joseph King, Ron Rawson.
Music: Charles Paul
Length: 30 and 15 minute versions.
NBC (1942), CBS (1950).
First Broadcast: 1942. In 1950, the series
switched to a fifteen-minute weeknight
show (as opposed to its previous weekly
half-hour format) featuring the cast of the
television version (Richard Denning and
Barbara Britton). In 1949, the principals
of the radio version (Joseph Curtin and
Alice Frost) appeared in a short-lived television version of "Mr. and Mrs. North."

Mr. Broadway

Type: Drama
Format: A Broadway columnist with a
penchant for spinning yarns about the
Great White Way told his story to a
night-club chanteuse, who interrupted
the story four times for a song.
Cast: The Broadway
          Columnist   Anthony Ross
        The Night Club
          Singer   Irene Manning
Orchestra: Glenn Osser.
Length: 30 minutes.
Network: ABC.
First Broadcast: 1952.

Mr. Chameleon

Type: Crime Drama
Format: The exploits of Mr. Chameleon, a
master New York City police detective
who used ingenious disguises to fool evil-
doers and bring them to justice.
Cast: Mr. Chameleon   Karl Swenson
        Dave Arnold, his
          assistant   Frank Butler
        The Police Com-
          missioner   Richard Keith
Announcer: Howard Claney.
Orchestra: Victor Arden.
Length: 30 minutes.
Network: CBS.
First Broadcast: 1948.

Mr. District Attorney. Left to right: Len Doyle, Vicki Vola, and Jay Jostyn.

Mr. District Attorney

Type: Crime Drama

Format: Dramatizations based on the files of the District Attorney's office. Became the basis for a television series of the same title.

Cast: Paul Garrett,
the D.A.   Dwight Weist
                  Raymond Edward
                     Johnson
                  Jay Jostyn
                  David Brian

Edith Miller, his
   secretary   Vicki Vola
Harington, his
   investigator   Jay Jostyn
                  Walter Kinsella
Miss Rand   Eleanor Silver
                  Arlene Francis
Voice of the Law: Maurice Franklin, Jay

Jostyn, David Brian.

Announcer: Fred Uttal, Mark Hawley, Ed Herlihy.

Orchestra: Harry Salter, Peter Van Steeden.

Sponsor: Ipana and Sal Hepatica (Bristol-Myers products).

Program Opening:

Announcer: Mr. District Attorney, champion of the people, defender of truth, guardian of our fundamental rights to life, liberty, and the pursuit of happiness.

Mr. D.A.:   And it shall be my duty as District Attorney not only to prosecute to the limit of the law all persons accused of crimes perpetrated within this county but to defend with equal vigor the rights and privileges of all its citizens.

Length: 15, then 30 minutes.

Network: NBC.

First Broadcast: 1939.

Mr. Feather

Type: Comedy
Format: The misadventures of Mr. Feather, an elderly soda-jerker in a drug store who yearns to become a pharmacist. His antics, as he goes about dispensing his discovery, a cure-all salve, and free advice, were the show's highlights.
Cast: Mr. Feather   Parker Fennelly
            His employer   Don Ralph Locke
Also: Don Briggs, Bob Dryden, Elinor Phelps, Mert Caplin.
Announcer: Bob Emerick.
Orchestra: Bernard Ludlow.
Length: 30 minutes.
Network: Mutual.
First Broadcast: 1949.

Mr. Keen, Tracer of Lost Persons

Type: Mystery
Format: The story of a sure-footed sleuth who undertook cases involving the recovery of a missing person.
Cast: Mr. Keen   Bennett Kilpack
                                Philip Clarke
                                Arthur Hughes
            Mike Clancy, his
                sidekick   Jim Kelly
            Miss Ellis, his
                secretary   Florence Malone
Announcer: Larry Elliott, James Fleming.
Orchestra: Al Rickey.
Organist: John Winters.
Program Opening:
Announcer (over music):   Mr. Keen, Tracer of Lost Persons is based on the novel, *Mr. Keen*.
Length: 30, then 15, then 30 minutes.
Network: NBC Blue (1937), CBS (1947).
First Broadcast: 1937.

Mr. Mercury

Type: Adventure
Format: The story of Mr. Mercury, a circus acrobat who doubled as a secret investigator.
Starring: John Larkin as Mr. Mercury.

Music: John Gart.
Length: 30 minutes.
Network: ABC.
First Broadcast: 1951.

Mr. Moto

Type: Crime Drama
Format: The investigations of Mr. Moto, J.P. Marquand's Japanese detective.
Starring: James Monks as Mr. Moto.
Length: 30 minutes.
Network: NBC.
First Broadcast: 1951.

Mr. President

Type: Anthology
Format: Weekly dramatizations based on the lives of U.S. Presidents.
Starring: Edward Arnold as The President.
Length: 30 minutes.
Network: ABC.
First Broadcast: 1947.

Mrs. Eleanor Roosevelt

Type: Talk-Variety
Format: Informal conversation on topics of special interest to American women.
Hostess: Eleanor Roosevelt.
Vocalist: Lee Wiley.
Orchestra: Leo Reisman.
Length: 15 minutes.
Network: NBC.
First Broadcast: 1932.

Mrs. Miniver

Type: Serial
Format: The story, which began where the film and book ended, followed the Miniver family's move from war-torn England to America, where their struggles to begin a new life were dramatized.
Cast: Kay Miniver   Judith Evelyn
                                Gertrude Warner

Kay's husband	Karl Swenson
	John Moore
Their daughter	Betty Jane Tyler
Their son	Alister Kay
Carl Bixby, their	
friend	Carl Eastman
Carl's wife	Sara Burton

Narrator: Arnold Moss.
Orchestra: Nathan Van Cleave.
Length: 30 minutes.
Network: CBS.
First Broadcast: 1943.

Mrs. Wiggs of the Cabbage Patch

Type: Serial
Format: The struggles of the very poor
   Wiggs Family, who live in the Cabbage
   Patch, a polite term for a slum-like area
   outside a fashionable city or town of the
   early 1900s. Based on the novel by Alice
   Caldwell Rice.

Cast:	Mrs. Wiggs	Betty Garde
		Eva Condon
	Pa Wiggs	Robert Strauss
	Billy Wiggs, their	
	son	Andy Donnelly
	Miss Hazy, their	
	neighbor	Agnes Young
		Alice Frost
	Miss Lucy Red-	
	ding, the rich	
	girl who be-	
	friends the	
	Wiggs family	Marjorie Ander-
		son
	Mr. Bob, Lucy's	
	beau	Frank Provo
		Bill Johnstone

Announcer: George Ansbro.
Length: 15 minutes.
Network: CBS, then NBC.
First Broadcast: 1936.

Murder and Mr. Malone

Type: Crime Drama
Format: The cases of John J. Malone, a
   criminal lawyer practicing in Chicago. Became the basis for "The Amazing Mr. Malone" TV series.

Starring: Frank Lovejoy as John J.
   Malone.
Length: 30 minutes.
Network: ABC.
First Broadcast: 1946.

Murder at Midnight

Type: Anthology
Format: Spine-tingling dramatizations.
Host-Announcer: Raymond Morgan.
Music: Charles Paul.
Program Opening:
Announcer: Murder at Midnight! Mid-
   night, when the graves gape open and
   death strikes. How? You'll learn the ans-
   wers in just a moment in "The Man with
   the Black Beard."
Length: 30 minutes.
Syndicated (1946), Mutual (1950).
First Broadcast: 1946.

Murder by Experts

Type: Anthology
Format: Mystery presentations; tales of
   murder and mayhem.
Host-Narrator: John Dickson Carr.
Length: 30 minutes.
Network: Mutual.
First Broadcast: 1949.

Murder Clinic

Type: Anthology
Format: A series of mysteries featuring
   a different cast and story each week.
Length: 30 minutes.
Network: Mutual.
First Broadcast: 1942.

Murder Is My Hobby

Type: Crime Drama
Format: The cases of Barton Drake, a po-
   lice inspector.
Starring: Glenn Langan as Barton Drake.
Announcer: Rod O'Connor.

Length: 30 minutes.
Network: Mutual.
First Broadcast: 1945.

Music America Loves Best

Type: Musical Variety
Starring: Louise Calhern, Jan Peerce, Sigmund Romberg, Martha Stewart.
Orchestra: Jay Blackton.
Length: 30 minutes.
Network: NBC.
First Broadcast: 1944.

Music by Camarata

Type: Musical Variety
Host-Orchestra: Tutti Camarata.
Length: 30 minutes.
Network: ABC.
First Broadcast: 1954.

Music by Gershwin

Type: Musical Variety.
Host: George Gershwin.
Announcer: Don Wilson.
Sponsor: Feen-A-Mint.
Length: 15 minutes.
First Broadcast: 1934.

Music for Moderns

Type: Musical Variety
Host: Clarence Fuhrman.
Announcer: Gulliver (as identified on the program).
Orchestra: Clarence Fuhrman.
Length: 30 minutes.
Network: NBC.
First Broadcast: 1940.

Music for You

Type: Musical Variety
Host: Earl Nightingale.

Regulars: Billy Leach, Joe Rumoro, Elaine Rodgers.
Orchestra: Caesar Petrillo.
Length: 30 minutes.
Network: CBS.
First Broadcast: 1949.

Music in the Moonlight

Type: Musical Variety
Hostess: Jane Grant.
Regulars: Lionel Reiger, The Moonlighters.
Orchestra: Beasley Smith.
Length: 25 minutes.
Network: NBC.
First Broadcast: 1941.

The Music of Andre Kostelanetz

Type: Musical Variety
Host: Andre Kostelanetz.
Narrator: Alexander Scott.
Announcer: Larry Elliott.
Orchestra: Andre Kostelanetz.
Length: 30 minutes.
Network: CBS.
First Broadcast: 1945.

Music of Manhattan

Type: Musical Variety
Hostess: Louise Carlyle.
Announcer: William Young.
Orchestra: Norman Cloutier.
Length: 30 minutes.
Syndicated.
First Broadcast: 1945.

Music Tent

Type: Variety
Host: Dirk Fredericks.
Regulars: Joyce Krause, Barbara Buchanan, Clarence Day, Jr., Elaine Spaulding, Vincent Lopez, Robert K. Adams.
Announcer: Doug Browning.

Orchestra: Glenn Osser.
Length: 25 minutes.
Network: ABC.
First Broadcast: 1955.

Music That Satisfies

Type: Musical Variety
Hostess: Ruth Etting.
Regulars: Arthur Tracy, The Boswell Sisters.
Orchestra: Nat Shilkret.
Sponsor: Chesterfield cigarettes.
Length: 30 minutes.
Network: NBC.
First Broadcast: 1932.

Music with the Hormel Girls

Type: Musical Variety
Hostesses: Betty Dougherty, Elina Hart.
Announcer: Marilyn Wilson.
Orchestra-Chorus: The Hormel Girls.
Sponsor: Hormel food products.
Length: 30 minutes.
Network: CBS.
First Broadcast: 1950.

Musical Story Lady

Type: Children
Format: A Sunday morning show of musical stories for children.
Starring: Alice Remsen as the Musical Story Lady.
Length: 10 minutes.
Network: Blue.
First Broadcast: 1937 (ended in 1941).

Musical Millwheel

Type: Musical Variety
Host: Walter Patterson.
Announcer: Dan Donaldson.
Music: The Pillsbury Besters.
Sponsor: Pillsbury.
Length: 30 minutes.

Network: NBC.
First Broadcast: 1941.

Musical Mock Trial

Type: Musical Quiz
Format: Six players, chosen from the studio audience, were designated as jurors; musical tunes were the plaintiff and defendant. A mystery musical selection was followed by the judge's reading of a short story about it. The jurors then had to determine if the defendant (the mystery song) was guilty or innocent (whether or not the song related to the story). If the jurors found the song innocent they received one dollar; if they found the song guilty, and were correct, they won ten dollars to be split among them. No matter what the decision, jurors received three dollars per minute of jury duty.
Host-Judge: Ben Bernie.
Regulars: Dinah Shore, Lew Lehr, The Bailey sisters.
Announcer: Ernest Chappell.
Length: 30 minutes.
Network: CBS.
First Broadcast: 1940.

Musical Steelmakers

Type: Musical Variety
Host: John Winchell (as The Old Timer).
Regulars: Ardene White, Dorothy Anne Crowe, Regina Colbert, The Singing Millmen, The Steele Sisters, Lois MacNoble, The Evans Sisters, Earl Summers, Carolyn Lee.
Announcer: Thomas Whitley.
Music: The Steelmakers Orchestra, The Lew Davis Orchestra.
Length: 30 minutes.
Network: Mutual (1939), Blue (1943).
First Broadcast: 1939.

Musical Treasure Chest

Type: Quiz

Format: Selected studio audience members competed in a musically oriented question and answer session in return for cash prizes.
Host-Orchestra: Horace Heidt.
Length: 30 minutes.
Network: NBC.
First Broadcast: 1940.

Musicomedy

Type: Variety
Host: Johnny Desmond.
Regulars: Julie Conway, Kenny Bowen, Don Appell, The Escorts Quartet.
Announcer: Dan Seymour.
Orchestra: Raymond Paige.
Length: 30 minutes.
Network: CBS.
First Broadcast: 1948.

My Best Girls

Type: Comedy
Format: Events in the lives of the Bartlett family, a family of four who lived in the outskirts of Chicago.
Cast: Russell Bartlett,
          a widower   John Griggs
                             Roland Winters
        Linda Bartlett, his
          17-year-old
          daughter   Mary Shipp
        Penny Bartlett,
          his 14-year-old
          daughter   Mary Mason
        Jill Bartlett, his 9-
          year-old
          daughter   Lorna Lynn
Also: Ogden Miles.
Announcer: Dan Seymour.
Organist: Don Baker.
Length: 30 minutes.
Network: Blue.
First Broadcast: 1944.

My Children

Type: Serial

My Friend Irma. Marie Wilson.

Format: The dramatic story of the Gilman family.
Cast: Mr. Gilman   Sydney Rogers
        Mrs. Gilman   Mary Parker
        Their daughter   Grace Holtby
        Their daughter   Lelah McNair
        Mr. Singleton,
        Gilman's
        employer   Max West
Orchestra: Dick Aurandt.
Length: 15 minutes.
Syndicated.
First Broadcast: 1939.

My Favorite Husband

Type: Comedy
Format: The trials and tribulations of the Coopers: George, a bank executive, and his scatterbrained wife, Liz. Became the basis for a television series of the same title.
Cast: George Cooper   Lee Bowman
                           Richard Denning
        Liz Cooper   Lucille Ball
        Katie, their maid   Ruth Perrott
Also: Hal March, Veola Vonn, James Scott.

Orchestra: Wilbur Hatch.
Length: 30 minutes.
Network: CBS.
First Broadcast: 1948.

My Friend Irma

Type: Comedy
Format: The story of New York secretaries Irma Peterson, a beautiful but dumb blonde, and Jane Stacey, her roommate, a level-headed girl who was constantly plagued by Irma's scatter-brained antics. Focal point of the series was a depiction of their romantic heartaches: Irma and her boyfriend, the impoverished and jobless Al, and Jane and her multi-millionaire employer, Richard Rhinelander III, an investment counselor whom she struggled to impress and hoped one day to marry. Became the basis for the television series of the same title.

Cast: Irma Peterson   Marie Wilson
        Jane Stacey   Cathy Lewis
                             Joan Banks
        Richard Rhine-
          lander III   Leif Erickson
        Al   John Brown
        Mrs. O'Reilly, the
          owner of the
          boarding house   Gloria Gordon
        Professor Kropot-
          kin, the girl's
          friend, a viol-
          inist   Hans Conried
                             Benny Rubin
        Mr. Clyde,
          Irma's boss   Alan Reed
        Richard's mother   Myra Marsh
Announcer: Wendell Niles, Frank Bingman, Johnny Jacobs.
Vocalists: The Sportsmen Quartet.
Orchestra: Lud Gluskin.
Program Opening:
Announcer: The Columbia Broadcasting System presents a new comedy —
Jane: My Friend Irma —
Announcer: Starring Marie Wilson as Irma and Cathy Lewis as Jane with John Brown as Al.
Length: 30 minutes.

My Little Margie. Charles Farrell and Gale Storm.

Network: CBS.
First Broadcast: 1947.

My Good Wife

Type: Comedy
Format: Events in the life of a young married couple.
Cast: The wife   Arlene Francis
        The husband   John Conte
Length: 30 minutes.
Network: NBC.
First Broadcast: 1949.

My Little Margie

Type: Comedy
Format: The series centered on the lives of Vernon Albright, widower, the vice-president of an investment firm, and his beautiful, unpredictable twenty-one-year-old daughter, Margie. Became the basis for a television series of the same title.
Cast: Margie Albright   Gale Storm
        Vernon Albright   Charles Farrell

Freddie Wilson,
Margie's im-
poverished boy-
friend   Gil Stratton, Jr.
Roberta Town-
send, Vern's
girlfriend   Doris Singleton
George Honey-
well, Vern's
employer   Will Wright
Orchestra: Lud Gluskin.
Length: 30 minutes.
Network: CBS.
First Broadcast: 1952.

My Mother's Husband

Type: Comedy-Drama
Format: The series, set in St. Louis, Mis-
souri, at the turn of the century, revolved
around a rambunctious father, his tactful
wife, and their related family problems.
Cast: The father   William Powell
His wife   Sarah Selby
Their daughter   Sharon Douglas
Their son   Willie Barley
Their maid   Lillian Randolph
Their neighbors   Joseph Kearns
                        Verna Felton
Announcer: Jack McCoy.
Music: Jeff Alexander and His Mellowmen
Quintet.
Length: 30 minutes.
Network: NBC.
First Broadcast: 1950.

My Secret Story

Type: Anthology
Format: Dramatizations of stories that
stressed human emotion.
Hostess-Narrator: Anne Seymour.
Length: 30 minutes.
Network: NBC.
First Broadcast: 1951.

My Silent Partner

Type: Comedy

Format: The story of a small town girl
who established herself in business in
New York as a trouble consultant.
Cast: The girl   Faye Emerson
Her romantic in-
terest, a
lawyer   Lyle Sudrow
The janitor   Cameron
                        Andrews
The soda fountain
counterman   Harold Stone
The public sten-
ographer   Ruth Gilbert
Announcer: Dick Dudley.
Length: 30 minutes.
Network: NBC.
First Broadcast: 1949.

My Son and I

Type: Serial
Format: Following the death of her husband, Connie Watson, a vaudeville actress (stage name Connie Vance) lost a
court case to retain custody of her son,
Buddy, who was reared in the wings. The
court, feeling that theatre life was unsuit-
able for the child, assigned him to the cus-
tody of Addy Owens, Connie's husband's
aunt. The series focused on Connie's at-
tempts to appeal the decision and prove
to the court that she could provide a
decent life for Buddy.
Cast: Connie Watson   Betty Garde
Buddy Watson   Kingsley Colton
Addy Owens   Agnes Young
Kent Davis   Alan Hewitt
Also: Gladys Thornton.
Announcer: Andre Baruch.
Length: 15 minutes.
Network: CBS.
First Broadcast: 1939.

My Son Jeep

Type: Comedy
Format: The story of Doc Allison, a small-
town doctor, and his attempts to recon-
struct his life after the death of his wife.
Episodes focused on the antics of Jeep,

his mischievous ten-year-old son. Became the basis for a television series of the same title.

Cast:

Doc Allison	Donald Cook
	Paul McGrath
Jeep Allison	Martin Houston
	Bobby Alford
Peggy Allison, Jeep's sister	Joan Lazer
Barbara, Doc's receptionist	Lynne Allen
	Joyce Gordon
Mrs. Birby, Doc's housekeeper	Leona Powers

Also: Cameron Andrews.
Announcer: Fred Collins, Gaylord Avery.
Music: John Geller.
Length: 30 and 15 minute versions.
Network: CBS.
First Broadcast: 1954.

Myrt and Marge. Vinton Hayworth.

My True Story

Type: Anthology
Format: Dramatic adaptations of stories from *My True Story* magazine. Became the basis for a television series of the same title.
Announcer: Glenn Riggs.
Organist: Rosa Rio.
Length: 30 minutes.
Network: ABC.
First Broadcast: 1945.

Myrt and Marge

Type: Serial
Format: The dramatic story of Myrt Spear and Marge Minter, two show business girls, and the problems each faced in making a career for herself.

Cast:

Myrt Spear	Myrtle Vail
	Alice Yourman
Marge Minter	Donna Damerel Flick
	Helen Mack
	Alice Goodkin
Jack Arnold	Vinton Hayworth
Clarence Tiffing-tuffer	Ray Hedge
Lee Kirby	Santos Ortega
Pat Hargate	Jackson Beck
Billie	Eleanor Rella
Edna	Lucy Gilman
Jimmy Kent	Michael Fitz-maurice
Pop	Joe Latham
Paula Kirby	Lucille Fenton
Phyllis Rogers	Dorothy Day
Jimmy Minter	Ray Appleton
Maggie	Marie Nelson

Announcer: David Ross, Tom Shirley, Andre Baruch.
Organist: John Winters, Rosa Rio.
Program Opening:
Announcer: The story of Myrt and Marge. Myrt and Marge is a story of Broadway, a story that goes beyond the lights of the Great White Way into the lives of two chorus girls; two girls from the cast of that most glittering of all Broadway extravaganzas, "Hayfield's Pleasures." The house lights go down; the footlights go on. In a moment the curtain will go up on the first chapter in the story of Myrt and Marge.
Length: 15 minutes.
Network: CBS (1931-1945), Syndicated (1946).
First Broadcast: 1931.

The Mysterious Traveler

Type: Anthology
Format: Supernatural stories.
Starring: Maurice Tarplin as The Mysterious Traveler.
Announcer: Jimmy Wallington.
Music: Doc Whipple.
Program Opening:
Announcer (over train sounds and eerie music):
  Mutual presents The Mysterious Traveler.
Mysterious Traveler: This is The Mysterious Traveler inviting you to join me on another journey into the realm of the strange and terrifying. I hope that you will enjoy the trip, that it will thrill you a little and chill you a little. So settle back, get a grip on your nerves and be comfortable, if you can.
Length: 30 minutes.
Network: Mutual.
First Broadcast: 1943.

Mystery Chef

Type: Cooking
Host: John MacPherson (originally not identified, hence the title).
Length: 30 minutes.
Network: NBC.
First Broadcast: 1950.

Mystery File

Type: Game
Format: A criminal case was reenacted, then stopped prior to its conclusion. Players had to determine the culprit on the basis of clues presented in the case. Winners received a cash prize.
Host: Walter Kiernan.
Announcer: Charles Woods.
Length: 30 minutes.
Network: ABC.
First Broadcast: 1950.

Mystery House

Type: Anthology
Format: Varied mystery presentations enacted by a regular cast.
The Cast: Nanette Sargeant, Forrest Lewis.
Length: 30 minutes.
Syndicated.
First Broadcast: 1946.

Mystery in the Air

Type: Crime Drama
Format: The investigations of detective Stonewall Scott.
Cast: Stonewall Scott   Stephen Courtleigh

  Dr. Alison, his
    beautiful aide   Joan Vitey
Length: 30 minutes.
Network: NBC.
First Broadcast: 1945.

Mystery in the Air

Type: Anthology
Format: Mystery stories set in the 19th Century.
Host—Occasional Performer: Peter Lorre.
Included:
The Lodger. A retelling of the Jack-the-Ripper story; the true story of a mysterious killer of young women.
Starring: Peter Lorre, Agnes Moorehead.
Challenge to Listeners. An unusual story in which one of the two leads is murdered, but his identity is not revealed. The program challenged listeners to guess which one it was.
Starring: Richard Widmark, Everett Sloane.
The Horla. The eerie tale of a Frenchman haunted by an evil invisible spirit known as the Horla.
Starring: Peter Lorre.

The Black Cat. While intoxicated, a man sees the reincarnation of his pet cat, which he strangled long ago. In a fit of rage, he kills his wife, then finds his life haunted by both her spirit and the cat's.
Starring: Peter Lorre.
Length: 30 minutes.
Network: NBC.
First Broadcast: 1947.

Mystery Is My Hobby

Type: Crime Drama
Format: The story of Barton Drake, a mystery writer who worked with the police in an attempt to find material.
Cast: Barton Drake   Glenn Langan
        The Police In-
            spector   Norman Field
Length: 30 minutes.
Syndicated.
First Broadcast: 1949.

Mystery Theatre

Type: Crime Drama
Format One:
(Under title "Molle Mystery Theatre.") A weekly anthology of crime and detective stories.
Host: Bernard Lenrow.
Announcer: Dan Seymour.
Orchestra: Jack Miller.
Sponsor: Molle Shave Cream.
Length: 30 minutes.
Network: NBC.
First Broadcast: 1943.
Format Two:
(Under title "Inspector Hearthstone of the Death Squad.") The cases of Inspector Hearthstone of Scotland Yard's Death Squad.
Starring: Alfred   Shirley   as   Inspector Hearthstone.
Orchestra: Alexander Semander.
Length: 30 minutes.

Network: NBC.
First Broadcast: 1945.
Format Three:
(Under title "Inspector Mark Saber.") The cases of Mark Saber, a New York City police inspector. Became the basis for a television series of the same title.
Cast: Mark Saber   Les Damon
        His assistant   Walter Burke
Music: Jacques Press.
Length: 30 minutes.
Network: ABC.
First Broadcast: 1953.

Mystery Without Murder

Type: Crime Drama
Format: The investigations of Peter Gentle, a private detective who was opposed to violence.
Cast: Peter Gentle   Luther Adler
        His secretary   Terry Keane
Length: 30 minutes.
Network: NBC.
First Broadcast: 1947.

Name the Place

Type: Quiz
Format: Called for players to identify locales (cities, countries, or states) from brief descriptions read to them by the host.
Host: Ben Grauer.
Announcer: Charles O'Connor.
Length: 30 minutes.
Network: NBC.
First Broadcast: 1939.

Name That Movie

Host: Clark Dennis

Vocalists: Peggy Mann, The Starlighters.
Announcer: Marvin Miller.
Orchestra: Edward Gilbert.
Length: 30 minutes.
Network: Mutual.
First Broadcast: 1949.

Name That Tune

Type: Quiz
Format: Two contestants competed in a game designed to test musical knowledge. Brief musical selections were played, after which contestants had to identify their titles. Five such rounds were played, worth $5, $10, $30, $40, and $50. The winner received a chance to play the jackpot round and win $500 by identifying three mystery tunes. Became the basis for a television series of the same title.
Host: Red Benson.
Announcer: Wayne Howell.
Vocalist: June Valli.
Orchestra: Harry Salter.
Length: 30 minutes.
Network: NBC.
First Broadcast: 1952.

The National Lampoon Radio Hour

Type: Satire
Format: If it could be made fun of, it was. Outrageous spoofs of anything—radio, TV, films, music, people, countries, etc.
The Cast: Polly Beard, Chevy Chase, Christopher Guest, Janet Hirsch, Lou Holtzman, Paul Jacobs, Judy Chafman, Bruce McCall, Bob Perry, Bob Tishler, Shawn Kelly, Tony Shearin, John Wald, Andrew Duncan, Doug Kenny, Bob Michaelson, Emily Praeger, Vernon Taft, Sidney Taft, Sam Sawyer, Richard Belzer, Bob Dryden, Ed Zubinski.
Sponsor: The National Lampoon Magazine.
Program Opening (each episode had its own unique opening; the following represents one such opening—a spoof of TV's "The Outer Limits"):
Announcer (over tuning frequency noises):

There is nothing wrong with your radio; do not attempt to change the station. We are controlling the transmission. We control the volume. We can change the tone to a fuzzy bass, or focus it to a tinny treble. We can speed things up so fast that you can hardly understand what is being said; or we can make things so s-l-o-w y-o-u d-o-n-'t c-a-r-e. We control the content. We can make it boring...or hilarious...We can make it stupid...or moronic...It's our show, we can do anything we want...Because this is The National Lampoon Radio Hour.
Length: 30 minutes.
Syndicated.
First Broadcast: 1974.

NBC Radio Theatre

Type: Anthology
Format: Varying dramas that featured one of four stars.
Host: Lee Bowman.
Rotating Performers: Gloria DeHaven, Celeste Holm, Lee Bowman, Madeleine Carroll.
Length: 30 minutes.
Network: NBC.
First Broadcast: 1950s.

NBC Star Playhouse

Type: Anthology
Format: Dramatic presentations.
Host: John Chapman.
Length: 60 minutes.
Network: NBC.
First Broadcast: 1953.

The NBC Symphony Orchestra

Type: Music
Host-Announcer: Ben Grauer.
Music: The NBC Symphony Orchestra.
Conductor: Arturo Toscanini, Pierre Monteaux, Dr. Frank Black.
Length: 30 minutes.
Network: NBC.
First Broadcast: 1936.

The Nebbs

Type: Comedy
Format: Events in the lives of the Nebbs family. Based on the comic strip by Sol Hess.
Cast: The father   Gene Lockhart
His wife   Kathleen Lockhart
Junior, their son   Conrad Binyon
Also: Billy Roy, Dink Trout, Dick Ryan, Ruth Perrott.
Announcer: Tom Dixon.
Orchestra: Bud Carlton.
Length: 30 minutes.
Network: Mutual.
First Broadcast: 1945.

Ned Jordan, Secret Agent

Type: Adventure
Format: The exploits of Ned Jordan, a Federal agent who worked undercover on a railroad. Stories depicted his adventures as he attempted to prevent ill will between the U.S. and friendly nations.
Starring: Jack McCarthy as Ned Jordan.
Length: 30 minutes.
Network: Mutual.
First Broadcast: 1939. The series originally began as a local entry over station WX-YZ in Detroit, Michigan, in 1938.

The Nelson Eddy Show

Type: Musical Variety
Host: Nelson Eddy.
Orchestra-Chorus: Robert Armstrong.
Length: 30 minutes.
Network: CBS.
First Broadcast: 1942.

Nero Wolfe

Type: Mystery
Format: The exploits of Nero Wolfe, the fictional detective made famous by Rex Stout.
Cast: Nero Wolfe   Francis X. Bushman
Santos Ortega
Sydney Greenstreet
Archie, his assistant   Elliott Lewis
Wally Maher
Gerald Mohr
Announcer: Don Stanley.
Length: 30 minutes.
Network: ABC (1943), NBC (1950).
First Broadcast: 1943. Also titled (1950) "The New Adventures of Nero Wolfe."

The New Junior Junction

Type: Variety
Format: Music, songs, and quizzes for children.
Host: Jack Lester.
Regulars: Bill Snary, Peggy Murdock.
Orchestra: Bruce Case.
Length: 30 minutes.
Network: ABC.
First Broadcast: 1950.

News and Rhythm

Type: Music-Information
Host-Reporter: Todd Hunter.
Featured: Dave Bacal.
Announcer: Tommy Bartlett.
Orchestra: Carl Hohengarten.
Length: 30 minutes.
Network: CBS.
First Broadcast: 1939.

News Game

Type: Quiz
Format: Guest news experts answered questions against a ticking clock. Their cash prizes were awarded to a hospitalized G.I.
Host: Kenneth Banghart.
Length: 30 minutes.
Network: NBC.
First Broadcast: 1954.

Newsstand Theatre

Type: Anthology
Format: Dramatizations of stories from the Crowell-Collier Publishing Syndicate.
Length: 30 minutes.
Network: ABC.
First Broadcast: 1951.

Next, Dave Garroway

See title: "Dave Garroway."

Nick Carter, Master Detective

Crime Drama
Format: The exploits of private detective Nick Carter.
Cast: Nick Carter   Lon Clark
        Patsy Bowen,
          his secretary   Helen Choate
                             Charlotte Manson
        Sgt. "Matty"
          Mathison   Ed Latimer
        Scubby, the
          reporter   John Kane
Announcer: Michael Fitzmaurice.
Organist: Hank Sylvern.
Sponsor: Lin-X Home Brighteners.
Program Opening:
Sound effect: Knocks and bangs at a door.
Woman's Voice: What's the matter? What is it?
Man's Voice: Another case for Nick Carter, Master Detective!
Announcer: Yes, it's another case for that most famous of all manhunters ... the detective whose ability at solving crime is unequaled in the history of detective fiction, Nick Carter, Master Detective.
Length: 30 minutes.
Network: Mutual.
First Broadcast: 1943. Spin-off series: "Chick Carter, Boy Detective," which see.

Night Beat

Type: Drama
Format: The exploits of Randy Stone, a Chicago-based newspaper reporter who combed the streets at night seeking material.
Starring: Frank Lovejoy as Randy Stone.
Announcer: Donald Rickles.
Length: 30 minutes.
Network: NBC.
First Broadcast: 1950.

Night Editor

Type: Anthology
Format: Dramatizations of actual newspaper stories.
Newsman-Storyteller: Hal Burdick.
Sponsor: Edwards' Coffee.
Length: 15 minutes.
Network: Blue.
First Broadcast: 1943.

Night Life

Type: Musical Variety
Host: Willie Brandt.
Regulars: Maxine Sullivan, The Lamuel Morgan Trio, Pete Johnson.
Announcer: Bob Hite.
Orchestra: Teddy Wilson.
Length: 30 minutes.
Network: CBS.
First Broadcast: 1946.

Night Life

Type: Jazz Music
Host: Ken Nordine.
Featured: Bobby Gibson.
Music: The Fred Kaz Trio.
Length: 30 minutes.
Network: NBC.
First Broadcast: 1955.

Nitwit Court

Type: Comedy
Format: A problem was read by the bailiff (host) to a trio of jurors: Hornblower, a fumbling motor boatist; Bubbles Lowbridge, a less than intelligent woman; and

Willow, a lisping man, who provided comic responses. A take-off on "It Pays to Be Ignorant."
Host: Ransom Sherman.
Cast: Willow   Arthur Q. Bryan
     Hornblower   Mel Blanc
     Bubbles Low-
       bridge   Sara Berner
Vocalists: Jimmie Dodd, Johnny "Scat" Davis.
Orchestra: Jack Rose.
Length: 25 minutes.
Network: Blue.
First Broadcast: 1944.

No School Today

Type: Children's
Format: Music, songs, and sketches set against the background of the Pumpkin Crossing General Store.
Hosts: Arthur Fields, Fred Hall.
The Newsman (Jolly Bill): Bill Steinke.
Length: 30 minutes.
Network: CBS.
First Broadcast: 1938.

Noah Webster Says

Type: Quiz
Format: Selected member of the studio audience defined words in return for cash prizes (up to $50).
Host: Haven MacQuarrie.
Judge: Dr. Charles F. Lindsley.
Announcer: John Frazer.
Length: 30 minutes.
Network: NBC.
First Broadcast: 1943.

Nobody's Children

Type: Human Interest
Format: Dramatizations intended to make listeners aware of the plight of orphans. The orphans, who appeared with guest celebrities, were available for adoption.
Host-Narrator: Walter White, Jr.
The Matron: Georgia Fifield.

Announcer: Bill Kennedy.
Length: 30 minutes.
Network: Mutual.
First Broadcast: 1939.

Nona from Nowhere

Type: Serial
Format: The story, set against the background of Hollywood, followed the career of Nona Dutell, a twenty-three-year-old actress with one ambition—to find her real parents. (Adopted as a young girl, she felt she had no real past; hence the title).
Cast: Nona Dutell   Toni Darnay
     Vernon Dutell,
      her foster
      father   Karl Weber
     Patrick Brady,
      the producer   James Kelly
     Gwen Parker   Florence
          Robinson
     Thelma Powell   Mitzi Gould
Announcer: Ford Bond.
Length: 15 minutes.
Network: CBS.
First Broadcast: 1949.

The Norman Brokenshire Show

Type: Musical Variety
Host: Norman Brokenshire.
Regulars: Martha Lou Harp, Bob Huston.
Orchestra: Bernie Green.
Length: 30 minutes.
Network: ABC.
First Broadcast: 1950.

Official Detective

Type: Crime Drama
Format: The cases of Dan Britt, a detective lieutenant.
Cast: Dan Britt   Ed Begley
          Craig McDonnell
     The Police
      Sergeant   Louis Nye
Announcer: Jack Irish.

Orchestra: Sylvan Levin.
Program Opening:
Announcer: Official Detective, dedicated to the men who guard your safety and protect your home, your police department. Official Detective, presented by the Mutual Broadcasting System in cooperation with *Official Detective Stories* magazine and starring Craig McDonnell as Detective Lieutenant Dan Britt.
Length: 30 minutes.
Network: Mutual.
First Broadcast: 1946.

O'Hara

Type: Adventure
Format: The exploits of Bob O'Hara, a newspaper correspondent in the Far East.
Starring: Jack Moyles as Bob O'Hara.
Length: 25 minutes.
Network: CBS.
First Broadcast: 1956.

Oklahoma Roundup

Type: Country-Western Musical Variety
Host: Hiram Higsby.
Regulars: Dick Reinhart, Ann Bond, Mary Lou, Lem Hawkins.
Announcer: Alan Page.
Length: 30 minutes.
Network: CBS.
First Broadcast: 1946.

The Old Gold Show

Type: Comedy-Variety
Starring: Don Ameche and Frances Langford (as John and Blanche Bickerson), Frank Morgan, Marvin Miller.
Announcer: Marvin Miller.
Orchestra: Carmen Dragon.
Sponsor: Old Gold cigarettes.
Length: 30 minutes.
Network: CBS.
First Broadcast: 1947.

Olmsted and Company

Type: Variety
Host: Nelson Olmsted.
Announcer: Tom Scott.
Orchestra: Norman Cloutier.
Length: 30 minutes.
Network: NBC.
First Broadcast: 1948.

On a Sunday Afternoon

Type: Variety
Host: Byron Palmer.
Regulars: Joan Weldon, The Pied Pipers.
Orchestra: Wilbur Hatch.
Length: 30 minutes.
Network: CBS.
First Broadcast: 1955.

On Stage

Type: Anthology
Format: Comedy and drama presentations.
Hosts-Performers: Cathy Lewis, Elliott Lewis.
Included:
Public Furlough. The story of a serviceman's attempts to land a date with a glamorous movie star.
Starring: Cathy and Elliott Lewis.
The Strange Bow Tie. The hazards that result when George Hapsmith's picture appears on a cologne and women being swooning over him.
Starring: Cathy and Elliott Lewis, Sheldon Leonard.
Length: 30 minutes.
Network: CBS.
First Broadcast: 1953.

On Stage America

Type: Variety
Format: Performance by both professional and non-professional talent.
Host: Paul Whiteman.

On Stage. Cathy Lewis.

Orchestra: Paul Whiteman.
Length: 30 minutes.
Network: ABC.
First Broadcast: 1945.

On the Town

Type: Variety
Host: Eddie Mayehoff.
Orchestra: Tommy Dorsey.
Length: 15 minutes.
Network: Mutual.
First Broadcast: 1940.

One Foot in Heaven

Type: Serial
Format: The dramatic story of Reverend
  Spence and the problems faced by a small
  community during World War II.
Cast: The Reverend
  Spence   Philip Merivale
Also: Muriel Kirkland, Evelyn Varden,
  Doris Dalton, Peggy Allenby, Edwin
  Cooper, John McGovern, Raymond Ives,

Bobby Readick, Peter Fernandez.
Orchestra: Joseph Stopak.
Length: 30 minutes.
Network: Blue.
First Broadcast: 1945.

One Man's Family

Type: Serial
Format: The dramatic story of the Bar-
  bour family: Henry, a stockbroker, his
  wife Frances, and their children Paul,
  Hazel, Clifford and Claudia (twins), and
  Jack. Became the basis for a television
  series of the same title.
Cast: Henry Barbour   J. Anthony
                              Smythe
       Frances Barbour   Minetta Ellen
                          Mary Adams
       Claudia Barbour   Kathleen Wilson
                          Barbara Fuller
                          Laurette Fill-
                          brandt
       Paul Barbour   Michael Raffetto
                          Russell Thorson
       Hazel Barbour   Bernice Berwin
       Clifford Barbour   Barton Yar-
                          borough
       Jack Barbour   Page Gilman
Announcer: William Andrews, Ken Car-
  penter, Frank Barton.
Organist: Paul Carson, Sybil Chism, Mar-
  tha Green.
Sponsor: Miles Laboratories.
Program Opening:
Announcer: This is One Man's Family. One
  Man's Family is dedicated to the mothers
  and fathers of the younger generation
  and to their bewildering offspring. Today,
  transcribed, we present Chapter 12, Book
  72 entitled "A Touch of Christmas Spirit."
Length: 30 and 15 minute versions.
Network: NBC.
First Broadcast: 1932.

$1,000 Reward

Type: Quiz
Format: A whodunit drama was enacted

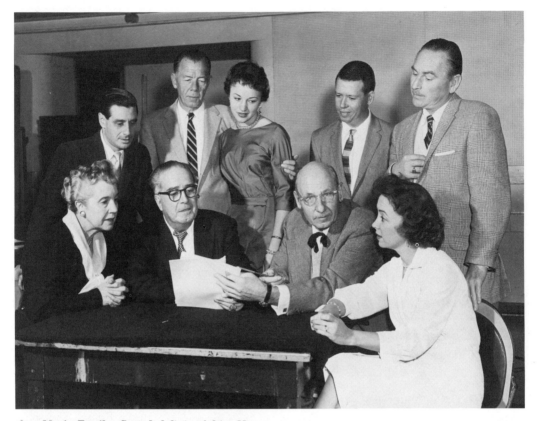

One Man's Family. Seated, left to right: Mary Adams, J. Anthony Smythe, Carlton E. Morse (the creator-writer), and Barbara Fuller. Standing, left to right: George Pirrone (Pinky), Russell Thorson (Paul Barbour), Anne Whitefield (Penny Lacey), Billy Idelson (William Murray), and Ben Wright (Nicholas Lacey).

and stopped prior to the denouncement. A telephone call was placed to a listener who could win $1,000 if he identified the killer.

Host: John Sylvester.

Dramatic Cast: Ralph Bell, Ethel Everett, Bill Smith, Ken Lynch.

Announcer: Ken Roberts.

Length: 30 minutes.

Network: NBC.

First Broadcast: 1950.

The O'Neills

Type: Serial

Format: The dramatic story of the O'Neill family. Became the basis for a television series of the same title.

Cast:

Mrs. O'Neill	Kate McComb
	Luise Barclay
Eddie O'Neill	Jimmy Donnelly
	Nick Dawson
Peggy O'Neill	Betty Caine
	Violet Dunn
	Claire Niesen
	Betty Garde
Janice O'Neill	Janice Gilbert
Danny O'Neill	James Tansey
Sally O'Neill	Helen Claire
	Betty Winkler

Announcer: Ed Herlihy, Craig McDonnell.

Organist: Herbert Little.

Length: 15 minutes.

Network: CBS (1934), NBC (1942).

First Broadcast: 1934.

Only Yesterday

Type: Variety
Format: The music and songs of the 1920's.
Starring: Benny Rubin, Mary Small.
Orchestra: Van Alexander.
Length: 30 minutes.
Network: CBS.
First Broadcast: 1943.

The Open Door

Type: Drama
Format: The story of Professor Erik Hansen, the dean of students at Vernon University. The program was actually a series of vignettes of the lives of the students who sought Hansen's comfort and advice.
Cast: Dean Erik
       Hansen   Dr. Alfred T. Dorf
       Corey Lehman,
       his secretary   Charlotte Holland
Length: 15 minutes.
Network: NBC.
First Broadcast: 1943.

Open House

Type: Musical Variety
Hostess: Helen Morgan.
Regulars: Frank Barton, Helen Kleeb, Charles Bernard, Sam Moore, Gladys Simpson, Monty Mohn.
Orchestra: Ruordo.
Length: 30 minutes.
Network: NBC.
First Broadcast: 1941.

The Opie Cates Show

Type: Comedy
Format: The misadventures of Opie Cates, a well-meaning but trouble-prone young man.
Cast: Opie Cates   Himself
       Cathy, his girl-
       friend   Noreen Gommill

Ma Buskirk, the
owner of a
boarding house
in Clinton,
Arkansas   Barbara Fuller
Pa Buskirk   Fred Howard
Music: Basil Adlam.
Length: 30 minutes.
Network: ABC.
First Broadcast: 1947.

Opry House Matinee

Type: Country-Western Musical Variety
Host: Eddy Arnold.
Regulars: Ernest Tubb, Lorue Buck, Jud Collins, Becky Barfield, Mack McGarr, Jack Baker, Owen Bradley and His Tennessians, The Short Brothers, The Old Hickory Singers, Rod Bradfield and His Sweetheart Susie, The Tennessee Playboys, The Troubadours.
Length: 60 minutes.
Network: Mutual.
First Broadcast: 1946.

The Original Amateur Hour

See title: "Major Bowes and the Original Amateur Hour."

Orson Welles' Almanac

Type: Variety
Host: Orson Welles.
Regulars: Groucho Marx, Agnes Moorehead, Arthur Q. Bryan, Martha Stewart, Ray Collins.
Orchestra: Lud Gluskin.
Length: 30 minutes.
Network: CBS (broadcast over Arizona and Los Angeles stations only).
First Broadcast: 1944.

Our Gal Sunday

Type: Serial

Orson Welles' Almanac. Orson Welles.

Format: Events in the life of an or-
phaned girl named Sunday—a small-
town Virginia girl who married a
wealthy English Lord in an attempt to
find happiness.

Cast: Sunday
    Brinthrope   Dorothy Lowell
                           Vivian Smolen

    Lord Henry
    Brinthrope,
      her husband   Karl Swenson
                           Alistair Duncan
    Elaine   Vicki Vola
    Barbara   Kay Brinker
    Jackie   Jay Jostyn
    Kathy   Ruth Russell
    Madelyn
      Travers   Joan Tompkins
    Slim Delaney   Van Heflin
    Rose Hunt   Florence
                           Robinson
    Charlotte   Elaine Kent
Announcer: James Fleming, Bert Parks,
   Charles Stark, John Reed King.
Length: 15 minutes.
Network: CBS.
First Broadcast: 1937.

Our Miss Brooks

Type: Comedy
Format: The trials and tribulations of
   Connie Brooks, English teacher at
   Madison High School. Stories depicted
   her romantic misadventures as she strug-
   gled to impress Philip Boynton, the
   Biology instructor. Became the basis for
   the television series of the same title.

Cast: Connie Brooks   Eve Arden
      Philip Boynton   Jeff Chandler
      Osgood Conklin,
        the principal   Joe Forte
                           Gale Gordon

      Walter Denton,
      the problem
      student   Richard Crenna
      Harriet Conklin,
      Osgood's
      daughter   Gloria McMillan
      Mrs. Davis,
      Connie's land-
      lady   Jane Morgan
      Stretch
      Snodgrass, a
      student   Leonard Smith
Announcer: Verne Smith, Bob Lemond.
Orchestra: Wilbur Hatch.
Sponsor: Colgate-Palmolive products.
Length: 30 minutes.
Network: CBS.
First Broadcast: 1948.

Our Secret World

Type: Serial
Format: The story focuses on the lives
   of Michael and Irene, two young marrieds
   separated by the outbreak of World War
   I. He is stationed with the AEF in
   England; she remains at home in
   America. At a fixed time each evening,
   Michael and Irene thought of each other.
   Through "soliloquies-by-telepathy" each
   relates daily happenings: Irene speaks
   first, assuring Michael of her love for him,
   of the sense of his presence, and of her
   sustained hope and faith that they will
   soon be together again. As Irene finishes

telling Michael about how her previously meaningless daily activities have suddenly taken on a new meaning, Michael speaks from England. He relates the bitterness of war, his thoughts of her, his loneliness, his anxiety, and his one desire — to return home to her. The series, with its sketchy backgrounds and characterizations, was designed to let the listener identify with its sentimental or romantic nature through personal daydreaming.

Cast: Michael   Milton Stanley
       Irene   Ann Starrett
Length: 30 minutes.
Network: Mutual.
First Broadcast: 1947.

Out of the Deep

Type: Drama
Format: Supposedly true adventures of famed sea captain Gunnar Carlyle, a deep-sea diver and sometime soldier of fortune.
Starring: Ted Maxwell as Gunnar H. Carlyle.
Announcer: Robert Campbell.
Organist: Joe Enos.
Length: 30 minutes.
Network: NBC.
First Broadcast: 1945.

Ozark Jubilee

Type: Country-Western Musical Variety
Host: Red Foley.
Featured: Grady Martin's Crossroads Gang.
Length: 25 minutes.
Network: ABC.
First Broadcast: 1954.

The Ozzie Nelson-Harriet Hilliard Show

See title: "The Adventures of Ozzie and Harriet."

Packham Inn

Type: Musical Variety
Host: Bill Packham.
Regulars: Ilene Woods, Fred Casper, The Four Vagabonds.
Orchestra: Rex Maupin.
Length: 30 minutes.
Network: NBC.
First Broadcast: 1946.

Paging the Judge

Type: Quiz
Format: Selected studio audience members were placed in prearranged situations that tested their ability to solve problems. Winners, determined by a panel of guest judges, received prizes.
Host: Robert Paige.
Length: 15 minutes.
Network: ABC.
First Broadcast: 1953.

Paging Mike McNally

Type: Comedy
Format: The misadventures of Mike McNally, a department store manager.
Starring: Walter Kinsella as Mike McNally.
Also: Joan Alexander, Hope Emerson, Alan Bunce.
Length: 30 minutes.
Network: Mutual.
First Broadcast: 1945.

Palmolive Beauty Box Theatre

Type: Anthology
Format: Musical adaptations of classic stories.
Hostess-Occasional Performer: Jessica Dragonette.
Regular Performer: Charles Kuhlman.
Sponsor: The Palmolive Soap Company.
Included:
The Chocolate Soldier. Oskar Straus'

operetta about a Serbian spy who seeks refuge in the enemy's house and falls in love with a beautiful young girl.

Starring: Jessica Dragonette, Charles Kuhlman.

The Vagabond King. The story of Francois Villon, the rogue poet of France.

Starring: Jessica Dragonette, Charles Kuhlman.

The Lady in Ermine. A beautiful girl captures the heart of a soldier heading the occupation forces in her country.

Starring: Jessica Dragonette, Thomas L. Thomas.

Length: 30 minutes.
Network: NBC.
First Broadcast: 1937.

Panorama Time

Type: Variety
Host: Johnny Desmond.
Music: Recorded.
Length: 25 minutes.
Network: Mutual.
First Broadcast: 1955.

The Parker Family

Type: Comedy
Format: Events in the lives of the Parkers, a not-so-typical American family.

Cast:		
Mr. Parker		Jay Jostyn
Mrs. Parker		Linda Carlon-Reid
		Marjorie Anderson
Nancy Parker, their daughter		Mitzi Gould
Richard Parker, their son		Leon Janney
		Michael O'Day
Elly Parker, their daughter		Patricia Ryan
Grandfather Parker		Roy Fant

Announcer: Hugh James.
Length: 15 minutes.
Network: CBS (1939), Blue (1943).
First Broadcast: 1939.

The Passing Parade

Type: Documentary
Format: Strange but true stories of unusual happenings.
Host-Narrator: John Nesbitt.
Announcer: Ken Carpenter, Harlow Wilcox.
Orchestra: Meredith Wilson, Carmen Dragon.
Program Opening:
Announcer: The Passing Parade. Your favorite stories as told by your favorite storyteller, John Nesbitt.
Program Closing:
Announcer: You have been listening to your favorite stories as told by America's favorite storyteller, John Nesbitt. Be with us the next time we move to the reviewing stand for yet another glimpse of The Passing Parade.
Length: 15 minutes.
Network: CBS.
First Broadcast: 1944.

Passport for Adams

Type: Drama
Format: The story of Jeff Adams, a small town editor from Centerville, and Perry "Quiz" Quisinberry, a New York photographer, as they visit and report on the principal allies of the U.S. during World War II for the Consolidated Syndicate.

Cast:	
Jeff Adams (later Doug Adams)	Robert Young
	Myron McCormick
Perry Quisinberry	Dane Clark
	Paul Mann

Length: 30 minutes.
Syndicated.
First Broadcast: 1943.

Passport to Romance

Type: Comedy
Format: The story of two singing stewards aboard the S.S. Harmonia.

Cast: The girl   Mitzi Green
      The boy   Larry Brooks
Length: 30 minutes.
Network: Mutual.
First Broadcast: 1946.

Pat Novak for Hire

Type: Crime Drama
Format: The story of Pat Novak, a tough-guy private detective who is independent of everyone and everything.
Cast: Pat Novak   Jack Webb
      The Police
        Sergeant   Raymond Burr
                      John Galbraith
Announcer: George Fenneman.
Length: 30 minutes.
Network: ABC.
First Broadcast: 1949.

The Patti Clayton Show

Type: Musical Variety
Hostess: Patti Clayton.
Announcer: Bill Cullen.
Orchestra: Archie Bleyer.
Length: 15 minutes.
Network: CBS.
First Broadcast: 1945.

The Paul Whiteman Hour

Type: Musical Variety
Host: Paul Whiteman.
Regulars: Eugene Baird, Johnny Thompson, The Joe Mooney Quartet, Duffy's Swinging Strings Choir.
Orchestra: Paul Whiteman.
Length: 60 minutes.
Network: ABC.
First Broadcast: 1946.

Paul Whiteman Presents

Type: Variety
Format: Performances by undiscovered professional talent.

The Paul Whiteman Hour. Paul Whiteman.

Host: Glenn Osser.
Regulars: Dinah Shore, The Modernaires.
Orchestra: Paul Whiteman.
Length: 30 minutes.
Network: NBC (1943), ABC (1950). Later titled "Paul Whiteman's Teen Club."

The Paul Winchell-Jerry Mahoney Show

Type: Comedy-Variety
Format: Music, songs, and comedy sketches that revolved around Jerry Mahoney, the mischievous wooden dummy of ventriloquist Paul Winchell.
Host: Paul Winchell (and Jerry Mahoney).
Vocalist: Vera Barton.
Orchestra: Bob Stanley.
Program Opening:
Announcer: Yes, it's The Paul Winchell-Jerry Mahoney Show featuring that lovely young singing star Vera Barton and Bob Stanley and his orchestra. And here's that talented young ventriloquist Paul Winchell and his little wooden dummy friend Jerry Mahoney.
Length: 30 minutes.
Network: Mutual.
First Broadcast: 1944.

The Paula Stone-Phil Brito Show

Type: Variety
Hosts: Paula Stone, Phil Brito.
Announcer: Tom Shirley.
Orchestra: Doc Whipple.
Length: 15 minutes.
Network: NBC.
First Broadcast: 1944.

The Pause That Refreshes

Type: Musical Variety
Host: Roger Pryor.
Vocalist: Ginny Simms.
Orchestra: Percy Faith.
Sponsor: Coca-Cola.
Length: 30 minutes.
Network: CBS.
First Broadcast: 1947.

Payroll Party

Type: Game
Format: Housewives, selected from the studio audience, competed in various humiliating stunts.
Host: Nicholas Girrard.
Length: 25 minutes.
Network: ABC.
First Broadcast: 1952.

The Peabodys

Type: Comedy
Format: The story of Harvey Peabody, a not-so-bright businessman, his wife Helen, and their daughter Harriet, and the problems that befall the family due to Harvey's antics.
Cast:
Harvey Peabody, the father	Norman Gottschalk
Helen Peabody, his wife	Fran Allison
Harriet Peabody, their daughter	Joan Alt
The sister-in-law	Elmira Roessler

Announcer: Bob Cunningham.

Organist: Dave Bacall.
Length: 15 minutes.
Syndicated.
First Broadcast: 1946.

The Peg LaCentra Show

Type: Musical Variety
Hostess: Peg LaCentra.
Music: John Gart; The Jesters.
Length: 15 minutes.
Network: NBC.
First Broadcast: 1938.

The Peggy Lee Show

Type: Musical Variety
Hostess: Peggy Lee.
Announcer: Bill Adams.
Orchestra: Russ Case.
Length: 30 minutes.
Network: CBS.
First Broadcast: 1951.

The Penny Singleton Show

Type: Comedy-Drama
Format: The story of Penny Williamson, a war widow and the mother of two children, Sue and Dorothy, and her struggles to provide a decent life for herself and family while working as a real estate salesperson in the town of Middletown.
Cast:
Penny Williamson	Penny Singleton
Sue Williamson	Sheila James
Dorothy "D.G." Williamson	Marylee Robb
Margaret, Penny's cook	Bea Benaderet
Horace Wiggins, Penny's partner	Jim Backus
Judge Beshomer Grundell	Gale Gordon

Announcer: Frank Martin.
Orchestra: Von Urbanski.
Length: 30 minutes.
Network: NBC.
First Broadcast: 1950.

Penthouse Blues

Type: Musical Variety
Hostess: Judith Arlen.
Length: 15 minutes.
Network: CBS.
First Broadcast: 1939.

People Are Funny

Type: Audience Participation
Format: Put selected studio audience members into screwball situations designed to test their willingness to make fools of themselves in return for money. Became the basis for a television series of the same title.
Host: Art Baker, Art Linkletter.
Announcer: Rod O'Connor, Ted Myers, Herb Allen.
Length: 30 minutes.
Network: NBC.
First Broadcast: 1942.

Pepper Young's Family

Type: Serial
Format: The story of the Young family, in particular Larry, nicknamed "Pepper," an oil field worker in the town of Elmwood.
Cast: Larry "Pepper"
Young   Curtis Arnall
                  Lawson Zerbe
                  Mason Adams
                  Peter Fernandez
Sam Young   Jack Roseleigh
                  Bill Adams
                  Thomas Chalmers
                  Bill Johnstone
Peggy Young   Elizabeth Wragge
Mary Young   Marion Barney
Linda Young   Eunice Howard
Sally Young   Maureen McManus
Hattie, the maid   Greta Kvalden
Announcer: Alan Kent, Martin Block, Richard Stark.
Music: William Meader.

Sponsor: Camay Soap.
Program Opening:
Announcer: Pepper Young's Family. The story of your friends the Youngs is brought to you by Camay, the mild beauty soap for a smoother, softer complexion. . .
Length: 15 minutes.
Network: NBC Blue (1936), Syndicated (1965).
First Broadcast: 1936.

The Percy Faith Orchestra

Type: Musical Variety
Host-Orchestra: Percy Faith.
Length: 30 minutes.
Network: Mutual.
First Broadcast: 1939.

The Perry Como Show

Type: Musical Variety
Host: Perry Como.
Vocalists: The Three Sisters.
Orchestra: Paul Baron.
Length: 15 minutes.
Network: CBS.
First Broadcast: 1944.

Perry Mason

Type: Crime Drama
Format: The cases of Perry Mason, a criminal attorney. Based on the character created by Erle Stanley Gardner. Became the basis for a television series of the same title.
Cast: Perry Mason   Bartlett Robinson
                       Santos Ortega
                       Donald Briggs
                       John Larkin
Della Street, his
   secretary   Gertrude Warner
                       Jan Miner
                       Joan Alexander
Paul Drake, his
   investigator   Matt Crowley

Lt. Arthur Tragg,
       L.A.P.D.   Mandel Kramer
                        Frank Dane
    Sgt. Dorsett   Arthur Vinton
Announcer: Alan Kent, Richard Stark, Bob Dixon.
Organist: William Meader.
Musical Director: Paul Taubman.
Length: 15 minutes.
Network: CBS.
First Broadcast: 1943.

The Pet Milk Show

Type: Musical Variety
Host: Jack Pearl.
Regulars: Mimi Benzell, Cliff Hall, Russ Emery.
Announcer: Ed Herlihy.
Orchestra: Gus Haenschen.
Sponsor: Pet Milk.
Length: 30 minutes.
Network: NBC.
First Broadcast: 1951.

Pete Kelly's Blues

Type: Drama
Format: The story of Pete Kelly, a tough jazz musician and leader of the Big Seven, a jazz band, during the Roaring 20s. Became the basis for a feature film, then a television series.
Cast: Pete Kelly   Jack Webb
      Maggi Jackson,
        the vocalist   Meredith Howard
The Big Seven Band members: Matty Matlock, Elmer Schneider, Ray Schneider, Bill Newman, Marty Carb, Nick Fatool.
Also: Peggy Webber, William Conrad, Vic Perrin, Whitfield Connor, Herb Butterfield, Jack Kruschen.
Musical Background: Dick Cathcart.
Length: 30 minutes.
Network: NBC.
First Broadcast: 1951.

The Peter Lind Hayes Show

Type: Variety
Host: Peter Lind Hayes.
Regulars: Mary Healy, Jerry Vale, Leslie Uggams, Harry Snow, The Toppers.
Announcer: George Bryan, Jack Haskell.
Music: The Norman Leyden Orchestra, The Norman Paris Trio.
Length: 25 minutes.
Network: CBS.
First Broadcast: 1954.

Peter Quill

Type: Mystery
Format: The exploits of Peter Quill, a detective who used scientific knowledge to apprehend evildoers.
Cast: Peter Quill   Marvin Miller
      Gail Carson, his
        aide   Alice Hill
      Police Capt.
        Roger Dorn   Ken Griffin
Length: 30 minutes.
Network: Mutual.
First Broadcast: 1940.

The Phil Baker Show

Type: Comedy-Variety
Host: Phil Baker.
Regulars: Harry McNaughton, Ward Wilson, The Andrews Sisters, The Seven G's.
Announcer: Harry Von Zell.
Orchestra: Eddie deLange, Frank Shields, Hal Kemp.
Length: 30 minutes.
Network: CBS.
First Broadcast: 1933.

The Phil Harris-Alice Faye Show

Type: Comedy-Variety
Format: Music and songs coupled with comedy sketches revolving around the

The Phil Baker Show. Phil Baker.

hectic lives of Phil Harris and his wife
Alice Faye.

Cast: Phil Harris   Himself
       Alice Faye Harris Herself
       Little Alice Har-
           ris, their daugh-
           ter   Jeanine Roos
       Phyllis Harris,
           their daughter Anne Whitfield
       Mr. Scott, Phil's
           sponsor's rep-
           resentative   Gale Gordon
       Julius, the deliv-
           ery boy   Walter Tetley
       Frankie Remley,
           Phil's friend   Elliott Lewis
Also: John Hubbard.
Announcer: Bill Forman.
Orchestra: Phil Harris, Walter Scharf.
Program Opening:
Announcer: Yes, it's Sunday, time for The
   Phil Harris-Alice Faye Show, presented
   by the makers of Rexall drug products
   and your Rexall family druggist...
Length: 30 minutes.
Network: NBC.
First Broadcast: 1946.

The Phil Silvers Show

Type: Variety
Host: Phil Silvers.
Regulars: Betty Garde, Jean Gillespie,
   Roger deKoven, Danny Ocko, William
   Keane, Jack Hartley, Lee Brady, Beryl
   Davis.
Orchestra: Ralph Norman.
Length: 30 minutes.
Network: ABC.
First Broadcast: 1947.

The Phil Spitalny Show

Type: Variety
Host: Phil Spitalny.
Regulars: Dorothy Thompson, John An-
   derson, The Three Little Words.
Announcer: Del Sharbutt.
Music: Phil Spitalny and His All-Girl Or-
   chestra.
Length: 30 minutes.
Network: NBC.
First Broadcast: 1936.

Philco Radio Playhouse

Type: Anthology
Format: Radio adaptations of plays origin-
   ally broadcast over "The Philco Television
   Playhouse."
Host-Narrator: Joseph Cotten.
Sponsor: Philco.
Length: 30 minutes.
Network: ABC.
First Broadcast: 1953.

Philco Radio Time

Type: Variety
Host: Bing Crosby
Regulars: Al Jolson, John Charles Thom-
   as, Connie Russell, Skitch Henderson.
Announcer: Glenn Riggs.
Orchestra: John Scott Trotter.

Sponsor: Philco appliances.
Program Opening:
Announcer: This is Glenn Riggs welcom-
   ing you to Philco Radio Time, produced
   and transcribed in New York, with John
   Scott Trotter and his orchestra, Skitch
   Henderson, and Bing's guests Fred Allen
   and Connee Boswell . . .
Length: 30 minutes.
Network: ABC.
First Broadcast: 1946.

Philip Marlowe

See title: "The Adventures of Philip Marlowe."

The Philip Morris Follies of 1946

Type: Musical Variety
Host: Johnny Desmond.
Regulars: Margaret Whiting, Herb Shri-
   ner.
Announcer: Ken Roberts.
Orchestra-Chorus: Jerry Gray.
Sponsor: Philip Morris cigarettes.
Length: 30 minutes.
Network: NBC.
First Broadcast: 1946.

The Philip Morris Playhouse

Type: Anthology
Format: Dramatic presentations.
Host: Charles Martin.
Announcer: Joe King, Bud Collyer, Ken
   Roberts.
Orchestra: Russ Morgan, Johnny Green,
   Ray Bloch.
Sponsor: Philip Morris cigarettes.
Length: 30 minutes.
Network: CBS.
First Broadcast: 1941.

Philo Vance

Type: Crime Drama

Format: The cases of private detective
   Philo Vance. Based on the character
   created by S.S. Van Dine.
Cast: Philo Vance   Jackson Beck
                               Jose Ferrer
         His secretary   Joan Alexander
                               Florence Robin-
                                  son
         District Attorney
            Markham   George Petrie
         Police Sgt. Heath   Humphrey Davis
Orchestra: Henry Sylvern.
Length: 30 minutes.
Network: NBC.
First Broadcast: 1945.

Phone Again Finnegan

Type: Comedy
Format: The misadventures of Finnegan,
   the inept manager of the Welcome Arms
   Apartments.
Cast: Finnegan   Stu Erwin
         The Swedish
            janitor   Harry Stewart
         The switchboard
            girl   Florence Halop
Also: Marlene Ames.
Announcer: Ken Niles.
Orchestra: Lou Kosloff.
Length: 30 minutes.
Syndicated.
First Broadcast: 1946.

The Phrase That Pays

Type: Quiz
Format: A contestant chosen from the studio audience was presented with three
   clues to the identity of a well-known
   phrase. Prizes were awarded based on
   which clue led to the identification; if the
   player failed to identify the phrase, the
   listener who submitted it won a prize.
Host: Red Benson.
Length: 15 minutes.
Network: NBC.
First Broadcast: 1953.

Pick a Date

Type: Interview-Quiz
Format: A woman selected from the studio audience was asked to state a memorable year in her life. She related the reason for its selection and answered questions about incidents that occurred during that year in return for merchandise prizes.
Host: Buddy Rogers.
Length: 30 minutes.
Network: ABC.
First Broadcast: 1949.

Pick and Pat Time

Type: Variety
Hosts: Pick Malone, Pat Padgett.
Regulars: Mary Small, Bruce Hayes, Tiny Ruffner, Diane Courtney, The Jesters.
Announcer: Paul Douglas, Tiny Ruffner.
Orchestra: Vincent Lopez.
Network: Mutual (1944), ABC (1945).
First Broadcast: 1944.

Pick and Play with Bob and Ray

See title: "Bob and Ray."

Pipe Dreams

Type: Comedy Sketch
Format: The tall tales of Willoughby Fibbe, M.P. (Master Prevaricator).
Starring: Alan Reed as Willoughby Fibbe.
Length: 5 minutes.
Network: NBC.
First Broadcast: 1939.

Pipe Smoking Time

Type: Musical Variety
Format: Invited male listeners to "light up, lean back, and listen."
Host: Arthur Fields.
Regulars: Fred Hall, Woody Guthrie, Edmund C. Roecker.

Orchestra: Ray Bloch.
Length: 25 minutes.
Network: CBS.
First Broadcast: 1940.

Pitching Horseshoes

Type: Anthology
Format: Capsule dramatizations of stories that appeared in Billy Rose's "Pitching Horseshoes" newspaper column.
Host: Billy Rose.
Announcer: Frank Waldecker.
Length: 55 minutes.
Network: Mutual.
First Broadcast: 1941.

Plantation Party

Type: Country-Western Musical Variety
Host: Whitey Ford (as the Duke of Paducah).
Regulars: Michael Stewart, Dolly and Milly Good, Tom, Dick, and Harry, Louise Massey and the Westerners, The Doring Sisters, The Plantation Choir.
Announcer: Charles Lyon.
Music: The Range Riders.
Length: 30 minutes.
Network: NBC.
First Broadcast: 1938.

The Player

Type: Anthology
Format: Dramatizations of various stories.
Performing all roles: Paul Frees.
Included:
Jack the Giant Killer. The tale of a little man whose big reputation is put to the test.
Murder At Tammerlane. The story of a girl, missing for five years, who suddenly turns up at an old mansion inhabited by an invalid old lady who loves Edgar Allan Poe stories.
Length: 15 minutes.
Syndicated.
First Broadcast: 1951.

Pleasure Parade

Type: Musical Variety
Hostess: Lillian Carroll.
Regulars: Dick Brown, Paula Kelly, The Modernaires.
Orchestra: Vincent Lopez.
Length: 15 minutes.
Syndicated.
First Broadcast: 1945.

Point Sublime

Type: Comedy
Format: Events in the life of Ben Willett, the friendly, philosophical owner of a general store in the town of Point Sublime.

Cast: Ben Willett   Cliff Arquette
His helper   Mel Blanc
Evelyn, Ben's
girlfriend   Jane Morgan
                  Verna Felton
Also: Lou Merrill, Earle Ross, Charles Seel.
Orchestra: Bud Dant.
Sponsor: The John Hancock Insurance Company.
Length: 30 minutes.
Network: NBC (1941), ABC (1944).
First Broadcast: 1941.

Police Headquarters

Type: Anthology
Format: Dramatizations of police law enforcement in action. Varying presentations and casts.
Length: 15 minutes.
Network: NBC.
First Broadcast: 1931.

Police Woman

Type: Crime Drama
Format: Dramatizations based on actual incidents in the life of Mary Sullivan, a New York City police woman for thirty-five years and the former director of the Police Woman's Bureau.

Cast: Mary Sullivan   Herself
                           Betty Garde
Announcer: Walter Herlihy, Dick Dunham.
Music: Jessie Crawford.
Length: 15 minutes.
Network: ABC.
First Broadcast: 1946.

The Ponds Program

See title: "Mrs. Eleanor Roosevelt."

Popeye the Sailor

Type: Children's
Format: The exploits of Popeye, the spinach eating sailor, as he struggled to protect his friends from harm. Based on the characters created by E.C. Segar.

Cast: Popeye   Det Poppen
                        Floyd Buckley
                        Jack Mercer

Olive Oyl,
his girl
friend   Olive La Moy
                Mae Questel

Bluto, his
arch enemy   Jackson Beck
J. Wellington
Wimpy, Pop-
eye's friend   Charles
                Lawrence

Matey,
Popeye's ward   Jim Donnelly
Swee'pea, the
foundling
left on
Olive's door-
step   Mae Questel
Sinbad, the
hulking, un-
kempt brute   Jackson Beck
Announcer: Kelvin Keech.
Music: Victor Erwin.
Sponsor: Wheatena.
Program Opening:
Announcer: All hands on deck, here's Popeye....Wheatena is his diet, he asks you to try it...with Popeye the Sailor man.

Portia Faces Life. Left to right: Esther Ralston, Donald Briggs, and Lucille Wall.

Length: 15 minutes.
Network: NBC.
First Broadcast: 1935.

Port of Missing Hits

Type: Musical Variety
Hostess: Edna Phillips.
Chorus: Thomas Haywood.
Orchestra: Milton Katims.
Length: 30 minutes.
Network: NBC.
First Broadcast: 1945.

Portia Faces Life

Type: Serial
Format: The dramatic story of Portia Blake, a widowed attorney and the mother of a young son.
Cast: Portia Blake   Lucille Wall
   Dickie Blake,
    her son   Raymond Ives

	Larry Robinson
	Edwin Bruce
Walter Manning	Myron McCormick
	Bartlett Robinson
Arlene Manning	Joan Banks
Portia's aunt	Frances Woodbury
Kirk Roder	Carleton Young
Dr. Holton	Donald Briggs
Kathy Marsh	Marjorie Anderson
	Esther Ralston
	Rosaline Greene
	Anne Seymour
Miss Daisey	Henrietta Tedro
Joan	Ginger Jones

Announcer: George Putnam, Ron Rawson.
Length: 15 minutes.
Network: CBS.
First Broadcast: 1940. The series originally began as a local entry over station KTSA in San Antonio. Also titled "Portia Blake Faces Life."

Postcard Serenade

Type: Musical Variety
Hostess: Judy Lang (accompanying herself on the piano).
Announcer: Frank Waldecker.
Length: 15 minutes.
Network: Mutual.
First Broadcast: 1945.

Pot O' Gold

Type: Quiz
Format: Listeners received the opportunity to win cash by correctly answering questions when telephoned by the host.
Host: Ben Grauer, Happy Felton.
Vocalists: Verna Holly, Amy Arnell, Don Brown, Jimmy Carroll.
Announcer: Bob Shepherd, Len Sterling.
Orchestra: Horace Heidt, Tommy Tucker, Harry Salter.
Length: 30 minutes.
Network: NBC (1939), ABC (1946).
First Broadcast: 1939.

Powers Charm School

Type: Women
Format: Beauty tips and advice.
Host: John Robert Powers.
Regulars: Peggy Allenby, Pat Hosley, Ken Lynch.
Announcer: Walter Herlihy.
Length: 25 minutes.
Network: ABC.
First Broadcast: 1946.

Prairie Folks

Type: Serial
Format: The saga of the pioneers and the settling of Minnesota during the 1800s.

Cast:
Thor Nielsen	Erik Rolf
Anna Nielsen, his wife	Helen Warren
Hancey Nielsen, their son	Kingsley Colton
Smiley	Parker Fennelly

Pretty Kitty Kelly. Lucille Wall.

Adam Bassett	Morris Carnovsky
Curtis Bassett	Cliff Carpenter
Anne Anders	Josephine Fox
Arnie Anders	Joe Helgeson

Length: 30 minutes.
Network: NBC.
First Broadcast: 1940.

Press Club

Type: Adventure
Format: The exploits of Mark Brandon, a newspaper reporter.
Starring: Marvin Miller as Mark Brandon.
Length: 30 minutes.
Network: CBS.
First Broadcast: 1944.

Pretty Kitty Kelly

Type: Serial
Format: Events in the life of Kitty Kelly, a spirited Irish girl.

Cast:
Kitty Kelly	Arline Blackburn
Michael Conway	Bud Collyer

Byron Welby	Bartlett Robinson
Isabel Andrews	Lucille Wall
Dennis Pierce	Richard Kollmar
Bunny Wilson	Helen Choate

Announcer-Narrator: Matt Crowley.
Length: 15 minutes.
Network: CBS.
First Broadcast: 1937.

The Private Files of Matthew Bell

Type: Crime Drama
Format: The exploits of Police Surgeon Matthew Bell, a man whose detection involved an understanding of the characters with whom he became involved.
Starring: Joseph Cotten as Matthew Bell.
Announcer: Phil Tonken.
Music: Recorded.
Length: 25 minutes.
Network: Mutual.
First Broadcast: 1952.

Private Showing

Type: Anthology
Format: Dramatizations suggested by famous paintings.
Host-Performer: Walter Hampden.
Included:
The Rehearsal on Stage. Based on a Degas painting, a story of murder in the French ballet.
The Poorhouse on the Hill. A story of greed suggested by a Cezanne painting.
Length: 30 minutes.
Network: Mutual.
First Broadcast: 1946.

Professor Quiz

Type: Quiz
Format: A series of question and answer rounds in which selected studio audience members competed for cash prizes.
Host: Craig Earl.
Announcer: Robert Trout, Gene Hamilton.
Sponsor: Noxzema Skin Cream.
Length: 30 minutes.

Network: CBS.
First Broadcast: 1936.

The Prudential Family Hour

Type: Music
Host: Deems Taylor.
Regulars: Gladys Swarthout, Ross Graham, Jack Smith.
Announcer: Frank Gallop.
Orchestra: Al Goodman.
Length: 45 minutes.
Network: CBS.
First Broadcast: 1941.

Pursuit

Type: Drama
Format: The exploits of Peter Black, a Chief Inspector for Scotland Yard, as he pursued and tracked down criminals.

Cast: Peter Black	Ted de Corsia
	John Dehner

Announcer: Don Baker, Bob Stevenson.
Orchestra: Marlen Skiles.
Length: 30 minutes.
Network: CBS.
First Broadcast: 1949.

Queen for a Day

Type: Audience Participation
Format: Preselected women were interviewed and asked to explain why they were in need of one specific item. One woman, whose response best impressed a panel of studio audience judges, was crowned "Queen for a Day" and received not only the prize she sought, but several others: a night club reservation, a Fifth Avenue beauty parlor appointment, and a shopping spree in a New York department store. Became the basis for the television series of the same title.
Host: Dud Williamson, Jack Bailey.
Announcer: Bob Bunce, Gene Baker.
Length: 30 minutes.
Network: Mutual.
First Broadcast: 1945.

Quick as a Flash

Type: Quiz
Format: Each of the six players that competed were assigned a specific light color. The host read a question; the first players to press a button and flash his light signal received a chance to answer and a cash prize if he responded correctly. Became the basis for the television series of the same title.
Host: Ken Roberts, Win Elliot, Bill Cullen.
Announcer: Frank Gallop, Cy Harrice.
Orchestra: Ray Bloch.
Length: 30 minutes.
Network: Mutual.
First Broadcast: 1944.

Quicksilver

Type: Quiz
Format: A microphone was concealed somewhere at a busy locale. A passerby was approached and asked to answer a riddle that has been submitted by a listener (who received $5). The participant received $5 also if he correctly answered the riddle; if not, he received one silver dollar.
Host: Ransom Sherman, Bob Brown.
Length: 30 minutes.
Network: NBC.
First Broadcast: 1939.

Quiet Please

Type: Anthology
Format: Mystery presentations. Became the basis for a television series of the same title.
Narrator: Ernest Chappell.
Announcer: Ed Michael.
Organist: Gene Perrazzo, Albert Buhrmann.
Length: 30 minutes.
Network: Mutual (1947), ABC (1948).
First Broadcast: 1947.

Quixie Doodle

Type: Quiz
Format: Two teams, the Submitters vs. the Answerers, competed in a ten-question game. For each correct response, the Answerers scored $10; each incorrect answer won the Submitters $10.
Host: Bob Hawk, Frederick Chase Taylor.
Announcer: Alan Reed.
Length: 30 minutes.
Network: Mutual.
First Broadcast: 1938. Originally titled "Bob Hawk's Quixie Doodle Quiz."

The Quiz Kids

Type: Quiz
Format: Had a panel of exceptionally bright children answering difficult questions. Became the basis for a television series of the same title.
Host: Joe Kelly.
Announcer: Fort Pearson, Roger Krupp, Ed Scott.
Sponsor: Alka-Seltzer.
Length: 30 minutes.
Network: NBC.
First Broadcast: 1940.

Quizzer's Baseball

Type: Quiz
Format: Two three-member teams competed in a question and answer session patterned after the game of baseball. Answers were scored from a base hit to a home run depending on the rapidity with which a player answered. The team scoring the most runs received one hundred dollars.
Host: Harry Von Zell.
Team One Captain: Glenda Farrell.
Team Two Captain: Budd Hulick.
Announcer: Harry Von Zell.
Orchestra: Peter Van Steeden.
Length: 30 minutes.
Network: CBS.
First Broadcast: 1941.

Radio City Playhouse

Type: Anthology
Format: Dramatic presentations.
Announcer: Fred Collins.
Orchestra: Roy Shields.
Length: 15 minutes.
Network: NBC.
First Broadcast: 1948.

Radio Reader's Digest

Type: Anthology
Format: Adaptations of stories from *Reader's Digest* magazine.
Host: Richard Kollmar.
Narrator: Conrad Nagel.
Music: Nathan Van Cleave.
Length: 30 minutes.
Network: CBS.
First Broadcast: 1942.

Radio Theatre of Famous Classics

Type: Anthology
Format: Varied dramas and casts.
Organist: Eddie Baker.
Length: 30 minutes.
Syndicated.
First Broadcast: 1946.

The Railroad Hour

Type: Musical Variety-Drama
Host: Gordon MacRae.
Regulars: Lurelle Norman, Billie Burke, The Sportsmen.
Announcer: Marvin Miller.
Orchestra: John Rarig, Carmen Dragon.
Sponsor: The Association of American Railroads.
Included:
New Moon. The story of a pirate who falls in love with a lady of nobility.
Starring: Gordon MacRae, Mimi Benzell.
The Merry Widow. The story of a prince who must court and wed a rich widow to save his country from financial ruin.

Starring: Gordon MacRae, Dorothy Kirsten, Jack Kirkwood.
Sari. The tale of a famed Gypsy violinist, his daughter, and a would-be fiddler as they seek fame and fortune.
Starring: Gordon MacRae, Margaret Truman.
Showboat. The story of a riverboat gambler and his lady love.
Starring: Gordon MacRae, Dorothy Kinsella.
Length: 45 and 30 minute versions.
Network: ABC (1948), NBC (1949).
First Broadcast: 1948.

Rainbow House

Type: Children's
Host: Bob Emery.
Orchestra: Dolphe Martin.
Length: 15 minutes.
Network: Mutual.
First Broadcast: 1942.

The Raleigh Room

Type: Talk-Variety
Hostess: Hildegarde Loretta Sell.
Orchestra: Harry Sosnik.
Sponsor: Raleigh cigarettes.
Length: 30 minutes.
Network: NBC.
First Broadcast: 1944.

The Ralph Edwards Show

See title: "Truth or Consequences."

The Ransom Sherman Show

Type: Variety
Format: Music, comedy, and dramatic sketches.
Host: Ransom Sherman.
Regulars: Bill Thompson, Wayne Van Dyne, Fran Allison.
Orchestra: Rex Maupin.

Length: 30 minutes.
Network: NBC.
First Broadcast: 1939.

Rate Your Mate

Type: Quiz
Format: Married couples competed. While one mate was isolated in a soundproof booth, the other had to predict whether or not his or her spouse could answer a specific question. A cash prize (up to $100) was awarded depending on the accuracy of the prediction.
Host: Joey Adams.
Announcer: Hal Simms.
Length: 30 minutes.
Network: CBS.
First Broadcast: 1950.

The Ray Bolger Show

Type: Variety
Host: Ray Bolger.
Regulars: Elvia Allman, Harry Lang, Verna Felton, Jeri Sullivan.
Announcer: Howard Petrie.
Orchestra: Roy Bargy.
Length: 30 minutes.
Network: CBS.
First Broadcast: 1945.

The Raymond Paige Orchestra

Type: Musical Variety
Host: Milton Cross.
Commentator: Deems Taylor.
Vocalists: The Mixed Choir.
Orchestra: Raymond Paige.
Length: 30 minutes.
Network: NBC.
First Broadcast: 1940.

The Raymond Scott Show

Type: Musical Variety
Host: Raymond Scott.

Vocalist: Dorothy Collins.
Orchestra-Chorus: Raymond Scott.
Length: 15 minutes.
Network: CBS.
First Broadcast: 1943.

The R.C.A. Victor Show

Type: Musical Variety
Host: Deems Taylor, Leonardo Feather, Robert Merrill.
Announcer: Kenny Delmar.
Orchestra: Raymond Paige, Arthur Fiedler and the Boston Pops Orchestra.
Sponsor: R.C.A. Victor.
Length: 30 minutes.
Network: NBC.
First Broadcast: 1945.

Red Benson's Movie Matinee

Type: Quiz
Format: Called for contestants to answer questions based on film titles in return for cash prizes.
Host: Red Benson.
Announcer: Carl Warren.
Length: 30 minutes.
Network: Mutual.
First Broadcast: 1949.

Red Hook 31

Type: Chatter
Format: The series focused on the exchange of conversations between Woody Klose, a radio scriptwriter, and his wife, Virginia, as they discussed their life, in particular their move from the city to the 102-acre Echo Valley Farm in Dutchess County, New York. (Red Hook 31: their telephone number.)
Cast: Woody Klose   Himself
           Virginia Klose   Herself
Length: 15 minutes.
Network: Mutual.
First Broadcast: 1947.

Red Ryder

Type: Western
Format: Set in various locales throughout the West, the series followed the exploits of Red Ryder, a roving cowboy, and his sidekick Little Beaver as they strove to maintain law and order. Based on the comic strip by Fred Harman.
Cast: Red Ryder   Reed Hadley
                         Carlton KaDell
                         Brooke Temple
      Little Beaver   Tommy Cook
                         Henry Blair
Also (various roles): Charles Lung, Lurene Tuttle, Fred Shields, Victor Rodman.
Red Ryder's Horse: Thunder.
Announcer: Ben Alexander.
Orchestra: Robert Armbruster.
Program Opening:
Announcer: From out of the West comes America's famous fighting cowboy, Red Ryder.
Length: 30 minutes.
Network: Mutual.
First Broadcast: 1942.

The Red Skelton Show

Type: Comedy-Variety
Host: Red Skelton.
Regulars: Gee Gee Pearson, Ozzie Nelson, Harriet Hilliard, Lurene Tuttle, Verna Felton, Anita Ellis, Wonderful Smith, The Four Knights, Pat McGeehan.
Announcer: John Holbrook, Truman Bradley, Marvin Miller, Rod O'Connor, Jean Paul King.
Orchestra: Ozzie Nelson, Dave Forrester, David Rose.
Sponsor: Raleigh Cigarettes.
Length: 30 minutes.
Network: NBC.
First Broadcast: 1941. Also titled "Red Skelton's Scrapbook." Became the basis for a television series of the same title.

The Redhead

Type: Comedy

The Red Skelton Show. Red Skelton.

Format: The adventures of a brash, wise-cracking young girl from a small town in Nebraska as she struggled to achieve fame and fortune as a model in New York City.
Cast: The would-be model   Mary McCarthy
      Her romantic interest   Dick Van Patten
Length: 30 minutes.
Network: ABC.
First Broadcast: 1952.

Refreshment Time

Type: Musical Variety
Host: Morton Downey.
Regulars: Stan Freeman, Kitty Kallen.
Announcer: Ray Morgan.
Orchestra: Carmen Mastren.
Sponsor: Coca Cola.
Length: 30 minutes.
Network: CBS.
First Broadcast: 1950.

Relaxation in Music

Type: Musical Variety
Hosts: Jean Tighe, Bob Bary.
Orchestra: Dick Adams.
Length: 15 minutes.
Network: Mutual.
First Broadcast: 1944.

The Remarkable Miss Tuttle

Type: Drama
Format: The story of Miss Tuttle, a re-
   sourceful, spinster who helped people
   solve their problems.
Cast: Miss Tuttle   Edna Mae Oliver
   Her nephew   Arnold Stang
   Her maid   Lillian Randolph
   Judge Carter   Cy Kendall
Also: Howard Harris, Martin Gosch.
Announcer: Murray Boler.
Length: 30 minutes.
Network: NBC.
First Broadcast: 1942.

Reminiscin' with Singin' Sam

Type: Musical Variety
Host: Harry Frankel (Singin' Sam).
Vocalists: The Mullin Sisters.
Orchestra: Charles Magnoule.
Length: 15 minutes.
Syndicated.
First Broadcast: 1946. See also: "Singin'
   Sam."

Renfrew of the Mounted

Type: Adventure
Format: The exploits of Inspector Doug-
   las Renfrew of the Royal Canadian
   Mounted Police. Became the basis for a
   television series of the same title.
Cast: Inspector Doug-
      las Renfrew   House Jameson
   Carol Girard,
      his romantic
      interest   Joan Baker

Announcer: Bert Parks.
Length: 30 minutes.
Network: CBS.
First Broadcast: 1936.

Reserved for Garroway

See title: "The Dave Garroway Show."

Results, Inc.

Type: Drama
Format: The cases of Johnny Strange and
   Terry Travers, partners in a detective
   agency that guaranteed to do anything,
   solve any problem, or remedy any difficul-
   ty.
Cast: Johnny Strange   Lloyd Nolan
   Terry Travers   Claire Trevor
Length: 30 minutes.
Network: NBC.
First Broadcast: 1944.

Reveille Round-Up

Type: Country-Western Musical Variety
Host: Tom Wallace.
Regulars: Louise Massey, The Westerners
   (Milt Mobie, Larry Wellington, Allen
   Massey, Curt Massey).
Length: 15 minutes.
Network: NBC.
First Broadcast: 1941.

Revere All Star Revue

Type: Musical Variety
Host: Andy Russell.
Regulars: Marion Hutton, The Pied Pip-
   ers.
Announcer: Toby Reed.
Orchestra: Ray Sinatra.
Sponsor: Revere cameras.
Length: 15 minutes.
Network: Mutual.
First Broadcast: 1948.

Rhapsody in Rhythm

Type: Musical Variety
Hostess: Connie Haines (1946), Peggy Lee (1947).
Host: Johnny Johnston (1947).
Regulars: Skitch Henderson, The Golden Gate Quartet, The Pied Pipers.
Announcer: Art Gilmore.
Orchestra: Jan Savitt.
Length: 30 minutes.
Network: NBC (1946), CBS (1947).
First Broadcast: 1946.

Rhythm On the Road

Type: Variety
Host-Announcer: Bob Dixon.
Vocalists: The Honeydreamers.
Orchestra: Elliott Lawrence.
Length: 60 minutes.
Network: CBS.
First Broadcast: 1955.

Rhythm Road

Type: Musical Variety
Host: Johnny Morgan.
Regulars: Ann Thomas, Alastair Kyle, Victoria Cordova, Sidney Fields, Glenn Riggs.
Orchestra: Jimmy Lytell.
Length: 30 minutes.
Network: CBS.
First Broadcast: 1943.

Richard Diamond, Private Detective

Type: Crime Drama
Format: The cases of private detective Richard Diamond. Became the basis for a television series of the same title.
Cast: Richard Diamond   Dick Powell
   Lieutenant
   Levinson   Ed Begley
Orchestra: Frank Worth.

Sponsor: Rexall Drugs.
Program Opening:
Announcer: Here's Dick Powell as Richard Diamond, Private Detective.
Length: 30 minutes.
Network: NBC.
First Broadcast: 1949.

Richard Lawless

Type: Adventure
Format: The series, set in 17th Century England, depicted the turbulence that existed during the period of Charles II.
Starring: Keven McCarthy as Richard Lawless.
Also: Kathleen Fordell, Neil Fitzgerald, Peter Bayne.
Orchestra: John Gart.
Length: 30 minutes.
Network: CBS.
First Broadcast: 1946.

The Richard Maxwell Show

Type: Talk-Variety
Host: Richard Maxwell.
Announcer: John Harper.
Length: 15 minutes.
Network: CBS.
First Broadcast: 1938.

The Right to Happiness

Type: Serial
Format: The dramatic story of the Kramers, a family that moved from the slums to a respectable neighborhood, and their attempts to find happiness.
Cast: Carolyn Kramer   Claudia Morgan
                        Eloise Kummer
        Carolyn's mother   Leora Thatcher
        Carolyn's father   Julian Noa
        Doris Cameron   Selena Royle
                        Constance Crowder
                        Irene Hubbard
        Rose Kransky   Ruth Bailey

| Fred Minturn | Charles Webster |
| Art Kohl |
Richard Campbell	Les Damon
	Alexander Scourby
Ginny	Anne Sterrett
Constance Wake-	
field	Violet Heming
	Luise Barclay
Susan Wakefield	Charita Bauer
Bill Walker	Reese Taylor
Ted Wakefield	Jimmy Dobson
	Billy Redfield
Alex	Staats Cotsworth
Jane	Ginger Jones
Skip	Peter Fernandez

Also: Bernadine Flynn, Carl Kroenke, Nancy Hurdle, Pat Murphy, Carlton KaDell, Lucille Gilman, Seymour Young.
Narrator: Marvin Miller.
Announcer: Ron Rawson, Michael Fitzmaurice, Hugh Conover.
Music: William Meeder.
Sponsor: Spic and Span, Cheer.
Length: 15 minutes.
Network: NBC (1939), CBS (1940).
First Broadcast: 1939.

The Rise Stevens Show

Type: Musical Variety
Hostess: Rise Stevens.
Announcer: Lou Crosby.
Orchestra: Under the direction of guest conductors.
Length: 30 minutes.
Network: NBC.
First Broadcast: 1945.

River Boat Revels

Type: Musical Variety
Hostess: Kay Carlisle.
Regulars: Joseph MacPherson, Minnie Pearl, Frank Marlowe, David Cobb, The Old Timers Quartet.
Orchestra: Peitro Brescia.
Length: 30 minutes.
Network: NBC.
First Broadcast: 1941.

The Robert Benchley Show

Type: Musical Variety
Host: Robert Benchley.
Announcer: Del Sharbutt.
Orchestra: Artie Shaw.
Length: 30 minutes.
Network: NBC.
First Broadcast: 1939.

The Robert Merrill Show

Type: Musical Variety
Host: Robert Merrill.
Announcer: Robert Denton.
Orchestra: Leopold Spitalny.
Length: 30 minutes.
Network: NBC.
First Broadcast: 1945.

The Robert Q. Lewis Show

Type: Variety
Host: Robert Q. Lewis.
Regulars: Earl Wrightson, Lois Hunt, Jan Arden, Jaye P. Morgan, William Keene, The Ames Brothers, Eugene Baird, Kathy Norman, Herb Sheldon, Toby David, Phil Kramer, Bill Wyatt, Billy Williams, Florence Robinson, Jackson Beck, The Chordettes, The Mixed Choir, Judy Johnson, Richard Hayes.
Announcer: Lee Vines, Kenneth Banghart, Warren Sweeney.
Orchestra: Ray Bloch, Howard Smith, Dave Grupp, George Wright, Milton Kaye, Lee Irwin.
Length: 15, 30, and 60 minute versions.
Network: NBC (1945), CBS (1947).
First Broadcast: 1945. Also titled: "Robert Q.'s Waxworks." Became the basis for a television series of the same title.

Rock 'n' Roll Dance Party

Type: Variety
Host: Joe Williams.
Announcer: Bern Bennett.
Music: The Count Basie Band.

Length: 30 minutes.
Network: CBS.
First Broadcast: 1956.

Rocky Fortune

Type: Crime Drama
Format: The exploits of Rocky Fortune, a private detective who would undertake any case for money.
Starring: Frank Sinatra as Rocky Fortune.
Narrator: Frank Sinatra.
Length: 25 minutes.
Network: NBC.
First Broadcast: 1953.

Rocky Jordan

Type: Adventure
Format: The story of Rocky Jordan, the owner-operator of the Cafe Tambourine (a night club in Cairo, Egypt), as he involved himself with and attempted to solve the problems of others.
Cast: Rocky Jordan   Jack Moyles
                          George Raft
       The Police Chief   Jay Novello
Announcer-Narrator: Larry Dobkin.
Orchestra: Richard Aurandt.
Sponsor: Del Monte Foods.
Length: 30 minutes.
Network: CBS.
First Broadcast: 1951. Originally titled "A Man Called Jordan."

Roger Kilgore—Public Defender

Type: Drama
Format: The cases and courtroom defenses of Roger Kilgore, a public defender.
Cast: Roger Kilgore   Raymond
                          Edward
                          Johnson
       The District
          Attorney   Santos Ortega
Orchestra: Sylvan Levin.
Length: 30 minutes.
Network: Mutual.
First Broadcast: 1948.

Rogers of the *Gazette*

Type: Comedy-Drama
Format: The story of an editor of a small town newspaper.
Cast: Will Rogers,
          the editor   Will Rogers, Jr.
       His assistant   Georgia Ellis
       The doctor   Parley Baer
Orchestra: Wilbur Hatch.
Length: 30 minutes.
Network: CBS.
First Broadcast: 1953.

Rogue's Gallery

Type: Crime Drama
Format: The cases of Richard Rogue, a private detective with a knack for solving crimes before the police.
Cast: Richard Rogue   Dick Powell
                          Barry Sullivan
Announcer: Jim Doyle.
Orchestra: Leith Stevens.
Length: 30 minutes.
Network: NBC.
First Broadcast: 1945.

Romance

Type: Anthology
Format: Romantic presentations.
Host-Narrator (The Voice of Romance): Doris Dalton, Kay Brinker.
Announcer: Roy Rowan.
Organist: Charles Paul.
Length: 30 minutes.
Network: CBS.
First Broadcast: 1943.

The Romance of Helen Trent

Type: Serial
Format: The dramatic story of Helen Trent, a thirty-five-year-old fashion designer.
Cast: Helen Trent   Virginia Clark
                          Betty Ruth Smith
                          Julie Stevens

Monica Smith	Audrey McGrath
Philip King	David Gothard
Cherry Martin	Marilyn Erskine
Cynthia Carter	Mary Jane Higby
Nancy Granger	Lucy Gilman
Tony Griffin	Louis Krugman
Agatha	Marie Nelson
	Katherine
	Emmet
	Bess McCammon
Drew Sinclair	Reese Taylor
Alice Carroll	Ginger Jones
Karl Dorn	Alan Hewitt
Roy Gabler	John Larkin
Margot	Alice Hill
Jeanette	Vivian Fridell
Jonathan Hay-	
ward	Bret Morrison

Announcer: Don Hancock, Pierre Andre.
Program Opening:
Announcer: The Romance of Helen Trent. The real life drama of Helen Trent who, when life mocks her, breaks her hopes, dashes her against the rocks of despair, fights back bravely, successfully, to prove what so many women long to prove in their own lives, that because a woman is thirty-five or more romance in life need not be over; that romance can begin at thirty-five.
Length: 15 minutes.
Network: CBS.
First Broadcast: 1933.

Rookies

Type: Comedy
Format: The bickering relationship between a training camp sergeant and a bumbling bootcamp trainee.
Cast: The Sergeant — Jay C. Flippen
The Trainee — Joey Faye
The camp hostess — Loulie Jean
Orchestra: Bob Stanley.
Length: 30 minutes.
Network: Mutual.
First Broadcast: 1941.

Roosty of the AAF

Type: Music and Drama
Format: An Army Air Force program of music and drama.
Host: William Tracy as Roosty.
Vocalist: Bob Carroll.
Orchestra: Felix Slatkin.
Length: 30 minutes.
Network: Mutual.
First Broadcast: 1944.

Rosemary

Type: Serial
Format: The dramatic adventures of Rosemary Dawson, a stenographer.

Cast:	
Rosemary Dawson	Betty Winkler
Her mother	Marion Barney
Patty Dawson, her sister	Jone Allison
	Patsy Campbell
The lawyer	Lawson Zerbe
Peter Harvey	Sidney Smith
Dick Phillips	James Van Dyke
Audrey Roberts	Lesley Woods
	Joan Alexander
Bill Roberts	George Keane
Tommy Taylor	Jackie Kelk
Joyce Miller	Helen Choate

Announcer: Joe O'Brien, Ed Herlihy, Fran Barber, Bob Dixon.
Music: Paul Taubman.
Length: 15 minutes.
Network: NBC.
First Broadcast: 1944.

The Rosemary Clooney Show

Type: Variety
Hostess: Rosemary Clooney.
Announcer: Johnny Jacobs.
Orchestra: Buddy Cole.
Length: 15 minutes.
Network: CBS.
First Broadcast: 1954.

Rosemary. The cast grouped around the show's author Elaine Carrington (seated).

Rose of My Dreams

Type: Serial
Format: The dramatic story of two sisters: Rose, who is sweet and kind, and Sarah, who is devious and scheming, and their attempts to win the heart of an Englishman—a man who toys with both of them.
Cast: Rose   Mary Rolfe
        Sarah   Charita Bauer
        The Englishman Joseph Curtin
        The producer   James Burke
Also: William Smith.
Announcer: Larry Elliott.
Length: 15 minutes.
Network: CBS.
First Broadcast: 1946.

The Roy Rogers Show

Type: Western
Format: Musical variety coupled with dramatic sketches.
Starring: Roy Rogers.
Regulars: Dale Evans, Gabby Hayes, Pat Brady, Forrest Lewis, The Whipoorwills, Bob Nolan, The Sons of the Pioneers.
Narrator: Frank Hemingway.
Announcer: Verne Smith, Lou Crosby.
Orchestra: Perry Botkin.
Sponsor: Goodyear products, Quaker oats, Post Sugar-Crisp, Dodge automobiles.
Length: 30 minutes.
Network: Mutual (1944), NBC (1946).
First Broadcast: 1944.

Royal Theatre

Type: Anthology
Format: Dramatic presentations broad-
cast from England.
Host: Laurence Olivier.
Music: Sidney Torch.
Length: 30 minutes.
Network: NBC.
First Broadcast: 1953.

The Rudy Vallee Show

Type: Variety
Host: Rudy Vallee.
Regulars: Virginia Gregg, Andy Devine,
Mary Boland, Abe Reynolds, Billie Burke,
Sara Berner.
Announcer: Frank Graham, Truman Brad-
ley, Jimmy Wallington, Carol Hurst, Mar-
vin Miller.
Orchestra: Benny Krueger, Ken Darby,
Xavier Cugat.
Chorus: Elliot Daniel, Benny Krueger.
Length: 60 and 30 minute versions.
Network: NBC.
First Broadcast: 1938.

Rumpus Room

Type: Variety
Host: Johnny Olsen.
Regulars: Kay Armen, Gene Kirby, Hal
McIntyre.
Music: The Buddy Weed Trio, The Hank
D'Amico Orchestra.
Length: 30 minutes.
Network: ABC.
First Broadcast: 1946.

The Russ Brown Show

Type: Musical Variety
Host: Russ Brown.
Regulars: The Cadets, The Bennett Sis-
ters.
Length: 15 minutes.
Syndicated.
First Broadcast: 1945.

The Rudy Vallee Show. Rudy Vallee.

The Sad Sack

Type: Comedy
Format: The misadventures of the Sad
Sack, the pathetic G.I. created by George
Baker, in the pages of wartime *Yank*
magazine.
Cast: The Sad Sack   Herb Vigran
        His girlfriend   Patsy Morgan
Also: Jim Backus, Doris Singleton.
Announcer: Dick Joy.
Orchestra: Lou Kosloff.
Length: 30 minutes.
Network: CBS.
First Broadcast: 1946.

The Saint

Type: Adventure
Format: The exploits of Simon Templar,
the Saint, a swashbuckling, devil-may-
care Robin Hood type who, in his attempt
to help people, remained just one step
ahead of the police and crooks—both of
whom he combatted.

Cast: Simon Templar,
       the Saint   Edgar Barrier
                         Brian Aherne
                         Vincent Price
                         Tom Conway
                         Barry Sullivan
       Happy, his
          houseboy   Ken Christy
       Police Inspector
          Fernak   John Brown
                         Theodore von
                          Eltz
       Patricia Holmes,
          Simon's girl-
          friend   Louise Arthur

Announcer: Don Stanley, Harold Ross, Carlton KaDell, Dick Joy.

Orchestra: Louis Adrian, Harry Zimmerman.

Program Opening:

Announcer: The Adventures of the Saint, starring Vincent Price. The Saint, based on characters created by Leslie Charteris and known to millions from books, magazines, and motion pictures. The Robin Hood of modern crime now comes to radio, starring Hollywood's brilliant and talented actor, Vincent Price, The Saint.

Length: 30 minutes.

Network: NBC.

First Broadcast: 1944.

Sam Spade

Type: Crime Drama

Format: The cases of Sam Spade, a private detective working out of San Francisco. Based on the character created by Dashiell Hammett.

Cast: Sam Spade   Howard Duff
                         Steve Dunne
       Effie, his
          secretary   Lurene Tuttle

Announcer: Dick Joy.

Sponsor: Wildroot Cream Oil Hair Tonic.

Program Opening:

Announcer: The Adventures of Sam Spade, Detective, brought to you by Wildroot Cream Oil Hair Tonic.

Sound Effect: Telephone rings.

Girl's Voice (after picking up receiver): Sam Spade Detective Agency.

Sam: Hello, sweetheart, it's only me.

Girl: Oh Sam, why so modest?

Sam: If you will only contain your feminine curiosity for a few moments, I'll be right over to dictate my report of "The Bow Window Case."

Length: 30 minutes.

Network: CBS (1945), NBC (1949).

First Broadcast: 1945.

The Sammy Kaye Show

Type: Musical Variety

Host: Sammy Kaye.

Regulars: Red Barber, Billy Williams, Tommy Ryan, Arthur Wright, Don Connell, Tony Alamo, Laura Leslie, Barbara Benson, Tony Russo, Don Rogers, Sally Stewart, Clyde Burke, Tommy Ryan, Jimmy Bram, The Vass Family, The Kaydettes, The Kay Choir.

Announcer: Gene Hamilton.

Orchestra: Sammy Kaye.

Length-Network-First Broadcast: NBC Blue (1944, 30 minutes), CBS (1949, 30 minutes), ABC (1949, 15 minutes, 1951, 30 minutes, 1954, 25 minutes). Also titled: "Sammy Kaye's Showroom" (1949), "Sammy Kaye's Sunday Serenade Room" (1954).

Satan's Waitin'

Type: Anthology

Format: Dramatizations depicting the Devil as the plot manipulator.

Host-Announcer: Frank Graham.

Length: 30 minutes.

Network: CBS.

First Broadcast: 1950.

The Saturday Morning Vaudeville Theatre

Type: Musical Comedy Revue

Starring: Charles Kemper, Jess Mack, Dick Todd, The Polka Dots, Anita Boyer,

Joan Shea, Jim Ameche, The Symphon-
ettes.
Orchestra: D'Artega.
Length: 30 minutes.
Network: NBC.
First Broadcast: 1941.

The Saturday Night Revue

Type: Musical Variety
Host: Robert Q. Lewis
Regulars: Bill Harrington, Elsa Mirande,
Henny Youngman, Vera Holley, Art Ta-
tum.
Announcer: Ted Brown.
Orchestra: John Gart.
Length: 30 minutes.
Network: CBS.
First Broadcast: 1946.

The Saturday Senior Swing

Type: Musical Variety
Format: A musical variety session geared
to selling war bonds.
Hostess: Jill Warren.
Regulars: Jack Manning, Patsy Garrett.
Music: The Hank D'Amico Quintet, The
Bill Dornell Orchestra under the direction
of Ray Carter.
Length: 30 minutes.
Network: NBC.
First Broadcast: 1945.

The Saturday Showcase

Type: Musical Variety
Host: Snooky Lanson.
Regulars: Evelyn Parker, Bradley Kin-
caid, The Varieteers.
Orchestra: Owen Bradley.
Length: 30 minutes.
Network: NBC.
First Broadcast: 1946.

Saturday Showdown

Type: Variety

Host: John Gibson.
Regulars: Ted de Corsia, Tommy Taylor,
The Murtok Sisters.
Orchestra-Chorus: Irving Miller.
Length: 30 minutes.
Network: NBC.
First Broadcast: 1943.

Saturday Theatre

Type: Anthology
Format: Dramatic presentations.
Host-Announcer: George Walsh.
Length: 30 minutes.
Network: CBS.
First Broadcast: 1954.

The Scarlet Pimpernel

See title: "The Adventures of the Scarlet
Pimpernel."

Scattergood Baines

Type: Drama
Format: The story of Scattergood Baines,
a well-meaning old gentleman who, in his
attempt to help people, found his intentions causing more problems than solu-
tions. Based on the *Saturday Evening
Post* comic by Clarence Buddington
Kelland.

Cast:	Scattergood Baines	Jess Pugh
		Wendell Holmes
	Hippocrates Brown	John Hearne
	Plinky Pickett	Francis Trout
	Mirandy	Viola Berwick
	Barbara Calkins	Barbara Fuller
	Clara Potts	Catherine Mc-Cune
	J. Wellington Keats	Forrest Lewis
	Beth Reed	Norma Jean Ross
	Margie	Jean McCoy
	Eloise Comstock	Louise Fitch

Announcer: George Walsh, Roger Krupp, Bob Emerick.
Music: Ben Ludlow.
Length: 15 and 25 minute versions.
Network: CBS (1938), Mutual (1944).
First Broadcast: 1938.

Scotland Yard

Type: Crime Drama
Format: The cases of Inspector Burke of Scotland Yard.
Starring: Basil Rathbone as Inspector Burke.
Announcer: Phil Tompkins.
Music: Sylvan Levin.
Length: 30 minutes.
Network: Mutual.

Scout About Town

Type: Variety
Format: Performances by undiscovered talent.
Hosts: Hunt Stromberg, Jr., Anna May Dickey.
Announcer: Ralph Paul.
Orchestra: Sylvan Levin.
Length: 15 minutes.
Network: Mutual.
First Broadcast: 1946.

Scramby Amby

Type: Quiz
Format: Selected studio audience members were presented with a series of scrambled words and three clues: a musical and/or vocal selection, a daffy rhyme, and the dictionary definitions of the words. The first player to unscramble the words (e.g. BATLES should be STABLE) received a cash prize.
Host: Perry Ward.
Vocalist: Lynn Martin.
Announcer: Larry Keating.
Orchestra: Charles "Bud" Dant.
Length: 30 minutes.

Network: Blue.
First Broadcast: 1944.

Screen Director's Playhouse

Type: Anthology Drama. Became the basis for the television series of the same title.
Included:
Appointment for Love. The story of a girl who, after marrying, insists that she and her husband retain their individuality.
Starring: Charles Boyer, Gale Storm.
Miracle on 34th Street. The story of a man who believes he is the real Santa Claus.
Starring: Edmund Gwenn.
Criss Cross. The story of an armoured car guard who plans to rob his company so he can finance the life he longs to live with his fiancee.
Starring: Burt Lancaster.
The Uninvited. The story of two spirits seeking revenge on the granddaughter of the original owner of the mansion they now haunt.
Starring: Ray Milland.
Length: 30 minutes.
First Broadcast: 1948.

Screen Guild Theatre

Type: Anthology
Format: Radio adaptations of motion pictures.
Host: Roger Pryor.
Orchestra: Oscar Bradley.
Included:
The Bells of St. Mary's. The story of Father O'Malley and his attempts to acquire financial aid for St. Mary's school.
Starring: Bing Crosby, Ingrid Bergman.
Laura. While investigating the murder of a beautiful woman by a shotgun blast, the detective falls in love with the image of the dead girl.
Starring: Dana Andrews, Gene Tierney, Clifton Webb.
Length: 30 minutes.
Network: CBS.
First Broadcast: 1938.

Screen Test

Type: Variety-Drama
Format: Would-be actors and actresses appeared with name celebrities in short dramatizations designed to act as screen tests.
Host: John Conte.
Orchestra: Ted Steele.
Sponsor: M-G-M Films.
Length: 15 minutes.
First Broadcast: 1944.

The Sea Has a Story

Type: Anthology
Format: Dramatizations of man's struggle against the sea.
Host-Narrator: Pat O'Brien.
Orchestra: Lud Gluskin.
Length: 30 minutes.
Network: CBS.
First Broadcast: 1945.

The Sea Hound

Type: Adventure
Format: The exploits of Captain Silver, of the ship *Sea Hound*, as he roamed the globe searching for new adventures.

Cast:
Captain Silver	Ken Daigneau
Carol Anderson	Janice Gilbert
Jerry	Bob Hastings
Kukai	Alan Devitt

Length: 15 and 30 minute versions.
Network: Blue (then ABC).
First Broadcast: 1942.

The Sealtest Variety Show

See title: "The Dorothy Lamour Show."

The Sears Radio Theatre

Type: Anthology
Format: Varied presentations, including Gothic chillers, comedies, westerns, romantic and adventure stories.
Hosts: Vincent Price, Richard Widmark, Andy Griffith, Cicely Tyson, Lorne Greene.
Announcer: Art Gilmore.
Music: Nelson Riddle.
Executive Producer: Elliott Lewis.
Sponsor: Sears, Roebuck and Company.
Length: 55 minutes.
Syndicated on a barter basis (Sears supplies the program free to stations who, in turn, agree to air the Sears commercials contained within it.).
First Broadcast: 1979.

Second Honeymoon

Type: Game
Format: Seven wives competed, each stating why she would like a second honeymoon. A panel of five judges chose the wife whom they believed related the best story. The winner received that second honeymoon plus a new wardrobe.
Host: Bert Parks.
Announcer: Ed Michael.
Organist: Rosa Rio.
Sponsor: Lustre Creme Shampoo, Miller beer, Doan's pills.
Length: 30 minutes.
Network: ABC.
First Broadcast: 1948.

Second Husband

Type: Serial
Format: The dramatic story of Brenda Cummings and the problems that arise within her family when she marries Grant Cummings, her second husband.

Cast:
Brenda Cummings	Helen Menken
	Cathleen Cordell
Grant Cummings	Joseph Curtin
	Richard Waring
Bill Cummings	Carleton Young
	Ralph Lee Robertson
Fran Cummings	Janice Gilbert
	Mercer McCloud
Dick Cummings	Tom Donnelly
	Jackie Kelk

Marion Jennings	Arlene Francis
	Madaline Belgrad
Ben Porter	Jay Jostyn
Louise	Ethel Wilson
Irma	Joy Hathaway
The butler	William Podmore
Valerie	Jacqueline DeWit
Marsha	Judy Blake

Announcer: Andre Baruch.

Length: 30 and 15 minute versions.

Network: CBS.

First Broadcast: 1937.

The Second Mrs. Burton

Type: Serial

Format: The dramatic story of marrieds Brad and Terry Burton. The title refers to Terry; the first Mrs. Burton was Brad's mother — a "bad mother-in-law" to Terry who always caused trouble.

Cast:	Brad Burton	Dix Davis
		Karl Weber
		Ben Cooper
		Larry Robinson
	Terry Burton	Sharon Douglas
		Claire Niesen
		Patsy Campbell
		Teri Keane
	Brad's mother	Evelyn Varden
		Ethel Owen
	Marion Sullivan	Joan Alexander
		Cathleen Cordell
	James Anderson	King Calder
	Lillian Anderson	Elspeth Eric
	Greg Martin	Alexander Scourby
	Jack Mason	Staats Cotsworth
		Les Tremayne
	Elizabeth Miller	Betty Caine
	Stan Burton	Dwight Weist
	Jane Waters	Lois Holmes
	Wendy Burton	Madaline Lee
	Stan	Gary Merrill

Announcer: Hugh James, Harry Clark.

Organist: Chet Kingsbury, Richard Leibert.

Length: 15 minutes.

Network: CBS.

First Broadcast: 1946 (ended in 1960).

Secret City

Type: Mystery

Format: The cases of private detective Ben Clark and his friend and assistant, Jeff Wilson, a mechanic.

Cast:	Ben Clark	Bill Idelson
	Jeff Wilson	Jerry Spellman

Length: 15 minutes.

Network: Blue.

First Broadcast: 1941.

Secret Missions

Type: Anthology

Format: Dramatizations based on the files of Ellis M. Zacharias, World War II deputy chief of the Office of Naval Intelligence.

Host-Narrator: Admiral Ellis M. Zacharias.

Announcer: Bill Hightower.

Orchestra: Elliot Jacoby.

Length: 30 minutes.

Network: Mutual.

First Broadcast: 1948.

Serenade to Loveliness

Type: Women's Variety

Host: John Stanton.

Vocalist: Andrew Gainey.

Announcer: Gil Berkley.

Orchestra: Milton Sherdnick.

Sponsor: Chamberlain Lotion.

Length: 30 minutes.

Network: NBC.

First Broadcast: 1940.

Sergeant Preston of the Yukon

Type: Adventure

Format: The story of Sgt. William Preston, of the Northwest Mounted Police, his dog Yukon King, and their attempts to maintain law and order in the Gold Rush days of the Yukon (1890s). Became the basis for a television series of the same title.

Cast: Sgt. William
        Preston   Jay Michael
                         Paul Sutton
        Inspector Conrad,
        Preston's super-
        ior at Dawson
        city   John Todd
Commentator: John Slagle, Jay Michael.
Announcer: Bob Hite, Fred Foy, Jay Mich-
ael.
Music: Benny Kyte's Band.
Sponsor: Quaker Puffed Wheat and Rice.
Program Opening:
Announcer: Now, as howling winds echo a-
    cross the snow-covered reaches of the
    wild Northwest, the Quaker Oats Com-
    pany, makers of Quaker Puffed Wheat
    and Quaker Puffed Rice, the delicious
    cereal shot from guns, presents Sergeant
    Preston of the Yukon. (over dog barks):
    It's Yukon King, swiftest and strongest
    lead dog of the Northwest, breaking the
    trail for Sergeant Preston of the North-
    west Mounted Police in his relentless pur-
    suit of lawbreakers. . . The adventures of
    Sergeant Preston and his wonder dog
    Yukon King as they meet the challenge of
    the Yukon.
Program Closing:
Announcer: These Sergeant Preston of
    the Yukon adventures are brought to you
    Monday through Friday at this time by
    the Quaker Oats Company . . . by special
    recording in cooperation with the Mutual
    Broadcasting System. They are a copy-
    right feature of Sergeant Preston of the
    Yukon, Inc. Created by George W. Tren-
    dle, Produced by Trendle-Campbell-Muir
    Inc. and directed by Fred Flowerday. The
    part of Sergeant Preston is played by
    Paul Sutton. This is Jay Michael wishing
    you good luck and good health from
    Quaker Puffed Wheat and Quaker Puffed
    Rice. So long. This is Mutual, radio net-
    work for all America.
Length: 15 and 30 minute versions.
Network: Mutual (1947), ABC (1950).
First Broadcast: 1939 — locally over
    WXYZ in Detroit. Original title: "Chal-
    lenge of the Yukon."

Service with a Smile

Type: Variety
Format: Performances by servicemen,
    broadcast from army camps.
Host: Garry Moore.
Announcer: Ben Grauer.
Length: 30 minutes.
Network: NBC.
First Broadcast: 1941.

Seven Front Street

Type: Anthology
Format: Mystery presentations set a-
    gainst the background of 7 Front Street,
    a waterfront dive. Varying casts.
Host-Narrator: Kenneth King.
Announcer: Ralph Paul.
Length: 30 minutes.
Syndicated.
First Broadcast: 1947.

The Shadow

Type: Mystery
Format: The story of Lamont Cranston, a
    wealthy man-about-town who was actu-
    ally The Shadow, a mysterious figure
    who aids the forces of law and order.
    Years ago, while in the Orient, Cranston
    had learned the secret of a hypnotic pow-
    er to cloud men's minds so they could not
    see him. Margot Lane, his lovely friend
    and companion, was the only person who
    knew of Cranston's secret ability to turn
    himself into The Shadow.
Cast: Lamont Cranston   James LaCurto*
                          Frank Readick*
                          Robert Hardy
                           Andrews
                          Orson Welles
                          Bill Johnstone
                          Bret Morrison
        Margot Lane   Agnes Moore-
                           head
                          Marjorie Ander-
                           son

The Shadow. Bret Morrison.

Program Opening:
Shadow: Who knows what evil lurks in the hearts of men? The Shadow knows (laughs).
Program Closing:
Shadow: The weed of crime bears bitter fruit. Crime does not pay. The Shadow knows (laughs).
Length: 30 minutes.
Network: Mutual.
First Broadcast: 1930.
*From 1930-1936 when The Shadow served only as the narrator. The Lamont Cranston character evolved in 1936.

The Shadow of Fu Manchu

Type: Adventure
Format: The story of Dr. Fu Manchu, an evil Chinese physician who strove to destroy mankind after his wife and son were inadvertently killed by Jack Petrie, a British officer, during the Boxer Rebellion. Stories depicted his attempts to achieve vengeance, and the efforts of Sir Dennis Nyland Smith, a Scotland Yard Inspector, to thwart his plans. Based on the character created by Sax Rohmer.

	Gertrude Warner	
	Grace Matthews	
	Lesley Woods	
Police Commissoner Weston	Dwight Weist	
	Ken Roberts	
	Arthur Vinton	
	Kenny Delmar	
	Santos Ortega	
	Ted de Corsia	
Shrevie, Lamont's friend the cab driver	Keenan Wynn	
	Alan Reed	
	Mandel Kramer	
Blue Coal's Heating Expert (sponsor's spokesman)	John Barclay	

Announcer: Andre Baruch, Don Hancock, Carl Caruso, Sandy Beck, Ken Roberts, Frank McCarthy.
Organist: Elsie Thompson, Rosa Rio, Charles Paul.
Sponsor: Blue Coal.

Cast: Fu Manchu   John C. Daly
                              Harold Huber

        Sir Dennis
           Nyland Smith   Charles Warburton

        Dr. Jack Petrie   Bob White
        Karameneh, the
           slave girl   Sunda Love
Length: 15 minutes.
Network: CBS.
First Broadcast: 1932.

Sheaffer Parade

Type: Musical Variety
Host: Fort Pearson.
Orchestra: Eddy Howard.
Sponsor: The Sheaffer Pen Company.
Length: 30 minutes.
Network: NBC.
First Broadcast: 1947.

Shell Chateau

Type: Variety
Host: Al Jolson.
Orchestra: Victor Young.
Sponsor: Shell Gasoline.
Length: 60 minutes.
Network: NBC.
First Broadcast: 1935.

The Sheriff

See title: "Death Valley Sheriff."

Sherlock Holmes

Type: Crime Drama
Format: The story of Sherlock Holmes, a
   consulting detective (a man who inter-
   venes in baffling police matters) and his
   roommate and biographer, Dr. John H.
   Watson. Stories depicted their attempts
   to solve baffling acts of criminal injustice
   through deductive reasoning and scientific evaluation. Based on the characters
   created by Sir Arthur Conan Doyle.
Cast: Sherlock Holmes   Richard Gordon
                          Louis Hector
                          Basil Rathbone
                          Tom Conway
                          Ben Wright
                          John Stanley
                          Morry Powell*
                          Carlton Hobbs†
                          Sir John Gielgud

         Dr. John H.
            Watson   Leigh Powell
                        Nigel Bruce
                        Eric Snowden
                        Alfred Shirley
                        Ian Martin
                        Peter Bathurst*
                        Norman Sheary†
                        Sir Ralph
                           Richardson
         Professor Mori-
            arity, Holmes'
            nemesis   Louis Hector
Announcer: Joseph Bell, Harry Bartlett, Herb Allen, Cy Harrice.

Organist: Albert Buhrman.
Orchestra: Graham Harris, Lou Kosloff.
Violinist: Alfred Campoli.
Length: 30 minutes.
Network-First   Broadcast: NBC   (1930),
   Mutual (1945), ABC (1946), Mutual (1948),
   ABC (1949), NBC (1955).
*Stars of a 1949 Australian version. †Stars
of the British version.

Short, Short Stories

Type: Anthology
Format: Capsule dramatic presentations.
Host-Announcer: George Putnam.
Length: 15 minutes.
Network: CBS.
First Broadcast: 1940.

Shorty Bell

Type: Comedy
Format: The misadventures of Shorty
   Bell, an eager-beaver young man strug-
   gling to succeed as a newspaper reporter.
Starring: Mickey Rooney as Shorty Bell.
Length: 30 minutes.
Network: CBS.
First Broadcast: 1947.

The Show Shop

Type: Musical Variety
Hostess: Gertrude Niesen.
Announcer: Ray Nelson.
Orchestra: Ray Nelson.
Length: 30 minutes.
Network: NBC.
First Broadcast: 1942.

Sidewalk Interviews

See title: "Vox Pop."

The Silent Men

Type: Anthology

Format: Dramatizations based on the investigations of various U.S. agents.
Starring: Douglas Fairbanks, Jr.
Length: 30 minutes.
Network: NBC.
First Broadcast: 1951.

Silver Eagle

Type: Adventure
Format: The story of Jim West, a Canadian Northwest Mounted Policeman whose exploits earned him the name Silver Eagle.
Cast: Jim West — Jim Ameche
Joe Bideaux, his
    side-kick — Mike Romano
         Jack Lester
Inspector Argyle — John Barclay
         Jess Pugh
Doc — Clarence Hartzell
Narrator: Ed Prentiss, Bill O'Connor.
Announcer: Ken Nordine, Ed Cooper.
Music: Richard Dix.
Length: 30 minutes.
Network: ABC.
First Broadcast: 1951.

Silver Theatre

Type: Anthology
Format: Dramatic presentations. Became the basis for a television series of the same title.
Host: Conrad Nagel.
Announcer: John Conte, Roger Krupp, Dick Joy.
Sponsor: The International Silver Company.
Length: 30 minutes.
Network: CBS.
First Broadcast: 1939.

Sincerely, Kenny Baker

Type: Musical Variety
Host: Kenny Baker.
Vocalist: Donna Dae.

Announcer: Jimmy Wallington.
Music: The Buddy Cole Trio.
Length: 15 minutes.
Syndicated.
First Broadcast: 1945.

Sing Along

Type: Musical Variety
Host-Announcer: Ken Roberts.
Music: The Landt Trio.
Length: 15 minutes.
Network: CBS.
First Broadcast: 1942.

Sing for Your Dough

Type: Game
Format: Before the broadcast, microphones were placed before selected members of the studio audience. Once on the air, the host led the audience in a community sing. After a given time, the host cued the audience to stop. If the person (or persons) stationed near a microphone continued the song, they received two dollars.
Host: Lew Valentine.
Organist: Don Baker.
Length: 30 minutes.
Network: CBS.
First Broadcast: 1942.

Sing for Your Supper

Type: Quiz
Format: Four contestants, chosen from the studio audience, sang a song while performing a stunt. The best performer received a prize.
Host: Tommy Tucker.
Regulars: Nancy Donovin, Tom Mahoney, The Ray Charles Quartet.
Announcer: Phil Tonkin.
Orchestra: Tommy Tucker.
Length: 30 minutes.
Network: Mutual.
First Broadcast: 1949.

Sing It Again

Type: Variety-Quiz
Format: The variety segment featured the works of songwriters who had refurbished the lyrics of standard popular songs; the quiz segment had contestants attempting to identify a recorded phantom voice through a series of rhyming clues.
Host: Dan Seymour.
Regulars: Alan Dale, Patti Clayton, Bob Howard, The Riddlers.
Orchestra: Ray Bloch.
Length: 60 minutes.
Network: CBS.
First Broadcast: 1948.

Singin' Sam

Type: Variety
Host: Harry Frankel (Singin' Sam), a baritone who sang new and old ballads.
Sponsor: Barbasol Shave Cream.
Length: 15 minutes.
Network: CBS.
First Broadcast: 1930. See also "Reminiscin' with Singin' Sam."

The Singing Lady

Type: Children
Format: Stories and songs for children.
Hostess: Irene Wicker.
Announcer: Bob Brown.
Music: Milton Rettenberg.
Length: 15 minutes.
Network: Blue (1931), ABC (1945).
First Broadcast: 1931.

The Six Shooter

Type: Western
Format: The exploits of Britt Poncett, a wandering Texan with a fast gun who lent a helping hand to people in need.
Starring: Jimmy Stewart as Britt Poncett.
Narrator: Jimmy Stewart.
Announcer: Hal Gibney.

Length: 30 minutes.
Network: NBC.
First Broadcast: 1953.

The $64.00 Question

See title: "Take It or Leave It."

The $64,000 Question

Type: Game
Format: A simulcast of the TV series. Players first choose a subject category, then answer related questions beginning at the one dollar level. Each correct response doubles a question's value from one dollar to $64,000. Players have the option to continue, risking loss of their winnings if an incorrect response is given, or stop and leave with what they have earned. Based on the radio series "Take It or Leave It" (a.k.a. "The $64.00 Question).
Host: Hal March.
Assistant: Lynn Dollar.
Announcer: Wayne Howell.
Music: Norman Leyden.
Sponsor: Revlon cosmetics.
Length: 30 minutes.
Network: CBS.
First Broadcast: 1955.

The Skip Farrell Show

Type: Musical Variety
Host: Skip Farrell.
Vocalists: The Honeydreamers.
Announcer: Jack Lester.
Music: The George Barnes Trio.
Length: 15 minutes.
Network: ABC.
First Broadcast: 1947.

Skippy

Type-Format: A children's adventure based on the Percy Crosby comic strip (and the 1931 movie with Jackie Coogan).
Cast: Skippy   Franklin Adams, Jr.

Socky, his friend   Francis Smith
Carol, his girl-
    friend   Patricia Ryan
Length: 15 minutes.
Network: NBC (later Syndicated).
First Broadcast: 1930s.

The Skippy Hollywood Theatre

Type: Anthology
Format: Dramatizations enacted by a reg-
ular cast.
Cast: Charles Starrett, Rosemary Red-
dins, Robert Clarke, Tyler McVey,
Howard Cowan.
Announcer: Van Resautel.
Music: Del Castillo.
Sponsor: Skippy Peanut Butter.
Length: 30 minutes.
Syndicated (1945), CBS (1949).
First Broadcast: 1945.

Sky King

Type: Adventure
Format: The exploits of Sky King, an ex-
F.B.I. agent, Navy pilot, and cowboy turn-
ed rancher as he battled the forces of evil
in the West. Became the basis for a tele-
vision series of the same title.
Cast: Sky King   Jack Lester
                      Earl Nightingale
                      Roy Engel
   Penny, his niece   Beryl Vaughn
   Clipper, his
      nephew   Johnny Coons
                      Jack Bivens
   The ranch fore-
      man   Cliff Soubier
Length: 15 and 25 minute versions.
Network: ABC (1946), Mutual (1950).
First Broadcast: 1946.

Skyline Roof

Type: Musical Variety
Host: Gordon MacRae.
Announcer: Harry Clark.
Orchestra: Archie Bleyer.

Length: 15 minutes.
Network: CBS.
First Broadcast: 1946.

The Slapsie Maxie Show

Type: Comedy
Format: A somewhat exaggerated at-
tempt to show the problems faced by
Slapsie Maxie Rosenbloom, a real ex-
prizefighter, as he strove to crack radio.
Cast: Maxie   Maxie Rosen-
                        bloom
   His girlfriend   Patricia Bright
Also: Betty Harris, Florence MacMichael,
Phil Kramer, Bernie West.
Orchestra: Norman Cloutier.
Length: 30 minutes.
Network: NBC.
First Broadcast: 1948.

A Slight Case of Ivory

Type: Musical Variety
Host: Walter Gross.
Regulars: Anita Boyer, Bob Hanna.
Orchestra: Walter Gross.
Length: 30 minutes.
Network: CBS.
First Broadcast: 1941.

The Sloan Simpson Show

Type: Interview-Variety
Hostess: Sloan Simpson.
Length: 30 minutes.
Network: Mutal.
First Broadcast: 1954.

The Smile Parade

Type: Variety
Host: Ransom Sherman.
Regulars: Paul Paige, Lillian Carroll.
Music: The Vagabonds.
Length: 30 minutes.
Network: NBC.
First Broadcast: 1939.

Smile Time

Type: Comedy-Variety
Host: Steve Allen.
Regulars: Wendell Noble, June Foray.
Music: Skitch Henderson.
Length: 30 minutes.
Network: Mutual.
First Broadcast: 1940.

The Smilin' Ed McConnell Show

Type: Children
Format: Stories, songs, and comedy sketches that featured such characters as Froggie the Gremlin, Midnight the Cat, and Squeaky the Mouse. Became the basis for the "Andy's Gang" television series.

Cast: Smilin' Ed (host)   Ed McConnell
      Buster Brown   Jerry Marin
      Tige, his dog   Bud Tollefson
      Froggie the
        Gremlin   Ed McConnell
      Grandie, the talk-
        ing piano   June Foray
      Midnight, the Cat   June Foray
Also, various roles: Billy Gilbert, Alan Reed.
Announcer: Arch Presby.
Sponsor: Buster Brown Shoes.
Program Opening:
Smilin' Ed: Hi kids, you better come runnin', it's old Smilin' Ed and his Buster Brown Gang...Yes sir-reee, Buster Brown Shoes are on the air with Smilin' Ed, Squeaky the Mouse, Grandie the Piano, Midnight the Cat, and Froggie the Gremlin out here in Hollywood all ready for another good old Saturday morning hullabaloo.
Length: 30 minutes.
Network: NBC.
First Broadcast: 1943. Also known as "The Buster Brown Gang Starring Smilin' Ed McConnell," and "The Buster Brown Gang."

Smilin' Jack

Type: Adventure
Format: Aviation adventures based on the comic strip by Zack Mosley.
Starring: Frank Readick as Smilin' Jack.
Length: 15 minutes.
Network: Mutual.
First Broadcast: 1939.

Smoke Dreams

Type: Variety
Format: Had the listener visualize a man seated in his easy chair in the living room; as he blew smoke rings, he reminisced about the past—which was presented in musical numbers.
Host: Tom Moore (as The Dreamer).
Regulars: Virginia Speaker, Wayne Van Dyne.
Orchestra: Frank Worth.
Sponsor: Chesterfield cigarettes ("Smoke dreams from smoke rings as a Chesterfield burns").
Length: 30 minutes.
Network: ABC.
First Broadcast: 1945.

Snow Village Sketches

Type: Drama
Format: Set against the background of a New Hampshire town, the series presented incidents in the lives of its citizens. Based on characters created by William Ford Manley.
Cast: Dan'l Dickey   Arthur Allen
      Old Hiram Nev-
        ille   Parker Fennelly
      Marge   Jean McCoy
      Wilbur   John Thomas
      Hattie   Agnes Young
      Carrie   Katherine Raht
Also: Kate McComb, William Adams, Joseph Latham.

The Smilin' Ed McConnell Show. Ed McConnell. Froggie the Gremlin is to his left.

Length: 30 minutes.
Network: Mutual.
First Broadcast: 1930.

So the Story Goes

Type: Anthology
Format: Dramatizations of little-known events that changed the destinies of famous men and women. Supposedly based on fact.
Host-Narrator: John Nesbitt.
Organist: Dick Platt.
Length: 15 minutes.
Syndicated.
First Broadcast: 1945.

So You Think You Know Music

Type: Quiz

Format: Called for contestants to answer questions based on music and composers in return for merchandise prizes.
Host: Ted Cott.
Regulars: Kitty Carlisle, Richard Dyer-Bennett, Felix Knight, Leonard Lieblin, Percy Grainger, Alan Dinehart.
Announcer: John Reed King, Jack Barry.
Orchestra: Henry Sylvern, Allen Roth.
Length: 25 minutes.
Network: CBS (1939), Mutual (1945).
First Broadcast: 1939.

Solitaire Time

Type: Musical Variety
Host: Warde Donovan.
Announcer: Tex Antoine.
Orchestra: Ving Merlin.
Length: 15 minutes.
Network: ABC.
First Broadcast: 1946.

Somebody Knows

Type: Anthology
Format: Dramatizations of actual, unsolved murder cases. Following the broadcast, a description of the killer was given to the radio audience in the hopes that someone might possess knowledge and contact the police.
Host-Narrator: Jack Johnstone.
Length: 30 minutes.
Network: CBS.
First Broadcast: 1950.

The Somerset Maugham Theatre

Type: Anthology
Format: Dramatizations of stories by W. Somerset Maugham. Became the basis for the "Teller of Tales" television series.
Host: W. Somerset Maugham.
Length: 30 minutes.
Network: CBS.
First Broadcast: 1951.

Song of Your Life

Type: Musical Variety
Host: Harry Salter
Regulars: Jack Arthur, Clark Dennis, Gwen Williams.
Orchestra: Harry Salter.
Length: 30 minutes.
Network: NBC.
First Broadcast: 1940.

Songs by Eddie Fisher

Type: Musical Variety
Host: Eddie Fisher.
Orchestra: Alvy West.
Length: 15 minutes.
Network: NBC.
First Broadcast: 1950.

Songs by George Byran

Type: Musical Variety

Host: George Byran.
Announcer: Dan Seymour.
Orchestra: Jeff Alexander.
Length: 15 minutes.
Syndicated.
First Broadcast: 1946.

Songs by Marcia Neil

Type: Musical Variety
Hostess: Marcia Neil.
Orchestra: Irving Miller.
Length: 15 minutes.
Network: NBC.
First Broadcast: 1942.

Songs by Morton Downey

Type: Musical Variety
Host: Morton Downey.
Announcer: Joe King.
Orchestra: Carmen Mastren.
Length: 15 minutes.
Network: CBS.
First Broadcast: 1948.

Songs by Sinatra

Type: Musical Variety
Host: Frank Sinatra.
Vocalists: The Pied Pipers, The Bobby Tucker Chorus.
Announcer: Marvin Miller, Jerry Lawrence.
Orchestra: Axel Stordahl.
Program Opening:
Announcer: Songs by Sinatra. Columbia invites you to another informal session in which there'll be Songs by Sinatra and The Bobby Tucker Chorus, and the music of Axel Stordahl.
Length: 15 minutes.
Network: CBS (1943), NBC (1954).
First Broadcast: 1943. In 1947 the series title became "Songs for Sinatra."

Songs for Sale

Type: Variety

Songs By Sinatra. Frank Sinatra.

Format: Presented the material of amateur songwriters whose work was performed by professionals, then judged, evaluated, and offered for sale. Became the basis for a television series of the same title.
Hosts: Jan Murray, Richard Hayes.
Vocalists: Tony Bennett, Rosemary Clooney.
Orchestra: Ray Bloch.
Length: 60 minutes.
Network: CBS.
First Broadcast: 1950.

Songs for Sinatra

See title: "Songs by Sinatra."

Songs of a Dreamer

Type: Variety
Format: A romantic interlude slanted to women.
Hostess: Doris Moore.
Vocalist: Gene Baker.
Organist: Larry Larsen.
Length: 15 minutes.
Syndicated.
First Broadcast: 1940.

Songs of the B-Bar-B

See title: "Bobby Benson's Adventures."

Sonny Skylar's Serenade

Type: Musical Variety
Host: Sonny Skylar.
Orchestra: Henry Sylvern.
Length: 15 minutes.
Network: Mutual.
First Broadcast: 1944.

The Space Adventures of Super Noodle

Type: Science Fiction Adventure
Format: The exploits of Super Noodle and his friend Rik, who, projected five hundred years into the future, battled the sinister forces of evil. The title was derived from a tie-in with the sponsor, the I.J. Gross Noodle Company.
Cast: Super Noodle   Charles Flynn
      Rik   Robert Englund
Also: Tomi Thurston, Everett Clarke.
Length: 15 minutes.
Network: CBS.
First Broadcast: 1952.

Space Patrol

Type: Science Fiction Adventure
Format: Earth in the 21st Century. The battle against celestial dangers as seen through the assignments of Buzz Corey, the commander-in-chief of the Space Patrol, an earth-based organization responsible for the safety of the United Planets (Earth, Mars, Venus, Jupiter, and Mercury). Based on the television series of the same title.
Cast: Buzz Corey   Ed Kemmer
      Cadet Happy, his
        co-pilot   Lyn Osborn
      Carol Karlyle,
        daughter of the
        secretary Gen-
        eral   Virginia Hewitt

Dr. Van Meter,
the scientist   Rudolph Anders
Tonga, a Space
Patrol ally   Nina Bara
Sponsor: Ralston cereals; Nestle's chocolate.
Length: 30 minutes.
Network: ABC.
First Broadcast: 1950.

Spade Cooley and His Dance Group

Type: Musical Variety
Host: Spade Cooley.
Regulars: Tex Williams, Precious Price.
Orchestra: Spade Cooley.
Length: 15 minutes.
Syndicated.
First Broadcast: 1946.

The Spade Cooley Show

Type: Variety
Host: Spade Cooley.
Regulars: Ginny Jackson, Phil Gray, Freddie Love, Hank Penny, Wally Ruth.
Announcer: Bob Lemond.
Length: 60 minutes.
Network: CBS.
First Broadcast: 1951.

Sparkle Time

Type: Musical Variety
Host: Ben Gage.
Vocalist: Annette Warren.
Announcer: Ben Gage.
Music: The Vivian Gray Trio.
Length: 30 minutes.
Network: CBS.
First Broadcast: 1946.

The Sparrow and the Hawk

Type: Adventure
Format: The exploits of Spencer Mallory, a lieutenant colonel with the Army Air Corps who was discharged due to combat injuries, and his ten-year-old nephew, Barney, a flying enthusiast, as they assisted people in distress.
Cast: Spencer Mallory,
"The Hawk"   Michael Fitzmaurice
Barney Mallory,
"The Sparrow" Donald Buka
Laura Weatherby, Spencer's romantic interest Susan Douglas
Tony, Spencer's friend   Joseph Julian
Mrs. Mallory,
Spencer's mother   Mary Hunter
Length: 30 minutes.
Network: CBS.
First Broadcast: 1945.

Special Agent

Type: Crime Drama
Format: The exploits of Alan Drake, an investigator working for his father's firm and specializing in marine/ocean insurance claims.
Cast: Alan Drake   James Meighan
His side-kick   Lyle Sudrow
Orchestra: Chet Kingsbury.
Length: 30 minutes.
Network: Mutual.
First Broadcast: 1948. Originally titled "The Gentleman Adventurer."

Spend a Million

Type: Game
Format: Contestants, chosen from the studio audience, each received $1,000. The first player to correctly answer a question received the opportunity to purchase merchandise at varying prices. The first player to spend all his money won what he had purchased.
Host: Joey Adams.
Announcer: Fred Collins.
Length: 30 minutes.
Network: NBC.
First Broadcast: 1954.

The Spike Jones Show. Left to right: Dick Morgan, Freddy Morgan, Sir Fredric Gas, Spike Jones.

The Spike Jones Show

Type: Comedy-Variety
Host: Spike Jones.
Regulars: Doodles Weaver (as Prof. Feedlebaum), Dick and Freddy Morgan, Sir Fredric Gas, The City Slickers, Dorothy Shay.
Music Conductor: Henizi Rene'.
Length: 30 minutes.
Network: NBC.
First Broadcast: 1940s.

Spin to Win

Type: Game
Format: A recorded song was played, and a telephone call placed to a listener, who was asked to name the title and the type of song (dance, ballad, jazz, etc.). If he answered correctly he won a prize and received the opportunity to crack the $15,-000 jackpot by identifying the title of a song that was played backwards.
Host: Warren Hull.
Length: 45 minutes.
Network: CBS.
First Broadcast: 1949.

Spotlight on Paris

Type: Variety
Format: Various entertainment acts broadcast from Paris in cooperation with the French Broadcasting System.
Host: Gregoire Aslan.
Length: 30 minutes.
Network: NBC.
First Broadcast: 1954.

The Spike Jones Show. Henizi Rene (left) and Spike Jones.

Spotlight Revue

Type: Variety
Hostess: Margaret Whiting.
Regulars: Jimmy Castle, Al Galante, The Joe Mooney Quartet.
Announcer: Joe King.
Orchestra: Dick Jurgens.
Length: 30 minutes.
Network: CBS.
First Broadcast: 1948.

Squad Car

Type: Anthology
Format: Dramatizations of cases from the files of the Louisville Police Department.
Narrator: Peter French.
Announcer: James Van Sickle.
Length: 15 minutes.
Syndicated.
First Broadcast: 1954.

The Squeaking Door

See title "Inner Sanctum Mysteries."

S.R.O.

Type: Quiz
Format: Four panelists attempted to answer questions submitted by listeners. Those whose questions stumped the panel received their choice of theatre tickets or a savings bond as a prize.
Hostess: Betty Furness.
Panelists: Eloise McElhone, Jean Meegan, Jimmy Cannon, Whitney Bolton.
Announcer: Douglas Browning.
Length: 30 minutes.
Network: ABC.
First Broadcast: 1953.

Stag Party

Type: Musical Variety
Host: Alan Young.
Regulars: Freddy Hill, Bill Herbert.
Orchestra: Harry Price.
Length: 30 minutes.
Network: NBC.
First Broadcast: 1942.

Stage Door Canteen

Type: Variety
Format: The program, set against the background of a World War II canteen, presented performances by top name entertainers.
Host: Bert Lytell.
Orchestra: Raymond Paige.
Program Opening:
Announcer: Corn Products presents Stage Door Canteen, starring tonight Louella Parsons, Connee Boswell, Bob Benchley, Benny Goodman, Eddie Green, and Raymond Paige and the Canteen Orchestra. Stand by—curtain up for victory!
Length: 30 minutes.
Network: CBS.
First Broadcast: 1942.

Stairway to the Stars

Type: Musical Variety

Hostess: Martha Tilton.
Announcer: Glenn Riggs.
Orchestra: Paul Whiteman.
Length: 30 minutes.
Network: ABC.
First Broadcast: 1946.

The Stan Freberg Show

Type: Satire
Host: Stan Freberg.
Regulars: Peggy Taylor, Daws Butler, June Foray, Peter Leeds, Jud Conlon's Rhythmaires.
Orchestra: Billy May.
Length: 30 minutes.
Network: CBS.
First Broadcast: 1957 (July 14 to October 20.)

The Star and the Story

Type: Anthology
Format: Dramatic presentations.
Host: Walter Pidgeon.
Announcer: Toby Reed.
Length: 30 minutes.
Network: CBS.
First Broadcast: 1944.

Star for a Night

Type: Game
Format: Called for contestants to perform in comedy skits in return for merchandise prizes.
Host: Paul Douglas.
Assistant: Wendy Barrie.
Announcer: Hugh James.
Length: 30 minutes.
Network: Blue.
First Broadcast: 1943.

Starlight Concert

Type: Musical Variety
Host: Eloise Dragon.
Choir: Norman Luboff.
Announcer: Don Wilson.

Orchestra: Carmen Dragon.
Length: 30 minutes.
Network: CBS.
First Broadcast: 1950.

Starlight Serenade

Type: Musical Variety
Starring: Victoria Cordova, Harrison Knox, Bernard Dudley, Nestor Chayres, Bea Wain.
Announcer: Del Sharbutt.
Orchestra: Alfredo Antonini.
Length: 30 minutes.
Network: Mutual.
First Broadcast: 1944.

Starring Boris Karloff

Type: Anthology
Format: Mystery-suspense presentations. Became the basis for a television series of the same title.
Host-Performer: Boris Karloff.
Announcer: George Gunn.
Organist: George Henniger.
Length: 30 minutes.
Network: ABC.
First Broadcast: 1949.

Starr of Space

Type: Science Fiction Adventure
Format: The exploits of Rocky Starr, a space policeman, as he battled evil throughout the universe.
Cast: Rocky Starr   John Larch
His female assistant   Jane Harlan
His male assistant   Tom Hubbard
Announcer: Lou Cook.
Length: 30 minutes.
Network: ABC.
First Broadcast: 1953.

Stars and Starters

Type: Variety

Format: Spotlighted undiscovered professional talent.
Host: Jack Barry.
Orchestra: Norman Cloutier.
Length: 30 minutes.
Network: NBC.
First Broadcast: 1950.

Stars in Khaki 'n' Blue

Type: Variety
Format: Spotlighted army talent.
Hostess: Arlene Francis.
Announcer: Jack Costello.
Orchestra: Bernie Leighton.
Length: 30 minutes.
Network: NBC.
First Broadcast: 1952.

Stars in the Air

See title: "The Lady Esther Screen Guild Theatre."

Stars Over Hollywood

Type: Anthology
Format: Dramatic presentations.
Host: Knox Manning.
Announcer: Frank Goss, Marvin Miller.
Orchestra: Del Castillo.
Included:
When the Police Arrive. The story of a couple who murdered an old woman, then plotted to cover it up.
Starring: Joan Crawford.
The Perfect Mate. An editor attempts to build up his magazine's circulation by running a perfect-mate-by-computer contest.
Starring: Jack Paar.
Length: 30 minutes.
Network: CBS.
First Broadcast: 1941.

Station EZRA

Type: Comedy
Format: A satirization of small town rad-
io outlets as heard through the antics of the staff of station E-Z-R-A, "a powerful little five watter down in Rosedale."

Cast: Uncle Ezra   Pat Barrett
       Cecelia   Nora Cunneen
       Aunt Fanny   Fran Allison
Also: Cliff Soubier, The Hoosier Hot Shots (Gabe Ward, Hezzie and Kenny Triesch, Frank Kettering), The Sons of the Pioneers.
Sponsor: Alka-Seltzer, Camel cigarettes.
Length-Network-First Broadcast: NBC (15 min. 1934-1938, 30 min. 1940-1941). Also titled "Uncle Ezra's Radio Station."

Stay Tuned for Terror

Type: Anthology
Format: Varied mystery-suspense presentations enacted by a regular cast.
Cast: Craig Dennis, Din Doolittle, Frances Spencer.
Organist: Romelle Fay.
Length: 15 minutes.
Syndicated.
First Broadcast: 1945.

Stella Dallas

Type: Serial
Format: The dramatic story of Stella Dallas, a seamstress in a small shop in Boston. Based on the novel by Olive Higgins Prouty.

Cast:		
Stella Dallas	Anne Elstner
Stephen Dallas, her husband	Frederick Tozere
Laurel Dallas Grosvenor, their married daughter	Joy Hathaway
	Vivian Smolen
Dick Grosvenor, Laurel's husband	Carleton Young
	Macdonald Carey
	Spencer Bentley
	George Lambert
Helen Dallas, Stella's daughter	Julie Benell

Stella Dallas. Left to right, bottom: Vivian Smolen, Anne Elstner, Jane Houston. Top, left to right: Bert Cowlan, Helen Claire, Stanley Warren.

Mrs. Grosvenor, Dick's mother	Jane Houston
Beatrice Martin	Mary Jane Higby
Charles Martin	Frank Lovejoy
	Tom Tully
Ada Dexter	Helen Claire
Minnie Grady	Grace Valentine
Lewis Johnson	Raymond Bramley
Vera Johnson	Helen Carew
Nellie Ellis	Barbara Barton
Sam Ellis	Mandel Kramer

Also: Stanley Warner, Bert Cowlan, Bill Quinn.

Announcer: Ford Bond, Frank Gallop, Jimmy Wallington, Roger Krupp, Howard Claney, Jack Costello.

Organist: Richard Leibert.

Program Opening:

Announcer: ....Stella Dallas...a true-to-life story of mother love and sacrifice, in which Stella Dallas saw her own beloved daughter Laurel marry into wealth and society and, realizing the difference in their...worlds, went out of Laurel's life. These episodes in the life of Stella Dallas are based on the novel by Olive Higgins Prouty.

Length: 15 minutes.

Network: CBS.

First Broadcast: 1937 (ended in 1956).

Stepping Out

Type: Musical Variety

Hostess: Rosemary Clooney.

Vocalist: Tony Bennett.

Announcer: Sandy Becker.

Orchestra: Johnny Guarneri.

Length: 15 minutes.

Network: CBS.

First Broadcast: 1950.

The Steve Allen Show

Type: Comedy-Variety

Host: Steve Allen.

Vocalist: Ilene Wood.

Announcer: Johnny Jacobs, Hal Simms.

Music: The Jerry Shard Trio, The Bobby Sherwood Trio.

Length: 30 minutes.

Network: CBS.

First Broadcast: 1952.

Steve Canyon

Type: Adventure

Format: The exploits of Steve Canyon, an air charter pilot whose service was available to anyone with the price. Based on comic strip by Milton Caniff.

Starring: Barry Sullivan as Steve Canyon.

Length: 30 minutes.

Syndicated.

First Broadcast: 1949.

Stop and Go

Type: Quiz

Format: Servicemen were assigned a category in which to answer questions that take the form of a mythical journey. A correct response afforded the player a chance to move one step in his journey, and a cash prize of two dollars. The first player to acquire eight dollars completed his journey and won the game.

Host: Joe E. Brown.
Orchestra: Matty Malneck.
Length: 30 minutes.
Network: Blue.
First Broadcast: 1944.

Stop Me If You've Heard This One

Type: Comedy
Format: A gag, submitted by a listener, was related to a panel of experts who were to interrupt and supply an appropriate answer before the punch line was given; if they failed, the listener received five dollars. Became the basis for a television series of the same title.
Host: Milton Berle, Roger Bower.
Panelists: Jay C. Flippen, Harry Hershfield, Morey Amsterdam, Lew Lehr.
Announcer: Dan Seymour, Ted Brown.
Orchestra: Joe Rines, Horace Heidt.
Length: 30 minutes.
Network: NBC (1939), Mutual (1947).
First Broadcast: 1939.

Stop the Music

Type: Game
Format: As a song played, a telephone call was placed to a listener. When the connection was made, the music stopped. If the listener could identify the song he won a $1000 bond. Became the basis for a television series of the same title.
Host: Bert Parks, Bill Cullen.
Vocalists: Jack Haskell, Jill Corey, Kay Armen, Dick Brown.
Announcer: Hal Simms, Doug Browning.
Orchestra: Ray Bloch, Harry Salter.
Length: 60 minutes.
Network: ABC (1948), CBS (1954).
First Broadcast: 1948.

Stories by Olmsted

Type: Readings

Format: The host simply read a story.
Host: Nelson Olmsted.
Length: 15 minutes.
Network: NBC.
First Broadcast: 1941.

The Story of Bess Johnson

Type: Serial
Format: A spin-off from "Hilltop House." Basically the same format, focusing on the struggles of Bess Johnson, the superintendant of a boarding school.
Cast: Bess Johnson   Herself
        Mr. Jordan   Joseph Curtin
        Mrs. Jordan   Irene Winston
        Barbara Bartlett   Mitzi Gould
        Natalie Holt   Nancy Marshall
        Patricia Jordan   Adrienne Marden
        Mrs. Townsend   Agnes Moore-
                             head
Length: 15 minutes.
Network: CBS.
First Broadcast: 1941.

The Story of Bud Barton

See title: "The Barton Family."

The Story of Dr. Kildare

Type: Medical Drama
Format: The life and loves of James Kildare, a young medical doctor. Based on the movie series.
Cast: Dr. James
        Kildare   Lew Ayres
        Dr. Leonard Gil-
        lespie, his
        mentor   Lionel Barrymore
Also: Lurene Tuttle, Lee Gregg.
Orchestra: Joey Harmon.
Program Opening:
Announcer: The Story of Dr. Kildare, starring Lew Ayres and Lionel Barrymore. Metro-Goldwyn-Mayer brought you those famous motion pictures; now this exciting, heartwarming series is

The Story of Mary Marlin. This photo, dated August 2, 1937, is the first photograph made of Anne Seymour and Bob Griffin together.

heard on radio. In just a moment, The Story of Dr. Kildare.
Length: 30 minutes.
Syndicated.
First Broadcast: 1949.

The Story of Ellen Randolph

Type: Serial
Format: The story followed the private life and the personal problems of Ellen Randolph.
Cast: Ellen Randolph   Elsie Hitz
      Her husband   John McGovern
      The doctor   Mark Smith
      Her friend   Ethel Owen
Announcer: Ford Bond.
Length: 15 minutes.
Network: NBC.
First Broadcast: 1939.

The Story of Kate Hopkins

See title: "Kate Hopkins, Angel of Mercy."

The Story of Mary Marlin

Type: Serial
Format: The dramatic story of Mary Marlin, a U.S. Senator.
Cast: Mary Marlin   Joan Blaine
      Anne Seymour
      Betty Lou Gerson
      Muriel Kirkland
      Eloise Kummer
      Linda Carlon
    Joe Marlin, her
      husband   Bob Griffin
    Bunny Mitchell   Fran Carlon
      Templeton Fox
    Frazier Mitchell   Phillips H. Lord
      Fred Sullivan
    Michael Dorne   Francis X. Bushman
    Annie   Judith Lowry
      Betty Caine
    Henry Matthews   Raymond Edward Johnson
    Sally Gibbons   Elinor Harriot
    Cynthia Adams   Loretta Poynton
    Giles   Arnold Moss

Also, various roles: Isabel Randolph, Frank Dane, Murray Forbes, Billy Lee.

Announcer: Truman Bradley, Les Griffith, Nelson Case, John Tillman.

Music: Joseph Kahn.

Sponsor: Proctor and Gamble.

Length: 15 minutes.

Network: NBC Red and Blue.

First Broadcast: 1935.

The Story of Ruby Valentine

Type: Serial

Format: A spin-off from "As the Twig is Bent." Set against the background of Harlem, the story focused on Ruby Valentine, the owner of a beauty parlor. The series featured an all-Black cast.

Starring: Juanita Hall as Ruby Valentine.

Also: Viola Dean, Earl Hyman, Ruby Dee.

Music: Luther Henderson.

Length: 15 minutes.

Network: CBS.

First Broadcast: 1955.

The Stradivari Orchestra

Type: Musical Variety

Host: Paul LaValle.

Regulars: Jacques Gasselen, Harrison Knox.

Announcer: Jack Costello.

Orchestra: Stradivari.

Length: 30 minutes.

Network: NBC.

First Broadcast: 1943.

Straight Arrow

Type: Western

Format: The story of Indian-born Steve Adams, a peaceful citizen who owned the Broken Bow Ranch. However, whenever injustice arose, Steve donned Comanche war paint and appeared as the mysterious Straight Arrow who, with his great horse Fury, rode hell bent for leather to stamp out evil.

Starring: Howard Culver as Steve Adams/Straight Arrow.

Announcer: Frank Bingman.

Organist: Not identified.

Sponsor: Nabisco.

Program Opening:

Announcer: Keen eyes fixed on a flying target, a gleaming arrow set against a rawhide string, a strong bow bent almost to the breaking point, and then...Straight Arrow! Nabisco Shredded Wheat presents Straight Arrow, a new and thrilling adventure story from the exciting days of the Old West . . .

Length: 30 minutes.

Network: Mutual.

First Broadcast: 1948.

Strange

Type: Anthology

Format: Stories of the supernatural.

Host-Announcer: Charles Woods.

Narrator: Walter Gibson.

Length: 15 minutes.

Network: ABC.

First Broadcast: 1955.

Strange As It Seems

Type: Anthology

Format: Dramatizations based on the newspaper strip, **Strange As It Seems,** by John Hix.

Host-Narrator: Patrick McGeehan, Gayne Whitman.

Length: 15 minutes.

Network: CBS.

First Broadcast: 1939.

The Strange Dr. Karnac

Type: Mystery

Format: The story of Dr. Karnac, a sleuth, and his female assistant, Dr. Watson, as they investigated supernatural crimes.

Cast: Dr. Karnac   James Van Dyke
      Dr. Watson   Jean Ellyn

Announcer: Fred Cole.
Organist: Bob Hamilton.
Length: 30 minutes.
Network: Blue.
First Broadcast: 1943.

The Strange Dr. Weird

Type: Anthology
Format: Chilling dramatizations of the supernatural.
Starring: Maurice Tarplin as the host, Dr. Weird.
Announcer: Dick Willard.
Sponsor: Adam Hats.
Length: 15 minutes.
Network: Mutual.
First Broadcast: 1944.

The Strange Romance of Evelyn Winters

Type: Serial
Format: Following his medical discharge from the service during World War II, Gary Bennett, a successful Broadway playwright, found that he had been named guardian of Evelyn Winters, the attractive, twenty-three year old daughter of his former colonel who was killed in action. The story followed the events in their lives—and the romance that developed between Evelyn and Gary.
Cast: Evelyn Winters Toni Darnay
     Gary Bennett Karl Weber
                  Martin Blaine
     Janice King Flora Campbell
     Charles Gleason Ralph Bell
     Maggie Kate McComb
     Edith Winters Helen Claire
     Ginny Roberts Mary Mason
Announcer: Larry Elliott.
Program Opening:
Announcer: We now present The Strange Romance of Evelyn Winters, the story of Gary Bennett, playwright, who suddenly and unexpectedly finds himself the guardian of lovely Evelyn Winters.
Length: 15 minutes.

Network: CBS.
First Broadcast: 1944.

Strange Wills

Type: Anthology
Format: Dramatizations of cases in which missing heirs were sought.
Host (The Investigator): Warren William.
Announcer: Marvin Miller.
Orchestra: Del Castillo.
Length: 30 minutes.
Syndicated.
First Broadcast: 1946.

Streamline Journal

Type: Variety
Hostess: Alma Kitchell.
Orchestra: Irving Miller.
Length: 30 minutes.
Network: NBC.
First Broadcast: 1940.

Strictly Business

Type: Drama
Format: The cases of a sophisticated press agent.
Cast: The Press Agent Lawson Zerbe
     His assistant Shirley Booth
Music: Paul LaValle.
Length: 30 minutes.
Network: NBC.
First Broadcast: 1940.

Strictly from Dixie

Type: Variety
Format: The music and songs of the deep South.
Host: Helena Horne, John Hicks.
Vocalist: Elizabeth Council.
Orchestra: Henry Levine.
Length: 15 and 25 minute versions.
Network: NBC (1941), ABC (1954).
First Broadcast: 1941.

Strike It Rich

Type: Audience Participation
Format: Four contestants related their hardships, stating their single most-needed possession. Home listeners were then invited to call in and donate money to a Heartline. The person with the saddest story, as determined by studio audience applause, received the cash in the Heartline. At one point in the series, it was also a quiz wherein players strove to win $800 by correctly answering five straight questions. The first format description became the basis for a television series of the same title.
Host: Todd Russell, Warren Hull.
Announcer: Don Baker, Ralph Paul.
Organist: Hank Sylvern.
Sponsor: The Colgate-Palmolive Company.
Length: 30 minutes.
Network: CBS.
First Broadcast: 1947.

Stroke of Fate

Type: Anthology
Format: Dramatized the effects the Hand of Fate has on the lives of ordinary people.
Host-Narrator: Walter Kiernan.
Commentator: Allan Nevin.
Length: 30 minutes.
Network: NBC.
First Broadcast: 1953.

The Stu Erwin Show

Type: Comedy-Variety
Host: Stu Erwin.
Regulars: Peggy Conklin, Pert Kelton, Cameron Andrews.
Vocalist: Milena Miller.
Announcer: John Reed King.
Orchestra: Jay Blackton.
Length: 30 minutes.
Network: CBS.
First Broadcast: 1945.

Studio One

Type: Anthology
Format: Stylish adaptations of well-known stories and plays. Became the basis for a television series of the same title.
Host: Fletcher Markle.
Music: Alexander Semmler.
Length: 60 minutes.
Network: CBS.
First Broadcast: 1947.

Summer Cruise

Type: Musical Variety
Host: Johnny Andrews.
Vocalist: Marilyn Ross.
Orchestra: Ralph Norman.
Length: 30 minutes.
Network: ABC.
First Broadcast: 1952.

Summerfield Bandstand

Type: Comedy-Variety
Format: The summer replacement for "The Great Gildersleeve" featured cast members from the series in various sketches. The title was derived from the series locale, Summerfield.
Starring: Ken Carson, Richard Legrand, Earle Ross, Walter Tetley.
Announcer: John Wald.
Orchestra: Jack Meakin.
Sponsor: The Kraft Foods Company.
Length: 30 minutes.
Network: NBC.
First Broadcast: 1947.

Sunday at Home

Type: Variety
Host: Jan Murray.
Regulars: Frank Stevens, Pat O'Day, Vic Marsallo, The Toppers.
Orchestra: Elliot Lawrence.
Length: 30 minutes.

Network: NBC.
First Broadcast: 1954.

Sunday Dinner at Aunt Fanny's

Type: Variety
Format: Featured Fran Allison, in her "Breakfast Club" role of Aunt Fanny, hosting a Sunday dinner party with guests from that program.
Length: 30 minutes.
Network: NBC.
First Broadcast: 1939.

Sunday Evening Party

Type: Musical Variety
Hostess: Louise Carlisle.
Featured: Donald Dane.
Announcer: Charles Stark.
Orchestra: Phil Davis.
Length: 30 minutes.
Network: ABC.
First Broadcast: 1945.

Sunday Night Serenade

Type: Musical Variety
Starring: Kitty Killand, Cecil Bailey, Snooky Lyman.
Orchestra: Francis Craig.
Length: 30 minutes.
Network: CBS.
First Broadcast: 1940.

Sunday on the N.K. Ranch

Type: Country-Western Musical Variety
Hostess: Carol Bruce.
Regulars: Curt Massey, The Charles Doucet Mixed Choir, The N.K. Ranch Hands.
Orchestra: Harry Sosnik.
Sponsor: Nash-Kelvinator Home Appliances.
Length: 30 minutes.
Network: ABC.
First Broadcast: 1945.

Sunday with Garroway

See title: "Dave Garroway."

Superman

See title: "The Adventures of Superman."

Superstition

Type: Anthology
Format: Dramatizations based on familiar fetishes.
Voice of Superstition (Narrator-Advisor-Confidant): Ralph Bell.
Announcer: Jimmy Blaine.
Orchestra: Bernie Green.
Length: 30 minutes.
Network: ABC.
First Broadcast: 1948.

Surprise Package

Type: Game
Format: Studio audience members competed in various stunt contests in return for prizes.
Host: Jay Stewart.
Length: 30 minutes.
Network: ABC.
First Broadcast: 1950.

Surprise Serenade

Type: Musical Variety
Host: Don Gordon, Ed Davies.
Announcer: Hugh Downs.
Orchestra: Joseph Gallichio.
Length: 30 minutes.
Network: NBC.
First Broadcast: 1949.

Suspense

Type: Anthology
Format: Mystery-suspense stories.

Cast: The Man in Black
      (host)   Joseph Kearns
                       Ted Osborne
Narrator: Paul Frees.
Announcer: Truman Bradley, Bob Stevenson, Harlow Wilcox, Larry Thor.
Orchestra: Lud Gluskin.
Sponsor: Roma Wines, Cresta Blanca, Auto-Lite.
Program Opening:
Announcer: Suspense.
Man in Black: This is the Man in Black here again to introduce Columbia's program, Suspense . . . If you have been with us on these Tuesday nights you well know that Suspense is compounded of mystery and suspicion, of dangerous adventure. In this series are tales calculated to intrigue you, stir your nerves, to offer you a precarious situation and then withhold the solution until the last possible moment. And so it is with "Sorry, Wrong Number," and the performance of Agnes Moorehead. We again hope to keep you in Suspense.
Included:
The Man Who Thought He Was Edward G. Robinson. The story of a meek man who, to escape his nagging wife and friends and solve his problems, adopted the tough guy characterization of Edward G. Robinson.
Starring: Edward G. Robinson.
Commuter's Ticket. A frustrated husband, after murdering his philandering wife, seeks to arrange the perfect alibi.
Starring: Jim Backus, Howard Duff, J. Carrol Naish.
Love's Lovely Counterfeit. A hoodlum, after a brief touch with decency, reverts to his past criminal activities.
Starring: James Cagney, Robert Montgomery.
Star Over Hong Kong. A lighthearted tale of a young movie star who is kidnapped while on a publicity tour of the Orient.
Starring: Marie Wilson.
The Jolly Death Riders. The story of a San Francisco Police Commissioner and his attempts to apprehend a woman's murderer.

Starring: William Holden.
Length: 30 and 55 minute versons.
Network: CBS.
First Broadcast: 1942 (ended in 1963). Became the basis for a television series of the same title.

Sweeney and March

Type: Comedy
Format: The misadventures of two small-town boys trying to make it in the big city.
Cast: Sweeney   Bob Sweeney
      March   Hal March
Vocalist: Patsy Bolton.
Announcer: George Ansbro.
Organist: Rosa Rio.
Orchestra: Irving Miller.
Length: 25 minutes.
Network: CBS.
First Broadcast: 1946.

Sweet River

Type: Serial
Format: The dramatic story of a minister in the town of Sweet River and his involvement with a woman of questionable character.
Cast: The minister   Ed Prentiss
       The woman   Betty Arnold
Also: Carl Kroenke, Kay Campbell, Helen Van Trupl, Dickie Turner.
Narrator: Howard Hoffman.
Length: 15 minutes.
Network: Blue, then ABC.
First Broadcast: 1944.

Swingtime at the Savoy

Type: Musical Variety
Host: Noble Sissle.
Regulars: Lucky Millinder, Jackie (Moms) Mabley, Paul Breckenridge, Miller and Lee, The Hall Sisters.
Music: The King Adum Quartet.
Length: 30 minutes.

Network: NBC.
First Broadcast: 1948.

Take a Card

Type: Quiz
Format: Four studio audience members competed. Each in turn drew four cards from a deck of fifty-two playing cards. The host related a question pertaining to one of the chosen cards. The player who possessed that card and was able to correctly answer the question received money according to the face value of the card.
Host: Wally Butterworth.
Assistant: Margaret Johnson.
Length: 30 minutes.
Network: Mutual.
First Broadcast: 1943.

Take a Number

Type: Quiz
Format: Questions submitted by listeners were put to selected members of the studio audience. If a player answered correctly he won five dollars, if not, the listeners received the money. The player with the most correct answers competed in the jackpot round by choosing a number from a board. If he answered the rather difficult question associated with the number, he won the money that had been accumulated through the defeats of other players.
Host: Bob Shepherd.
Announcer: Jack Irish.
Length::   30 minutes.
Network: Mutual.
First Broadcast: 1948.

Take It Easy

Type: Musical Variety.
Host: Ed Drew.
Vocalist: Haron Hyde.
Announcer: Ed Pearson.

Orchestra: Ed Drew.
Length: 30 minutes.
Network: CBS.
First Broadcast: 1940.

Take It Easy Time

Type: Musical Variety
Host: Dick Willard.
Vocalists: The Song Chiefs.
Orchestra: Frank Novak.
Length: 15 minutes.
Network: Mutual.
First Broadcast: 1945.

Take It Or Leave It

Type: Quiz
Format: One player at a time competed in a series of question and answer rounds— each worth from one dollar doubled to sixty four dollars. At any point in the game, the player could take what he had already earned, or leave it and attempt to double his winnings by answering another question—risking loss of everything if he should fail. Became the basis for TV's "The $64,000 Question."
Host: Phil Baker, Bob Hawk, Garry Moore, Jack Paar, Eddie Cantor.
Announcer: Ken Roberts.
Orchestra: Eversharp.
Length: 30 minutes.
Network: CBS (1940), NBC (1949).
First Broadcast: 1940. Later titled "The "The $64,000 Question."

Talent Search, Country Style

Type: Variety
Format: Showcased undiscovered professional Country and Western performers.
Host: Tom George.
Announcer: Ray Barrett.
Length: 30 minutes.
Network: NBC.
First Broadcast: 1951.

Tales of Fatima

Type: Drama
Format: The cases of Basil Rathbone as a private detective who drew his inspiration by dreaming of the fabulous Princess Fatima; he also recalled romantic flights of poetry with his idol.
Starring: Basil Rathbone as himself.
Orchestra: Carl Hoff.
Length: 30 minutes.
Network: CBS.
First Broadcast: 1949.

Tales of the Texas Rangers

Type: Western
Format: The exploits of Jace Pearson, a Texas Ranger, one of fifty men using time-honored methods to battle crime. Became the basis for a television series of the same title.
Starring: Joel McCrae as Ranger Jace Pearson.
Program Opening:
Announcer: The Tales of the Texas Rangers, starring Joel McCrae as Ranger Jace Pearson. Texas, more than 260 square miles, and fifty men who make up the most famous and oldest law enforcement body in North America. Now, from the files of the Texas Rangers, come these stories based on fact; only names, dates, and places are fictitious for obvious reasons. The events themselves are a matter of record.
Length: 30 minutes.
Network: NBC.
First Broadcast: 1950.

Tales of Willie Piper

Type: Comedy
Format: The misadventures of a timid man named Willie Piper.
Cast: Willie Piper   Billy Redfield
        His wife   Elaine Rost
Announcer: Win Elliot.
Music: Ralph Norman.
Length: 30 minutes.

Network: ABC.
First Broadcast: 1947.

Tangee Varieties

Type: Musical Variety.
Host: Paul Winchell.
Orchestra: Sammy Kaye.
Sponsor: Tangee Cosmetics.
Length: 30 minutes.
Network: Mutal.
First Broadcast: 1944.

Tarzan

Type: Adventure
Format: Put ashore in Africa by the mutinous crew of a ship bound for England, Lord John Greystoke and his wife Alice, left with tools and firearms, construct a small shack near the sea when all attempts to escape fail. One year later, a son is born to them.

Shortly after, their cabin is attacked by a tribe of bull apes. John and Alice are savagely slaughtered and little Lord Greystoke is taken by Kalah, a young female ape who raises him as Tarzan, Lord of the Jungle.

Twenty years later, a young girl named Jane Parker strays from the safari she is with and is suddenly propelled into a web of impending death: a rampaging elephant and savage pygmies. She is rescued by Tarzan, whom she befriends, teaches to speak, and decides to remain within the jungle. Stories depicted Tarzan's attempts to protect his adopted homeland from the forces of evil.
Cast: Tarzan   James Pierce
                          Calton KaDell
                          Lamont Johnson
        Jane   Joan Burroughs
Narrator: Charles Arlington.
Music: Albert Glasser.
Program Opening:
Announcer: From the black core of dark Africa, land of enchantment, mystery, and violence, comes one of the most colorful figures of all time; transcribed from the immortal pen of Edgar Rice Bur-

roughs—Tarzan, the bronzed, white son of the jungle.
Length: 30 minutes.
Network: CBS.
First Broadcast: 1932 (to 1935, 1951 to 1952).

Tea Time at Morrell's

Type: Variety
Host: Don McNeill.
Regulars: Gale Page, Charles Sears.
Orchestra: Joseph Gallichio.
Sponsor: The John Morrell Company.
Length: 30 minutes.
Network: NBC.
First Broadcast: 1936.

Ted Drake, Guardian of the Big Top

Type: Adventure
Format: The story of Ted Drake, a circus detective for a traveling tent show.
Cast: Ted Drake   Vince Harding
        His side-kick   Fred Rains
Announcer: Bob Larrimore.
Music: Recorded.
Length: 30 minutes.
Network: Mutual.
First Broadcast: 1949.

The Ted Lewis Show

Type: Musical Variety
Host: Ted Lewis.
Vocalist: Geraldine DuBois.
Orchestra: Paul Arnold.
Length: 30 minutes.
Syndicated.
First Broadcast: 1947.

The Ted Mack Family Hour

Type: Variety
Host: Ted Mack.
Sponsor: General Mills and Swanson Foods.

Length: 30 minutes.
Network: ABC.
First Broadcast: 1951.

The Ted Steele Show

Type: Variety
Host: Ted Steele.
Regulars: Rita Grande, The Five Marshalls.
Orchestra: Paul LaValle.
Length: 30 minutes.
Network: NBC.
First Broadcast: 1942.

Ted Steele's Novatones

Type: Musical Variety
Host: Ted Steele.
Music: The Ted Steele Trio (Ted Steele on novachord, Doc Whipple on electric organ, and Howard Smith on drums).
Length: 15 minutes.
Network: NBC.
First Broadcast: 1939.

Teen Town

Type: Musical Variety
Format: Showcased teenage performers.
Host: Dick York.
Vocalists: Tony Frantina, Jackie Dvorak.
Orchestra: Mary Hartline.
Length: 30 minutes.
Network: ABC.
First Broadcast: 1946.

The Teentimers Club

Type: Musical Variety
Host: Johnny Desmond.
Regulars: J. Scott Smart, Phil Kramer, Jr., Ray Ives, Hope Emerson, Susan Douglas.
Announcer: Tom Hudson.
Orchestra: Johnny Long.
Length: 30 minutes.
Network: NBC.
First Broadcast: 1945.

Tena and Tim

Type: Comedy
Format: The mishaps of Tena, a Swedish maid and cook, and her devoted friend and admirer, Tim, an Irish janitor.
Cast: Tena — Peggy Beckmark
Tim — James Gardner
George Cisar

Mr. Hutchinson, Tena's employer — John Goldsworthy

Mrs. Hutchinson, his wife — Gladys Heen
Also: Claire Baum, Arthur Young.
Length: 15 minutes.
Syndicated (1939), CBS (1944).
First Broadcast: 1939. The series was originally broadcast locally over Station WCCO in Minneapolis.

The Tennessee Ernie Ford Show

Type: Variety
Host: Tennessee Ernie Ford.
Announcer: Jack Narz.
Orchestra: Cliff Stone.
Length: 15 minutes.
Network: CBS.
First Broadcast: 1954.

Tennessee Jed

Type: Adventure
Format: The exploits of Tennessee Jed Sloan, an undercover agent for President Grant.
Cast: Tennessee Jed Sloan — Johnny Thomas
Don MacLaughlin
Sheriff Jackson — Humphrey Davis
His deputy — Jim Boles
Announcer-Narrator: Court Benson.
Sponsor: Tip Top Bread.
Program Opening:
Man: There he goes Tennessee, get him. (Gun shot is heard), Got him, dead center!
Announcer: That's Jed Sloan, Tennessee Jed, deadliest man ever to ride the Wes-

tern Plains. Brought to you transcribed by the makers of Tip Top Bread.
Length: 15 minutes.
Network: ABC.
First Broadcast: 1945.

Terkel Time

Type: Variety
Host: Studs Terkel.
Regulars: John Conrad, Connie Russell, Jack Haskell.
Music: The Art Van Damme Quintet.
Length: 30 minutes.
Network: NBC.
First Broadcast: 1950.

Terry Allen and the Three Sisters

Type: Musical Variety
Host: Terry Allen.
Vocalists: Margie, Bea, and Geri Ross (the Three Sisters).
Music: The Captivators.
Length: 15 minutes.
Network: CBS.
First Broadcast: 1944.

Terry and the Pirates

Type: Adventure
Format: Inheriting an abandoned gold mine from his grandfather, Terry Lee, a U.S. Air Force Colonel, journeyed to the Orient to begin a search for it. Captured by a band of cutthroats and taken to a secret mountain hideaway, he met his evil Eurasian captor, Lai Choi San, alias The Dragon Lady, who planned to enslave him. Resisting and escaping her bonds, he remained in the Orient, where, while searching for the gold mine, he battled the evils of The Dragon Lady. Based on the comic strip character by Milton Caniff.
Cast: Terry Lee — Jackie Kelk
Cliff Carpenter
Owen Jordan

Patrick Ryan	Bud Collyer
	Lawrence Alexander
	Warner Anderson
	Bob Griffin
The Dragon Lady	Agnes Moorehead
	Adelaide Klein
	Marion Sweet
Hot Shot Charlie	Cameron Andrews
Connie	Cliff Norton
	Peter Donald
	John Gibson
Burma	Frances Chaney

Announcer: Douglas Browning.
Sponsor: Quaker Oats, Puffed Wheat, and Puffed Rice.
Length: 15 minutes.
Network: NBC, the ABC.
First Broadcast: 1937.

Terry's House Party

Type: Musical Variety
Host: Terry Pepin.
Featured: Ted Cole.
Orchestra: Bobby Norris.
Length: 30 minutes.
Network: Blue.
First Broadcast: 1944.

Tex and Jinx

Type: Variety
Hosts: Tex McCrary, Jinx Falkenberg.
Regulars: Mary Martin, Billy Rose, Helen Carroll and the Escorts.
Announcer: Dan Seymour.
Orchestra: Johnny Guarneri.
Length: 30 minutes.
Network: NBC.
First Broadcast: 1947. Became the basis for a television series of the same title.

Texaco Star Theatre

Type: Variety

Hosts: Kenny Baker, Jane Froman, Milton Berle.
Regulars: Arnold Stang, Pert Kelton, John Gibson, Al Kelly, Ken Murray, Frances Langford, Edward Trevor, Kay Armen, Bob Hanna, The Mixed Chorus.
Announcer: Frank Gallop, Jimmy Wallington.
Orchestra: Allen Roth, David Broekman, Al Goodman.
Sponsor: Texaco.
Length: 30 and 60 minute versions.
Network: CBS (1939), NBC (1948).
First Broadcast: 1939.

That Brewster Boy

Type: Comedy
Format: The adventures of Joey Brewster, a mischievous boy.

Cast:	
Joey Brewster	Eddie Firestone, Jr.
	Arnold Stang
	Dick York
James Brewster, his father	Hugh Studebaker
Jane Brewster, his mother	Constance Crowder
Nancy Brewster, his sister	Louise Fitch
	Patricia Dunlap

Announcer: Marvin Miller.
Length: 30 minutes.
Network: NBC.
First Broadcast: 1941.

That Hammer Guy

Type: Crime Drama
Format: The exploits of Mike Hammer, a tough, wandering private detective. Based on the character created by Mickey Spillane. Became the basis for the television series "Mike Hammer, Detective."
Starring: Larry Haines as Mike Hammer.
Length: 30 minutes.
Network: Mutual.
First Broadcast: 1953.

That's a Good One

Type: Variety
Format: Featured guest comedians in a joke-telling session.
Hostess: Faye Emerson.
Regulars: Ward Wilson, Art Elmer, Al Lee Reiser.
Announcer: Ed Herlihy.
Organist: John Gart.
Length: 15 mminutes.
Network: Blue.
First Broadcast: 1943.

That's Life

Type: Audience Participation
Format: Allowed anyone who wanted to get on the air to do so. Microphones were turned over to would-be performers, to people with gripes, and to people with a story to tell.
Host: Jay C. Flippen.
Announcer: Jay Stewart.
Length: 30 minutes.
Network: CBS.
First Broadcast: 1946.

That's My Pop

Type: Comedy
Format: The life of a loveable but lazy head of a houschold, a man whose last means of employment was selling sun glasses during the 1929 eclipse.
Cast: The father   Hugh Herbert
       His wife   Mary Wickes
       Their daughter Peggy Conklin
       Their son   Ronald Liss
Also: Jack Albertson, Ethel Owen, Toby David, Walter Kinsella.
Length: 30 minutes.
Network: CBS.
First Broadcast: 1945.

That's Rich

Type: Comedy

Format: The story of a wide-eyed, innocent young man; a man with a trivial job with a paper company whose sole interest in life is bird-watching.
Cast: The man   Stan Freberg
       The operator   Patte Chapman
Also: Patricia Dunlap, Les Tremayne, Bridgit McColland, Tony Kay, Bob Jellison, Will Wright, Martha Wentworth, Daws Butler, Peter Leeds.
Announcer: Roy Rowan.
Length: 30 minutes.
Network: CBS.
First Broadcast: 1954.

The Theatre Guild on the Air

See title: "The U.S. Steel Hour."

There's Music in the Air

Type: Musical Variety
Host: Donald Richards.
Regulars: Frances Greer, Nancy Evans, Clark Dennis.
Announcer: Olin Tice.
Orchestra: Alfredo Antonini.
Length: 30 minutes.
Network: CBS.
First Broadcast: 1953.

The Thin Man

Type: Crime Drama
Format: The story of the Norths: Nick, a private detective, and his beautiful, trouble-prone wife, Nora, and their investigations into acquired cases. Based on the characters created by Dashiell Hammett. Became the basis for the television series of the same title.
Cast: Nick Charles   Lester Damon
                       Les Tremayne
                       Joseph Curtin
                       David Gothard
                       Bill Smith
       Nora Charles   Claudia Morgan
Announcer: Tom Shirley, Ed Herlihy, Ron Rawson.

Orchestra: Fred Fradkin.
Sponsor: Pabst Blue Ribbon Beer.
Program Opening:
Announcer: Pabst Blue Ribbon Beer presents The New Adventures of the Thin Man, with Nick and Nora Charles, the happiest, merriest married couple in radio. Claudia Morgan as Nora and Les Tremayne as Nick in tonight's adventure of The Thin Man called "The Adventure of the Passionate Palooka."
Length: 30 minutes.
Network-First Broadcast: NBC (1941), CBS (1946), NBC (1948), ABC (1950). Also titled: "The New Adventures of the Thin Man."

This Day Is Ours

Type: Serial
Format: The dramatic story of Eleanor MacDonald, the daughter of a missionary, as she struggled to help people in war-torn China.
Cast:

Eleanor Mac-Donald	Templeton Fox
	Joan Banks
Curtis, a missionary	Jay Jostyn
Paul, the clerical worker	Frank Lovejoy
Wong, their Chinese friend	Alan Devitt
Pat Curtis, the missionary's wife	Patricia Dunlap

Announcer: Mel Allen.
Organist: Don Becker.
Length: 15 minutes.
Network: CBS.
First Broadcast: 1938.

This Is Broadway

Type: Variety
Host: Clifton Fadiman.
Regulars: Helen Hayes, George S. Kaufman, Adele Clark, Phil Foster, Nancy Franklin, Frank Parker, Mary McCarthy, Artie Shaw.

Orchestra: Ray Bloch.
Length: 60 minutes.
Network: CBS.
First Broadcast: 1949.

This Is Helen Hayes

Type: Anthology
Format: Dramatizations of the work and sacrifices of army and navy nurses.
Hostess-Narrator: Helen Hayes.
Announcer: Hal Lansing.
Length: 15 minutes.
Network: Mutual.
First Broadcast: 1945.

This Is My Best

Type: Anthology
Format: Dramatic presentations.
Host: Orson Welles.
Sponsor: Cresta Blanca.
Length: 30 minutes.
Syndicated.
First Broadcast: 1945.

This Is Nora Drake

Type: Serial
Format: The dramatic story of Nora Drake, a nurse in a metropolitan hospital.
Cast:

Nora Drake	Charlotte Holland
	Joan Tompkins
	Mary Jane Higby
Arthur Drake	Joseph Conway
	Everett Sloane
	Ralph Bell
Dorothy Stewart	Evelyn Varden
	Elspeth Eric
Dr. Jensen	Arnold Robertson
Peg Martinson	Lesley Woods
	Joan Alexander
	Mercedes McCambridge
Suzanne	Joan Lorring
Charles Dobbs	Grant Richards
Gillian Gray	Charlotte Manson

Announcer: Bill Cullen.

Organist: Charles Paul.
Sponsor: Toni Home Permanents.
Program Opening:
Announcer: Toni. . . Home   Permanents
   presents.
Woman's Voice: This Is Nora Drake.
Announcer: This Is Nora Drake, a modern
   story seen through the window of a
   woman's heart.
Length: 15 minutes.
Network: NBC.
First Broadcast: 1947.

This Is Paris

Type: Musical Variety
Host: Maurice Chevalier.
Regulars: Yves Montand, Claude Dauphin,
   Marjorie Dunton, Gaumont Lanvin, Liné
   Renaud.
Orchestra: Paul Baron.
Length: 30 minutes.
Network: Mutual.
First Broadcast: 1949.

This Is the Story

Type: Anthology
Format: Serialized dramatizations of nov-
   els.
Hostess: Madeleine Carroll.
Length: 25 minutes.
Network: Mutual.
First Broadcast: 1954.

This Is Your F.B.I.

Type: Anthology
Format: Dramatizations based on the files
   of the Federal Bureau of Investigation.
Host-Narrator: Frank Lovejoy.
Announcer: Milton Cross, Carl Frank, Lar-
   ry Keating.
Length: 30 minutes.
Network: ABC.
First Broadcast: 1945.

This Is Your Life

Type: Variety
Format: The series presented the life stor-
   ies of celebrities. Became the basis for a
   television series of the same title.
Host: Ralph Edwards.
Announcer: John Hollbrook.
Length: 30 minutes.
Network: NBC.
First Broadcast: 1948.

This Life Is Mine

Type: Serial
Format: The dramatic story of the Chan-
   ning family: Eden, the mother, a school
   teacher estranged from her husband, ac-
   tor Edwin Lorimer, her children David
   and Joe, and her younger sister, Jane.
Cast: Eden Channing   Betty Winkler
         David Channing   Henry M. Neeley
         Joe Channing   Raymond Ives,
                              Jr.
         Jane Channing   Ruth McDevitt
         Edwin Lorimer   Paul McGrath
Also: Jay Meredith, Philip Gordon, Bert
   Burnham.
Announcer: Tony Marvin.
Organist: John Gart.
Length: 15 minutes.
Network: CBS.
First Broadcast: 1943.

This Small Town

Type: Serial
Format: The story of young marrieds in
   a small New England town.
Cast: Carrie, the wife   Joan Banks
         Russ, the hus-
            band   Jay Jostyn
Also: Carl Eastman, Eleanor Audley.
Announcer: Ed Herlihy.
Length: 15 minutes.
Network: NBC.
First Broadcast: 1940.

Those We Love. Left to right: Helen Wood, Mary Gordon, Richard Cromwell, Ann Todd, Donald Woods, Anne Stone, Alma Kruger, Nan Grey, Eddie Cantor (not a cast member; "Those We Love" replaced his series for the summer), Francis X. Bushman, Virginia Sale.

Those Bartons

See title: "The Barton Family."

Those Good Old Days

Type: Musical Revue.
Format: The music, song, and comedy of the 1900s.
Host: Pat Barnes.
Regulars: Hal Willard, Ethel Gilbert, Lulu Bates, Aileen Stanley.
Orchestra: Joe Rines.
Length: 30 minutes.
Network: Blue.
First Broadcast: 1942.

Those We Love

Type: Serial
Format: The dramatic story of marrieds Kathy and John Marshall.
Cast:

Kathy Marshall	Nan Grey
John Marshall	Francis X. Bushman
Elaine Bascomb	Helen Wood
	Jean Rogers
Kit Marshall	Richard Cromwell
Amy Foster	Priscilla Lyon
	Ann Todd
Emily Mayfield	Alma Kruger
Lydia Dennison	Anne Stone
Martha	Virginia Sale

Leslie Foster	Donald Woods
Peggy Edwards	Lurene Tuttle
Mrs. Emmett	Mary Gordon

Announcer: Dick Joy.
Length: 15 minutes.
Network: NBC Blue.
First Broadcast: 1937.

Three City Byline

Type: Commentary
Host, New York: Hy Gardner.
Hostess, Hollywood: Sheilah Graham.
Host, Chicago: Irv Kupcinet.
Length: 15 minutes.
Network: ABC.
First Broadcast: 1953.

Three for the Money

Type: Quiz
Format: Of the three players competing in each round, only one emerged the winner during a question and answer session. The winner now had to predict how three tunes would score, based on studio audience applause. If his predictions were correct he won $300 and the opportunity to win $500 additional by predicting a second bracket of three tunes. If he was successful again, he attempted to predict a third grouping for a total of $5,000.
Host: Bud Collyer.
Vocalists: Mary Small, Russ Emery, The Stardusters Quartet.
Orchestra: Mark Warnow.
Length: 60 minutes.
Network: Mutual.
First Broadcast: 1948.

Three Sheets to the Wind

Type: Adventure
Format: The series presented a look into the sinister happenings that occurred during a world cruise on a luxury liner.
Cast:

The British Intelligence agent	Helga Moray

The American (posing as a habitual drunk to cover his secret intentions).	John Wayne

Announcer: Ray Garrett.
Length: 30 minutes.
Network: NBC.
First Broadcast: 1940 (a 26-episode series).

Thunder Over Paradise

Type: Drama
Format: The struggles of a woman rancher in Central America.
Cast:

The rancher	Laurette Fillbrandt
The aviator	Bill Crawford
The revolutionary general	Sid Ellstrom
The ranch hand	Mike Romane

Length: 15 minutes.
Network: NBC.
First Broadcast: 1939.

Thurston the Magician

Type: Adventure
Format: The exploits of Howard Thurston, a master magician.
Cast:

Howard Thurston	Cliff Soubier
His assistant	Carlton Brickert

Announcer: William Kephart.
Length: 15 minutes.
Network: Blue.
First Broadcast: 1932.

Tillie the Toiler

Type: Comedy
Format: Adopted from the comic strip by Russ Westover, the series followed the hectic life of a helpful woman named Tillie.
Cast:

Tillie	Caryl Smith
Simpkins, the absent-minded gentleman	John Brown

Mac, Tillie's faith-
ful swain   Billy Lynn
Tillie's mother   Margaret Burlen
Orchestra: Alexander Semmler.
Length: 30 minutes.
Network: CBS.
First Broadcast: 1942.

Time for Love

Type: Drama
Format: The exploits of Dianne LaVolte, a
   mysterious international figure for law
   and order, as she strove to protect the in-
   nocent and uncover the guilty.
Cast: Dianne LaVolte   Marlene Dietrich
   Her boyfriend, an
      American news-
      paperman   Robert Readick
Announcer: Lee Vines.
Music: Alec Wilder.
Length: 30 minutes.
Network: CBS.
First Broadcast: 1953.

Time to Smile

Type: Musical Variety
Host: Eddie Cantor.
Regulars: Bert Gordon, Nora Martin, Joan
   Davis, John Brown, Arthur Q. Bryan.
Announcer: Harry Von Zell.
Orchestra: Leonard Sues.
Length: 30 minutes.
Network: NBC.
First Broadcast: 1944.

Time's a Wastin'

Type: Quiz
Format: Selected studio audience members competed in a series of question and
   answer sessions designed to be played in
   ten second intervals. Each correct answer
   to a question earned a player a merchandise prize, the value of which began at
   $1,000 and decreased by $100 with each
   second the player used to answer.
Host: Bud Collyer.
Length: 30 minutes.

Time to Smile. Eddie Cantor.

Network: CBS.
First Broadcast: 1948.

The Timid Soul

Type: Comedy
Format: Based on the comic strip by H.T.
   Webster, the series followed the misad-
   ventures of Casper Milquetoast, the
   Timid Soul.
Cast: Casper Milque-
      toast   Billy Lynn
   Madge Milque-
      toast, his wife   Cecil Roy
Also: Jackson Beck, Katherine Renwick,
   Mona Moray.
Length: 30 minutes.
Network: Mutual.
First Broadcast: 1941.

Title Tales

Type: Game
Format: Called for a cast to relate a story
   based on five song titles submitted by a

listener. Their failure to relate a satisfactory story earned the listener $50.

Hostess: Sylvia Rhodes.

Cast: Bert Farber, Paul Jones, The Devere Sisters, The Marathon Melody Men.

Announcer: Bill Frost.

Orchestra: Jimmy James.

Length: 30 minutes.

Network: Mutual.

First Broadcast: 1940.

T-Man

Type: Drama

Format: Adaptations of cases from the files of the U.S. Treasury Department.

Starring: Dennis O'Keefe as Treasury Agent Larsen.

Announcer: Bob Lemond.

Length: 30 minutes.

Network: CBS.

First Broadcast: 1950.

Today at the Duncans

Type: Comedy

Format: Events in the life of the Duncan family.

Cast:
Mr. Duncan	Frank Nelson
Mrs. Duncan	Mary Lansing
Their son	Dix Davis

Length: 15 minutes.

Network: CBS.

First Broadcast: 1942.

Tom Corbett, Space Cadet

Type: Science Fiction Adventure

Format: Earth in the year 2350. The exploits of Tom Corbett, a space cadet at Space Academy, an earth-based West Point where young men and women trained to become Solar Guards, the agents of a celestial police force established to protect Earth, Mars, Venus, and Jupiter, the planets that comprise a universal council of peace known as the Solar Alliance. Based on the television series of the same title.

Cast:
Tom Corbett	Frankie Thomas
Astro, the Venusian	Al Markin
Cadet Roger Manning	Jan Merlin
Captain Larry Strong	Edwin Brice

Announcer: Jackson Beck.

Sponsor: Kellogg's Cereals.

Program Opening:

Announcer: Kellogg's Pep, the build-up wheat cereal, invites you to rocket into the future with Tom Corbett, Space Cadet... As roaring rockets blast off to distant planets and far flung stars, we take you to the age of the conquest of space with Tom Corbett, Space Cadet.

Length: 30 minutes.

Network: ABC.

First Broadcast: 1952.

The Tom Mix Straightshooters

Type: Western

Format: The exploits of Tom Mix, a daring crusader for justice and owner of the T-M Bar Ranch in Dobie Township.

Cast:
Tom Mix	Artells Dickson
	Russell Thorson
	Jack Holden
	Curley Bradley
Jane	Winifred Toomey
	Jane Webb
The Old Wrangler	Percy Hemus
Pecos	Curley Bradley
The Sheriff	Leo Curley
	DeWitt MacBride
	Hal Peary
	Willard Waterman
Amos Snood	Sidney Ellstrom
	Curley Bradley
Jimmy	Andy Donnelly
	George Gobel
	Hugh Rowlands
Calamity	Bob Jellison
Pat Curtis	Patricia Dunlap
Judge Parsons	Arthur Peterson

Announcer: Don Gordon, Les Griffith, Frank Ferguson.

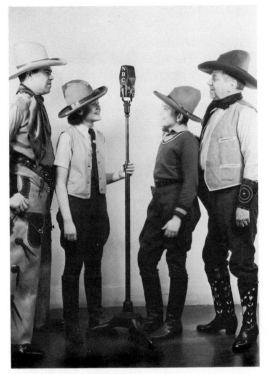

The Tom Mix Straightshooters. An early cast of the series.

Sponsor: Ralston Cereals.
Program Opening:
Announcer: The Tom Mix Ralston Straightshooters bring you action, mystery, and mile-a-minute thrills in radio's biggest western detective program. Tonight you're about to hear another episode in a baffling mystery — "Secret Mission"..."
Length: 15 minutes.
Network: NBC.
First Broadcast: 1933. Also known as "The Adventures of Tom Mix" and "The Tom Mix Ralston Straightshooters."

Tom, Timmy, and Mae

Type: Variety
Format: Music, songs, chatter, and skits.
Starring: Tom Glazzer (Tom), and Mae Questel (Timmy and Mae).
Length: 15 minutes.
Network: NBC.
First Broadcast: 1949.

The Tommy Riggs Show

Type: Musical Variety
Host: Tommy Riggs.
Regulars: Eileen Woods, Wally Maher, Jimmy Cash, Bill Goodwin, Bea Wain.
Announcer: Paul Masterson, Dan Seymour, Jack Mather.
Music: The Roy Whitaker Quartet, The Felix Mills Orchestra, The Larry Clifton Orchestra.
Length: 30 minutes.
Network: NBC (1938), ABC (1946).
First Broadcast: 1938.

Tonight On Broadway

Type: Musical Variety
Hostess: Connee Boswell.
Regulars: Ted Husing, Bob Doyle.
Announcer: Ken Roberts.
Orchestra-Chorus: Ray Bloch.
Length: 30 minutes.
Network: CBS.
First Broadcast: 1946.

The Tony Martin Show

Type: Musical Variety
Announcer: Jimmy Wallington, Bill Forman.
Chorus: Jeff Alexander.
Orchestra: Victor Young.
Length: 30 minutes.
Network: CBS (1947), NBC (1953).
First Broadcast: 1947.

Tony Wons Radio Scrapbook

Type: Poetry Readings
Host: Tony Wons.
Vocalist: Shirley Sadley.
Announcer: Lewis Rowen.
Organist: Irma Glenn.
Length: 30 minutes.
Network: CBS.
First Broadcast: 1940.

Tony Wons Radio Scrapbook. Tony Wons.

Too Many Cooks

Type: Comedy
Format: The story of a family with ten children.
Cast: Mr. Cook   Hal March
       Mrs. Cook   Mary Jane Croft
Also: Bob Sweeney, George Fenneman, Willard Waterman, Jerry Hausner.
Orchestra: Marlen Skiles.
Length: 30 minutes.
Network: CBS.
First Broadcast: 1950.

The Top Guy

Type: Crime Drama
Format: The story of a police commissioner and his battle against crime.
Cast: The Police
        Commissioner   J. Scott Smart
        His assistant   Ken Lynch
Length: 30 minutes.
Network: ABC.
First Broadcast: 1951.

Top Secret

Type: Adventure
Format: The exploits of a female U.S. undercover agent during World War II.
Starring: Ilona Massey as the agent.
Announcer: Fred Collins.
Music: Roy Shield.
Length: 30 minutes.
Network: NBC.
First Broadcast: 1950.

Topper

See title: "The Adventures of Topper."

Transatlantic Quiz

Type: Quiz
Format: The basis, similiar to that of "Information Please," had panels in the United States and Britain attempting to answer some rather difficult questions submitted by listeners.
Host, United States: Alistair Cooke.
Panel, U.S.:   Buck Crouse, Christopher Morley.
Host, Britain: Lionel Hale, Ronny Waldman.
Panel, Britain: Professor Dennis Brazan, Col. David Niven.
Length: 15 minutes.
Network: NBC Blue/B.B.C.
First Broadcast: 1944.

Travelin' Man

Type: Comedy
Format: The misadventures of two traveling salesmen.
Cast: The Salesman   Bill Adams
        The Yankee
        Peddler   Sam Winters
Length: 30 minutes.
Network: NBC.
First Broadcast: 1946.

Treasure House of Song

Type: Musical Variety
Starring: Lucia Albonese, Francescia Valentino, Alois Havrille.
Orchestra: Alfredo Antonini.
Length: 30 minutes.
Network: Mutual.
First Broadcast: 1943.

Treasure Trails of Song

Type: Country-Western Musical Variety
Starring: Mary Martha Briney, Dick Fulton, Paul Shannon, Peggy Nelson, The Kinder Sisters, The Pioneer Quartet.
Orchestra: Aneurin Bodycombe.
Length: 25 minutes.
Network: NBC.
First Broadcast: 1941.

Treasury Agent

Type: Drama
Format: The exploits of Joe Lincoln, the Chief Treasury Agent based on the official files of the Treasury Department.
Starring: Raymond Edward Johnson as Joe Lincoln.
Also: Elmer Lincoln Drey, retired chief coordinator of all law enforcement agencies in the Treasury Department.
Sponsor: Winston cigarettes, Ennds deodorant.
Length: 30 minutes.
Network: ABC.
First Broadcast: 1947.

Treat Time

Type: Variety
Host: Buddy Cole.
Announcer: Marvin Miller.
Orchestra: Caesar Petrillo.
Length: 15 minutes.
Network: CBS.
First Broadcast: 1941.

A Tree Grows In Brooklyn

Type: Drama
Format: The story of the Nolans, a poor but proud family living in a tenement in Brooklyn in 1912. Based on the book by Betty Smith.
Cast: Johnny Nolan, the charming, alcoholic father — John Larken
Katie Nolan, his strong-willed wife — Anne Seymour
Francie Nolan, their daughther — Denise Alexander
Neely Nolan, their son — Bernie Raeburn
Length: 30 minutes.
Network: NBC.
First Broadcast: 1949.

Tremendous Triffles

Type: Drama
Format: Capsule stories based on the syndicated newspaper column *Tremendous Triffles*.
Host-Narrator: George Hicks.
Length: 5 minutes.
Network: CBS.
First Broadcast: 1955.

True Detective Mysteries

Type: Anthology
Format: Dramatizations of stories from *True Detective* Magazine. Following each story, the editor of the magazine offered a $1,000 reward for information leading to the arrest of a wanted criminal.
Host-Narrator: John Shuttleworth, the editor of *True Detective* Magazine. When the series first began, Dick Keith portrayed the role of the editor.
Announcer: Hugh James, Frank Dunne.
Music: Chet Kingsbury.
Sponsor: Viceroy cigarettes, Baby Ruth

candy bars, Bisodol, Ex-Lax, O'Henry candy bars.

Program Opening:

Announcer: And now True Detective Mysteries. In cooperation with the editor of *True Detective* Magazine and the Mutual Broadcasting System, True Detective Mysteries...

Length: 30 minutes.

Network: CBS (1929), Mutual (1938).

First Broadcast: 1929.

True or False

Type: Quiz

Format: Two six-member teams, male vs. female, responded to true or false questions. The highest scoring team received $30 (the prize was later increased to $5 per correct response).

Host: Dr. Harry Hagen, Eddie Dunn, Bill Slater.

Announcer: Glenn Riggs.

Length: 30 minutes.

Network-First Broadcast: CBS (1933), Blue (1938), Mutual (1948).

The Truitts

Type: Comedy

Format: Events in the life of the Truitt family.

Cast: Elmer Truitt,
the father — John Dehner
Mother Truitt,
his wife — Constance Crowder
Gladys Truitt,
their daughter — Jane Webb
Dawn Bender
Clarence Truitt,
their son — Eddie Firestone
Grandpa Truitt — Parley Baer

Also: Charles Woolf, Mirian Jay.

Announcer: Arch Presby.

Length: 30 minutes.

Network: NBC.

First Broadcast: 1950.

Truth or Consequences

Type: Game

Format: Contestants attempted to answer a nonsense riddle which, of course, they couldn't, so had to pay the consequence: performing a stunt in return for prizes. Became the basis for a television series of the same title.

Host: Ralph Edwards.

Announcer: Bud Collyer, Mel Allen, Jay Stewart, Milton Cross, Harlow Wilcox, Ed Herlihy, Ken Carpenter, Verne Smith, Ken Roberts.

Music: Buddy Cole.

Length: 30 minutes.

Network: NBC (1940), CBS (1951).

First Broadcast: 1940.

Tune In With Lucie Arnaz

Type: Celebrity Interview

Hostess: Lucie Arnaz.

Producer-Sponsor: S.C. Johnson and Son.

Length: 5 minutes (a 26-program series).

Syndicated.

First Broadcast: 1978.

Tune Up Time

Type: Musical Variety

Host: Tony Martin

Regulars: Kay Thompson, David Loughlin, The Rhythm Singers.

Announcer: Dan Seymour.

Orchestra: Andre Kostelanetz.

Length: 30 minutes.

Network: CBS.

First Broadcast: 1939.

The 21st Precinct

Type: Crime Drama

Format: The series focused on the lives and experiences of the men of the 21st police precinct in New York City.

Cast: Captain Frank
Kennelly — Everett Sloane

The Lieutenant	Ken Lynch
The Sergeant	Harold J. Stone

Length: 30 minutes.
Network: CBS.
First Broadcast: 1953 (ended in 1956).

20 Questions

Type: Game
Format: Panelists attempted to identify persons, places, or objects within twenty questions. If the panel failed to do so, the listener who submitted the item won a prize. Became the basis for a television series of the same title.
Host: Bill Slater, Jay Jackson.
Panel: Herb Polesie, Fred Van Deventer, Florence Rinard, Bobby McGuire.
Mystery Voice (provided clues for the home audience): Bruce Elliott, Frank Waldecker.
Commercial Spokeswoman (for Ronson lighters): Charlotte Manson.
Announcer: Frank Waldecker.
Sponsor: *Pageant* magazine, Ronson lighters.
Length: 30 minutes.
Network: Mutual.
First Broadcast: 1946.

Twenty Thousand Years in Sing Sing

Type: Anthology
Format: Dramatizations from the files of Sing Sing Prison.
Host: Lewis E. Lawes, the Warden of Sing Sing.
Interviewer: Joseph Bell.
Announcer: Kelvin Keech.
Length: 30 minutes.
Network: Blue.
First Broadcast: 1933.

The Two Daffodils

Type: Variety
Hosts: Ken Gillum, Duke Attenbury.
Length: 15 minutes.

Syndicated.
First Broadcast: 1932.

Two on a Clue

Type: Crime Drama
Format: The series, which dramatized actual case histories, followed the investigations of Jeff and Debby Spencer, a husband and wife private detective team.

Cast:	Jeff Spencer	Ned Weaver
	Debby Spencer	Louise Fitch
	Sgt. Trumbull	John Gibson

Announcer: Alice Yourman.
Length: 15 minutes.
Network: CBS.
First Broadcast: 1944.

Two on a Shoestring

Type: Comedy-Drama
Format: The trials and tribulations of two small-town career girls as they struggled to succeed as radio personalities in New York City.

Cast:	Sally	Peggy Zinke
	Her friend	Eleanor Phelps
	The hotel manager	Dick Keith

Length: 15 minutes.
Network: Mutual.
First Broadcast: 1938.

Two Thousand Plus

Type: Anthology
Format: Science fiction tales set in the twenty-first century.
Orchestra: Emerson Buckley.
Length: 30 minutes.
Network: Mutual.
First Broadcast: 1950.

Uncle Don

Type: Children's
Host: Don Carney as Uncle Don.

Length: 30 minutes.

Network-First Broadcast: Basically it was a local New York program broadcast over WOR from 1925 to 1949. Briefly, in 1939, the program was carried over the full Mutual network, sponsored by Maltex.

Uncle Ezra's Radio Station

See title: "Station EZRA."

Uncle Jim's Question Bee

Type: Quiz

Format: Called for players to answer questions in return for cash prizes.

Host: Jim McWilliams (Uncle Jim), Bill Slater.

Length: 15 and 30 minute versions.

Network: Blue.

First Broadcast: 1936.

Uncle Walter's Dog House

Format One:

Type: Comedy-Variety

Format: Varied skits and musical numbers.

Host: Tom Wallace.

Vocalists: Mary Ann Mercer, The Dog House Chorus.

Orchestra: Phil Davis, Bob Strange.

Length: 30 minutes.

Network: NBC.

First Broadcast: 1939.

Format Two:

Type: Comedy

Format: Mishaps that befall the Wiggins family. Domestic family sketches interwoven with musical numbers.

Cast: Uncle Walter

Wiggins	Tom Wallace
Mr. Wiggins	Charles Penman
Mrs. Wiggins	Kathryn Card
Margie Wiggins, their daughter	Beryl Vaughn
Mrs. Dramp, a friend	Betty Arnold

Vocalist: Mary Ann Mercer.

Also: Frank Dane, Fred Brady, Marvin Miller.

Announcer: Charles Lyon.

Orchestra: Bob Strange.

Length: 30 minutes.

Network: NBC.

First Broadcast: 1942.

Under Arrest

Type: Crime Drama

Format: The exploits of Police Captain Drake as he battled gangsters (in later episodes, the exploits of Captain Jim Scott).

Cast: Captain Drake   Craig McDonnell
        Captain Jim Scott   Joe Di Santis

Announcer: Ted Brown.

Organist: Al Finelli.

Length: 30 minutes.

Network: Mutual.

First Broadcast: 1938.

The U.S. Steel Hour

Type: Anthology

Format: Dramatic presentations. Became the basis for a television series of the same title.

Host: Lawrence Langner.

Narrator: Roger Pryor.

Announcer: Norman Brokenshire, George Hicks.

Soloist: Bidu Sayo.

Music: The Howard Levey Orchestra; The NBC Symphony Orchestra.

Sponsor: The U.S. Steel Corporation.

Included:

The Glass Menagerie. Tennessee William's story of an aging Southern belle who struggled to keep her son and daughter close by her side.

Starring: Helen Hayes, Montgomery Clift, Karl Malden.

1984. A dramatization of Orwell's searing forecast of the future. In a dictatorship, one man finds brief happiness with a girl just before the police crush them forever.

Starring: Richard Widmark.

Length: 60 minutes.
Network: CBS (1943), NBC (1950).
First Broadcast: 1943. Also titled "The Theatre Guild on the Air."

Vacation Serenade

Type: Musical Variety
Hostess: Dorothy Kristen (1943), Rose Bampton (1944).
Featured: Reed Kennedy.
Announcer: Ben Grauer.
Orchestra: Wilfred Pelletier.
Length: 30 minutes.
Network: NBC.
First Broadcast: 1943.

Vacation with Music

Type: Musical Variety
Host: Phil Brete.
Regulars: Liza Morrow, Ed Herlihy.
Announcer: Jack Costello.
Orchestra: Harry Sosnik.
Length: 30 minutes.
Network: NBC.
First Broadcast: 1946.

Valentino

Type: Women's
Format: Radio's answer to television's "The Continental." The format had Barry Valentino, "The Prisoner of Romance," bring "love and romance to a housewife's dreary afternoon" through songs and poetry.
Length: 25 minutes.
Network: ABC.
First Broadcast: 1952.

Valiant Lady

Type: Serial
Format: The dramatic story of Joan Scott, the "Valiant Lady" of the title, as she struggled to help her unstable husband, Truman, "keep his feet planted firmly upon the pathway to success."

Valiant Lady. Joan Blaine.

Cast:	Joan Scott	Joan Blaine
		Joan Banks
		Florence Freeman
	Truman Scott	Bartlett Robinson
		Martin Blaine
	Margie Cook	Jean Ellyn
	Jim Barnett	Richard Gordon
		Bill Johnstone
		Gene Leonard
	Agnes Westcott	Linda Carlon
	Abby Trow-bridge	Ethel Owen
	Dudley Trow-bridge	Shirling Oliver
	Jeffrey Clark	Lawson Zerbe
	Lester Brennan	Everett Sloane
	Colin Kirby	Ned Weaver
	Estelle Cummings	Elsie Mae Gordon
	Eleanor Richards	Elspeth Eric
	Myra Gordon	Irene Winston
	Monica Brewster	Cathleen Cordell
	Chris Ellerbe	Frank Lovejoy
	Norman Price	Albert Hayes
	Emma Stevens	Judith Lowry

Announcer: Dwight Weist.
Organist: Jesse Crawford.
Sponsor: General Mills.
Program Opening:
Announcer: Thursday, October 2nd, 1941, time for Valiant Lady. General Mills' new Bisquick presents Joan Blaine in Valiant Lady, the story of a brave woman and her brilliant but unstable husband. The story of her struggle to keep his feet planted firmly upon the pathway to success.
Length: 15 minutes.
Network: CBS.
First Broadcast: 1938.

Variety Fair

Type: Musical Variety
Host: Holland Engle.
Regulars: Elmira Roessler, The Spotlighters.
Length: 15 minutes.
Syndicated.
First Broadcast: 1946.

The Vaughn Monroe Show

Type: Musical Variety
Host: Vaughn Monroe.
Regulars: Marilyn Duke, Tom Shirley.
Orchestra: Vaughn Monroe.
Length: 30 minutes.
Network: CBS.
First Broadcast: 1942.

The Vera Burton Show

Type: Musical Variety
Hostess: Vera Burton.
Orchestra: Walter Gross.
Length: 15 minutes.
Network: CBS.
First Broadcast: 1942.

The Vera Vague Show

Type: Musical Variety

Hostess: Vera Vague (played by Barbara Jo Allen).
Announcer: Owen James.
Length: 15 minutes.
Network: ABC.
First Broadcast: 1949.

Vi and Velma Vernon

Type: Variety
Hosts: Vi and Velma Vernon.
Pianist: Glenn Hurley.
Length: 15 minutes.
Network: NBC.
First Broadcast: 1942.

Vic and Sade

Type: Comedy-Serial
Format: Events in the lives of the eccentric Gook family, residents of the small town of Crooper, Illinois.

Cast:

Vic Gook, the husband	Art Van Harvey
Sade Gook, his wife	Bernardine Flynn
Rush Gook, their son	Billy Idelson
	Johnny Coons
	Sid Koss
Uncle Fletcher	Clarence Hartzell
Chuck Brainfeeble, their friend	Carl Kroenke
Dottie Brainfeeble, his wife	Ruth Perrott
	Dorothy Day

Announcer: Charles Irving, Clarence Hartzell, Ralph Edwards, Bob Brown, Ed Herlihy, Glenn Riggs, Roger Krupp, Ken Roberts.
Music: Walter Blaufuss.
Sponsor: Crisco Oil, Ivory Snow Flakes, Fitch's Cocoanut Shampoo.
Program Opening:
Announcer: And now get ready to smile again with radio's home folks, Vic and Sade...

Length: 15 and 30 minute versions.
Network-First Broadcast: Blue (1932), CBS (1945), Mutual (1946), Syndicated (1947).

The Vic Damone Show

Type: Musical Variety
Host: Vic Damone.
Announcer: Dan Frederick.
Orchestra: Sylvan Levin.
Length: 15 minutes.
Network: Mutual.
First Broadcast: 1947. Also known as "The Voice of Vic Damone."

The Victor Borge Show

Type: Variety
Host: Victor Borge.
Regulars: Pat Friday, The Henry Russell Chorus.
Announcer: Ken Roberts, Harlow Wilcox, John Reed King.
Orchestra: Billy Mills.
Length: 30 minutes.
Network: Blue.
First Broadcast: 1945.

The Village Store

Type: Variety
Format: Music, songs, and comedy sketches set against the background of the Sealtest Village Store.
Hostess: Eve Arden (proprietress of the store).
Host: Jack Haley (proprietor of the store).
Regulars: Bob Stanton, Jack Carson, Joan Davis, John Barrymore, Rudy Vallee, The Fountainaires.
Announcer: Hy Averback.
Orchestra: Frank DeVol.
Sponsor: Sealtest products.
Length: 30 minutes.
Network: NBC.
First Broadcast: 1947.

The Voice of Broadway

Type: Gossip
Format: Inside news about show business personalities.
Hostess: Dorothy Kilgallen.
Announcer: Allan Stuart.
Length: 15 minutes.
Network: CBS.
First Broadcast: 1941.

The Voice of Vic Damone

See title: "The Vic Damone Show."

The Voyage of the Scarlet Queen

Type: Adeventure
Format: The exploits of Philip Carney, captain of the schooner *Scarlet Queen*, as it roamed the South Pacific.
Starring: Elliott Lewis as Capt. Philip Carney.
Length: 30 minutes.
Network: Mutual.
First Broadcast: 1951.

Vox Pop

Type: Interview
Format: Travelers, passing through New York City, were met, interviewed, and awarded a merchandise prize for relating their experience of the city.
Host: Parks Johnson, Jerry Belcher, Wallace Butterworth, Warren Hull.
Announcer: Graham McNamee, Roger Krupp, Dick Joy.
Sponsor: Kentucky Club Tobacco.
Length: 30 minutes.
Network: NBC (1935), CBS (1935).
First Broadcast: 1933. Originally titled: "Sidewalk Interviews."

Wake Up and Smile

Type: Musical Variety

Vox Pop. Parks Johnson (left) and Jerry Belcher.

Host: Hal O'Holloron.
Regulars: Boyce Smith, Kay Armen, Patsy Montana, Salty Holme.
Orchestra: Rex Maupin.
Length: 30 minutes.
Network: ABC.
First Broadcast: 1946.

Walk a Mile

Type: Quiz
Format: Had contestants answer general knowledge questions in return for a carton of cigarettes. The title was derived from the sponsor's slogan—"I'd Walk a Mile for a Camel."
Host: Win Elliot, John Henry Faulk.
Announcer: Ralph Paul, Mort Lawrence, Joe King, Joe Ripley.
Orchestra: Peter Van Steeden.
Sponsor: Camel cigarettes.
Length: 30 minutes.
Network: CBS.
First Broadcast: 1952.

The Walt Disney Song Parade

Type: Children
Format: Soundtracks from various Disney films, linked together with odd bits of chatter by an announcer.
Length: 15 minutes.
Network: Mutual.
First Broadcast: 1941.

The Walter O'Keefe Show

Type: Variety
Host: Walter O'Keefe.
Regulars: Lily Pons, The Kay Thompson Singers.
Orchestra: Andre Kostelanetz.
Length: 45 minutes.
Network: CBS.
First Broadcast: 1938.

The Walter Winchell Show

Type: Commentary
Host: Walter Winchell.
Announcer: Hugh James, Ben Grauer, Richard Stark, Cy Harrice.
Length: 15 minutes.
Network: NBC.
First Broadcast: 1930. Also titled "The Jergens Journal" (when sponsored by Jergens Lotion) and "The Lucky Strike Magic Carpet" (under the sponsorship of Lucky Strike cigarettes).

Wanted

Type: Anthology
Format: Dramatizations of actual police cases. Became the basis for a television series of the same title.
Narrator: Walter McGraw.
Announcer: Fred Collins.
Music: Morris Mamorsky.
Length: 30 minutes.
Network: NBC.
First Broadcast: 1949.

The Walter Winchell Show. Walter Winchell.

The Wayne and Shuster Show

Type: Variety
Host: Johnny Wayne and Frank Shuster.
Vocalist: Georgia Dey.
Announcer: Herb May.
Orchestra: Samuel Hersenhoren.
Length: 30 minutes.
Network: NBC.
First Broadcast: 1947.

The Wayne King Orchestra

Type: Musical Variety
Host: Wayne King.
Vocalist: Buddy Clarke.
Orchestra: Wayne King.
Length: 25 minutes.
Network: CBS.
First Broadcast: 1939.

We Are Four

Type: Drama

Format: Events in the lives of the Webster family.
Cast: Tony Webster,
      the father   Charles Flynn
      Nancy Webster,
      his wife   Marjorie Hannan
      Lydia Webster,
      their daughter   Alice Hill
      Priscilla Webster
      their daughter   Sally Smith
Announcer: Ed Smith.
Length: 15 minutes.
Network: CBS.
First Broadcast: 1935.

We Love and Learn

Type: Serial
Format: The story of Barbara Weeks, a small town schoolteacher, and her struggles to succeed as a model. A spin-off from "As the Twig Is Bent."
Cast: Barbara Weeks   Ann Thomas
      The lawyer   Arthur Vinton
      The possessive
      mother   Charme Allen
      The juvenile   Jim Carlton
      Barbara's friend   Sue Reed
Announcer: Adele Ronson.
Organist: Herschel Leucke.
Length: 15 minutes.
Network: NBC.
First Broadcast: 1948.

We, the Abbotts

Type: Comedy
Format: Events in the lives of the Abbotts, a not-so-typical American family of five.
Cast: John Abbott, the
      father, a school
      teacher   John McIntire
      Emily Abbott,
      his wife   Betty Garde
            Ethel Everett
      Linda Abbott,
      their seventeen-
      year-old
      daughter   Betty Jane Tyler
            Betty Philson

Barbara Abbott,	
Linda's twin	
sister	Audrey Egan
Jack Abbott,	
their son	Cliff Carpenter
Hilda, their maid	Adelaide Klein

Announcer: Ted Pearson.
Length: 15 minutes.
Network: CBS.
First Broadcast: 1940.

We Who Dream

Type: Serial
Format: The story of a childless wife who yearns to have her own home and children.
Starring: Claire Niessen.
Length: 15 minutes.
Network: CBS.
First Broadcast: 1944.

Wednesday With You

Type: Musical Variety
Hostess: Nora Martin.
Vocalist: Freddie Martel.
Announcer: Harry Von Zell.
Orchestra: Leonard Sues.
Length: 30 minutes.
Network: NBC.
First Broadcast: 1945.

Weekend Whimsy

Type: Musical Variety
Starring: Loulie Jean, Sylvia Marlowe, Brad Reynolds.
Announcer: Red Hall.
Orchestra: Dick Dinsmore.
Length: 15 minutes.
Network: NBC.
First Broadcast: 1941.

Welcome Travelers

Type: Interview

Format: Travelers, passing through Chicago were met at bus, train, and plane terminals and brought before a microphone to relate their impressions of the Windy City. Became the basis for a television series of the same title.
Host: Tommy Bartlett.
Announcer: Jim Ameche.
Length: 30 minutes.
Network: ABC.
First Broadcast: 1947.

Western Caravan

Type: Anthology
Format: Western dramatizations. Varying casts and stories.
Orchestra: Robert Armbruster.
Length: 30 minutes.
Network: NBC.
First Broadcast: 1950.

What Makes You Tick?

Type: Quiz
Format: Following their responses to a series of ten psychological questions, contestants' answers were appraised by two guest psychologists.
Host: John K.M. McCaffery (1948).
Hostess: Gypsy Rose Lee (1950).
Announcer: George Ansbro.
Length: 30 minutes.
Network: CBS (1948), ABC (1950).
First Broadcast: 1948.

What Would You Have Done?

Type: Quiz
Format: Selected members of the studio audience, posed with a dilemma, had to solve it to the best of their abilities. Winners, determined by studio audience applause, received merchandise prizes.
Host: Ben Grauer.
Announcer: Jack Costello.
Length: 30 minutes.
Network: NBC.
First Broadcast: 1940.

What's My Name? Arlene Francis.

What's Cooking?

Type: Cooking
Hostess: Beulah Karney.
Assistant: Earl Tanner.
Announcer: Dick Dowd.
Orchestra: Harry Kogen.
Length: 25 minutes.
Network: Blue.
First Broadcast: 1944.

What's My Line?

Type: Game
Format: A panel of four regulars identified the occupations of guests through a series of questions. Based on the television series of the same title.
Host: John Daly.
Panel: Arlene Francis, Dorothy Kilgallen, Hal Brock, Bennett Cerf.
Announcer: Don Briggs.
Length: 30 minutes.
Network: NBC.
First Broadcast: 1952.

What's My Name?

Type: Quiz
Format: Selected members of the studio audience competed. Four clues to the identity of a famous person were related. Players received money based on the clue at which the identity was made (first clue, ten dollars; second clue, nine dollars; third, eight dollars; fourth, seven dollars). Later formats raised the cash prize to $15, then $100 on the first clue.
Hostess: Arlene Francis.
Host: Fred Uttal, Budd Hulick, Ward Wilson.
Announcer: John Reed King, Ken Roberts.
Orchestra: Walter Gross.
Length: 30 minutes.
Network-First Broadcast: Mutual (1939), NBC (1939), ABC (1948).

What's New?

Type: Variety
Host: Don Ameche.
Length: 60 minutes.
Network: Blue.
First Broadcast: 1943.

What's the Name of That Song?

Type: Quiz
Format: Selected members of the studio audience competed to identify a tune played by the host on a piano. Correct answers netted the players five dollars. If a player could sing the first line, his money was doubled; if he could sing the chorus, his money was tripled.
Host: Dud Williamson, Bill Gwinn.
Length: 30 minutes.
Network: Mutual.
First Broadcast: 1944.

When a Girl Marries

Type: Serial

Format: The story of young marrieds Joan and Harry Davis.

Cast:
Joan Davis	Noel Mills
	Mary Jane Higby
Harry Davis	John Raby
	Robert Haag
	Whitfield Connor
	Lyle Sudrow
Lillie	Georgia Burke
Sylvia Field	Joan Tetzel
	Jone Allison
	Toni Darney
Kathy Cameron	Anne Francis
	Rosemary Rice
Irma Cameron	Jeanette Dowling
Betty McDonald	Eunice Hall
	Helen Dumas
Chick Norris	John Kane
Phil Stanley	Michael Fitz-maurice
	Richard Kollmar
	Staats Cotsworth
	Karl Weber
	Paul McGrath
Angie	Mary Jane Higby
	Wynne Gibson
Steve	Jack Arthur

Announcer: Charles Stark, Frank Gallop, Richard Stark, Hugh James, Wendell Niles.
Organist: Richard Leibert, Rosa Rio.
Sponsor: Maxwell House Coffee.
Program Opening:
Announcer: When a Girl Marries. Maxwell House, that ripe, mellow, satisfying coffee that's good to the last drop, presents When A Girl Marries, a tender, human story of young married life, dedicated to everyone who has ever been in love.
Length: 15 minutes.
Network: CBS.
First Broadcast: 1939.

Where Have You Been?

Type: Game
Format: A celebrity panel had to guess where (city, country, state) a guest contestant had been. A prize is awarded to the contestant if the panel failed to uncover the locale.
Host: Horace Sutton.
Panelists: Harriet Van Horne, Marc Connelly, Ernie Kovacs, Peggy McKay.
Announcer: Jack Costello.
Length: 30 minutes.
Network: NBC.
First Broadcast: 1954.

Which Is Which?

Type: Quiz
Format: Members of the studio audience attempted to identify radio and screen stars, who appeared as guests, from their voices only. Prizes were awarded to successful players.
Host: Ken Murray.
Orchestra: Richard Himber.
Length: 30 minutes.
Network: CBS.
First Broadcast: 1944.

Whispering Streets

Type: Serial
Format: A drama of life as seen through the narration of a female authoress.
Narrator: Gertrude Warner, Bette Davis.
Length: 20 minutes.
Network: ABC (1952), CBS (1957).
First Broadcast: 1952.

The Whisper Men

Type: Adventure
Format: The exploits of Max Chandler, a crusading radio commentator who fought the Whisper Men—communist infiltrators of the underworld.
Cast:
Max Chandler	Karl Swenson
	Joseph Curtin
Rod Buchanan, his assistant	Kermit Murdock
The newspaper-woman	Betty Caine

Music: Chet Kingsbury.
Length: 30 minutes.
Network: Mutual.
First Broadcast: 1945.

The Whistler

Type: Anthology
Format: Mystery presentations. Stories of people who were suddenly caught in a destructive web of their own misdeeds. The Whistler, identified by the mournful whistling of the theme music, never appeared in the stories. His observations on the vices and virtues of the individuals were heard throughout each drama. Became the basis for a television series of the same title.
Cast: The Whistler   Joseph Kearns
                     Bill Forman
                     Marvin Miller
                     Everett Clarke
Announcer: Bob Venables, Bob Lemond, Donald Rickles, Marvin Miller.
Orchestra: Wilbur Hatch, Hunter Taylor.
Whistling: Dorothy Roberts.
Program Opening:
The Whistler: I am the Whistler. And I know many things, for I walk by night. I know many strange tales hidden in the hearts of men and women who have stepped into the shadows. Yes, I know the nameless terrors of which they dare not speak.
Included:
Mirage. The story of an underworld attorney who shuns the beautiful woman who gave him his start, and of the woman's attempts to seek revenge.
Starring: Gerald Mohr, Wally Maher.
The Morrison Affair. A childless English bride passes an adopted child off as her own when her husband returns from the war.
Starring: Madeleine Carroll, Gerald Mohr.
Ghost Hunt. The adventures of a radio disc jockey who agrees to stay in a haunted house to gain publicity.
Starring: Ralph Edwards.

The Wages of Sin. The story of a hooker who blackmails gangsters after they use her apartment for a murder.
Starring: Barbara Stanwyck.
Length: 30 minutes.
Network: CBS.
First Broadcast: 1942.

Whitehall 1212

See title: "The Black Museum."

The Whiteman Varieties

Type: Variety
Format: Presented young performers.
Host: Paul Whiteman.
Length: 60 minutes.
Network: ABC.
First Broadcast: 1954.

Whiz Quiz

Type: Quiz
Format: Called for studio audience members to answer general knowledge questions in return for merchandise prizes.
Host: Johnny Olsen.
Announcer: Sidney Walton.
Length: 30 minutes.
Network: ABC.
First Broadcast: 1948.

Who-Dun-It?

Type: Game
Format: A mystery case was enacted. Selected members of the studio audience who were able to identify the culprit won $100. If the culprit was not uncovered, the money was placed in a jackpot. The player with the most correct identifications received a chance to crack the jackpot by solving a case based on one musical clue.
Host: Bob Dixon.

Inspector Slade: Santos Ortega. (Inspector Slade's personal files were the source for the capsule mysteries).
Orchestra: Jack Miller.
Length: 30 minutes.
Network: CBS.
First Broadcast: 1948.

Who Knows?

Type: Anthology
Format: Mystery-suspense presentations that concerned psychic phenomena.
Host: Dr. Hereward Carrington.
Announcer: Jack Johnstone.
Length: 15 minutes.
Network: Mutual.
First Broadcast: 1940.

Who Said That?

Type: Quiz
Format: Had a panel of experts attempting to answer questions based on current news events. Became the basis for a television series of the same title.
Host: Robert Trout.
Panel: H.V. Kaltenborn, John Cameron Swayze, plus guests.
Announcer: Peter Roberts.
Length: 30 minutes.
Network: NBC.
First Broadcast: 1948.

Wild Bill Hickok

Type: Western
Format: The exploits of Wild Bill Hickok, a U.S. Marshal, and his side-kick, Jingles P. Jones, as they dispensed justice on the Southwestern frontier during the 1870s. Became the basis for a television series of the same title.
Cast: Wild Bill Hickok   Guy Madison
        Jingles P. Jones   Andy Devine
Announcer: Charles Lyon.
Length: 30 minutes.
Network: Mutual.
First Broadcast: 1952.

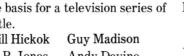

Wild Bill Hickok. Guy Madison.

Wilderness Road

Type: Drama
Format: The struggles of the pioneering Weston family during the late 1890s.
Cast: Daniel Boone,
            the trailblazer   Ray Collins
        *The Weston
        Family:*
        Ann   Vivian Block
        Sam   Lon Clark
        Mary   Anne Elstner
        Peter   Jimmy Donnelly
        John   Chester Stratton
        James   James McCallion
        Simon   William
                           Johnson
Length: 30 minutes.
Network: CBS.
First Broadcast: 1936.

Will Bradley and His Orchestra

Type: Musical Variety
Host: Will Bradley.
Vocalists: Carlotta Dale, Ray McKinley.

Orchestra: Will Bradley.
Length: 30 minutes.
Network: NBC.
First Broadcast: 1940.

The Will Rogers Show

Type: Commentary
Format: A transcribed series of 130 three-minute capsule episodes featuring the wit of Will Rogers. The programs were made using recordings of earlier Rogers' broadcasts.
Starring: Will Rogers.
Host-Announcer: John Cannon.
Length: 3 minutes.
Network: ABC.
First Broadcast: 1951. In 1933 Will Rogers appeared on "The Gulf Program," a thirty minute series for Gulf Oil on CBS.

Willie Piper

Type: Comedy
Format: The story of Willie Piper, a naive, unpredictable young grocery clerk, and his misguided attempts to succeed in the business world.
Cast: Willie Piper   Dick Nelson
    Martha Piper,
      his wife   Jean Gillespie
    Mr. Bissell,
      Willie's friend   Stewart
                              McIntosh
Announcer: Jack McCarthy.
Music: Ralph Norman.
Length: 30 minutes.
Network: ABC.
First Broadcast: 1946.

The Windy City

Type: Musical Variety
Host: Lee Bennett.
Vocalists: The Dinning Sisters.
Orchestra: Robert Trendler.
Length: 30 minutes.
Network: Mutual.
First Broadcast: 1949.

Wings of Destiny

Type: Adventure
Format: The exploits of pilot Steve Benton.
Cast: Steve Benton   Carlton KaDell
                              John Hodiak
    Peggy Banning,
      his girlfriend   Betty Arnold
    Brooklyn, the
      mechanic   Henry Hunter
Announcer: Marvin Miller.
Length: 30 minutes.
Network: NBC.
First Broadcast: 1940.

Winner Take All

Type: Quiz
Format: Consisted of a three match question and answer session wherein the player with the most correct answers received merchandise prizes.
Host: Bill Cullen, Ward Wilson, Bud Collyer.
Announcer: Bern Bennett, Bill Cullen.
Music: Chet Kingsbury.
Length: 30 minutes.
Network: CBS.
First Broadcast: 1946.

The Witch's Tale

Type: Anthology
Format: Chilling stories narrated by Nancy, a 117-year-old witch, and her yowling black cat, Satan.
Host: Alonzo Deen Cole.
Nancy: Adelaide Fritz, Miriam Wolfe, Martha Wentworth.
Program Opening:
Announcer: The Witch's Tale. The fascination for the eerie, weird, blood chilling tales told by old Nancy, the witch of Salem, and Satan, the wise black cat. They're waiting, waiting for you now...
Length: 15 minutes.
Network: Mutual.
First Broadcast: 1934.

The Wizard of Odds

Type: Game
Format: Selected members of the studio audience were each given five dollars bidding money. The highest bidding player received a chance to answer a question. A correct response added money to his total based on previously announced odds; an incorrect answer deducted the bet amount. Winners were the highest cash scorers.
Host: Walter O'Keefe.
Length: 15 minutes.
Network: CBS.
First Broadcast: 1953.

The Woman

Type: Variety
Format: Songs, sketches, and dramatizations based on stories appearing in women's magazines.
Hostess: Lorna Farrell.
Regulars: Harry Elders, Sylvia Reigh, Bryna Raeburn, Rita Ascot.
Announcer: John Reed King.
Orchestra: Henry Sylvern.
Length: 30 minutes.
Syndicated.
First Broadcast: 1946.

Woman from Nowhere

Type: Serial
Format: The story of a courageous and lofty sprite with a mysterious past.
The Woman: Irene Rich.
The Swain: Bill Johnstone.
Narrator: Gerald Mohr.
Also: Ann Sloane, Herb Allen, Dean Fossler.
Announcer: Marvin Miller.
Length: 15 minutes.
Network: CBS.
First Broadcast: 1944.

The Woman in My House

Type: Drama

Format: The story of the Carter family.
Cast: Mr. Carter   Forrest Lewis
        Mrs. Carter   Janet Scott
        Sandy Carter,
          their daughter   Peggy Webber
Announcer: Charles Lyon.
Music: Paul Carson.
Length: 15 minutes.
Network: NBC.
First Broadcast: 1951.

A Woman of America

Type: Drama
Format One:
The series focused on the life of Prudence Dane, a widow and the mother of three children, as she struggled to begin a new life in Kansas following the Civil War. Her wagon-train journey from western Pennsylvania to Kansas had been the original concept of the series.
Cast: Prudence Dane   Anne Seymour
        Linda Dane,
          her daughter   Coletta McMahon
        Tommy Dane,
          her son   Ogden Miles
        Wade Douglas,
          the wagon
          master   James Monks
Announcer: Frank Gallop.
Organist: Richard Leibert.
Length: 15 minutes.
Network: NBC.
First Broadcast: 1943.
Format Two:
Set in 1943, the dramatic story of Prudence Dane, the editor of a newspaper. In both versions, the intent was to dramatize the struggles of the American woman.
Starring: Florence Freeman as Prudence Dane.
Also: Santos Ortega, Cliff Carpenter, Joan Tetzel, Ogden Miles, Coleen Ward, Ken Lynch, Linda Ward, Wilfred Lytell, Charles Webster.
Announcer: Frank Gallop.
Organist: Richard Leibert.
Length: 15 minutes.
Network: NBC.
First Broadcast: 1943.

Women in White

Type: Serial
Format: The dramatic story of the women of the nursing profession. The series later dramatized the work of both doctors and nurses.

Cast:
Eileen Holmes	Sarajane Wells
Dr. Paul Burton	Ken Griffin
Helen Bradley	Muriel Bremner
Dr. Purdy	Hugh Studebaker
Karen Harding	Luise Barclay
	Peggy Knudsen
Rosemary Hemingway	Irene Winston
	Genelle Gibbs
Betty Adams	Toni Gilman
	Louise Fitch
Dr. Lee Markham	MacDonald Carey
	Marvin Miller
Dr. Kirk Harding	Karl Weber
Alice Day	Ruth Bailey
Myra Walker	Betty Ruth Smith
Alice Hendricks	Beverly Taylor
Anne Templeton	Louise Arthur
Dr. Jack Landis	Harry Elders
Janet Adams	Lesley Woods

Length: 15 minutes.
Network: NBC.
First Broadcast: 1937.

Women's Club

Type: Women
Hostess: Isobel Leighton.
Announcer: George Byron.
Length: 15 minutes.
Network: CBS.
First Broadcast: 1946.

Wonderful City

Type: Human Interest
Format: Revolved around the theory of New York's warm heart. The program presented people with worthy or humane causes.
Host: Harry Wismer.
Vocalists: Jimmy Carroll, Lois Hunt.
Orchestra: Nat Brandwynne.
Length: 25 minutes.
Network: CBS.
First Broadcast: 1953.

The Woody Herman Show

Type: Musical Variety
Host: Woody Herman.
Regulars: Frances Wayne, Joe "Flip" Phillips, Bill Harris, Chubby Jackson.
Orchestra: Woody Herman.
Length: 30 minutes.
Network: ABC.
First Broadcast: 1945.

The Woolworth Hour

Type: Variety
Host: Donald Woods.
Orchestra: Percy Faith.
Sponsor: F.W. Woolworth and Company.
Length: 60 minutes.
Network: CBS.
First Broadcast: 1955.

The World's Greatest Short Stories

Type: Anthology
Format: Dramatic presentations.
Host-Narrator: Nelson Olmsted.
Announcer: John Holten.
Length: 15 minutes.
Network: NBC.
First Broadcast: 1946.

The Xavier Cugat Show

Type: Musical Variety
Host: Xavier Cugat.
Regulars: Lina Romay, Bert Parks, Yvette Harris, Bob Graham, Nita Rose, Carmen Castillo, The Art Ballinger Chorus, The Don Rodney Chorus.

Orchestra: Xavier Cugat, Art Ballinger.
Length: 30 minutes.
Network: NBC (1941), CBS (1947).
First Broadcast: 1941. Also titled: "Casa Cugat."

X Minus One

Type: Anthology
Format: Science fiction dramas.
Host: Norman Rose.
Announcer: Bob Warren, Fred Collins.
Program Opening:
Announcer: Count down for blast-off: X Minus five . . . Four . . . Three . . . Two . . . X Minus One; fire! (a rocket is heard blasting off). From the far horizons of the unknown come tales of new dimensions in time and space. These are stories of the future; adventures in which you'll live in a million could-be years on a thousand maybe worlds. The National Broadcasting Company in cooperation with *Galaxy* science fiction magazine presents (in echo effect) X-x-x-x MINUS-minus-minus ONE-one-one.
Included:
Hallucination Orbit. The story concerned the hallucinations experienced by an astronaut as he mans an asteroid space station. Called "soliticisis" by psychiatrists, it is a condition where, in prolonged situations, the mind imagines sensual women and all things that cannot be.
Starring: William Redfield.
The Old Die Rich. After several elderly people have been found dead of starvation, yet in the possession of considerable sums of money, a police detective's investigation uncovers a girl who perfected a machine that can send people back into time. He then discovers that the girl uses elderly people to invest money in a past era so she can reap rewards in the present (1956), and the reason for the deaths: the machine deprives the body of nutrition.
Starring: Jim Boles, Jan Miner, Ivor Francis.
Real Game. The story concerned the mys-

terious power of a sculptor who can make the most perfect miniatures in the world — by shrinking himself to the size of an ant and carving the works on an even eye basis.
Starring: Al Collins.
Length: 30 minutes.
Network: NBC.
First Broadcast: 1955 (April 22, 1955 to January 9, 1958). Originally titled "Dimension X," which ran from 1950 to 1955.

Yesterday and Today

Type: Musical Variety
Host: Blue Barron.
Regulars: Alec Templeton, Billy Kover, Clyde Burke, Charlie Fisher, The Blue Barron Glee Club.
Orchestra: Blue Barron.
Length: 30 minutes.
Network: NBC.
First Broadcast: 1942.

You Are There

Type: Drama
Format: CBS news correspondents described reenactments of historical events, using modern broadcasting techniques. Became the basis for a television series of the same title.
Host: John Daly.
Regulars: Ken Roberts, Quincy Howe, Don Hollenbeck, Ned Calmer, Harry Marble.
Announcer: Ken Roberts, Stuart Metz.
Length: 30 minutes.
Network: CBS.
First Broadcast: 1947. Also titled: "CBS Is There."

You Bet Your Life

Type: Game
Format: Contestants were first comically interviewed, then competed in a quiz wherein, after choosing a category, they

answered a series of questions. The players (called couples as two compete as a team) first received $100, then selected a question according to its cash value ($10 to $100). If the question was correctly answered, the money was added to their score; if not, they lost half of the original amount. The object was to build the highest cash score ($440 by choosing and correctly answering the $100, $90, $80, and $70 questions); the couple with the highest score returned at the end of the program to answer the jackpot question, which began at $500 and increased by $500 with each couple's failure to win it. Became the basis for a television series of the same title.

Host: Groucho Marx.

Announcer: Jack Slattery, George Fenneman.

Orchestra: Billy May, Jerry Fielding, Stan Myersand, Jack Meakin.

Length: 30 minutes.

Network: ABC (1947), CBS (1949), NBC (1950).

First Broadcast: 1947.

Young Dr. Malone

Type: Serial

Format: The dramatic story of Dr. Jerry Malone, a physician at the Three Oaks Medical Center. Became the basis for a television series of the same title.

Cast:

Dr. Jerry Malone	Alan Bunce
	Carl Frank
	Charles Irving
	Sandy Becker
Ann Malone	Elizabeth Reller
	Barbara Weeks
Dr. David Malone	Bill Lipton
Jill Malone	Joan Lazer
	Rosemary Rice
Alice Hughes	Nancy Coleman
Robbie Hughes	Richard Coogan
Dr. Dunham	James Van Dyk
Dr. Harrison	Richard Barrows
Daisy	Ethel Morrison
Marsha	Elspeth Eric
Dr. Crawford	Paul McGrath
Christine Taylor	Betty Pratt
Phyllis	Joan Banks
Tracy Malone	Jone Allison
	Joan Alexander
	Gertrude Warner
Lynne	Donna Keith
Jessie Hughes	Isabel Elsom
Veronica	Helene Dumas
Miss Burns	Katharine Raht
Horace Sutton	Ian Martin
Shari	Joy Terry
Lucille Crawford	Janet McGraw
David Crawford	Jack Manning
Carl Ward	Larry Haines

Announcer: Ron Rawson.

Organist: Charles Paul.

Sponsor: Dr. Caldwell's Laxative, Sta-Puf Laundry Rinse, 4-Way Cold Tablets, Crisco oil, Joy dishwashing liquid.

Length: 15 minutes.

Network: Blue.

First Broadcast: 1939.

Young Love

Type: Comedy

Format: The story revolved around the misadventures of Jimmy and Janet, two young college students who married against school regulations and struggled to keep it a secret.

Cast:

Jimmy	Jimmy Lydon
Janet	Janet Waldo
Professor Mitchell	John Heistand
Dean Ferguson	Herb Butterfield
Molly Belle, Janet's Southern classmate	Shirley Mitchell

Also: Hal March, Jerry Hausner.

Announcer: Ron Rowan.

Sponsor: The Ford Motor Company.

Length: 30 minutes.

Network: CBS.

First Broadcast: 1949 (ended in 1950).

Young Widder Brown. Ned Weaver and Wendy Drew.

Young Widder Brown

Type: Serial
Format: The story of Ellen Brown, widow and owner of a tea shop, and her romantic interest, Dr. Anthony Lorring.

Cast:		
Ellen Brown	Florence Freeman	
	Wendy Drew	
Anthony Lorring	Ned Weaver	
Marjorie Williams	Toni Gilman	
Victoria Lorring	Ethel Remey	
	Riza Joyce	
Joyce Turner	Joan Tompkins	
	Helen Shields	
Peter Turner	Bud Collyer	
Barbara Storm	Arline Blackburn	
Mark Brown	Tom Donnelley	
Jane Brown	Marilyn Erskine	
Herb Temple	House Jameson	
	Eric Dressler	
	Alexander Scourby	
Olivia	Bess McCammon	
Mark	Dick Van Patten	
Alicia	Eva Parnell	

Announcer: George Ansbro.
Music: John Winters.
Length: 15 minutes.
Network: NBC.
First Broadcast: 1938.

Your Hit Parade

Type: Musical Variety
Format: Presented the top songs of the week as determined by record and sheet music sales and by songs played over the air and in juke boxes. Became the basis for a television series of the same title.
Host (CBS version):   Andre Baruch.
Vocalists: Frank Sinatra, Marie Greene, Jerry Wayne, Buddy Clark, Joan Edwards, Georgia Gibbs, Jeff Clark, Eileen Wilson, Doris Day, Lanny Ross, Johnny Hauser, Bonnie Baker, Dinah Shore, Andy Russell, Kay Lorraine, Bea Wain, Margaret McCrea, Kay Thompson, Gogo De Lys, Lawrence Tibbett.
Chorus: Mark Warnow, Lyn Murray, Ken Lane.
Announcer: Martin Block, Del Sharbutt, Andre Baruch, Milton Cross, Kenny Delmar, Basil Ruysdael.
Also: Milton Cross.
Orchestra: Freddie Rich, Lennie Hayton, Johnny Green, Leo Reisman, Richard Himber, Al Goodman, Orrin Tucker, Axel Stordahl, Harry Sosnik, Carl Hoff, Mark Warnow, Raymond Scott.
Organist: Ethel Smith.
Sponsor: Lucky Strike cigarettes.
Length: 30 minutes.
Network: NBC.
First Broadcast: 1935. Also titled "Your Hit Parade On Parade." A new version of the series appeared on CBS in 1955 with Andre Baruch presenting the top tunes via recordings.

Your Hit Parade on Parade

Type: Musical Variety
Format: Showcased the top tunes previously presented over the fourteen year

period in which Lucky Strike sponsored "Your Hit Parade" on NBC.
Host: Russ Case.
Regulars: Marjorie Hughes, Stewart Foster.
Orchestra: Russ Case.
Length: 30 minutes.
Network: CBS.
First Broadcast: 1949.

Your Home Beautiful

Type: Women's
Format: Home decorating and furnishing advice.
Hostess: Vicki Vola.
Assistant: Johnny Thompson.
Announcer: Bob Shepherd.
Orchestra: Paul Taubman.
Length: 15 minutes.
Network: Mutual.
First Broadcast: 1950.

Your Lucky Strike

Type: Variety
Format: Presented undiscovered professional talent.
Host: Don Ameche.
Announcer: Frank Martin.
Sponsor: Lucky Strike cigarettes.
Length: 30 minutes.
Network: CBS.
First Broadcast: 1948.

Your Radio Theatre

Type: Anthology Drama
Host-Narrator: Herbert Marshall.
Announcer: Don Stanley.
Length: 55 minutes.
Network: NBC.
First Broadcast: 1955.

Your Song and Mine

Type: Musical Variety
Host: Thomas L. Thomas.

Regulars: Mary Martha Briney, Felix Knight, Edward Slattery, Charles Meynante.
Announcer: Andre Baruch.
Pianist: Enrico Wahl.
Length: 30 minutes.
Network: CBS.
First Broadcast: 1948.

You're the Expert

Type: Game
Format: Six players, chosen from the studio audience, answered a problem question (e.g. "Should you tell your best friend that her husband is getting involved with another woman?"). The player with the best response, as determined by a guest judge, won $25; $10 was awarded to the player with the second-best response; and $5 to the player with the third.
Host: Fred Uttal.
Announcer: Del Sharbutt.
Length: 15 minutes.
Network: CBS.
First Broadcast: 1941.

Yours for a Song

Type: Musical Variety
Hostess: Jane Froman.
Featured: Robert Weede.
Announcer: Bernard Dudley.
Orchestra: Alfredo Antonini.
Length: 25 minutes.
Network: Mutual.
First Broadcast: 1948.

Yours Truly, Johnny Dollar

Type: Drama
Format: The exploits of Johnny-Dollar, a highly priced freelance insurance investigator.
Cast: Johnny Dollar Charles Russell
         Edmond O'Brien
         John Lund
         Bob Bailey

294 YOUTH VS. AGE

Bob Readick
Mandel Kramer

Announcer: Charles Lyon, Roy Rowan.
Orchestra: Eddie Dunstedder, Rick Marino.
Sponsor: Pepsi-Cola, Ex-Lax, Kent cigarettes.
Length: 30 and 15 minute versions.
Network: CBS.
First Broadcast: 1949.

Youth vs. Age

Type: Quiz
Format: Had two teams, the Juvenile vs. the Adult, answer questions submitted by listeners. The team that scored highest received one dollar per correct response.
Host: Cal Tinney.
Announcer: High McDerevy.
Length: 30 minutes.
Network: NBC.
First Broadcast: 1939.

Yvette

Type: Variety
Hostess: Yvette Harris.

Announcer: Ben Grauer.
Length: 15 minutes.
Network: NBC.
First Broadcast: 1940.

The Zero Hour

Type: Anthology
Format: Five-part mystery-suspense presentations. Stories ran one week, Monday through Friday, with a new mystery beginning the following Monday.
Host: Rod Serling.
Producer-Director: Elliott Lewis.
Music: Ferrante and Teicher.
Length: 30 minutes.
Syndicated. The series also appeared briefly on Mutual in 1973.
First Broadcast: 1973.

The Ziegfeld Follies of the Air

Type: Variety
Host: James Melton.
Orchestra: Al Goodman.
Sponsor: Palmolive.
Length: 60 minutes.
Network: CBS.
First Broadcast: 1936.

INDEX